THE FLEXIBLE ECONOMY

The turbulence and accelerating pace of change in the world economy requires national economies to be adaptable. Inflexibility has led to economic crisis in communist Eastern Europe and in Africa, while adaptability has characterised the 'economic miracle' of East Asia. The adoption of 'structural adjustment' programmes in many developing countries shows that the importance of these issues is now being recognised.

However, this book is the first explicitly to address the nature and determinants of economic adaptability. This multi-disciplinary collection of specially commissioned chapters explores the subject from a wide variety of perspectives. Conceptual chapters discuss treatment of the topic in economic theory and in the literature on economic development. There are case studies of Africa, East Asia and Eastern Europe, and a comparative study of responses to oil shocks. Other chapters examine the topic as it relates to the industrial and financial sectors; another studies the political determinants of economic flexibility; and the final chapter draws general conclusions.

Largely non-technical, this unique study will be of great interest to the wide range of people concerned with long-run development, comparative economic performance and the problems of economic transition.

Tony Killick is Senior Research Fellow and former Director of the Overseas Development Institute, London, and Visiting Professor of the University of Surrey.

THE FLEXIBLE ECONOMY

Causes and consequences of the adaptability
of national economies

Edited by Tony Killick

London and New York

First published 1995
by Routledge
11 New Fetter Lane, London EC4P 4EE

Simultaneously published in the USA and Canada
by Routledge
29 West 35th Street, New York, NY 10001

© 1995 Overseas Development Institute

Typeset in Garamond 10/12 by
Florencetype Ltd, Stoodleigh, Devon

Printed and bound in Great Britain by
Biddles Ltd, Guildford and King's Lynn

British Library Cataloguing in Publication Data
A catalogue record for this book is available from the British Library

Library of Congress Cataloging in Publication Data
A catalogue record for this book has been requested

ISBN 0–415–11775–5 (hbk)
ISBN 0–415–11776–3 (pbk)

CONTENTS

v

LIST OF ILLUSTRATIONS

FIGURES

TABLES

CONTRIBUTORS

Kaushik Basu, Delhi School of Economics, University of Delhi, Delhi, India

Tim Belton-Jones, School of Development Studies, University of East Anglia, Norwich, UK

Ha-Joon Chang, Faculty of Economics and Politics, University of Cambridge, Cambridge, UK

Maxwell J. Fry, International Finance Group, University of Birmingham, Birmingham, UK

E.L. Jones, School of Economics and Commerce, Department of Economic History, La Trobe University, Bundoora, Victoria, Australia

Tony Killick, Overseas Development Institute, London, UK

Sanjaya Lall, International Development Centre, Queen Elizabeth House, University of Oxford, Oxford, UK

Alexander Neuber, Kennedy School of Government, Harvard University, Cambridge, MA, USA

David Seddon, School of Development Studies, University of East Anglia, Norwich, UK

Peter Smith, Department of Economics, University of Southampton, Southampton, UK

Moshe Syrquin, Department of Economics and Business Administration, Bar-Ilan University, Ramat Gan, Israel

Alistair Ulph, Department of Economics, University of Southampton, Southampton, UK

FOREWORD

This book is a major step in redirecting attention to exploring the nature of the dynamics of economic, political, and social change which is surely the great frontier of social science analysis. The theory that we use in economic analysis is static. I do not mean that as a pejorative term. Neoclassical economic theory provides valuable insights into the operations of markets; valuable enough so that it is correctly viewed as the queen of the social sciences. But when it comes to dealing with problems of change, with analysis of the way economies evolved through time, that body of theory is woefully inadequate. What we need is a body of theory that analyses the way in which economies adjust to the shocks and changes of all kinds that are an inevitable part of the process of economic change. This study is an important initial effort at exploring the way in which the flexibility of economies affects economic performance over time.

As a number of the chapters make clear, the issue of flexibility is a delicate one in the sense that economies that are going to be able to evolve, not only must have flexibility, but the flexibility must be traded off against stability and credible commitment that is essential to economic development. It would be too much to say that the chapters in this volume solve the problems that are dealt with, but they do ask all the right questions, and they do provide a number of valuable insights into the process of change and the way in which flexibility may work. They are both theoretical in terms of analysing the economic and political theory entailed in flexibility and empirical in analysing flexibility, or the lack of it, in Asia, Africa and Eastern Europe.

Douglass C. North

PREFACE

A few years ago I was commissioned by the World Bank's Economic Development Institute to write an informal textbook on the principles of adjustment policies. In setting about this, I wanted to be able to relate the programmes of 'structural adjustment' which became so widespread in developing countries during the 1980s to longer-term processes of economic development. The link, it seemed to me, was in the patterns of structural change which had been observed as intrinsic to what Kuznets labelled 'modern economic growth'. I saw the 1980s push as simply an episode in the continuous adaptation of national economies to changing circumstances and emerging opportunities, albeit an episode of particular intensity for many countries, reflecting the accelerating pace of change in the world.

However, to someone who has worked most on the economic problems of Africa, it was clear that flexibility is not an attribute shared equally among nations, for over the last fifteen years African governments have found adjustment more difficult than most others. In preparing that book I therefore searched the literature to see what could be gleaned about the flexibility of national economies, and why some are more adaptable than others. Little was found, however, and the resulting book, *The Adaptive Economy*, was unable to take the flexibility idea much further. The present volume tries to reduce this gap in understanding.

A good many debts of gratitude have been incurred during this project. The principal funding was provided by a grant from the Ford Foundation. I should like to express gratitude to them, and especially to the Foundation's Seamus O'Cleireacain for his personal encouragement. Thanks also to the Overseas Development Administration, which covered the costs of a workshop at Bisham Abbey, near Oxford, held to consider first drafts. In addition to chapter authors, gratitude is due to others who were generous enough to sacrifice a precious weekend to attend the workshop, which benefited greatly from their interventions: Walter Elkan, John Henley, Adrian Hewitt, Helga Hoffman, Ian Little, Machiko Nissanke and Rachel Phillipson.

For organising the workshop so efficiently, dealing with a dozen or so authors scattered around the globe and contributing greatly to the final outcome of the project, special thanks go to Jane Horsfield. Margaret Cornell, ODI's enduring editor, went through the entire manuscript with a skill and tact that is standard for her but for few others, and Helen Cleasby did an excellent job in making the script ready for the publishers. My thanks also to John Howell, ODI's Director, for his encouragement when I was ready to abandon attempts to get the project off the ground, and for his support throughout. Finally, the warmest appreciation to my wife, Inge, for her unwavering support at all times, even when it must seem that I prefer my scribblings.

None of the above, of course, have any responsibility for the final product. That buck stops with me.

Tony Killick
Overseas Development Institute, London
February 1994

1

RELEVANCE, MEANING AND DETERMINANTS OF FLEXIBILITY

Tony Killick

I INTRODUCTION

This volume is based on two propositions, the first innocuous, the second less so.

(i) An economy with a flexible structure, which can readily adjust to the needs of the time, will achieve faster development than an economy with a rigid structure. Inflexible economies can expect retarded growth, with disjunctures between demand and supply creating bottlenecks, balance-of-payments strains, inflationary pressures and other economic dislocations.

(ii) The flexibility of national economies is a distinctive concept, worthy of separate study, which is not adequately treated within the present literature on market efficiency or long-run development.

If the *prima facie* importance of economic flexibility is accepted as a working hypothesis, we need to clarify what it means, what determines it and how government policies can influence it. This volume attempts such clarification.

Although this project arose from practical questions about the design of adjustment policies, and of supporting measures by the industrial world, it is perhaps not too fanciful to relate our enquiries also to the limited explanatory power of modern models of economic growth. Empirical tests of neoclassical-type growth models invariably result in only very partial explanations of growth, with a mysterious 'residual' factor called in aid to explain the balance. Even some of the more recent 'endogenous' growth models posit the existence of some special growth factor raising the total productivity of other factors of production (see Boltho and Holtham, 1992: 9).

Various contents have been packed into this black box: technological progress; education and the stock of knowledge; public investment. The flexibility of the national economy is hereby volunteered as another

1

candidate, although we shall see that this attribute is closely related to others just mentioned.

The focus here on the national economy needs explaining, not least because a good argument could be made for the proposition that the sovereign state is an outmoded entity and that the future lies with regional and other supranational units of economic co-operation. At the other end of the spectrum, we could be criticised for neglecting the micro foundations of economic adaptability. Our defence is purely pragmatic: the task is already dauntingly large without extending our enquiries forward into the global system or backward into firm- or industry-level issues (although see Chapter 9 on industrial adaptation and technological capabilities). Boundaries had to be set. We drew them around the nation-state, which, in a world going through a distinctly nationalistic phase, shows great tenacity as an economic entity.

The remainder of this introductory chapter is taken up with elaborating the *prima facie* case for regarding flexibility as important; with trying to sort out some of the conceptual issues that arise; and with the presentation of hypotheses concerning the determinants of national economic flexibility.

II THE *PRIMA FACIE* CASE: THE PERMANENCE OF CHANGE

All economies are constantly in a state of flux, buffeted by developments in the rest of the world, by shifts in the composition of demand, by technological changes. There is thus an ever-present need to respond to – and take advantage of – such changes in the economic environment. The imperative to do so has been intensified in recent decades as economic interdependence among nations has increased, with the rise of trade and international capital movements relative to domestic economic activity. There are rich rewards for those who find ways of leading this expansion; increasingly, none can afford to be left out.

An analogy suggests itself here with the concept of 'fitness' in Darwinian theories of evolution. We can view economic competition among nations as a kind of survival of the fittest, where fitness is determined by the speed with which economies can respond to shocks, and can move to take advantage of new technologies or markets, and adjust to the actions of others. The greater the ease, and the lower the costs, with which an economy can adjust, the more it is likely to prosper.

It is useful, if rather arbitrary, to think of changes in the economic environment as falling into two classes: relatively unpredictable and short-term shocks and longer-term trends.

Shocks

Most of these are external to the national economy. The most obvious are terms-of-trade shocks. The first two oil shocks of 1973–4 and 1979–80 are classic examples, bringing about large deteriorations in the commodity terms of trade of many oil-importing countries, massive improvements in the terms of trade of major oil exporters and large, if unsustained, redistributions of world income (see Chapter 8 on this). Countries dependent on the exportation of other primary products have frequently had to cope with further terms-of-trade shocks, due to the abnormal instability (around trend values) of the world prices of many such commodities, often a magnified reflection of cyclical fluctuations in levels of economic activity in industrial countries.

However, the outside world may impinge by way of financial shocks as well as through merchandise trade. An obvious example is the unexpected rise in world interest rates in the early 1980s, from negative to substantially positive real levels, and the serious difficulties this created for countries which had entered into large variable-interest debt commitments. A related development was the sudden diminution after 1982 in developing-country access to world savings, especially commercial bank credits – sparked off by the debt crisis but also linked to the emergence of the USA as a large-scale net borrower.

There may be domestic shocks to cope with as well. In fact, natural disasters are a frequent source of economic crises in developing countries.[1] The vagaries of the weather are a potent factor in agriculturally based economies, increasing the riskiness of farming and the dangers of famine.[2] We may also mention the frequency of organised violence and the large economic costs that often result from civil and international disturbances and wars. It may seem to strain the language to think of economies adapting to such violence and yet we do talk about economies' resilience in the face of the depredations of war. We should mention too the large-scale migrations that often result from both violence and famine. The need to care for these large, frequently sudden, influxes of people into regions often already poor can impose major economic strains.

Further weight is added to the importance of shocks for economic performance by an interesting study of long-term growth trends by Easterly *et al.* (1993), which points out that growth models seek to explain economic performance by reference to country attributes. These attributes are only slow-changing, however, whereas there are large observed variations in country growth rates over time. The authors argue that these facts can only be reconciled by the influence of exogenous shocks: 'Shocks, especially those to terms of trade, play a much larger role in explaining variance in growth rates than previously acknowledged' (p. 1). To this they might have added 'and the ability to respond to these shocks'.

3

Trends

What, now, of the trends to which economies need to adapt during their development? The most fundamental are long-run changes in the composition of final demand of the type postulated in Engel's Law. In fact, the evidence suggests a rather richer menu of generalisations about income elasticities of demand. Cross-country studies by Theil and his associates show remarkably similar patterns of preference across widely varied economic and cultural conditions (see Clements, Suhm and Theil, 1979; Finke, Rosalsky and Theil, 1983; and Theil and Seale, 1987). Of course, if we use broad categories, such as 'food' or 'consumer durables', the composition of demand appears to change only slowly. But within these categories the pace of change can be much faster, as is most obviously the case with fashion goods. Productive structures need to adapt to such movements in the composition of final demand.

International trade modifies this necessity in important ways, breaking the link between domestic demand and production. However, it provides only a partial escape, since the composition of trade also reflects trends in final demand. Recent decades have witnessed marked changes in the composition of merchandise trade, notably the rise of manufactures relative to primary commodities. Figure 1.1 shows the relative growth of trade in manufactures, mineral and agricultural products since 1950. We can see that the growth of manufactured exports has consistently been faster than for primary products, and often much faster. In consequence, the share of primary products in total world merchandise exports fell from 57 per cent in 1950 to 26 per cent in 1991, with manufactures growing from 43 per cent to 74 per cent.[3] Were the data better, they might well show that the most recent decades have also seen a sharp relative rise in trade in services.

Technological progress is another potent influence to which productive structures must respond, and one of growing importance because of the accelerating pace of technological advances. Indeed, one of the challenges of adaptation facing many developing countries in the late twentieth century is to reduce the widening technology gap between themselves and industrial countries. Here again, however, the hidden hand of demand is pulling some of the levers, for technological progress is not independent of market forces. Rather, it – and the investments in R&D which underlie it – are sensitive to market conditions, with the high income elasticities of demand for manufactures relative to agricultural products probably contributing to the tendency for manufacturing to achieve faster improvements in total factor productivity (Syrquin, 1988: 225).

Reversion to historically more normal rates of economic growth is a further apparent trend of large importance: it appears that the extraordinarily rapid growth among OECD countries in the 1950s through the 1970s has given way to slower growth since, with an associated rise in long-term

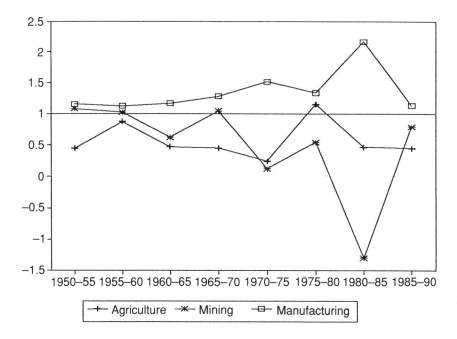

Figure 1.1 Relative growth rates of world exports by commodity groups (1 = sub-period average of total world exports)

Source: GATT, 1985 and GATT, 1991.

unemployment.[4] One of the dangers here is that social pressures will lead to intensified protectionist responses which, by further slowing the expansion of world trade, retard necessary structural adaptation.

Global warming is a (probable) development of more recent provenance to which, if its existence is confirmed, national economies will need to respond in future, particularly those which remain agriculturally-based and already have large areas of marginal land.[5] It is tempting to add other environmental problems as further constraining sustainable development paths in ways that call for structural and policy responses.

Some examples

Take now some contemporary examples of the evident importance of flexibility for human welfare and the development of national economies:

- The well-known success of the newly industrialising countries (NICs) of East and South-East Asia in taking advantage of opportunities in world markets for manufactured goods. Thus, in a study of the electronics

5

industry Mody (1990: 291) writes of firms in South Korea and Taiwan 'learning to manoeuvre in fast-changing markets by responding rapidly to new opportunities, taking greater risks, and meeting higher quality standards'. Indeed, this region has been characterised by the speed with which it has been able to accommodate rapid adjustment and structural change, and the apparently low social costs incurred in the process.[6]

- Related to the last point, the large implications for much of industrial activity of the rapid development and application of microelectronic information technology. This has reduced information costs and has introduced much greater diversity, complexity and flexibility when applied to the control mechanisms of machinery and inventory management. Indeed, some see this as rendering obsolete much industrial organisation based on techniques of mass production, giving way to much smaller units based on 'flexible specialisation' (Piore and Sabel, 1984). Their apparently superior capacity to adapt industrial structures to these technological developments is one of the principal ways in which East Asian countries have excelled.

- The starkly contrasting failures of the former Soviet Union and other ex-communist countries of Eastern Europe to keep abreast of modern industrial technologies, trading opportunities and changing consumer preferences, attributable in part to the rigidities of central planning (see Chapter 5).

- The great difficulties created for many of the economies of Africa by their failure to diversify their export bases in response to trend declines in world real prices for their traditional commodity exports. In consequence, the share of primary products in total African exports remained unchanged at 92 per cent between 1965 and 1991, in sharp contrast with other developing areas (see Table 6.1). In retrospect, Kindleberger's comment about countries which complain of adverse terms-of-trade trends has proved perceptive: 'The complaint will be true, but the difficulty will lie not in the manipulation of its terms of trade by the world beyond its frontiers, but in its incapacity to transform' (1962: 103).

- The widely varying responses and economic outcomes in oil-importing countries to the 1973–4 and 1979–80 oil shocks. For a sample of OECD countries, Black (1985) has shown a wide range of outcomes in terms of a 'misery index' (a combination of unemployment and inflation rates), identifying as among the most important determinants of country outcomes (a) the adaptability of the export sector (a highly positive factor for Japan; less so for certain European economies) and (b) the extent of labour market flexibility (again negative for some of the European countries in his sample). Chapter 8 provides an exploration of this topic.

- Similar contrasts in the costs suffered by countries heavily indebted to commercial banks, as a result of the post-1982 debt crisis. There is a large difference in the records of South Korea and indebted Latin American countries in this respect. Faced with a large incipient debt problem, Korea made an early decision to generate surpluses so as to retire much of its debt, through the restraint of domestic consumption and the aggressive promotion of exports. As a result, it reduced its debt–GNP ratio from 53 per cent in 1985 to 15 per cent in 1992, and its debt-servicing-to-exports ratio from 27 per cent to 7 per cent. Latin American debtors were slower to respond and suffered more prolonged recessions. Writing early in 1994, however, it appears that within Latin America too those who changed policies earliest and most vigorously – such as Chile and Mexico – were beginning to reap major benefits (aided by large capital inflows), by comparison with more reluctant adjusters such as Brazil and Peru.

It was in recognition of the importance of adaptation to both shocks and trends (as well as to past policy mistakes) that there occurred in the 1980s much increased attention to the adoption of 'adjustment programmes'. Thus, the World Bank moved heavily into the support of 'structural adjust-ment' policy packages in developing countries, together with the International Monetary Fund and various aid donor agencies. Other devel-oping countries designed their own policy responses, as did various indus-trial countries.[7] In enquiring into the determinants of the flexibility of economies we are thus implicitly agreeing on the importance of adjustment – but as a permanent condition rather than a creature of the 1980s – and exploring the conditions which determine the success of adjustment efforts and their costs.

The *prima facie* case in favour of studying flexibility is thus persuasive. At the same time, we should be aware of the pitfalls. The chief of these is the difficulty of defining flexibility in an operational way, to be taken up shortly: this is not a quality which can be readily quantified. It therefore cannot be accommodated in formal economic models. Some would argue that to be a sufficient reason for us to desist, on the grounds that scientific enquiry should be confined to the production of falsifiable hypotheses.[8]

Even though we reject this view as unnecessarily narrow, it must be admitted that the concept of economic flexibility is less than ideally sharp and that there is a constant danger of circularity: of using the expression as a near-synonym for growth or development, so that the claim that flexibility benefits development is reduced to mere tautology. Our next step, then, is to try to define flexibility and explicate its nature.

III CONCEPTUALISING FLEXIBILITY

Types and agents of change

Figure 1.2 attempts to capture various dimensions of the concept. This tableau is important for our purposes, for much of the rest of this chapter is organised around it. First, Figure 1.2 distinguishes between responsive

		Period of adjustment	
		short ————————— long	
		Type of flexibility	
		Responsive	Innovative
Agents	Individuals	**1** *Elasticity of demand* *Elasticity of supply* *of labour*	**4** *Investment in skills* *Entrepreneurship*
	Firms, other organisations	**2** *Elasticity of supply* *Imitation/adaptation* *of products and* *processes*	**5** *Investment, R&D,* *innovation*
	Institutions	**3** *Transactions costs* *Policy management*	**6** *Public investment* *(education, research,* *infrastructure)* *Socio-political innovation*
	Hypothesised determinants	7 Information Market efficiency Openness Political autonomy Population age structure	8 Education Technological capability/ industrialisation Historical and social influences

(Left margin: Ease of adjustment — easy / hard)

Figure 1.2 Dimensions of economic flexibility

(or passive) and innovatory flexibility. Responsive flexibility refers to the reaction of economic agents to altered relative prices or other economic stimuli. The reactions of savers to changes in interest rates, or of exporters to a devaluation, or of governments to a natural disaster are examples of responsive flexibility.

By contrast, innovatory flexibility refers to changes initiated by the exercise of entrepreneurship. Those who exercise this quality are the leaders, the visionaries, the shakers and movers of society. Individuals may display it by investing in training which anticipates the skills which will be in short supply in the future. Business people may display it through their spending on R&D and the resulting product or other innovations they introduce. Statesmen or women may display it through the introduction of institutions or policies which will help give the economy a competitive edge in the future, say by the creation of advanced educational or transportation infrastructures.

Figure 1.2 also indicates that there is a time dimension to these two classes of flexibility. Responsive flexibility might be thought of as exemplified by the demand and supply elasticities familiar in standard microeconomics, reactions to changes in relative prices. As such, it can be seen as short-to-medium-term, although time is needed for elasticities to take on their maximum values. In contrast, innovatory flexibility typically involves investment and longer gestation lags. It may also involve the creation of new, or substantially altered, institutions – generally a protracted process.

On its vertical our tableau identifies three types of agents of change: individuals, organisations and institutions, arranged in ascending order of the ease with which, in the general case, they are able to adapt. On this ranking, individuals come out on top. As is shown in later chapters, inflexibility among the economies of Africa or in the centrally planned economies of Eastern Europe cannot be attributed to unresponsiveness on the part of their populations. Evidence from another part of the world is on display in the vigour with which the population of southern China has taken advantage of economic liberalisation there. Despite large historical, cultural and geographical differences, people everywhere seem to belong to the species *homo economicus*, and to equate development with modernisation. Revealed patterns of income elasticities of consumer demand are much the same the world over,[9] and so are people's responsiveness to relative prices – if they are given the opportunity to take advantage of them.

This is not to say that everyone everywhere is equally adaptable. Adaptability is a capacity which diminishes with age. It is enhanced by education, an aspect we shall explore later. People do respond to incentives – but subject to the constraints upon them. Theodore Schultz postulates that:

> there are economic incentives to reallocate resources, that people respond to these incentives to the best of their ability, and that the difference in their performance is a measure of the difference among people with respect to the particular type of ability that is required.
>
> (Schultz, 1975: 834)

Lack of education is one constraint. Exploring others brings us to the second and third types of agents of change identified in Figure 1.2: organisations and institutions. In distinguishing between these we follow North, seeing institutions as:

> formal rules, informal constraints (norms of behavior, conventions, and self-imposed codes of conduct), and the enforcement characteristics of both. . . . If institutions are the rules of the game organizations are the players. Organizations consist of groups of individuals engaged in purposive activity. The constraints imposed by the institutional framework (together with the other standard constraints of economics) define the opportunity set and therefore the kind of organizations that will come into existence.
>
> (North, 1992: 9–10)

So it is to institutions that we must look in order to understand the constraints upon individual (and organisational) responsiveness. In support of this we can note that Morris and Adelman's 1988 study of comparative patterns of economic development concluded that institutions, and their adaptability, mattered most in explaining differential rates of diffusion of economic growth. Out-dated laws, a reactionary or corrupted judiciary resulting in unpredictable enforcement of contracts and property rights, or a hidebound public administration can be potent obstacles to responsiveness, frustrating entrepreneurs and others wishing to take advantage of new opportunities. The economic history of India provides a salutary illustration of this truth.

Tradition and religion nominate themselves as liable to be among the more important institutions, although they take an economist into treacherous waters. A flexible economy requires a population which is willing to take action to maximise whatever material benefits may be derived from changing conditions (or to minimise the costs). This points in favour of an individualistic (or family-based) welfare-maximising approach, and mobility in pursuit of this objective, since collective action is apt both to be slower and more uncertain. These attributes may clash with traditional values, however, which often place more stress on the value of collective well-being and erect obstacles to mobility.

The pursuit of economic self-improvement, for example, requires some faith that advancement will be on the basis of personal ability and effort. Traditional mores may undermine such faith, with promotion decided on the basis of seniority or caste. An attribute of many traditional societies is that they deny equality of opportunity to women, discouraging their education and thus weakening the economic incentives of half the population. Equality of opportunity is also often denied on ethnic grounds (although not just in traditional societies), where a dominant tribe or race holds down the progress of others and gives preferment to its own members.

Traditional values may also be opposed to the self-regarding pursuit of material well-being. Extended family obligations, for instance, can weaken incentives, because of the high implicit marginal rate of taxation imposed by customary obligations to numerous, more or less distant, relatives. There may be similar traditional influences standing in the way of, or weakening the incentives for, public servants adopting the role orientation necessary for the efficient conduct of their duties. In short, traditional values may be at odds with the 'modernisation' of outlook which is necessary for the flexible economy, and hence may dull responsiveness.

Religion may have a like effect. Perhaps the key question here is what a religion teaches concerning human beings' relationship to their environment. Some faiths see human fate as predetermined by God's will, and acceptance of poverty in this world as a mere prelude to a better life in the next. Such a faith is not likely to encourage enterprising self-help in response to a changing environment. The Buddhist and Hindu religions are perhaps most often associated with passive fatalism. Conversely, the Judæo–Christian traditions have been viewed as emphasising the individual's responsibility for his/her actions and well-being, with the 'Protestant ethic' sometimes particularly associated with capitalistic values. In view of the dynamism of the economies of Eastern Asia, Confucianism also tends nowadays to be awarded high marks! The Islamic faith is given an intermediate ranking.

Nonetheless, while religions have themselves proved mutable in face of the need to remain relevant in a changing world, the social and political structures they give rise to are often seen as conservative, protective of traditional values, resistant to modernisation and materialism. Some place limited value on secular education; many have resisted scientific explanations of the world's workings when these appear to conflict with religious teachings. The validity and influence of such tendencies remain highly controversial, of course, not least because of large differences within all the main religions.

The negative influences mentioned are best viewed as dampening responses and reducing elasticities, not usually as giving rise to perverse responses. The economic life of some traditional societies is often very vigorous, and highly resilient in the face of adversity – hence the persistence of extensive parallel markets and 'informal' sectors in many developing countries. There are obstacles to responsiveness within all societies and no form of cultural determinism is intended. But we persist in suggesting that tradition and religion are more likely than not to reduce receptivity to change.

While individual responsiveness is likely to be necessary for adaptive national economies, it is not a sufficient condition. Institutions and policies can prevent such responsiveness from translating into economy-wide flexibility, or perhaps can compensate for deficiencies at the micro level. The nature of governments is one such institutional factor of great importance. We have already cited the Indian state as one which has tended to stifle individual enterprise in the past. A government which is insecure, corrupt or repressive is unlikely to give much heed to economic performance, or to have the legitimacy necessary to carry through the policies needed to adapt the economy to changing circumstances. Special interest groups will obstruct the reform of policies from which they benefit.

However, change is not impossible even when the state is behoven to interest groups. There is evidence of a kind of cost-benefit logic at work, in which the economic deterioration resulting from anti-adaptation policies throws up a countervailing public discontent which will either impel the government to act or overthrow it for a more reform-minded alternative. When combined with strong leadership, public acceptance of the need for change can render politically feasible policy shifts that would formerly have been judged suicidal.

While considering political factors, we should also mention the delicate balance to be struck between flexibility and continuity in government policies. Modern macroeconomics teaches the importance for effective policy interventions of the ways in which the public reacts to – and anticipates – government actions, and of the techniques that it develops for frustrating government intentions. Corruption and parallel markets are examples of the latter. To be effective, policies must be credible; people must believe they will be implemented and will stick.[10] This is why unstable or inconsistent governments have difficulty in improving the performance of the economy: citizens do not believe that the government means what it says, or will enforce its decisions. This is a reason for valuing political stability, for who can plan on the reliability of some new policy signal when governments have only brief life expectancies?

We have suggested that institutions are the least adaptable of the three categories of agents of change identified in Figure 1.2. One reason for this is that almost invariably powerful groups grow up with vested interests in maintaining the status quo. Douglass North again:

> The process of change [of institutions] is overwhelmingly incremental. . . . The reason is that the economies of scope, complementarities, and network externalities that arise from a given matrix of formal rules, informal constraints, and enforcement characteristics will typically bias costs and benefits in favour of choices consistent with the existing framework. Therefore . . . institutional change will occur at those margins considered most pliable in the context of the bargaining power of interested parties.
>
> (North, 1992: 11)

Moreover, there is considerable scope for tension in the adaptation of institutions, resulting from the relative ease with which changes in formal rules may be legislated once a coalition for change has been assembled, as contrasted with the more obscure and osmotic ways in which informal constraints – reflecting value systems and social mores – alter over time. However, as North acknowledges, there are situations in which revolutionary change becomes possible and Chapter 5 of this volume, on Eastern Europe, is devoted to an exploration of precisely such a situation.

Responsive flexibility

Reverting again to Figure 1.2, entries in the cells numbered 1 to 6 signal ways in which the various forms of flexibility manifest themselves. Explanation of these, and their determinants, will throw additional light on the concept of flexibility.

Cell 1 needs little explication. Subject to the constraints acting upon them, individuals respond to changing relative prices, product innovations and real wages so as to improve or defend their welfare. Responses to alterations in relative prices are a form of flexibility which is familiar and can be measured, as price elasticities. These are rarely observed to have an 'incorrect' sign, although their values will depend upon the constraints faced by the individuals.

The notion of firms' elasticities of supply in *Cell 2* is also familiar and amenable to measurement. Leaving aside short-term factors, such as the availability of material inputs and the extent of prior unutilised capacity, and assuming that a price change is taken to be more than temporary, then for the economy as a whole supply elasticities will be strongly influenced by factor mobilities and the extent of competition.

Factor mobilities The ease with which labour and capital can move between alternative employments will be influenced by the efficiency of the factor markets, including the flexibility of wages and returns to capital, and the speed with which these markets clear. It will also be influenced by the degree of specificity of the factors: the extent to which they are versatile, or are trained or designed to perform a narrow range of tasks. Related to factor specificity is the extent to which technologies are embodied in production processes, as against being available as disembodied knowledge for a range of applications.

The extent of competition Elasticities of supply are larger in competitive firms and tend to be so for competitive industries. Conversely, a firm which is a sole producer has weaker incentives to respond to changed market conditions, for its monopoly power can already earn it acceptable rates of return. It can get away with avoidably high cost structures – X-inefficiency – and can postpone the discomforts of change.

We can also mention the state of the economy's basic infrastructure, which is often poor in developing countries. In such circumstances, it will be difficult to obtain ample and reliable additional input supplies and ready access to markets. The state of the infrastructure also has a direct bearing on the mobility of labour and, more generally, on the structural flexibility of an economy, for a well-developed infrastructure helps to integrate markets and raise their efficiency.

The inclusion of 'imitation and adaptation' in Cell 2 refers to firms' (and other organisations') abilities to assimilate innovations introduced by others, especially competitors, although pure imitation is rare and some adaptation to local circumstances is almost invariably required. At the level of national economies, Japan is often cited as having excelled at imitation in the earlier phases of its industrialisation, but they had earlier examples to follow. Francis Bacon long ago nominated gunpowder, printing and the compass as inventions which changed the world, but Rosenberg (1982) points out that, although these were widely adopted in, and exported from, Europe, in each

13

case the original invention was probably Chinese. It was the European response to these (foreign) inventions which was crucial: 'It may be seriously argued that, historically, European receptivity to new technologies, and the capacity to assimilate them whatever their origin, has been as important as inventiveness itself' (p. 245).

Cell 3 requires more explanation. First, the reference to transactions costs.[11] This is a catch-all expression referring to the costs of providing various services necessary for efficient transactions in a market economy: the provision and exchange of information and other actions necessary to bring buyers and sellers together; the measurement and inspection of goods; the preparation and enforcement of contracts; and so on. In less developed economies transactions costs are reduced by limited specialisation and face-to-face transactions, and enforcement achieved informally through customary practice and social pressures – although they are raised by poor information and weak institutions.

As an economy begins to modernise, so transactions costs tend to rise relative to total economic activity, unless there is a parallel development of institutions to offset this tendency. Specialisation increases, more transactions occur impersonally through the intermediation of markets, the necessary network of 'middlemen' becomes denser, there is more standardisation, more quality control, information needs multiply, custom becomes an inadequate means of enforcement. If rising transactions costs are not to frustrate economic development, institutions, particularly of the more formal type, need to develop to keep these costs to a minimum: 'Efficient markets are a consequence of institutions that provide low-cost measurement and enforcement of contracts. . . . Essential to efficiency over time are institutions that provide economic and political flexibility to adapt to new opportunities' (North, 1992: 9). This implies sufficient flows of information for agents to know about the opportunities open to them and be able to make rational decisions about them.

The invention of money and other financial instruments arguably did most to reduce transactions costs, permitting modern economic development. The development of the financial sector continues to offer large benefits for the flexibility of the economy for reasons expounded by Maxwell Fry in Chapter 10. By reducing risks and losses of liquidity, and by offering a financial reward, it tends to increase total saving. It thus also promotes capital formation, by increasing the supply of investible resources. Savings are transferred to investors with different needs, degrees of risk and prospective rates of return, thereby permitting more diversified and efficient investment. Through diversification of financial instruments and access to better information than individuals can readily obtain, financial institutions reduce, bear or transfer risks. Through maturity transformation, they allow savers to hold liquid assets while investors borrow long-term. They match savers and investors with congruent preferences for risk and return, and they bulk up the small-scale savings of households for investment in sometimes large projects, thereby increasing the volume of investment and enabling more risky investments with higher yields. Capital markets further exert pressure on investors to use resources for the maximum return, in order to be able to repay loans and qualify for new financing. Finally, financial institutions provide a safe, efficient payments system, permitting quick settlement of obligations, reducing risks and transactions costs.

Economic flexibility requires institutions to respond to the needs of modern economic growth by means that keep transactions costs to a minimum. However, there is no assurance that such a response will occur. Chapter 6 suggests that part of Africa's lagging development experience is explicable in terms of a failure of institutional adaptation. North gives an example from European history:

> Some economies evolved to produce a political structure that permitted the development of third-party enforcement and the complicated structure of institutions that characterizes the modern Western world. But even in Western Europe not all economies evolved in the same way. Rather, some, as in the case of Spain, came to a dead end as a consequence of political/economic policies that produced bankruptcy and disincentives to produce institutional innovation.
>
> (North, 1990: 122)

The entry 'policy management' in Cell 3 of Figure 1.2 covers a subset of the kind of institutional responsiveness discussed above, referring to the ability of the state to modify existing policies and introduce new ones in the light of emerging needs. The management of fiscal and monetary policy so as to reconcile competing inflation, balance-of-payments, employment and growth objectives is one example. Another is actions to offset the effects of terms-of-trade shocks, but there is a host of other ways in which governments need constantly to review their policies – on trade, taxation and public spending – in the light of changing external and internal conditions. The readiness and wisdom with which the state undertakes such policy management will have much to do with the creation of an environment conducive to adaptation on the part of other economic agents. State institutions in East Asia, for example, have a reputation for a high-quality responsiveness which has contributed much to the apparent flexibility of the economies of that region (see Chapter 7, and also World Bank, 1993b, Chapter 3).

Innovatory flexibility

Let us proceed next to the cells in Figure 1.2 under the heading of innovatory flexibility. *Cell 4* is straightforward. Perhaps the most common way in which individuals might be said to exhibit this form of flexibility is by investing, for themselves or their children, in the acquisition of knowledge and skills that they judge likely to be in scarce supply in the future and which, therefore, are likely to yield a superior income stream. The beneficial impact of education on people's economic adaptability is discussed later.

Similarly little persuasion is needed for the view that the exercise of entrepreneurship exemplifies innovatory flexibility *par excellence*. An entrepreneur thinks ahead; is alert to new information about economic and technical conditions; is particularly sensitive to the emergence of new market opportunities and tries to anticipate future ones; moves quickly in order to be a step ahead of competitors; is willing to take risks, to innovate, to embrace the unfamiliar.[12] As Etzioni (1987: 176) has put it, 'The societal function of entrepreneurship is . . . to *change* existing obsolescent societal patterns (of relations, organisations, modes of production) to render them more compatible with the changing environment.'

Hence, a society with a vigorous entrepreneurial culture is likely to have a flexible economy. Unfortunately, enterprise is unevenly distributed within and across peoples, notwithstanding the standard assumption of economics that it is a quality in unlimited supply and does not, therefore, constrain production. In reality there is no assurance that there will be an adequate supply of entrepreneurs and there can result what has been called a creative market failure to invest and innovate on an adequate scale (Kaldor, 1972, as discussed in Arndt, 1988).

The inclusion of firm- or organisation-level 'investment, R&D and innovation' in *Cell 5* need not detain us long. Product and process changes are self-evidently among the most important forms of innovatory flexibility, and it is at the level of the firm that most such changes are likely to be developed and applied.

But how can we differentiate between the entries in Cells 2 and 5? For this purpose Fransman's categorisation of forms of technological change is helpful:

(i)   The search for new products and processes developed by others.
(ii) The adaptation of externally generated innovations to local conditions.
(iii) Improvements to products and processes which go beyond adaptation.
(iv) The initiation and development of new products and processes.
(v)   Basic research, serving as a foundation for (iv).

(Fransman, 1986: 23–5)

There is an element of arbitrariness in the dividing line we choose to draw, since we are actually dealing with a continuum. Category (i) is clearly responsive rather than innovatory. However, the rarity of pure imitation, without need for any modification, suggests that we should realistically also include (ii): adaptation to local conditions. Categories (iii) to (v), on the other hand, involve higher levels of creativity and are best thought of as innovatory, involving the recognition of new opportunities for profitable or socially useful changes.

And investment? Well, a high proportion of technological advances are given material form in new equipment and other forms of capital accumulation. So-called endogenous growth theory, in fact, has rehabilitated investment as a growth agent precisely because of its crucial role in the creation and application of new knowledge. Beyond this, we have stressed that structural change is intrinsic to economic development and the importance therefore of an environment which facilitates such changes. These involve the relative, sometimes absolute, decline of some activities (agriculture, simple manufacturing, petty trade) and the rise of new ones (high-tech industries and a wide range of modern service activities). But the new leading sectors can only be created by investment, so that, over and above its role as a vehicle for technological progress, a high-investment economy is more likely to achieve necessary structural change.

Cell 6 may also be allowed largely to speak for itself. We are here essentially interested in whether the institutional and policy environment is an 'enabling' one – whether it encourages (or constrains) individuals, enterprises and other organisations to adapt and innovate. The case for public investments in education, research and physical infrastructure has already been made, or is implicit in the foregoing. The main point is that these can be seen as 'crowding-in', or stimulating, complementary investments by individuals and firms.[13]

As regards 'enabling' institutional innovations, North (1992: 21) gives examples from the USA of the passing of legislation in the nineteenth century for the creation of land-grant colleges to promote the development and dissemination of agricultural knowledge, and for the establishment of agricultural experimental stations in every state. Another example of an 'enabling' institutional innovation raising the flexibility of the economy is the introduction of state supervision of commercial banks. The existence of this supervision reduces the risk of banking instability, raising public confidence in the use of money and encouraging financial deepening by safeguarding against misuse of the public's deposits.

We should remember, finally, an implication of the location of these types of innovation in the bottom right-hand cell of Figure 1.2: that we expect that in general it will be difficult to achieve this type of change and that such adaptation is likely to be slow.

Defining a flexible economy

By now it will be evident that the notion of flexibility cannot readily be reduced to some brief, precise definition, let alone be quantified. Against this, we have made progress in identifying the characteristics of a flexible economy. Broadly expressed, *we can define a flexible economy as one in which individuals, organisations and institutions efficiently adjust their goals and resources to changing constraints and opportunities.*

Note from this that ends as well as means are adapted. Objectives can be made more ambitious as old constraints give way, say, to technological advances. Or objectives may need to be trimmed back as new constraints emerge, as when non-renewable resources become exhausted. And objectives are likely to need to be constantly redefined in the context of changing conditions and values. Note too that on our definition adjustment can be responsive, e.g. to changing competitive conditions or to exogenous shocks, or innovative, e.g. to take advantage of some advance in knowledge.

The key expression in the definition is the idea of the *efficient* adjustment of ends and means, but what does that mean? Part of the answer must refer to the speed with which agents are able to effect changes. An inflexible economy is one in which adjustment is slow. However, speed is not a sufficient condition, for it may be that rapid change can be achieved only by imposing large costs upon the population. Thus, a flexible economy is one in which there is both a relatively low-cost and a speedy movement of resources among alternative uses, leading to changing factor proportions, technologies and outputs in response to disequilibrium situations. On the demand side, this implies responsiveness by purchasers to changing relative prices, and comparative ease of substitution in the disposition of income as between consumption and saving.

For reasons already given, such an economy will be marked by a social, policy and institutional environment which will minimise transactions costs and the constraints acting upon agents' abilities to respond and innovate – what in another context has been called an 'enabling environment'.

Adjustment costs

We have now introduced an additional concept: the idea of adjustment costs. This too must be clarified. Various types of cost may be identified.

First there are what might be termed *absorption costs*. These arise in the common situation where a country's adjustment policies are addressed to reducing inflationary demand pressures or an unviable balance-of-payments deficit. Standard theory tells us that the country must reduce absorption (consumption plus investment) relative to income. In principle, it is possible to achieve this by increasing income while holding absorption constant, but in practice – and in the short term – countries are likely to have to cut back on consumption and/or investment in the public and/or private sectors. Such cuts can be seen as costs, resulting in less consumption or investment than would otherwise have occurred. In a sense, these costs are unavoidable in that they are part of the economic logic of the macroeconomic imbalances, although they can be minimised by doing everything possible to maximise the growth of output and income.[14]

A second category might be termed *frictional costs*. These refer to losses of output, employment and consumption resulting from shifts of resources from declining to expanding sectors. These arise because markets are imperfect: if they were everywhere perfect all prices would be flexible, resources would be completely homogeneous and mobile, and adjustment would be instantaneous. However, many types of labour, capital and natural resources are specific in their productive employment. An irrigation system cannot be used in factories; a miner cannot instantly be converted into a hotel worker; even within agriculture, land in a given ecological zone may not be suitable for conversion from cultivation of one crop to another.

Markets are imperfect in other ways, too. Prices are often sticky in the downward direction, none more so than in labour markets. In the face of such conditions, structural adaptation will be associated with frictional losses of employment and capacity utilisation – losses which may be large and persistent. Indeed, most of the discussion of adjustment costs in industrial countries is about unemployment.

A final, closely related, category is what we can call *distributional costs*. Absorption and frictional costs affect income distribution because they are not spread across the population in a manner exactly proportionate to the existing distribution of income. But there would be distributional consequences even in the absence of the other two categories, because adaptation affects the relative sizes of sectors of production and these employ differing factor proportions. Structural change thus gives rise to groups of gainers and losers whose short-term interests conflict with one another.

Net distributional costs might be said to arise when the value attached by society to the losses of those adversely affected exceeds the value placed upon the benefits of the gainers. Much of the discussion of the costs of adjustment is, in fact, about distributional aspects and, in particular, about the danger that vulnerable poverty groups will be disadvantaged. Implicit here is the idea that a dollar's worth of loss by the poor is not offset by a dollar gain by the rich, so that different weights should be placed on the income changes.

IV THE DETERMINANTS OF NATIONAL ECONOMIC FLEXIBILITY

The last task of this chapter is to present some hypotheses concerning the determinants of flexibility, summarised in Cells 7 and 8 of Figure 1.2.

Information

Cell 7 summarises the suggested determinants of economies' responsive flexibility and starts with information. The importance of information sounds so obvious that it can be taken for granted, but in many countries data are still sparse, unreliable and out-of-date. In such circumstances neither private nor government decision-makers can operate efficiently. Not a few governments lurched into a debt problem because they did not know the rate at which debts were being accumulated; businessmen have lost competitive advantage or failed to grasp new market opportunities because of ignorance about the possibilities open to them; peoples have experienced famines because 'early warning' information systems were not in place. Moreover, it cannot be assumed that market incentives will generate all the necessary information or make it available to all who can take advantage of it. Indeed, imperfect information, raising transactions costs, is seen as one of the key features which distinguish developing from developed economies (see in particular Stiglitz's essay in Chenery and Srinivasan, 1988, vol. 1, Chapter 5 and the references cited there).

Governments everywhere therefore include the gathering and dissemination of information as among their responsibilities. There is little controversy about this, but in many developing countries information flows often remain woefully inadequate. Flexibility is bound to be limited in the face of ignorance about changes in circumstance to which the economy – and policies – must adapt.[15] The flexible economy needs good intelligence: about changing conditions in world trade and finance; about developments within the domestic economy; about the ways in policy instruments impact upon the economy; about scientific matters, e.g. as they bear upon technological progress; and about how these and other variables interact with each other. In this way the transactions costs of adaptation will be reduced and the likelihood of change enhanced.

Market efficiency

Since transactions costs would be zero in a perfectly functioning market economy and imperfect information raises transactions costs, it follows that good, low-cost information flows are a necessary condition for market efficiency. Stiglitz and his associates have urged the importance of this factor and have fruitfully applied the concept of imperfect information to the analysis of rural credit markets in developing countries.[16] Thus, Hoff and Stiglitz (1990) show how the high costs of obtaining information about potential borrowers – reflecting weak formal institutional development in rural economies – lead to non-clearing and incomplete financial markets based on credit rationing. Because of their superior access to local-level knowledge, moneylenders and other informal financial institutions are better able to meet many of the population's demands for financial services.

Information is not enough, however, for it must also find reflection in people's incentives. Markets score heavily here, for they are the means of processing huge amounts of information about conditions of supply and demand. Their decentralised nature, and their ability to translate information into price incentives and to co-ordinate a huge number of individual decisions through an interacting network, places them well in advance of what state planners can hope to achieve. In short, we can hypothesise that a well-functioning market system is conducive to economic flexibility and that, by comparison, central planning creates rigidities. We would therefore expect an economy dominated by the state, with heavy public participation in production, to be less flexible than one with a productive system based on private enterprise.

This is a view to be explored later in this volume (especially in Chapter 5) but we can already quote two examples giving it a *prima facie* plausibility. At a superficial level, we can cite the remarkable recent economic progress of China, especially in the southern parts of the country. While this has been achieved with continuity in power of a government which is still in some attenuated sense communist, the essential point is that the economic transformation has been based on a movement away from central planning, to decentralisation and deregulation, and through the encouragement and rapid growth of private enterprise.[17]

Relatedly but at a different level, we can also refer to *a priori* expectations that public enterprises will be less responsive to changing market conditions and opportunities than their private sector counterparts. The especially large principal-agent problems that characterise many public enterprises – resulting particularly from the diffusion of property rights and resulting weak supervision of, and incentives for, managements – are one reason for this (see Adam *et al.*, 1992, on the principal-agent problem in public enterprises). When combined with the monopoly power characteristic of public enterprises, there are fewer incentives for public enterprise managers to maximise their firms' competitiveness. The mixture of market and 'social' objectives which governments commonly ask managements to pursue compounds the problem, leading, for example, to non-market employment practices – in plain language, over-manning.

In suggesting that a well-functioning market system is conducive to economic responsiveness, however, the key word is 'well-functioning', for all economies experience market failures, particularly in countries still at relatively early stages of development. Among the many conditions contributing to a well-functioning market system, the freedom of entry of new firms into existing markets is particularly important, encouraging the spread of successful ideas and safeguarding against industries becoming slow to take advantage of technological and other opportunities.

One, indeed about the only, aspect of the ways in which market efficiency bears upon the adaptability of an economy that has already been reasonably well researched concerns the operation of labour markets. The notion of labour market flexibility has been given differing meanings, but they revolve round the idea of the capacity to adapt to change (Meulders and Wilkin, 1987: 5). Klau and Mittelstädt (1986: 10) identify four aspects: (i) real labour cost flexibility at the economy-wide level; (ii) adaptability of relative labour costs across occupations and enterprises; (iii) labour mobility; and (iv) the flexibility of working time and work schedules. Inflexibility in labour markets is often linked in the literature to trade union militancy.

We can see from this that the idea of labour market flexibility shares with our more overarching notion of economic adaptability the qualities of being multi-faceted and difficult to distil into an operational definition. It is encouraging, therefore, that economists have been able to develop quantifiable indicators of the degree of labour market flexibility and to use these to assess the extent to which various labour markets possess the quality of flexibility, and changes in this situation over time. The results of one such exercise are reproduced in Table 1.1, which the authors interpret as supporting the general proposition that, at least during the 1970s, short-term labour market flexibility was greater in Japan and the USA than among European countries (Klau and Mittelstädt, 1986: 41).[18] The important thing for present purposes, however, is that flexibility is a feature of the efficiency of labour markets which has been found both important to study and amenable to empirical research. We have already cited Black's (1985) conclusion of the importance of labour market flexibility as a determinant of the costs of adjustment to oil shocks among OECD economies.

The efficiency of capital markets may also be expected to exert a strong influence on the flexibility of national economies. For reasons given earlier, the financial system is likely to have a strong influence on the performance of the rest of the economy. We see capital markets as having a large potential role in determining the mobility of capital, the responsiveness of suppliers to changing price relativities and the rate at which technical progress becomes incorporated into the productive system.

Openness

As a variable closely related to market efficiency, the degree of openness of an economy also has an important influence on its flexibility. The suggestion here is that international trade is a potent medium both for the transfer of information and for the transmission of incentives to adapt. Through contractual arrangements and visible embodiment in new goods, merchandise trade provides a flow of information about technological advances, changing tastes and product development. Transnational corporations are similarly a common means by which such changes are conveyed from investing to recipient countries. Learning-by-exporting has, for example, been an important way in which the new economic giants of East Asia have raised their productivities and the quality of their output.[19] Competition from imports ensures that domestic producers must keep abreast or lose markets. More generally, a society which is thoroughly exposed to commerce with, and

22

Table 1.1 Indicators of labour market flexibility (1970s and 1980s) – synoptic table

	USA	Japan	Germany	France	UK	Italy	Canada	Austria	Netherlands	Sweden
1 Short-run real wage rigidity[a]	low	low	low	high	high	intermediate	intermediate	intermediate	high	
2 Intersectoral labour cost differentials[b]	average	average	low	high	low	high	low			low
3 Change in (2)	rising	stable	rising	falling	falling	falling	rising			falling
4 Inter-industry wage differentials[c]	high	high	low	low	low	average	high			low
5 Change in (4)	rising	rising	rising	falling	falling	falling	stable			falling
6 Change in dispersion of intersectoral productivity differentials[d]	falling	stable	rising	rising	rising	falling				rising
7 Change in ratio of female to male wages[e]	falling	falling	rising	rising	rising	falling			rising	rising
8 Change in ratio of female to male unemployment rate	falling	rising	rising	stable	rising	rising	falling		rising	falling
9 Change in ratio of youth to adult wages	falling	stable	rising	stable	rising					rising
10 Change in ratio of youth to adult unemployment rates	falling	falling	rising	falling	rising	falling	stable			rising
11 Unemployment replacement rates[f]	low	low	high	high	low	low	high			average
12 Change in part-time employment relative to full-time employment	small increase	small increase	strong rise	strong rise	small absolute	small fall	average rise	average	strong rise	strong rise
13 Change in annual hours worked per employed person	small fall	small rise	average fall	strong decline	strong decline	small decline	average fall		average fall	average fall
14 Earnings exempt from employers' social security contributions	zero	intermediate	intermediate	zero	high	high	low			
15 Rise in unemployment relative to high capacity use (shift in 'Okun curve')	small	small	moderate	strong	strong	strong	moderate		strong	small

Notes:

a Short-run price coefficients divided by cyclical coefficient (money wage equations for private non-farm business sector). b Coefficient of variation of sectoral labour cost differentials (compensation per employed person). c Coefficient of variation of inter-industry hourly wage differentials (pay for time worked). d Coefficient of variation of sectoral output per employed person. e Hourly adult wages. f Unemployment benefits per unemployed person as a percentage of net income of average production worker.

Source: Klau and Mittelstädt, 1986: Table 11.

investments from, the rest of the world is more likely to be aware of the changes occurring around it, and more receptive to new ideas.

Governments that provide undiscriminating protection, which penalise exports or which discourage foreign investment thereby reduce the likelihood that their economies will prove adequately adaptable in the face of changing circumstances. Conversely, a country that pursues an open-economy stance arguably erects a safeguard against subsequent government policies that could inhibit flexibility, as Krueger has argued that:

> an export-promotion strategy appears to place certain kinds of constraints upon economic policy and its implementation; these constraints, in turn, limit the magnitude and duration of policy mistakes and also tend to force policies to work through pricing, rather than quantitative, interventions . . . a growth strategy oriented towards exports entails the development of policies that make markets and incentives function better . . .
>
> (Krueger, 1978: 284)

Indeed, so powerful are the incentive effects of exposure to international trade that it can plausibly be suggested that the trade creation resulting from the European Community has been a prime stimulus for the renewal of the economies of France and the UK, which in the years after World War II displayed decided symptoms of sclerosis.

Political autonomy

The way political power is distributed may easily act as a barrier to adaptation. Existing policies – however ill-chosen – often have large inertial force because those who benefit from them are powerful enough to block change. This has often led the IMF and the World Bank to blame inadequate 'political will' or 'political commitment' for disappointing implementation in developing-country adjustment programmes. Unfortunately, the notion of political will is too superficial to take us far. It is necessary to dig beneath this surface to discover the forces acting upon governments and, in particular, the degree of autonomy which the agencies of state enjoy from class and other interest group pressures when determining policies.

There is near unanimity that relative state autonomy is one of the factors that has worked to the advantage of the East Asian 'miracle' economies. Thus, Jenkins (1991) identifies the high degree of autonomy of East Asian states, by comparison with those of Latin America, as the chief explanation of the superior development record of the former, while Shams (1989) similarly sees the same factor as an important determinant of the region's implementation of adjustment programmes. The World Bank study of East Asia already cited sees 'technocratic insulation' as an institutional trait that has been crucial to the joint achievement of economic growth and improved income distribution in East Asia:

> technocratic insulation, the ability of economic technocrats to formulate and implement policies in keeping with politically formulated national goals with a minimum of lobbying for special favors from politicians and interest groups. Without it, technocrats in the high performing Asian economies would have been unable to introduce and sustain rational economic policies, and some vital wealth-sharing mechanisms would have been neutralized soon after their inception . . .
>
> (World Bank, 1993b: 167)

The importance of this, and how it was achieved, is a theme taken further in Chapter 11. The effects of its absence in Africa are likewise among the issues explored in Chapter 6.

V SOURCES OF INNOVATIVE FLEXIBILITY

In this discussion of the determinants of flexibility, the usefulness of our distinction between responsive and innovative flexibility becomes a little strained. All the hypotheses so far presented – about the importance of information, market efficiency, openness and political autonomy – are also relevant to an economy's innovatory flexibility. For example, we have earlier drawn attention to entrepreneurs as innovators *par excellence*. But they too are likely to flourish best when they have ready access to low-cost information, and operate in an open, competitive economic environment.

However, when we consider innovatory flexibility additional determinants suggest themselves, as identified in *Cell 8* of Figure 1.2, for we are here concerned with the institutional underpinnings of a society's capacity to 'turn a problem into an opportunity' and to achieve economic leadership.

Education

A population's access to education nominates itself as an important ingredient of this capacity. The educated person will understand more of his/her environment and the changing opportunities it offers and be more self-confident about being able to take advantage of them.[20] It is from the well-educated that an upwardly mobile middle class with capitalistic values is most likely to be created, and it is from this group that most modernisation is likely to originate. It is the educated who serve as exemplars to the rest of the population, implicitly inviting them to shed the influences of ignorance and tradition. Moreover, those with scientific and technical educations will go far to determine the ability of a country to take advantage of modern technologies.

In an interesting study of people's abilities to deal with disequilibria Theodore Schultz particularly stresses the value of education in enhancing the ability to adapt, by improving capacities to solve problems. He surveys a large number of empirical studies bearing upon the influence of education in developing-country agriculture and concludes that there is enough evidence 'to give validity to the hypothesis that the ability to deal successfully with disequilibria is enhanced by education . . .', adding that 'this ability is one of the major benefits accruing to people privately in a modernising economy' (1975: 843). (This latter remark can be taken to mean that increasing people's ability to adapt enhances their control over their own lives – their knowledge, and capacity to take advantage, of the possibilities open to them – which further points up the potential value of increasing our knowledge of the determinants of economic flexibility.)

Technological capabilities

Even countries with no aspirations to become leaders in basic research or in the development of new products nonetheless require a strong technological base if they are to be able to adapt foreign technologies to local needs (for some adaptation to local conditions is virtually always needed) and to search in a selective and discriminating manner for advances abroad which have potential for local application.[21] If they aspire to go beyond mere adaptation to a more innovatory mode – introducing more substantial improvements to existing products, or developing new products and processes – the depth of their technological capabilities will, we suggest, be even more crucial.

We can here follow Bell and Pavitt (1993: 261–2) in thinking of technological capabilities as referring to 'the resources needed to generate and manage technical change, including skills, knowledge and experience, and institutional structures and linkages'. Among the inputs they identify as determining the accumulation of technological capabilities are the human and other resources necessary for researching, designing and testing; R&D at the firm level (because it is at the firm level that most productive technology is developed); 'tacit knowledge', i.e. productive knowledge acquired through experience and embodied in people and institutions; and the external agglomeration economies secured from a growing volume of technology-based activities. Arguably, the emergence of manufacturing as a leading sector is a necessary condition for the development of an adequate technological capability, with its superior revealed capacity to generate technological advances which may then be applied to other parts of the economy, and to reap the economies of scale which remain such a feature of modern production.

In an increasingly science-based world, where the pace of change has so accelerated, the importance of national-level technological capabilities can hardly be exaggerated. As Rosenberg (1982: 271) has put it, 'Perhaps the most distinctive single factor determining the success of technology transfer is the early emergence of an indigenous technological capacity'. Such an emergence is, of course, closely tied up with the provision of education, discussed above.

Technological capabilities, in the context of industrial adaptation, are the subject of Chapter 9.

Social determinants

One of the premises of this study is that national economies – and their relative performance – can only be fully understood when viewed in their institutional and social context. They exist within societies and there is a powerful interplay between the variables we choose to label 'economic' and 'social'. At this very general level, the proposition that an economy's innovative flexibility will be strongly influenced by the nature of its culture and social organisation seems irresistible, a view which finds support in Chapter 4. The difficulty is in going beyond this unhelpfully large generalisation.

Some implicit suggestions are contained in the earlier discussion of societal constraints on individuals' abilities to adapt. This points to the superiority, for the fostering of flexibility, of value systems and social structures which encourage the idea that human beings are able to improve their own lot, which value education, promote individual (or household) self-improvement, and incorporate upward mobility based on merit, and which are outward- rather than inward-looking, embracing cultural diversity and open to external influences.

Finally, we might revert to political factors, specifically the quality of leadership. This is another criterion by which the nations of East Asia, for example, have scored well. Several commentators have noted the steadiness of purpose among the leaders of such countries as South Korea and Taiwan in giving the goal of economic development priority over more short-term and 'political' objectives, and their pragmatism in being willing to drop policies that did not promote this overriding objective. To quote the World Bank again:

> One of the hallmarks of economic policy making in the [high-performing Asian economies] was the pragmatic flexibility with which governments tried policy instruments in pursuit of economic objectives. Instruments that worked were retained. Instruments that failed or impeded other policy objectives were abandoned.
>
> (World Bank, 1993b: 86)

In her studies of the politics of economic policy reform programmes Nelson (1989, Chapter 1) also emphasises the importance of the quality of leadership, in which she includes a willingness on the part of heads of government and their colleagues to influence public opinion and initiate change, shrewdness in the phasing of policy changes to avoid upsetting too many groups at once and to keep potential opposition groups isolated from each other, and a willingness to offer compensation to those who may lose from the reforms and who are in a position to make political trouble.[22]

Whether the sagacity of a country's political leadership is just a matter of luck and history or whether it can be, if not engineered, at least encouraged by constitutional arrangements is less clear. North, for example, has suggested (1992: 17) that 'democratic politics and decentralized market economies with well-specified and enforced property rights are the closest approximation we know to an adaptively efficient institutional framework', and others have pointed to the incentives created for policy responsiveness by democratic mechanisms of public accountability. On the other hand, our earlier praise for the beneficial effects in East Asia and elsewhere of the insulation of policy-makers from pressures exerted by special interest groups and by the legislature sits uneasily with the concept of democratic accountability, as does Nelson's (1989: 12) identification of 'strong centralised authority' as conducive to successful adjustment policies in developing countries.

Thus, other than an insistence that social and political forces will be important determinants of a nation's capacity to adapt, we have no strong or precisely defined hypothesis to suggest here. The political aspects of the subject are carried further in Chapter 11.

VI THE STRUCTURE OF THE REMAINDER OF THIS BOOK

In varying ways, the following three chapters explore economic flexibility at the conceptual level. In Chapter 2 Moshe Syrquin approaches the subject from a broadly structuralist perspective, relating it to the studies of structural change with which his name is closely associated and paying particular attention to the long-term relations between flexibility and economic growth. This is followed by a provocative exploration by Kaushik Basu of the treatment of flexibility in economic theory. Chapter 4, by Eric Jones, approaches the subject from the viewpoint of an economic historian and insists that we should disregard neither the path-dependent nature of the flexibility (or otherwise) of national economies nor the social factors which contribute to this condition.

Chapters 5–7 present area studies. In the first, Alexander Neuber examines the situation of Eastern European countries currently in transition from a centrally planned to a market-oriented mode of economic organisation, dissecting the inflexibilities of central planning and examining the institutional and other forces conditioning these countries' abilities to achieve market orientation in a low-cost manner. In Chapter 6 I look at the economic problems of sub-Saharan Africa as a case study in inflexibility and try to throw light on the causes of this.

For our purposes, particular interest attaches to the countries of East Asia, already cited in this chapter as paragons of economic and policy flexibility. Ha-Joon Chang's interpretation of their case, in Chapter 7, offers a subtly different view, however, arguing that the neo-liberal school have misunderstood the nature of this case and that policy-induced rigidities have underlain the undoubted longer-term flexibility of these economies. This is followed in Chapter 8 by a case study of a different type, a comparative study of economies' responses to the oil shocks of the 1970s and 1980s. In this Peter Smith and Alistair Ulph approach their task from both micro and economy-wide perspectives, and for the latter task develop an index of economies' flexibility.

Chapter 9 takes the microeconomics of the topic further. Sanjaya Lall there takes up the important topic of the industrial adaptability and technological capabilities of developing countries, contrasting the situations of African and Asian countries and bringing out the complex, multifaceted nature of the subject. He too is critical of the neoclassical school, not because market forces do not matter but because of the importance of going beyond getting prices right.

Maxwell Fry takes a more neoclassical view. His Chapter 10 addresses the case of the financial sector, drawing attention to the importance of the financial system for the overall flexibility of the economy and examining the forces which prevent it from making its full contribution. He particularly stresses the adverse effects for financial markets of many state interventions, including interventions which impede the competitive efficiency of such markets.

In a contribution complementary to Chang's, David Seddon and Tim Belton-Jones come to grips with the political determinants of economic flexibility in Chapter 11, addressing this with special reference to the East Asian case but also surveying the wider literature bearing on the policy responsiveness of governments. Finally, the volume comes full circle in Chapter 12, where I attempt to distil general results from the preceding chapters, examine the extent to which they provide support for the hypotheses presented above, and explore policy inferences that might be drawn from the study.

NOTES

1 Thus, a study of country experiences with IMF programmes found that natural disasters had been an important, perhaps dominant, factor in decisions to turn to the IMF for help in six out of seventeen countries studied (see Killick and Malik, 1992: 604).

2 Bangladesh is the most spectacular example of a country prone to weather shocks,

recording in 1960–81 seventeen major floods and thirty-seven cyclones, and with many further disasters since.

3 Figures for 1950 are from Kenwood and Lougheed, 1993, Table 28 and those for 1991 are from World Bank, 1993c, Table 15.

4 Thus, the OECD economies recorded an average growth rate of 4.2 per cent in 1962–79, against 2.4 per cent in 1979–92, although there were admittedly considerable movements around these averages (World Bank 1993a, Table 6.2).

5 On this see Killick (1992), which explores the difficulties created for policy-makers by the large uncertainties but points out that in already marginal agricultural areas action may be needed quite soon.

6 Thus, a World Bank (1992) study of experiences with structural adjustment programmes singles out Korea, Indonesia and Thailand as among the few countries in which the adjustment process was followed by a swift transition to a new growth path (p. 3). On structural change in East Asia see Chowdhury and Islam, 1993, Chapter 1.

7 See the OECD (1983) for a discussion of the adjustment policies of industrial countries.

8 Thus Easterly and Levine (1993: 15) on their finding of a 'mysteriously poor performance of Africa', i.e. lower rates of growth than can be explained by standard growth models: 'The temptation will be strong to use words like "governance", "culture", and "institutions" to explain the unexplainable. We think the temptation should be resisted . . . to the extent that these concepts are unobservable and unmeasurable, they do not satisfy the basic scientific requirement that all hypotheses be falsifiable . . .'

9 For evidence see the earlier reference to the work of Theil and his associates p. 4.

10 See Lächler, 1988, for an exploration of this theme, applied to the question of anti-inflation policies in 'Southern Cone' Latin American countries.

11 The influence of North, 1990 and 1992, on the following must be acknowledged.

12 For a similar view see Kirzner (1986), who sees such entrepreneurial attributes as making the link between invention and innovation.

13 For evidence that public investment can have a stimulating effect on investments within the private sector see Blejer and Khan, 1984; and Greene and Villanueva, 1991.

14 The history of attempts to deal with the debt crisis of the heavily indebted Latin American countries after 1982 can be traced in these terms. The initial effort was focused on cutting absorption and both consumption and investment were reduced. As a result, there were major improvements in the trade balances of the debtor countries (necessary in order that they could make interest payments on their external debt) but at the cost of severely reduced living standards and investment levels. In the belief that such sacrifices were not indefinitely sustainable and could, in any case, prove counter-productive, from about 1987 international attention switched to 'adjustment with growth', with the intention of being able to ease up on the absorption variables. The 'Baker Plan' of that year was the catalyst, although only limited improvement was achieved in practice.

15 Thus, Mody (1990: 311) attributes much of the proven ability of Taiwan's electronics industry to respond successfully to the use in that country of various public productivity, research standardisation and marketing institutions to gather and disseminate information to private history.

16 See the September 1990 special issue of the *World Bank Economic Review* on imperfect information and rural credit markets.

17 For evidence on this and discussions of the complexities arising from the continuing coexistence of planning and market modes see Hussain and Stern (1991) and

Perkins (1988).

18 For a more sceptical view of this proposition and for further discussion of the meaning and measurement of labour market flexibility see Boyer, 1987.

19 Thus, a major World Bank study (1993b: 318–20) of the 'East Asian Miracle' argues the great importance of that region's manufactured exports for over-coming imperfect information by permitting the acquisition of the knowledge necessary for high productivity through the purchase of new equipment, direct foreign investment, the licensing of existing foreign technologies, information from customers and in other ways.

20 An interesting recent piece of evidence pointing to a connection between edu-cation and responsiveness is reported in Bernheim and Scholz (1993). They found that in the USA tax incentives to encourage saving are less effective for those without a college education because, though both those with and without college education responded in some degree, the elasticity of the college-educated to changes in the rate of return was roughly seven times larger.

21 See Rosenberg (1982) and Fransman (1986) for valuable surveys of the literature on innovation and technological change. Both these writers – and many others – stress the potentially high costs of the search process and that adaptation to local conditions is an almost invariable rule in the introduction of foreign technologies into the domestic productive system.

22 Consistent with this, Horowitz (1989: 207) suggests there is more scope for the exercise of political leadership in developing-country conditions, where the strength of the central government may be greater *vis-à-vis* organised interest groups than in the more highly articulated societies of the industrial world. Support for this proposition comes from a study of agricultural policy change in India by Varshney (1989) who argues that the state had considerable degrees of freedom to initiate changes (a) because existing policies were widely agreed to be failing and (b) because interest groups had not coalesced in defence of the status quo or in favour of particular solutions.

REFERENCES

Adam, C., W. Cavendish and P. Mistry (1992) *Adjusting Privatization*, London: James Currey.

Arndt, H.W. (1988) '"Market failure" and underdevelopment', *World Development* 16(2), February: 219–30.

Bell, Martin and Keith Pavitt (1993) 'Accumulating technological capability in developing countries', in *Proceedings of World Bank Annual Conference on Development Economics, 1992*, Washington, DC: World Bank.

Bernheim, Douglas and John Scholz (1993) 'Private saving and public policy', Working Paper no. 4215, Cambridge, MA: National Bureau of Economic Research.

Black, Stanley W. (1985) *Learning From Adversity: Policy Responses to Two Oil Shocks*, Essays in International Finance no. 160, Princeton, NJ: Princeton University, December.

Blejer, M. and M. Khan (1984) 'Government policy and private investment in developing countries', *IMF Staff Papers* 31(2), June: 378–403.

Boltho, Andrea and Gerald Holtham (1992) 'New approaches to economic growth', *Oxford Review of Economic Policy* 8(4), Winter: 1–14.

Boyer, Robert (1987) 'Labour flexibilities: many forms, uncertain effects', *Labour and Society* 12(1), January: 107–30.

Chenery, Hollis and T.N. Srinivasan (eds) (1988, 1989) *Handbook of Development*

Economics, vols I and II, Amsterdam: North-Holland.

Chowdhury, Anis and Iyanatul Islam (1993) *The Newly Industrialising Economies of East Asia*, London: Routledge.

Clements, Kenneth W., Frederick E. Suhm and Henri Theil (1979) 'A cross-country tabulation of income elasticities of demand', *Economic Letters 1979* no. 3: 199–202.

Easterly, William, Michael Kremer, Lant Pritchett and Lawrence Summers (1993) 'Good policy or good luck? Country growth performance and temporary shocks', Washington, DC: World Bank, mimeo.

Easterly, William and Ross Levine (1993) 'Is Africa different? Evidence from growth regressions', Washington, DC: World Bank, April, mimeo.

Etzioni, Amitai (1987) 'Entrepreneurship, adaptation and legitimisation', *Journal of Economic Behaviour and Organization 8*.

Finke, Renata, Mercedes C. Rosalsky and Henri Theil (1983) 'A new cross-country tabulation of income-elasticities of demand', *Economic Letters 1983* no. 12: 391–6.

Fransman, Martin (1986) *Technology and Economic Development*, Brighton: Wheatsheaf Books.

GATT (1985) *International Trade Report 1984–85*, Geneva: GATT.

—— (1991) *International Trade Report 1990–91*, Geneva: GATT.

Greene, J. and D. Villanueva (1991) 'Private investment in developing countries: an empirical analysis', *IMF Staff Papers* 38(1), March: 33–58.

Hoff, Karla and Joseph E. Stiglitz (1990) 'Introduction: imperfect information and rural credit markets – puzzles and policy perspectives', *World Bank Economic Review* 4(3), September: 235–50.

Horowitz, Donald L. (1989) 'Is there a Third-World policy process?', *Policy Sciences* 22(3–4), September.

Hussain, A. and N. Stern (1991) 'Effective demand, enterprise reforms, and public finance in China', *Economic Policy* 12, April: 141–86.

Jenkins, Rhys (1991) 'The political economy of industrialisation: a comparison of Latin American and East Asian newly industrialising countries', *Development and Change* 22(2), April: 197–232.

Kaldor, N. (1972) 'The irrelevance of equilibrium economics', *Economic Journal* 82(328), December.

Kenwood, A.G. and A.L. Lougheed (1993) *The Growth of the International Economy, 1820–1993*, 3rd edition, London and New York: Routledge.

Killick, Tony (1992) 'Policy-making under extreme uncertainty: developing country responses to global warming', *Journal of International Development* 4(1), January–February: 29–40.

Killick, Tony and Moazzam Malik (1992) 'Country experiences with IMF programmes', *World Economy* 15(5), September: 599–632.

Kindleberger, Charles P. (1962) *Foreign Trade and the National Economy*, New Haven, CT: Yale University Press.

Kirzner, I.M. (1986) *Discovery and the Capitalist Process*, Chicago: University of Chicago Press.

Klau, Friedrich and Axel Mittelstädt (1986) 'Labour market flexibility', *OECD Economic Studies* no. 6, Spring: 8–44.

Krueger, Anne O. (1978) *Liberalization Attempts and Consequences*, New York: Ballinger.

Lächler, Ulrich (1988) 'Credibility and the dynamics of disinflation in open economies', *Journal of Development Economics* 28(3), May: 285–308.

Meulders, Danièle and Luc Wilkin (1987) 'Labour market flexibility: critical introduction to the analysis of a concept', *Labour and Society* 12(1), January: 3–18.

Mody, Ashoka (1990) 'Institutions and dynamic comparative advantage: the electronics industry in South Korea and Taiwan', *Cambridge Journal of Economics* 14(3), September: 291–314.

Morris, C. and I. Adelman (1988) *Comparative Patterns of Economic Development 1850–1914*, Baltimore, MD: Johns Hopkins University Press.

Nelson, Joan M. (ed.) (1989) *Fragile Coalitions: The Politics of Economic Adjustment*, New Brunswick, NJ: Overseas Development Council and Transaction Books.

North, Douglass C. (1990) *Institutions, Institutional Change, and Economic Performance*, Cambridge: Cambridge University Press.

—— (1992) 'Transactions costs, institutions, and economic performance', *Occasional Paper no. 30*, San Francisco: International Center for Economic Growth.

Organisation for Economic Cooperation and Development (OECD) (1983) *Positive Adjustment Policies: Managing Structural Change*, Paris: OECD.

Perkins, Dwight (1988) 'Reforming China's economic system', *Journal of Economic Literature* XXVI(2), June: 601–45.

Piore, M.J. and C.F. Sabel (1984) *The Second Industrial Divide: Possibilities for Prosperity*, New York: Basic Books.

Rosenberg, Nathan (1982) *Inside the Black Box: Technology and Economics*, Cambridge: Cambridge University Press.

Schultz, Theodore W. (1975) 'The value of the ability to deal with disequilibria', *Journal of Economic Literature* XIII(3), September.

Shams, Rasul (1989) 'Adjustment constraints in developing countries – a comparative study', *Intereconomics* 24(2), March/April: 71–8.

Stiglitz, Joseph E. (1988) 'Economic organization, information and development', in Hollis Chenery and T.N. Srinivasan (eds) *Handbook of Development Economics*, Amsterdam: North-Holland.

Syrquin, Moshe (1988) 'Patterns of structural change', in Hollis Chenery and T.N. Srinivasan (eds) *Handbook of Development Economics*, Amsterdam: North-Holland, vol. I, Chapter 7.

Theil, Henri and James L. Seale (1987) 'Income elasticities at different price vectors', *Economics Letters 1987*: 24, 261–5.

Varshney, Ashutosh (1989) 'Ideas, interests and institutions in policy change: transformation of India's agricultural strategy in the mid-1960s', *Policy Sciences* 22(3–4), September.

World Bank (1990) *World Bank Economic Review* 4(3) (special issue).

—— (1992) *The Third Report on Adjustment Lending: Private and Public Resources for Growth*, Washington, DC: World Bank.

—— (1993a) *Global Economic Prospects and the Developing Countries, 1993*, Washington, DC: World Bank.

—— (1993b) *The East Asian Miracle: Economic Growth and Public Policy*, New York: Oxford University Press.

—— (1993c) *World Development Report 1993*, New York: Oxford University Press.

2

FLEXIBILITY AND LONG-TERM ECONOMIC DEVELOPMENT

Moshe Syrquin

I INTRODUCTION

Long-term economic growth is intrinsically a process of change. Associated with the rise in income are changes in composition of demand, international trade and factor use, all of which interact with the pattern of productivity growth, availability of natural resources and government policies in determining the pace and nature of industrial growth. This process of industrialisation is only one aspect of the general transformation which Kuznets (1966) identified as 'modern economic growth'.

The pervasive application of science-based technology, which according to Kuznets is the defining characteristic of the current economic epoch, has far-reaching implications. These include the concentration of economic activity in urban centres with the consequent displacement of population; a switch to large-scale enterprises, with a corresponding change from self-employment to employee status; and a move towards universal education. These and other such trends lead to changes in the structure of families and in their roles as providers of safety nets, and to changes in the social positions, expectations and aspirations of various groups in the population. 'Because the required adaptations can and do alter the positions, prospects, and power of established groups, conflict and resistance are intrinsic to the growth process' (Abramovitz, 1989: 354). Both Abramovitz and Kuznets emphasise the necessity of a mechanism for conflict resolution, and the emergence of the state as arbiter among group interests and mitigator of the adverse effects of economic change. 'Policy action and institutional changes are required [to minimise] the costs of, and resistance to, the structural shifts implicit in, and required for, a high rate of growth' (Kuznets, 1979: 130). Flexibility and adaptability appear to be key elements in facilitating the all-encompassing transformation required by modern economic growth, particularly in view of the conflictual nature of the process.

In this chapter I shall consider the relationship between flexibility and long-run structural transformation. Long-run patterns are at times punctuated by short-term shocks which, in the absence of the appropriate flexible

34

reactions, may derail the economy from its long-term growth path. However, in this chapter they are not considered except when they leave their mark through hysteresial effects. Part II starts with a discussion of some issues related to the concept of flexibility, followed in Part III by a selective review of the use of the concept in the literature relevant to economic development. In Part IV there is a brief presentation of the stylised facts of growth and structural transformation, with emphasis on those where flexibility appears to be most relevant. The final section offers a more extended discussion of the long-term relation of flexibility and growth.

II FLEXIBILITY – A PRELIMINARY DISCUSSION

The notion that flexibility contributes to growth does not appear to need much arguing. It appears in the context of developing countries, in the analysis of economies in transition between systems, and in explanations of the productivity slowdown in more advanced economies. However, in trying to define flexibility and to establish its relation to growth, it is all too easy to fall into a circularity trap by postulating that flexibility is positively associated with growth and therefore fast growing countries must somehow be flexible. And yet it is arguable that over the last twenty years economies in East Asia have been more flexible than economies in Africa. Large differences in growth performance may indicate where to look for measures of flexibility, but by themselves cannot be taken as such measures.

I shall not, therefore, attempt a formal definition of long-run flexibility but shall confine myself to some observations on essential elements in such a definition, relying on Killick's broad discussion of the issue in Chapter 1 and (1994). For this purpose it may be useful to start with a brief listing of his categories, to which I shall refer along the way. The level of flexibility of an economy can be said to depend on (a) informational and incentive systems and (b) factors bearing upon the responsiveness of economic agents to those systems. The first category refers to factors affecting the opportunity sets of economic agents, while the second focuses on agents' reactions. If flexibility is deemed to be below its potential (optimal?) level and amenable to be influenced by policy, it must be because of a government or market failure somewhere in the system. The above categories are useful in identifying the problem and determining the scope for action.[1]

The efficacy of an information system is clearly related to the level and spread of education and to the availability and quality of the means of mass diffusion. But information is also intimately tied with uncertainty. The individual agent may be uncertain about the nature of the constraints, about the persistence of changes in the economic environment, and about the intentions and credibility of other agents, including the government. The experience of the formerly socialist economies reminds us that misinformation is also a possibility, in which case the less diffusion the better, of course.

The incentive system, exogenous for the individual, is the principal channel through which flexibility can be enhanced. The crucial question is whether policy-makers have the ability and will to do so – a question further explored in the final section of this paper.

With regard to the responsiveness of individuals, there is a potential identification problem: a relatively low response may simply be a rational individual adjustment to constraints in accordance with his/her preferences. It is important to try and separate among the determinants of aggregate flexibility those related to initial conditions, or simply compositional effects, from market and government failures. For example, an observed low supply elasticity in agriculture could be the result of low elasticities at the product level, but also of a large weight in the sector of products where elasticities are inherently low even under the best circumstances. In the former case the observed low response may be a reflection of tastes or of undeveloped (though efficient) information systems, in which case there is no failure. But it could also be the result of imperfect capital markets (market failure), or of an irrational protection system (government failure).

In lieu of a definition

As a starting point flexibility can be identified with an ability to make the best out of a given situation. While this formulation also refers to static allocative efficiency, discussions of flexibility usually arise in dynamic contexts as efficient adjustments to changing circumstances, covering as a most important sub-case the ability to recognise mistakes and the willingness to do something about them. Furthermore, the constraints themselves, the external circumstances, are not always totally exogenous but may be amenable to change. For example, flexibility means being able to take advantage of an expanding international market, but it is also an ability to expand market share in a contracting market. More generally, it is also the ability to create new opportunities in addition to recognising and exploiting available ones.

This ambiguous working definition serves to highlight some of the key issues in the analysis of flexibility. Here I briefly discuss the main issues and then return in the final section of the chapter to their principal implications for the relation between flexibility and growth.

Flexibility of what or whom?

The focus in this chapter is on the flexibility of national economies. One aspect of this is market flexibility which one can associate with high elasticities of demand and supply. Low elasticities imply that large changes in price are needed to correct or reduce market disequilibria, which tend to distort the signalling role of the price mechanism (see Little, 1982). The issue of market flexibility, particularly in the labour market, figures prominently in the recent literature that tries to explain the productivity slowdown and the persistence of unemployment for the industrialised countries (see, for example, OECD, 1989 and essays in Lawrence and Schultze, 1987). This is undoubtedly an important facet of flexibility at the national level, but for the analysis of long-term development we may have to probe at lower and higher levels of aggregation.

National flexibility is clearly related to the pattern of responsiveness at the individual level, but the relation is not a simple one. Elastic responsiveness by individuals does not necessarily translate into high flexibility at the aggregate level (see Chapter 6 on the paradox of responsiveness in Africa). And, on the other hand, flexibility at the aggregate level may require constraining the range of choice of the individual. At the individual level choices may follow custom which may result in rigid behaviour, but this could help overcome inefficiencies associated with strategic behaviour in prisoner's dilemma situations.

Going beyond single markets, flexibility at the national level depends on the institutional framework governing economic activity and policy (the state). The paradox in Africa of apparently responsive farmers and yet inflexible economies is largely explained in terms of institutional failure. At this level the problem of simultaneity becomes most acute. Flexibility depends on institutions, but in turn it is a major determinant of institutional change.

Flexibility for what objective?

Once we have identified the decision-maker and the level of analysis, the next step is to clarify what the objective function might be. If we avoid the circularity trap in defining flexibility, then it is not necessarily the case that the more of it the better. This can be illustrated for the individual and at the macro level. Individuals, even if they are utility maximisers, may rationally choose to react to changes in the economic environment in a conservative way. In an uncertain world fraught with non-convexities and lock-in traps, seemingly inflexible responses may actually be socially optimal for the given environment. Adopting Killick's scheme, we can say that a judgement about flexibility being low would then refer to deficiencies in the transmission of information or in the incentive system, but not in the extent of responsiveness. However, in some cases it could be argued that a problem of rigidity was due to the individual response being sub-optimal according to some external criterion (clearly not according to the individual's own current preferences). At one level we search for institutional constraints on the capacity to adapt, but we (some of us?) may want to go beyond that and identify traits, norms, or customs that reduce flexibility.

One of Singer's (1950) arguments for advocating industrialisation was based on the externalities derived from the more progressive traits and outlook of an industrial labour force. Similarly, Hirschman argues that 'the very attitudes alleged to be preconditions of industrialization could be generated on the job and "on the way", by certain characteristics of the industrialization process' (1984: 89).

At the aggregate level we need to consider the aversion to undesirable outcomes such as inflation and unemployment (relevant for reforms in countries in transition). Differences in reaction to a shock may be due to differences in constraints or in preferences. Bruno and Sachs (1984) point out a major conceptual problem in cross-country comparisons of macro-economic trade-offs – that variations in these may be due to different structures or to different goals.

To conclude this section I mention two implications of recognising the multiplicity of objectives and their complex interrelations with flexibility. First, once it becomes clear that we may not want to do away with all rigidities, then it seems less puzzling to use an oxymoron such as 'flexible rigidities' (Dore, 1986; and Chapter 7 by Chang). Inertia in institutions, which provide the framework for economic activity, is not necessarily pathological: 'A completely flexible framework is a contradiction in terms' (Matthews, 1986: 914). We may even want to define efficient or optimal rigidities but without implying that inefficient or dysfunctional rigidities, or even institutions, will be selected against. I return to this issue in Part V.

The second observation is that focusing on the various competing ends brings out the various trade-offs implicit in the process of choice. Actions designed to increase flexibility have associated with them expected benefits but also expected costs. This seemingly trivial aspect is often ignored in discussions about flexibility and kindred concepts (Neuber's Chapter 5 is an exception).

III NOTES ON THE LITERATURE

The concept of flexibility has not been much analysed explicitly in the economic literature. In addition to the available explicit references, however, it is possible to identify various discussions of the topic but under different labels. Without attempting a thorough survey of the literature, in this part I present a brief and partial review of those studies particularly relevant for the long-term analysis of flexibility and growth.

Economic theory

The main instances in the economic theory literature with relevance for development fall mostly under two categories: first, keeping your options open to allow a better future choice or to prevent a potential disaster, and second, constraining your current options to make sure the choice is the right one.

Hysteresis and lock-in

Economic development is a dynamic process that takes place in an uncertain environment. Decisions at the individual or aggregate levels are made with limited and imperfect information, and often are, at least in part, irreversible. That is, the expenditures involved become largely sunk costs. Under such conditions and with information emerging with the passage of time, it may be optimal to adopt a 'flexible position' and wait before taking action (see among others, Hirshleifer and Riley, 1979; Pindyck, 1991; Dixit, 1992). Flexibility is relevant when there is a trade-off between the cost of waiting and a possible loss suffered from a mistaken early commitment. The case where an action has irreversible effects is particularly relevant to the environment, where the irreversibility may be absolute (Henry, 1974; Arrow and Fisher, 1974). But the point applies also to intermediate cases where the costs of reversal are positive but finite.

Every action has to a certain extent irreversible effects; hysteresis is the rule rather than an exception. The lesson for development is that efficiency may call for long-term flexibility, and this in turn may require action to slow down or block short-run reactions.

A similar related case is the one where the individual or the economy may become 'locked-in' into a sub-optimal local equilibrium. The necessary conditions for such an outcome were first spelled out in David's 'Clio and the economics of QWERTY' (1985), and later on in various publications by David and others, notably Arthur (1989). The structural elements leading to path-dependent outcomes are usually a combination of: (i) non-convexities (indivisibilities), (ii) learning effects, (iii) co-ordination and other externalities, and (iv) a degree of irreversibility of commitments (the list is based on David, 1988 and Arthur, 1988). All of these elements seem to recur with high frequency in the development process.

Commitments and compulsive sequences

The second category deals with cases where, contrary to standard micro-economic theory, enlarging the choice set does not necessarily increase welfare. One example refers to prisoner's dilemma situations where individual rationality leads to collective inefficiency. Restricting an individual's flexibility may lead to a Pareto-superior position. A second example is the 'rules vs discretion' debate. Because of the importance of credibility, authorities may choose to bind themselves by inflexible rules and thus avoid the problem of 'time inconsistency' (Kydland and Prescott, 1977). The increasing number of countries that have recently declared their intention to legislate the independence of their central bank attests to the relevance of the credibility issue for macroeconomic policy.

A related point comes from the development literature. A basic characteristic of developing countries is the existence of slack in the economy. In terms of Killick's analysis, there is a problem of signalling and of incentives which dampens the response of economic agents. To enhance flexibility we need inducement mechanisms that can help mobilise the underutilised resources. The search for such inducement mechanisms is the hallmark of Hirschman's approach. In his *Strategy of Economic Development* (1958) there are various passages relevant for flexibility and, characteristically, in a paradoxical way. In a number of activities in developing countries there is evidence of poor performance. Reducing its scope would improve the efficiency of the use of resources. One example discussed by Hirschman is the problem due to lack of proper maintenance. An obvious way of coping with it would be to select activities which do not require much maintenance. However, this solution, besides being potentially expensive or inapplicable, has the great drawback of perpetuating the problem. Hirschman's solution: choose activities in which maintenance is of supreme importance; where the failure to maintain could prove catastrophic, thus generating a compulsion to maintain, as would be true of airlines as compared with highways, for example. More generally, the suggestion is to reduce the latitude afforded to the individual, inducing him/her through a 'focusing device' or an almost compulsive sequence to choose the right path.[2]

Development economics

In the literature of development economics, broadly defined to include some economic history and more advanced economies, we do find extensive discussions of (in)flexibility even if the term is not always explicitly used. It figures prominently in the writings of structuralists, Keynesians, and in the quasi-medical diagnoses of eurosclerosis, Dutch disease and related maladies.

Structuralism

The structuralist view of the world is one of low elasticities, low mobility, imperfect or non-existent markets, rigid social structures, etc. In short, it is a view of low flexibility (Chenery, 1975, 1986; Little, 1982). Table 2.1 presents Chenery's (1986) characterisation of the contrast between the neoclassical view of the growth process and the structuralist view.[3]

Among those that we can identify as structuralists there is a broad spectrum of views ranging from the mild versions of Nurkse, Rosenstein-Rodan and Chenery to the extreme views of the 'dependencia' approach

40

Table 2.1 Alternative views of growth

Neoclassical approach	Structural approach
Assumptions	
Factor returns equal marginal productivity in all uses	Income-related changes in internal demand
No economies of scale	Constrained external markets and lags in adjustment
Perfect foresight and continuous equilibrium in all markets	Transformation of productive structure producing disequilibria in factor markets
Empirical implications	
Relatively high elasticities of substitution in demand and trade	Low price elasticities and lags in adjustment
Limited need for sector disaggregation	Segmented factor markets
	Lags in adopting new technology
Sources of growth	
Capital accumulation	Neoclassical sources plus:
Increase in labour quantity and quality	Reallocation of resources to higher-productivity sectors
Increase in intermediate inputs	Economies of scale and learning by doing
Total factor productivity growth within sectors	Reduction of internal and external bottlenecks

Source: Chenery, 1986.

represented in, for example, Baran, Cardoso and Frank (for references see Little, 1982). Accordingly, there is large variation in the diagnoses of the causes of low flexibility and in the remedies proposed. The causes mentioned include technological factors, an archaic social structure, and the network of trade which results in the underdevelopment of the periphery. Among the remedies suggested are tax reform, agrarian reform and various other reforms calling for changes that range from the innocuous to the overthrow of the system.

The experience with the industrialisation strategy based on import substitution (ISI), advocated by structuralists, suggests a distinction between reality and a perception of reality which at times becomes self-fulfilling. A perception of low flexibility and ubiquitous rigidities, even if imagined or ideologically based, may lead to policies that in effect end up reducing the system's capacity to adjust. That this was the case with the strategy of ISI was claimed by, among others, Little, Scitovsky and Scott (1970). The path dependence of an incentive structure and of the way it is perceived are an important ingredient of North's (1990) argument of why 'history matters' [and of Jones in Chapter 4].

41

Disequilibrium and demand effects

The concept of flexibility is particularly relevant in disequilibrium situations, but mainstream economics is not as developed in dealing with such situations as it is for the analysis of equilibrium.[4]

T.W. Schultz repeatedly stressed the importance of education for growth. A central component of the acquisition of human capital is 'The value of the ability to deal with disequilibria' (1975). This ability, which Schultz includes in an extended concept of entrepreneurship, is of little value in a traditional economy with a fixed supply of resources and no change; but it has a high premium in a modern economy where change is pervasive. His analysis has clear policy implications since education is shown to influence positively the ability to cope with change.

Another example is Hicks once he went beyond steady state growth. In 1976 he interpreted the chapter in *Capital and Growth* called 'Traverse' as a first attempt at building a theory of 'an economy which has a history, . . . a system in which . . . flexibility (which disappears from sight in the steady state) is a matter of major importance' (1976: 144).

References to disequilibrium are often associated with demand-side economics. Modern economic growth is a process of growth and transformation. In neoclassical growth theory the rate of growth of output is unrelated to the expansion of demand. Since the composition of demand and output follows the level of development, more flexibility has no effect on the speed of transformation in the neoclassical framework.

A different approach incorporates demand effects and their interactions with the supply side of the neoclassical approach (here I am lumping together very different approaches having in common only that they consider demand as well, or exclusively as with some Keynesians). The common elements in this approach are: it (a) disaggregates analysis, (b) considers disequilibrium in the form of inter-sectoral differences in factor productivities, (c) allows for less than full utilisation of resources and for this to affect the rate of total factor productivity growth (TFP). In development economics representatives include mild structuralists (Chenery, 1975; Chenery, Robinson and Syrquin, 1986). In the context of more advanced countries, reference to disequilibrium and demand reminds us of Kaldor. From the vast literature that stems from his approach probably the most useful recent reference that emphasises the crucial importance of flexibility for growth and transformation is Cornwall (1977).[5] In his study Cornwall focuses on the unbalanced nature of growth, which involves wide qualitative changes in a perpetual state of disequilibrium. In such a framework there is a stress on the stimulating effects of demand pressure and on the importance of flexibility, which is determined by capital accumulation and the growth of employment. In line with Kaldor–Verdoorn arguments, the analysis relies on dynamic economies of scale and considers the manufacturing sector as the engine of growth. A vigorous reallocation of labour from low productivity sectors to manufacturing is a sign of flexibility in the economy, as well as a determinant of flexibility in that sector.

On gout, senility and other perils of riches and maturity

The last group of studies in this literature review stresses the decline in flexibility that seems to take place in 'the aging economy' (Kindleberger, 1978), or the negative impact of sudden riches on the economy's capacity to adapt. In both cases the analysis moves rapidly into issues not usually studied by economists, without this necessarily making them not amenable to economic analysis. Both issues are dealt with in more detail in Part V.

IV STRUCTURAL TRANSFORMATION

The process of modern economic growth entails, and is almost synonymous with, a radical transformation in the structure of the economy. In this section I shall present a brief summary of some of the principal uniformities in the process of development that have been identified in studies of the long-term experience of the industrialised countries, and in cross-country comparisons for a given period for broader samples of economies that also include a large number of developing countries.[6] I shall emphasise aspects where flexibility appears to be of importance and refer mostly to the experience of semi-industrial countries, not of stagnant ones. As important as establishing the average patterns of development is the search for the sources of diversity around the average trends. Accordingly, the impact of initial conditions and policy on the uniform trends is also considered in this section.

Growth and structural change are strongly interrelated. Policy can try to anticipate structural change, facilitating it or accelerating it by removing obstacles and correcting for market failures. It can also hamper growth by blocking the required changes in structure or by attempting to dictate them, as in Cambodia in the 1970s. As the Soviet experience showed, forced industrialisation can accelerate recorded growth, but only for a while and at very high cost.

Flexibility, adaptability and a capacity to transform are therefore essential for growth and structural change to proceed smoothly. Are they more important today than they were in the growth experience of the industrialised countries? Starting with the opportunities for growth, it can be argued that these are larger today and growth is therefore unequivocally easier: 'not only could more growth be attained, but a lot more has been attained than a century ago' (Krueger, 1991: 460). Krueger mentions technological improvements but gives primacy to 'the availability and buoyancy of the international market, which have permitted a degree of reliance on comparative advantage and division of labour not possible in the nineteenth century' (Krueger, 1991: 460). However, while opportunity sets have been larger in recent decades, it can still be claimed that flexibility and adaptability have become more important today, and that because of three reasons. First, the rate of population growth has been much higher in the current developing countries than in the past;[7] second, growth and structural change have accelerated considerably in the postwar period; and finally, today a country in the early stages of modern economic growth faces a large number of more-developed countries and a growing number of newly industrialising countries. The necessity to respond quickly to changing circumstances seems therefore to have become more pressing, at a time when the consequences of failing to do so were also increasing.

A list of stylised facts

This section presents some stylised facts of long-run development, starting with the growth of output and productivity and followed by patterns of structural change.

Growth of output and productivity

In the early stages of the transition, the rate of growth has often shown a tendency to accelerate as a result of an increase in the rate of capital accumulation and of productivity growth, as well as of a reallocation of factors from lower to higher productivity activities.

Total factor productivity (TFP) growth shows a similar acceleration to output growth. Figure 2.1 summarises the contributions to growth of labour, capital and TFP for a large income range. (The numbers come from the cross-country simulation model presented in Chenery and Syrquin, 1986.) For higher-income countries the figure confirms the finding of TFP accounting for a large fraction of growth. However, at low income levels the largest source of growth is capital accumulation. The difference in results according to the level of development – one of many such instances – points to the danger of generalising from the experiences of one or a few case studies to the whole range of the transition.

Changes in the structures of production and factor use

A concise picture of the dimension of the transformation appears in Table 2.2. The figures in the table relate various structural characteristics to the level of development but in a timeless fashion. Absent from this presentation is the speed of the transformation, clearly an important aspect of the analysis of flexibility, but referred to only briefly in this paper.

The transformation in final demand is one of the most uniform features of

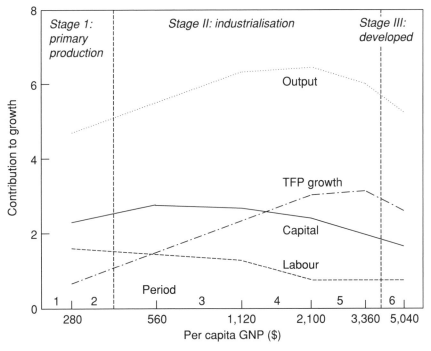

Figure 2.1 Factor contributions to growth

Source: Chenery and Syrquin, 1986.

the process of development. On average, the share of private consumption in GDP declines with the level of income, as the share of investment rises. Food consumption drops by about twenty percentage points, while non-food consumption (not shown separately) goes up.

Only a small part of the variation in aggregate trade can be related to income. Focusing on the commodity composition of exports, we find a fairly steady increase in the proportion accounted for by manufactures throughout the transition and a decline in the share of primary products (agriculture and mining) in the later stages. In the case of imports, both commodity groups show an increasing trend.

Changes in final demand and trade reinforce each other. They combine with complementary changes in intermediate uses and productivity growth to produce a more pronounced shift in the structures of production and labour use. The share of value added in agriculture declines sharply over the transition, whereas manufacturing, construction and utilities double their share and the services sector share rises by about 50 per cent. The decline in the share of agriculture in employment is more pronounced than the decline of its share in production, but since employment starts from a much higher level its percentage decline is smaller than for agricultural production. The

Table 2.2 Shares of economic structure associated with levels of per capita income (%)

Component of economic structure	Actual average <300[a]	Income per capita (1980 US$) Predicted[b]					Actual average >4,000[c]	Total change	Midpoint of change
		300	500	1,000	2,000	4,000			
Final demand									
Private consumption	79	73.3	70.2	66.4	63.1	60.3	60	−19	600
Government consumption	12	13.6	13.5	13.7	14.4	15.4	14	2	–
Investment	14	18.4	20.8	23.3	25.0	25.9	26	12	400
Exports	16	19.3	20.7	22.6	24.5	26.4	23	7	400
Imports	21	24.6	25.2	26.0	27.0	28.0	23	2	–
Food consumption	39	38.7	34.5	29.1	23.9	18.9	15	−24	1,200
Trade									
Merchandise exports	14	15.2	16.9	18.8	20.3	21.2	18	4	400
Primary	13	13.9	14.9	15.2	14.1	11.8	7	−6	–
Fuels	3	4.8	6.3	7.3	7.2	6.1	2	−1	–
Other	10	9.1	8.6	7.9	6.9	5.7	5	−5	1,250
Manufacturing	1	1.3	2.0	3.7	6.1	9.4	11	10	2,000
Merchandise imports	16	18.2	19.3	20.6	21.7	22.7	19	3	–
Primary	5	6.4	6.7	7.1	7.5	8.0	7	2	–
Manufacturing	11	11.8	12.6	13.5	14.2	14.7	12	1	–
Production (value-added)									
Agriculture	48	39.4	31.7	22.8	15.4	9.7	7	−41	700
Mining	1	5.0	6.6	7.7	7.5	6.1	1	0	–

Table 2.2 Continued

Component of economic structure	Actual average <300[a]	Predicted[b]					Actual average >4,000[c]	Total change	Midpoint of change
		300	500	1,000	2,000	4,000			
Manufacturing	10	12.1	14.8	18.1	21.0	23.6	28	18	1,200
Construction	4	4.4	4.9	5.5	6.1	6.7	7	3	1,000
Utilities	6	6.7	7.4	8.1	8.8	9.3	10	4	900
Services	31	32.4	34.6	37.8	41.2	44.7	47	16	1,300
Manufacturing									
Early	7	6.8	7.6	8.3	8.3	7.8	7	0	–
Middle	2	3.3	3.3	5.3	6.0	6.5	6	4	500
Late	3	1.8	3.2	5.3	7.6	10.2	13	10	2,500
Labour force									
Agriculture	81	74.9	65.1	51.7	38.1	24.2	13	-68	1,300
Industry	7	9.2	13.2	19.2	25.6	32.6	40	33	1,600
Services	12	15.9	21.7	29.1	36.3	43.2	47	35	1,000

Notes:
– Not applicable: change is not monotonic or significant.
Expressed as shares of GDP, except for labour force variables, which are expressed as shares of total labour force.
[a] Based on 1960–72 period for countries with per capita income less than $300 in 1970: mean approximately $180.
[b] Assumes average population (20 million).
[c] Based on 1960–72 period for countries with per capita income greater than $4,000 in 1970; mean $7,300.

Source: Syrquin and Chenery, 1989.

end result is that in spite of the rapid shift of labour out of agriculture, the inter-sectoral gap in average labour productivity initially widens before it starts to narrow down.

Changes in the use of intermediate inputs as income rises contribute to the decline in the share of agriculture in value added in two ways. First, producers in all sectors tend to substitute manufactured inputs for natural intermediates because of changes in prices and in technology. Second, producers in agriculture increase their use of inputs relative to output, reducing the ratio of value added to gross output (see Deutsch and Syrquin, 1989).

Figure 2.2 summarises the sectoral distribution of output, labour and capital for a wide income range.

Aggregate productivity

An important aspect of the development process where flexibility is of paramount importance, is the reallocation of resources from lower to higher productivity sectors. In middle-income countries this accounts for up to 30 per cent of measured TFP. This substantial contribution is estimated at a relatively high level of aggregation and is therefore just a lower bound of the real importance of inter-sectoral reallocation. Intra-sectoral shifts are probably a no less significant component of productivity growth. Ever since the detailed studies of Kuznets (1930) and Burns (1934), it has been recognised that relative stability in an aggregate quantity can hide very significant changes in its separate components.

In disaggregated cross-country comparisons or in a single country over time, one finds a high degree of uniformity of TFP across sectors for a given country or period. This country effect emerges much more clearly than does any sector or industry effect, suggesting that, in addition to any intrinsic productivity potential of an industry, the overall economic and institutional environment is important in explaining the general level of productivity growth.[8]

Variations in patterns of resource allocation

Many of the variations from the average patterns of growth are a reflection of the interaction of comparative advantage with policy. For example, a relative abundance of natural resources that are economical to exploit at given prices and technology, is expected to lead to a high share of primary exports. Although it is difficult to measure the availability of resources, a simple proxy for the proportion of resources to population is the density of the population. A high density has been shown to be significantly associated with lower trade shares and a higher share of manufactured goods in total exports (Perkins and Syrquin, 1989).

48

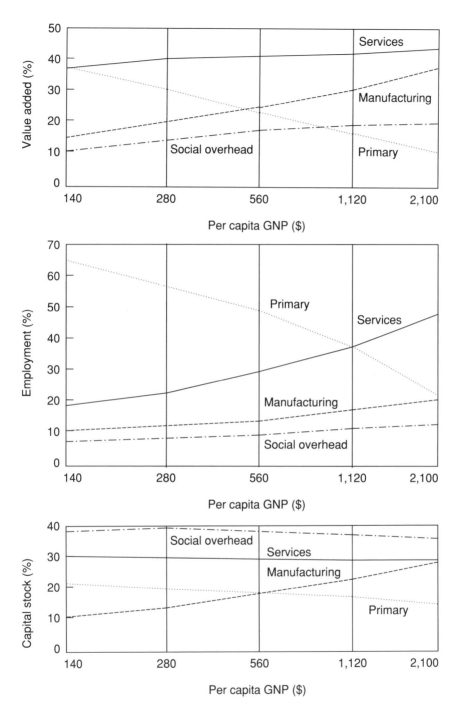

Figure 2.2 Simulations of value-added, employment and capital for cross-country model

Source: Chenery and Syrquin, 1986.

Besides the availability of resources, there are various other initial conditions that can influence the patterns of development. The size of the economy is significantly associated with the share of trade in output. Small countries are generally dependent on trade to a greater extent than are large countries, and they also tend to have higher degrees of concentration in production. The type of specialisation in small countries is determined largely by the availability of natural resources and by the policies adopted. The pattern of specialisation affects the timing of the transformation, but less so its overall nature. Thus, for example, in resource-rich countries, industrialisation is delayed in the early stages, but at the later stages the productive structure is not very different from that in the average resource-poor economy.

V FLEXIBILITY AND DEVELOPMENT

The preceding sections have argued the case for flexibility and presented some of the stylised facts of structural transformation which make flexibility so important for development. This final section focuses on the question: what kind of relation can we expect between flexibility and the level of development?

During the early stages of the transition from a poor primarily rural country to one which is mostly urban and with a much higher income, flexibility probably shows an increasing trend. The relation, however, is not a simple smooth one and over longer stretches of development it is most probably non-monotonic. As the level of income goes up we can expect flexibility to increase as a result of the following development-related changes: an improvement in the systems generating and disseminating information, a rise in the levels of education and skills of the labour force, a change in the attitudes of the population leading to a higher level of mobility and responsiveness in general, and a greater commitment to growth on the part of the government. At higher income levels, flexibility probably reaches a peak and then declines. The reasons for this slowing down in the capacity to respond to changes are mostly related to institutional rigidities that spread with maturity. (These are further discussed below in the section on institutions.)

I have just argued that the relation between flexibility and development is non-monotonic: positive in the earlier stages of development but only up to a point. In fact, even the positive association at low income levels is better seen not as a smooth upward trend but rather only as a likely outcome where positive effects on flexibility outweigh negative ones. Take education, for example; it adds to the ability to respond promptly but also to the capacity for rent-seeking and for other types of behaviour that are profitable to the individual but potentially detrimental socially. The balance between contradictory effects may be a precarious one and various elements, including

50

chance or just luck, could tilt it either way. The following sections look at some of the elements which influence the flexibility–income relation.

Time and the horizon

Most of the analysis in this chapter has involved the adequacy of the response, by an agent or by the economic system as a whole, to an exogenous shock. Time, mostly ignored so far, enters in various non-trivial ways. The response to a permanent, persistent change may increase with the length of the period; but we may also find the short-run reaction being partially or completely offset in the long run.

Speed as a decision variable

Over any given length of horizon the speed aspect of flexibility is to a large extent a decision variable rather than a datum. Speed can be increased, but only by incurring some costs. This means that, even ignoring the possibility of a fast reaction leading to sub-optimal results (see the section on lock-in), higher speed may not always be desirable.[9] In the context of structural transformation, speed can be considered excessive if it produces incongruences between demand and supply. For example, high labour mobility is a sign of flexibility, but very fast rural–urban migration can well exceed the capacity of the modern sectors to absorb the migrants, the result being unemployment, shanty towns, and other characteristics of 'overurbanisation'.

Short-run and long-run

The strength of the response to a stimulus may vary with time, as in the case of Marshallian elasticities which are assumed to increase with time. This is an instance of the Le Chatelier principle which states that the less constrained a system the more responsive it will be to exogenous changes. In our case, the longer the horizon the more degrees of freedom we have; fixed factors become variable, consumption habits can be modified, etc. However, short-run and long-run flexibility do not always go in the same direction. Various palliatives soften the blow of a shock in the short run but may reduce long-run flexibility: foreign aid and other capital inflows, for example, allow the economy to cope with an emergency without too much adjustment but, precisely because they reduce the necessity to adjust, may increase the vulnerability of the system to future shocks.

Time dependence

A policy instrument or a strategy instituted as a response to a certain change may have to wait before its full impact is felt, in accordance with the

51

expectation that elasticities increase with time. But simultaneously, the efficacy of that same policy measure may erode with time as circumstances change and agents learn how to protect themselves or even benefit from the measure. An important example may be the import-substitution strategy in Latin America – successful in the 1930s, but less so in the 1950s. The perception of a progressive erosion in the power of the strategy is reflected in numerous references since the 1950s to the 'exhaustion' of the 'easy' phase of import substitution. Similarly, Lindbeck (1985) has argued that the full employment policy in Europe, quite successful in the 1960s, by its very nature generated substantial disincentive effects and thus 'carried the seeds of its own destruction' (p. 155). However, it took some time and a deterioration in the international environment before these effects made themselves felt.

The above points to a very significant aspect of flexibility, namely, the ability to abandon a course of action if it turns out to have been a mistake, or once it ceases to be effective. In a study contrasting economic policies in Korea and Turkey, Krueger (1987) finds the principal difference in policy formulation between the two countries in 'the speed with which policy-makers recognized their mistakes and dealt with them' (p. 201). The choice of an outward-oriented trade strategy was itself the result of 'the Korean policy-makers' willingness to confront their problems and to recognize difficulties early which . . . led them to address perceived difficulties more quickly . . . than did the Turkish policy-makers' (pp. 201–2).

Initial conditions

The long-term relation between flexibility and development is in part a function of the set of initial conditions. Observed high flexibility in a certain setting may have much to do with suitable initial conditions, and this has important implications for the possibility of replication. For example, the East Asian success stories started this period of high growth with relatively high levels of human capital and adequate infrastructure (Ranis, 1989).

The best reaction to an exogenous change might depend on structural characteristics such as size and the availability of resources. Large countries in Latin America weathered the depression of the 1930s more successfully than smaller economies, for whom import substitution on a wide front was never (or should not have been) a real option. Similarly, when recommending how fast to proceed with liberalisation in economies in transition, there seems to be some schizophrenia (Singh, 1991): fast for Poland, less so for China. Taking into account the differences in size and in other initial conditions largely resolves that puzzle.

A particularly important initial condition is the availability of natural resources. Not only do resources influence the expected patterns of development, but they also affect in diverse ways the interrelations between flexibility, growth, and institutions. It has long been recognised that an abundance of resources is not always an unambiguous blessing. Rosenberg (1969) cites Marshall, Postan and Pirenne to the effect that a lack of resources contributed to the good performance of Holland, Flanders and Venice respectively. In each case the initial disadvantage was more than made up by the spur it gave to inventiveness for overcoming it.[10]

A resource-rich country, particularly in the early stages of development, may experience a mediocre growth performance because of problems related to the management of rents. This has a short-run and a long-run aspect. The short-run problems of relevance for our topic are nowadays associated with the Dutch-disease syndrome. The essential elements can be illustrated by the example of a sudden price boom or resource discovery. Initially foreign-exchange earnings go up sharply, but then the beneficial effects of the shock start to dissipate and may even become negative. Government expenditures and wages (primarily in the public sector) go up easily in the good times, but are hard to reduce afterwards should it become necessary. Rent-seeking activities proliferate, encouraged by the increase of funds in the public sector. These and other such effects tend to reduce the flexibility of the economy. Although they are not inevitable concomitants of a primary export boom, they occur with a high enough frequency to regard them as characteristic features (see, for example, Lewis, 1984). An additional effect of an inflow of foreign exchange, much emphasised in the literature, is the appreciation of the exchange rate which reduces the competitiveness of the tradable sectors. In the long run this effect may delay the process of industrialisation or even block it altogether.

For the long-run aspect of rent management in the primary export economy, we can refer to the 'staples approach' pioneered by economic historians. By the staples approach I mean those historically oriented export-based growth theories that focus on countries (or regions) exporting primary commodities (agriculture and mining), often specialising in one or a few goods. Starting from an exogenous export boom that occurs as a result of a resource discovery or increased demand, the main question asked is whether the staple industry remains an isolated enclave, or whether its stimulus spreads throughout the economy. Two features in the analysis are particularly relevant in the present context: the importance of the identity of the export commodity and the interrelations between the commodity, institutions and performance. The propagation of the stimulus is taken to depend on various technological characteristics associated with a commodity, such as capital intensity, economies of scale, skill requirements, income distribution and pattern of consumption. These are often summarised in the form of various potential linkages (see, for example, Watkins, 1963 and Hirschman, 1977). Given an institutional set-up, some commodities (wheat) are seen as more likely to lead to a successful propagation than others (sugar). The higher flexibility in such cases would to a large extent be a function of the identity of the staple. Analysis at the aggregate level, or even at the sector level, that did not identify the commodity in question would be inadequate. The idea that the type of commodity or of activity can influence attitudes, traits, and performance is not unique to the staple approach. Singer was cited above as claiming a superiority for manufacturing over agriculture for this reason. Rosenberg (1964) refers to Adam Smith and David Hume advocating commercial activity because of its character-forming impact, and himself regards the existence of a well developed capital goods sector as 'one of the most important factors contributing to viability and flexibility of industrial economies' (p. 71).

The technological relations embedded in the linkages represent only a permissive condition; the transmission of the initial stimulus is contingent on the absence of domestic impediments such as various market imperfections, barriers to mobility and other rigidities in the economic environment. In other words, it is contingent on a favourable institutional background (Watkins, 1963; Meier, 1984). Some authors go even further and regard the evolution of the institutional framework itself as being a function of the identity of the commodity. In a characteristic exploration into what he labels micro-Marxism, Hirschman (1977) conjectures that the emergence of a new mode of production (say, slavery) is intimately tied to the availability of an activity with strong affinity to that mode (say, sugar).

Institutions

The long-run evolution of flexibility is clearly influenced by the institutional framework whose evolution is, in turn, conditioned by the level of flexibility. The interrelations between the two are a book-length subject. This section attempts only to point to some key links and to pull together some scattered references on specific topics that seem particularly germane to the long-run flexibility of national economies.

More on ossification

Previous sections have already mentioned the thesis that long-term development, when not disrupted by war or revolution, promotes the creation of distributional coalitions and instils some inertia in methods and techniques which tends to retard further growth (Olson, 1982). Hodgson (1989), in a study of sixteen advanced economies, tested the dependence of productivity growth on the degrees of institutional flexibility and disruption. To measure flexibility, Hodgson postulated a bell-shaped relation with respect to time in order to capture the idea that 'the most flexible period for the more rapid development of new skills and routines is during the period at which industrialisation is proceeding at the fastest pace' (p. 89). Major disruptions such as revolutions and military occupations, are conducive to learning and establishing new habits and routines, but to qualify for the analysis the disruption must occur only after the process of economic and social transformation is under way. The impact of a particular disruption is measured as a function of the time which has elapsed from the beginning of the transformation to the actual time of the event. The regression results for 1960–84, and for two sub-periods, strongly supported both the flexibility and the disruption hypotheses.

Path dependence

The evolution of institutions is path-dependent and, as it proceeds in an uncertain world and in a framework of strong interdependences and economies of scale, it can lead to lock-in into less than optimal states (North, 1990). As argued above, an institutional response might be optimal in a given situation but it may become dysfunctional as circumstances change. The strategy of import substitution in Latin America has already been mentioned. A different example is the case of Israel. The economic challenges immediately after the establishment of the state were enormous, yet the performance surpassed all expectations. In recent decades a drastic reversal seems to have taken place: the growth of productivity slowed down considerably, inflation got out of hand (for a while at least), rent-seeking activities proliferated, and a certain paralysis seemed to have afflicted the government. In short, flexibility shrank from its former relatively high level. These long-run developments suggest that the institutions that are required for nation-building may not be the most appropriate in a world that needs quick response (see Ben-Porath, 1986).

A missing factor – some binary comparisons

A theme that runs through this chapter and much of the literature on institutions is the distinction between necessary and sufficient conditions or, in other formulations, between permissive and compulsive sequences, or between potential for growth and the conditions leading to its realisation. Often we find a case where the necessary conditions for success seemed to be present, and yet performance was disappointing. A certain factor seemed to have been missing after all. That factor usually represents some facet of the institutional set-up. It appears at times under labels such as social capability (Abramovitz, 1989), the managerial factor (Mason, 1984), or civic community (Putnam, 1993).

A useful way to get a glimpse of the missing factor is by comparing the experience of two economies with very different performance in spite of similar initial conditions (apart from the missing factor). In a previous section Krueger's contrasting of Korea and Turkey was presented. Korea also appears, with Egypt this time, in Mason's (1984) comparison of development policy and its implementation. In 1960 both countries were of similar size and had almost the same level of per capita income. Their subsequent performances were widely divergent. Among the various managerial factors considered to explain this difference, Mason regards government objectives as the single most important one: in Korea the primary purpose of government was to facilitate growth, while in Egypt it was not. Similarly, Adelman and Morris (1967) single out 'the leadership commitment to economic development' as the most important factor, while for Reynolds (1983) it is 'the political organization and the administrative competence of government'. The importance of these factors in explaining recent stagnation in Africa is a major conclusion of Killick (Chapter 6).

If Korea appears often as an example of success, it is in Latin America that we tend to find the disappointing case. Institutions figure prominently in studies that attempt to explain why the same staple (wool, wheat) was more successful in propagating growth in some countries (Australia, Canada) than in others (Argentina) (see various studies in Platt and di Tella, 1985). In a study contrasting long-term development in Latin America and in the USA, Mosk (1951) went back to institutional conditions established in the colonial period, such as the social structure and the system of landholding. More recently, North (1990) made use of this same case to illustrate path dependence. Both the Latin American republics and the USA began their independence with abundant resources, similar international opportunities and similar formal institutions. Many republics adopted US-inspired constitutions influenced by the ideology derived from the American and French Revolutions. The rules were the same, but little else was.

> In the case of Latin America, an alien set of rules was imposed on a long heritage of centralized bureaucratic controls and accompanying ideological perceptions of the issues. In consequence, Latin American federal schemes and efforts at decentralization did not work. . . . The persistence of the institutional patterns that had been imposed by Spain and Portugal continued to play a fundamental role in the evolution of . . . policies and perceptions.
>
> (North, 1990: 103)

The last example is a comparison by Putnam (1993)[11] of not one but twenty new regional governments created in Italy in 1970. As a test of the path dependence of institutions, the Italian case, as contrasted with the USA–Latin America comparison, seems more powerful analytically because more variables are held constant and because the North–South cleavage in Italy has endured longer than in America. Twenty years later it was evident that some governments had done better than others. The differences in performance could not be traced back to the level of development, nor to education or urbanisation. What seems to have accounted for the differences in performance and in citizens' levels of satisfaction was the regional level of 'civic community'. This represents the pattern of social co-operation based on tolerance, trust and widespread norms of active citizen participation. A main lesson from this study, which corroborates North's analysis, is that 'Social context and history profoundly condition the effectiveness of institutions' (p. 182). (See also Jones, Chapter 4.)

Another lesson from Putnam's study is that the 'civic community has deep historical roots' (p. 183). In stressing the tenacious past he echoes, among others, Abramovitz and North. In discussing catching up, Abramovitz argues that the realisation of a productivity potential depends on a host of societal characteristics which, following Ohkawa and Rosovsky, are called 'social capability'. Technological backwardness is not only not enough to assure a fast catching up, but is itself the result of the same 'tenacious social characteristics'. '. . . a country's potential for rapid growth is strong not when it is backward without qualification, but rather when it is technologically backward but socially advanced' (Abramovitz,1989: 222). For North 'the tenacious survival of institutional constraints in the face of radical alterations in the formal rules of the game is the best evidence of the increasing-returns characteristics of an institutional framework' (North, 1990: 101). Just how tenacious is the past? According to Putnam – very much so. The differences in civic community can be traced back to 'distinctive traditions that have endured for nearly a thousand years' (Putnam, 1993: 180). As Putnam is aware, 'This is a depressing observation . . . [as a] regional president in an uncivic region exclaimed. . . . "This is a counsel of despair! . . . The fate of the reform was sealed centuries ago"' (Putnam, 1993: 183).

Some qualifications

To conclude on a more positive note I now list some qualifications to the apparent fatalism in Putnam's analysis. First, the past is not always a good predictor of the future. Easterly *et al.* (1993) analyse growth in a large number of countries over the period 1960–88, sub-divided into various sub-periods. Their main conclusion is that growth rates are highly unstable over time, while country characteristics are highly persistent. A second key result is that fundamentals matter. In other words, investment in human capital and infrastructure, deepening of financial markets, absence of price and exchange controls, active participation in international trade, these and other such factors still account for a significant fraction of differences in performance across countries. The second qualification is simply a rephrasing of Gerschenkron's thesis, namely that 'preconditions' are not carved in stone; substitutes can usually be improvised or imposed to overcome a seemingly unpassable barrier. Which brings us to the third and final comment. Most change is gradual and lock-in is a frequent outcome; together they give the past its tenaciousness. But changes do take place, and at times they appear as discontinuous jumps which allow the system to escape any real or imaginary low-level equilibrium traps. In such cases the problem is one of perception, of overcoming the dissonance experienced when facing unexpected forward movement. Two examples, taken from Kindleberger are:

Adam Smith's failure to recognize the onset of the industrial revolution happening around him as *The Wealth of Nations* appeared in 1776 [and] . . . the resurgence of the French economy after World War II at a time when the analysts, including economic historians, were busy explaining French economic retardation.

(Kindleberger, 1990: 352)

VI CONCLUDING REMARKS

This chapter has presented some issues related to the nature, significance and determinants of flexibility. It turned out to be easier to discuss the nature of flexibility and to argue the case for its significance than to sort out its determinants. This is largely due to the difficulty of defining the concept in an unambiguous and measurable way. Its importance becomes apparent indirectly through some effects that depend on it, such as labour mobility: an adequate rate of mobility being an indication of the presence of flexibility. The ambiguity in defining the flexibility of national economies is in part due to the fact that we have to aggregate the responses of a variety of agents. Such responses reflect the constraints under which an agent operates, its objectives and agility in achieving them.

The adequacy of an economy's response to an external stimulus is a function of flexibility. Along the way from flexibility to the national response we find various facets of the ability of individuals: the ability to forecast economic events and reliance on the supply of information, and the ability to process and assess that information. Next, we require a capacity for making collective decisions and a mechanism for conflict resolution. An important aspect of this is the ability to recognise and correct mistakes. Finally, both at the individual and at the collective level there is the need for learning, that is, for adaptation of responses to changes in the environment and to the mere passage of time.

The way in which flexibility interacts with economic growth depends on the international environment and on initial conditions. In this last category we have the institutional set-up which, as argued above, evolves slowly and gradually. The tenacious past is very much present, making economic outcomes path-dependent. The response to an exogenous shock cannot be analysed in abstract terms: a variety of responses is possible, and even likely, depending on the specific conditions in each case.[12] A characteristic of the growth process, similar to path dependence but less well recognised, is the time dependence of policies or growth strategies. The efficacy of a flexible – successful – reaction to a change in circumstances, if not continuously adapted, can be expected to become eroded over time or even to reverse sign and become counterproductive. The duration of policy measures, or time elapsed since adoption need to be considered when discussing flexibility.

The main conclusion on the positive side is that flexibility can probably be enhanced by very prosaic methods. Foremost is education or more generally, the development of human capabilities, which ultimately determine the capacity to adapt and to transform. A key necessary factor for promoting flexibility and growth is a high level of capital formation. It is necessary, to serve as the carrier of new technologies and to allow resources to be reallocated from lower to higher productivity sectors. By itself, however, a high rate of investment is not sufficient: it will be translated into a high rate of growth only if the institutional framework is conducive to that. On the policy side it was argued that fundamentals matter: flexibility and growth cannot be promoted by ignoring the discipline of the marketplace. At the same time government intervention may be essential to anticipate and facilitate the process of structural transformation. Intervention works best when it is applied promotionally rather than restrictively (see Pack and Westphal, 1986), and this leads us back to flexibility which probably makes it more likely that the promotional type will prevail.

NOTES

I am grateful to Nicola De Liso for helpful comments on an earlier draft.

1 The categories resemble the analysis of Arndt (1988) of potential failures in the price mechanism. He identifies at least three components of the mechanism which may fail: signalling, response and mobility.

2 See Clague (1970) for additional aspects of reducing the latitude of agents, and Rosenberg (1969) for a discussion of compelling pressures in the area of technological change.

3 In the section on the irreversible effect mention was made of the environment. Current debates on sustainable growth bring to mind the earlier ones about structuralism. In both cases a major issue is the (mostly implicit) assumption about elasticities of substitution between various types of capital, or between types of capital and the environment. The 'economic' approach assumes positive elasticities which probably increase with time, in contrast with alternative approaches which tend to assume no substitutability.

4 Machlup (1963) is still worth reading for the various ways in which this and related terms (for example, structure and structural change) have been used and abused in economics.

5 Earlier references are Kindleberger (1967) with an application of the surplus labour model to explain European growth in the 1950s, and Svennilson's *Growth and Stagnation in the European Economy* (1954) – a key pioneer study on flexibility.

6 The exposition and the summary of results are based on studies that originate

with Simon Kuznets. They draw primarily from Kuznets (1966, 1971), Chenery, Robinson and Syrquin (1986), Syrquin and Chenery (1989) and Syrquin (1988).

7 Johnston (1970) has argued that, as compared with the experience of today's more advanced countries, the principal obstacle to sustained growth in developing countries is the much faster rate of population growth.

8 In a study of twenty-eight sectors in thirteen industrial countries, Dollar, Wolff and Baumol (1988) report a similar finding: countries with high relative labour productivity in one sector tend to have it in all of them. This result, they emphasise, goes against the predictions of the factor–price–equalisation model.

9 Speed in its relation to flexibility appears also in the analysis of socialist economies. An important feature of the socialist growth strategy has been labelled 'haste'. It is part of the explanation of the decline in productivity over time (see Ofer, 1987). In the literature on economies in transition the speed issue appears in the debate on gradualism versus shock treatment (see, for example, Fischer and Gelb, 1991 and Neuber in Chapter 5).

10 Adversity may stimulate inventiveness; but again it may not. In a related context, Kindleberger (1978) mentions the response a British civil servant gave to a question about the stimulation to industry after British entry into the Common Market: 'Not every kick in the pants galvanises; some merely hurt.'

11 A characteristically lucid book review in *The Economist* (6 February 1993) first brought this interesting book to my attention. The presentation in the text paraphrases some of the exposition in the review.

12 This point was forcefully argued in Kindleberger (1951), where he contrasted the very different responses of five European countries to the same stimulus – the decline in the price of wheat after 1870.

REFERENCES

Abramovitz, M. (1989) *Thinking About Growth and Other Essays on Economic Growth and Welfare*, Cambridge: Cambridge University Press.

Adelman, I. and C.T. Morris (1967) *Society, Politics and Economic Development: A Quantitative Approach*, Baltimore, MD: Johns Hopkins University Press.

Arndt, H.W. (1988) '"Market failure" and underdevelopment', *World Development* 16(2) February: 219–29.

Arrow, K.J. and A.C. Fisher (1974) 'Environmental preservation, uncertainty and irreversibility', *Quarterly Journal of Economics* 88: 312–19.

Arthur, W.B. (1988) 'Self-reinforcing mechanisms in economics', in P.W. Anderson, K.J. Arrow and D. Pines (eds) *The Economy as an Evolving Complex System*, New York: Addison–Wesley.

—— (1989) 'Competing technologies, increasing returns, and lock-in by historical events', *Economic Journal* 99: 116–31.

Ben-Porath, Y. (1986) 'Introduction', in Y. Ben-Porath (ed.) *The Israeli Economy: Maturing through Crises*, Cambridge, MA: Harvard University Press.

Bruno, M. and J. Sachs (1984) *Economics of Worldwide Stagflation*, Cambridge, MA: Harvard University Press.

Burns, A.F. (1934) *Production Trends in the United States Since 1870*, New York: National Bureau of Economic Research.

Chenery, H.B. (1975) 'The structuralist approach to development policy', *American Economic Review* 65: 310–16.

—— (1986) 'Growth and transformation', in H.B. Chenery, S. Robinson and M. Syrquin (eds) *Industrialization and Growth: A Comparative Study*, New York: Oxford University Press.

Chenery, H.B. and M. Syrquin (1986) 'Typical patterns of transformation', in H.B. Chenery, S. Robinson and M. Syrquin (eds) *Industrialization and Growth: A Comparative Study*, New York: Oxford University Press.

Chenery, H.B., S. Robinson and M. Syrquin (eds) (1986) *Industrialization and Growth: A Comparative Study*, New York: Oxford University Press.

Clague, C. (1970) 'The determinants of efficiency in manufacturing industries in an underdeveloped country', *Economic Development and Cultural Change* 18: 188–205.

Cornwall, J. (1977) *Modern Capitalism: Its Growth and Transformation*, London: Martin Robertson.

David, P.A. (1985) 'Clio and the economics of QWERTY', *American Economic Review Proceedings* 75: 332–7.

—— (1988) 'Path-dependence: putting the past into the future of economics', Institute for Mathematical Studies in the Social Sciences Technical Report 533, Stanford, CA: Stanford University, mimeo.

Deutsch, J. and M. Syrquin (1989) 'Economic development and the structure of production', *Economic Systems Research* 1: 447–64.

Dixit, A. (1992) 'Investment and hysteresis', *Journal of Economic Perspectives* 6: 107–32.

Dollar, D., E.N. Wolff and W.J. Baumol (1988) 'The factor–price equalization model and industry labour productivity: an empirical test across countries', in R.C. Feenstra (ed.) *Empirical Methods for International Trade*, Cambridge, MA: MIT Press.

Dore, R. (1986) *Flexible Rigidities: Industrial Policy and Structural Adjustment in the Japanese Economy 1970–80*, London: Athlone Press.

Easterly, W., M. Kremer, L. Pritchett and L.H. Summers (1993) 'Good policy or good luck? Country growth performance and temporary shocks', *Journal of Monetary Economics* 32: 459–83.

Fischer, S. and A. Gelb (1991) 'The process of socialist economic transformation', *Journal of Economic Perspectives* 5: 91–105.

Henry, C. (1974) 'Investment decisions under uncertainty: the "Irreversibility effect"', *American Economic Review* 64: 1006–12.

Hicks, J.R. (1976) 'Some Questions of Time in Economics', in A.M. Tang, F.M. Westfield and J.S. Worley (eds) *Evolution, Welfare and Time in Economics*, Lexington, MA: Lexington Books.

Hirschman, A.O. (1958) *The Strategy of Economic Development*, New Haven, CT: Yale University Press.

—— (1977) 'A generalized linkage approach to development, with special reference to staples', *Economic Development and Cultural Change* 25: 67–97.

—— (1984) 'A dissenter's confession: "The Strategy of economic development" revisited', in G.M. Meier and D. Seers (eds) *Pioneers in Development*, New York: Oxford University Press.

Hirshleifer, J. and J.G. Riley (1979) 'The analytics of uncertainty and information: an expository survey', *Journal of Economic Literature* 17: 1375–421.

Hodgson, G. (1989) 'Institutional rigidities and economic growth', *Cambridge Journal of Economics* 13: 79–101.

Johnston, B.F. (1970) 'Agriculture and structural transformation in developing countries: a survey of research', *Journal of Economic Literature* 3: 369–404.

Killick, T. (1994) 'The flexibility of national economies: a neglected attribute in economic development', in J.D. MacArthur and J. Weiss (eds) *Agriculture, Projects and Development*, Aldershot: Avebury.

Kindleberger, C.P. (1951) 'Group behavior and international trade', *Journal of*

Political Economy 59: 30–47.

—— (1967) *Europe's Postwar Growth: The Role of Labour Supply*, Cambridge, MA: Harvard University Press.

—— (1978) 'The aging economy', *Weltwirtschaftliches Archiv* 114: 407–21.

Krueger, A.O. (1987) 'The importance of economic policy in development: contrasts between Korea and Turkey', in H. Kierzkowski (ed.) *Protection and Competition in International Trade*, Oxford: Basil Blackwell.

—— (1991) 'Benefits and costs of late development', in P. Higonnet, D.S. Landes and H. Rosovsky (eds) *Favorites of Fortune: Technology, Growth, and Economic Development since the Industrial Revolution*, Cambridge, MA: Harvard University Press.

Kuznets, S. (1930) *Secular Movements in Production and Prices*, Boston, MA: Houghton Mifflin Co.

—— (1966) *Modern Economic Growth*, New Haven, CT: Yale University Press.

—— (1971) *Economic Growth of Nations: Total Output and Production Structure*, Cambridge, MA: Harvard University Press.

—— (1979) 'Growth and structural shifts', in W. Galenson (ed.) *Economic Growth and Structural Change in Taiwan: The Postwar Experience of the Republic of China*, Ithaca, NY: Cornell University Press.

Kydland, F. and E.C. Prescott (1977) 'Rules rather than discretion: the inconsistency of optimal plans', *Journal of Political Economy* 85: 473–92.

Lawrence, R.Z. and C.L. Schultze (1987) *Barriers to European Growth*, Washington DC: The Brookings Institution.

Lewis, S.R., Jr (1984) 'Development problems in the mineral-rich countries', in M. Syrquin, L. Taylor and L.E. Westphal (eds) *Economic Structure and Performance: Essays in Honor of Hollis B. Chenery*, New York: Academic Press.

Lindbeck, A. (1985) 'What is wrong with the West European economies?', *World Economy* 8: 153–70.

Little, I.M.D. (1982) *Economic Development: Theory, Policy and International Relations*, New York: Basic Books.

Little, I.M.D., T. Scitovsky and M. Scott (1970) *Industry and Trade in Some Developing Countries: A Comparative Study*, London: Oxford University Press.

Machlup, F. (1963) *Essays in Economic Semantics*, Englewood Cliffs, NJ: Prentice-Hall.

Mason, E.S. (1984) 'The Chenery Analysis and some other considerations', in M. Syrquin, L. Taylor and L.E. Westphal (eds) *Economic Structure and Performance: Essays in Honor of Hollis B. Chenery*, New York: Academic Press.

Matthews, R.C.O. (1986) 'The economics of institutions and the sources of growth', *Economic Journal* 96: 903–18.

Meier, G.M. (1984) 'Conditions of export-led development: note', in G.M. Meier, *Leading Issues in Economic Development*, 4th edition, New York: Oxford University Press.

Mosk, S.A. (1951) 'Latin America versus the United States', *American Economic Review* 41: 367–83.

North, D.C. (1990) *Institutions, Institutional Change and Economic Performance*, Cambridge: Cambridge University Press.

OECD (1989) *Economies in Transition: Structural Adjustment in OECD Countries*, Paris: OECD.

Ofer, G. (1987) 'Soviet economic growth: 1928–1985', *Journal of Economic Literature* 25: 1767–833.

Olson, M. (1982) *The Rise and Decline of Nations: Economic Growth, Stagflation and Social Rigidities*, New Haven, CT: Yale University Press.

Pack, H. and L.E. Westphal (1986) 'Industrial strategy and technological change: theory vs reality', *Journal of Development Economics* 22: 87–128.

Perkins, D.H. and M. Syrquin (1989) 'Large countries: the influence of size', in H.B. Chenery and T.N. Srinivasan (eds) *Handbook of Development Economics*, vol. II, Amsterdam: North-Holland.

Pindyck, R.S. (1991) 'Irreversibility, uncertainty and investment', *Journal of Economic Literature* 29: 1110–48.

Platt, D.C.M. and G. di Tella (eds) (1985) *Argentina, Australia and Canada: Studies in Comparative Development*, London: Macmillan.

Putnam, R.D. with R. Leonardi and R.Y. Nanetti (1993) *Making Democracy Work: Civic Traditions in Modern Italy*, Princeton, NJ: Princeton University Press.

Ranis, G. (1989) 'The role of institutions in transition growth: the East Asian newly industrializing countries', *World Development* 17(9): 1443–53.

Reynolds, L.G. (1983) 'The spread of economic growth in the Third World: 1850–1950', *Journal of Economic Literature* 21: 141–80.

Rosenberg, N. (1964) 'Neglected dimensions in the analysis of economic change', *Oxford Bulletin of Economics and Statistics* 26: 59–77.

—— (1969) 'The direction of technological change: inducement mechanisms and focusing devices', *Economic Development and Cultural Change* 18: 1–24.

Schultz, T.W. (1975) 'The value of the ability to deal with disequilibrium', *Journal of Economic Literature* 13: 827–46.

Singer, H.W. (1950) 'The distribution of gains between investing and borrowing countries', *American Economic Review* 40: 473–85.

Singh, I.J. (1991) 'Is there schizophrenia about socialist reform theory? Some thoughts about the two-track approach' (World Bank) *Transition Newsletter about Reforming Economics* 2(7): 1/3.

Svennilson, I. (1954) *Growth and Stagnation in the European Economy*, Geneva: United Nations Economic Commission for Europe.

Syrquin, M. (1988) 'Patterns of structural change', in H.B. Chenery and T.N. Srinivasan (eds) *Handbook of Development Economics*, vol. I, Amsterdam: North-Holland.

Syrquin, M. and H.B. Chenery (1989) 'Three decades of industrialization', *World Bank Economic Review* 3: 145–81.

Watkins, M.H. (1963) 'A staple theory of economic growth', *Canadian Journal of Economics and Political Science* 29: 141–58.

3

FLEXIBILITY IN ECONOMIC THEORY

Kaushik Basu

I INTRODUCTION

The *production* of fashion garments (not to be confused with *design*) is a fairly low-skill activity. Suppose shirts of a particular colour and cut are suddenly in vogue in New York. The department stores and suppliers will immediately transmit by some form of electronic mail the design and orders to their Asian suppliers. But the fashion, like many fashions, will last only for a few weeks or at most a few months. Manufacturing countries which can respond *promptly* are the ones which win such orders and rake in large profits. Other nations which are slow to respond (and, more importantly, have a reputation for slowness), either because they do not have the technology or because they do have the bureaucracy, will be the losers.

This is what happens in the multi-million dollar international garment industry. Clothesline, for instance, is a specialty store in the USA that has done outstandingly well by this method. It faxes to its Asian producers the colour and design of the clothes it needs (it is expected that it will soon be projecting the true colour and size on a television screen for the manufacturers to see) and expects the supplies to come in within weeks. By responding to the changing fashions quickly and not getting caught with large inventories of clothes which no one wants, Clothesline is subjecting the well-established, but also more inflexible, department stores to tough competition, and has been cited as a factor contributing to the high level of bankruptcy among them (Koshy, 1993). From the point of view of the producers, as just mentioned, this means that nations that can cut through their bureaucracy and respond with speed will get the orders; it is not simply a matter of low wages. Hong Kong and China have been doing very well in this regard.

This story illustrates the critical importance of suppleness or flexibility in economic functioning. Yet flexibility hardly figures in the writings of economists. In standard neoclassical models, flexibility is unimportant because it is total. In other models (such as fix-price equilibrium models) the extent of inflexibility is constant. In any event, the role of suppleness of action is minimal in textbook economics. My opening paragraph suggests that this should not be so. In making that case, however, it also seems to be making a case for flexibility, and that is not necessary. One of the objectives of this chapter will be to argue that the role of flexibility in economics is intriguing partly because of its ambiguity. Flexibility, of course, helps but, more interestingly, it can also hinder. To demonstrate this, one does not have to search for the proverbial needle in the haystack; in evolutionary game models, examples crop up often enough. The purpose of this chapter is to try to gather together various ideas of flexibility that have appeared in the literature on theoretical economics in different scattered places and in various guises.

As with several important phenomena in the social sciences, such as influence, power and coercion, 'flexibility in organisations' is difficult to define. Yet it is something that most of us can recognise when we see it. As with many other important ideas, this may well be a good enough starting point. Very often usage precedes definition. Thus, economists talked about luxury goods long before they were able to agree upon a formal definition based on the elasticity of demand. I therefore make no attempt here to define flexibility formally, but work on the assumption that, we can generally recognise flexibility when we see it even if we cannot offer a rigorous definition. In Part II, I shall review some of the broad ideas concerning flexibility that have occurred explicitly or implicitly in the standard theoretical schools of thought.

Organisations as well as organisms often have differing levels of adaptability. Is it always the case that the more adaptable agents do better? Modern evolutionary game theory provides an excellent framework for attempting to answer this question. Part III, therefore, introduces the reader to this kind of game theory and is the only section where flexibility is given a fairly rigorous characterisation.

Then comes a brief discussion in Part IV of what may be called 'natural' flexibility, showing how certain kinds of flexibility can emerge naturally through the pressures of market forces. This is illustrated by the example of share tenancy. Part V delves into the more down-to-earth subject of what makes for more flexibility in governments and organisations. It makes suggestions regarding the reorganisation of government decision structures. Since most of the ideas in this paper are introduced through examples, the concluding section attempts to draw together the general principles that emerge.

II THE IDEA OF FLEXIBILITY

Let us consider a standard neoclassical model. Firms have technologies and try to maximise profits and consumers have their preferences and try to maximise utility. Through their interaction prices emerge and firms earn equilibrium profits and consumers equilibrium utility. Now let us ask the question: What would happen in this model if producers were slow to respond to the prices or were inflexible in terms of the technology they use? Such a question is very difficult to answer within the confines of the neoclassical model, the reason being that in the standard neoclassical model perfect flexibility is a built-in assumption. To change this would require one to change the very framework of analysis. If one wants to go on to the larger question of the goodness or badness of flexibility in governments and organisations (the subject of Part V of this chapter) and the issue of whether a country ought to be flexible in terms of its macroeconomic policies, the standard neoclassical model turns out to be quite inadequate.

Let us, however, for the moment continue on the theme of microeconomic flexibility. What is important is that inflexibilty, of varying degrees, is an essential part of virtually all the components of real-life economic interactions. A producer can get locked into a technology or a management set-up which needs to be refashioned to meet the needs of a new market condition. There have been tales of consumers suffering starvation because the only food available is what they have traditionally considered to be inedible. And, thanks to the joint action of consumers and producers, prices often continue to be sticky even when demand outstrips supply or supply exceeds demand. On all these fronts, theorists have made occasional forays in an attempt to incorporate some of these inflexibilitites into the neoclassical models. One of the most celebrated efforts was that by the 'non-Walrasian' school (see, for example, Dreze, 1975; Malinvaud, 1977). Malinvaud, in particular, made it very clear that his real interest was not so much in the total rigidity of prices as in the fact that prices, in reality, were not completely flexible, as in the Walrasian model. However, when it came to modelling this formally, the literature began to specialise in completely fixed prices. Moreover, the rigidity of prices was compensated in these models by the flexibility of rations (supply quotas for producers and demand restrictions for consumers). So once again, from our present point of view, where the concern is with the extent of flexibility, this type of model is not of much use.

Among the many micro-level efforts, one interesting exercise is that in oligopoly theory, which studies 'supply-functions equilibria'. In traditional oligopoly theory, firms are assumed to choose either prices or quantities. Once a firm has made its choice, this is assumed to be fixed and other firms respond bearing this in mind. There has now emerged some work where firms are supposed to choose not just prices or quantities, but supply curves (see, for example, Klemperer and Meyer, 1989). The interesting feature of this is that it embodies a novel view of the organisation of the firm. We now have a firm which can adjust both prices and production plans. In brief, it has an organisation which is flexible but which can at the same time commit itself to a particular supply–response type of behaviour.

Finally, one may ask what the new institutional theories have to offer on this subject, since the question we are asking here is ultimately an institutional one. According to a class of writings loosely labelled the new institutional school, an institution emerges and persists when the benefits of such an institution exceed the costs (see Basu *et al.*, 1987 and Schlicht 1993 for discussions). This theory has a bearing on the subject of flexibility in two ways: first, an optimal institution must also be optimally flexible and, secondly, when an institution ceases to be the most apt because of changes in, for instance, the international environment, it will, according to this point of view, wither away and give rise, in its place, to a more suitable institution.

I have argued earlier (Basu, 1990) that this argument is flawed because for an institution to be changed there have to be individuals (a) who benefit from the change and (b) who have the power to bring it about. If the new institution is optimal for the new context, it is arguable that proposition (a) will be true, while it is entirely possible for (b) to be false. Most changes are not Pareto improvements. Hence, when somebody gains, there may well be somebody who loses, and the latter can thwart the change. Moreover, as we know from simple game-theoretical examples such as the prisoner's dilemma, even Pareto improvements may not always be possible because individual rationality can conflict with group rationality.

It now seems that one can draw a line between the automatic optimality of institutions and its critique as outlined in the preceeding paragraph. This entails bringing in arguments from evolutionary economics. If an institution is too sub-optimal, it is arguable that the society in which it functions will perish, and with it the institution. Hence, natural selection would require that institutions which persist should create benefits above a certain cut-off level. Evolution would thus ensure that even if institutions are not the best, they are reasonably good for *homo economicus*. Some agrarian institutions may be best understood in this light, as I try to demonstrate in Part IV.

The idea of evolution is important here not only from the point of view of new institutional economics but in general. Some of the most important recent advances in modelling flexibility have occurred in the newly emergent evolutionary game theory. The next section gives a brief introduction to this.

III FLEXIBILITY AND INFLEXIBILITY IN EVOLUTIONARY GAMES

Evolutionary game theory is one area where a sharp distinction can be drawn between flexibility and rigidity, and their advantages and disadvantages assessed.

The essential difference between the kind of game theory that economists are used to and evolutionary games as developed by Maynard Smith and Price (1973) (see also Maynard Smith, 1982) is that in an evolutionary game the strategy represents a phenotype, or a fixed behaviour pattern, and each player is, in turn, a phenotype. Consider the well-known Hawk–Dove game:

	Hawk	Dove
Hawk	−1, −1	2, 0
Dove	0, 2	1, 1

Consider a large number of agents (or players) where each agent is represented by a probability, p, of playing Hawk and a probability, $1-p$, of playing Dove. If an agent p is such that $p = 1$, we say the agent is a Hawk and if $p = 0$, we say that he is a Dove. Pairs of agents are drawn at random from the population of agents and as they play the pay-offs they get are represented in the pay-off matrix above.

Thus if a Hawk is matched against a Hawk their mutual aggression causes havoc to both and they each get −1 units of pay-off. If a Hawk is made to play a Dove, the Hawk's aggression meet with no defence and the Hawk gets hold of all the resources without having actually to fight; so the Hawk gets 2 and the Dove gets 0. If both players are Doves, they share the resources and get 1 each.

Check next that if a player of type p plays another player of type q, then the former player earns an expected pay-off of

$$A(p, q) = -pq + 2p(1-q) + (1-p)(1-q);$$

and player q earns

$$A(q, p) = -qp + 2q(1-p) + (1-q)(1-p)$$

The seminal equilibrium idea introduced by Maynard Smith and Price is that of evolutionary stability. Broadly speaking, a phenotype is an evolutionary stable strategy if a population of such phenotypes can destroy any mutant bridgeheads of other phenotypes that may enter into this society. More formally, a strategy, p, is an *evolutionarily stable strategy* (ESS) if, for all strategy q, which is distinct from p,

(1) $A(p, p) > A(q, p)$ or

(2) $A(p, p) = A(q, p)$ and $A(p, q) > A(q, q)$.

In other words, either p's pay-off against p is greater than q's pay-off against p or the two are the same but p's pay-off against q exceeds q's pay-off against q.

From the point of view of the present paper, note that an agent or player in an evolutionary game is a completely inflexible agent; being a phenotype he is locked into a strategy and cannot change this. This obviously raises the question as to how a rational agent, namely, one who can be flexible in terms of his choice of action, fares in such a framework. There has been some recent work where agents are allowed different degrees of flexibility (Banerjee and Weibull, 1991, 1993; Basu, 1992b).[1] To understand this, suppose S is the set of all possible actions or strategies potentially open to all agents. But depending on the nature of the agent and his training and history, only a subset of S would be open to him. Thus if the agent in question is a devout Hindu and one of the actions in S, say action a, is eating beef, then we may suppose that the agent chooses from a subset of S which excludes a.

Assume that agents 1 and 2 choose their actions from the sets X_1 and X_2, respectively, where X_1 and X_2 are subsets of S. Thus for agent 1 actions outside X_1 are simply considered out of bounds; he does not consider such actions when maximising utility. Thus, for instance, most of us would not consider picking another person's pocket even if that gave us a large pay-off. I shall call X_1 player 1's domain of choice or civil norm.[2] If X_1, is a proper subset of X_2, we shall say that 2 is a more flexible agent.

In Banerjee and Weibull's formulation they visualise an animal in the same way as in Maynard Smith's work; that is, as an agent with a singleton domain of choice, that is, a unique behaviour pattern, which is in fact tantamount to there being no choice. Its behaviour is fixed exogenously. Into such a kingdom of animals they introduce Adams and Eves, characterising them as agents who can freely choose from within S. In other words, they think of human beings as rational agents with a domain of choice equal to S. Would such rational agents have greater survival chances than animals? The answer is: Not necessarily. In an evolutionary context, being able to choose may well turn out to be a disadvantage. The process of natural selection may select against such agents. This is surprising at one level. If one agent can only choose action a and another agent can choose between actions a and b, surely the latter cannot do worse? In an immediate sense this is true. But in the long run, having a choice can weaken an agent's ability to precommit and therefore can hurt him.

This is easy to understand from an example. Consider the standard model of Cournot duopoly (that is, an industry which has two firms producing the same good with each firm deciding how much it should produce, leaving the determination of the price to the market). If two rational agents, who are free to choose any level of output play against each other, they will earn the usual Cournot profits. Now suppose one of these agents is inherently inflexible and can only produce the output of a Stackelberg leader (that is, someone who chooses first knowing that the other firm will not choose independently but will respond to it like a follower). In other words, his domain of choice is a singleton consisting of the Stackelberg leader's output. Seeing the inflexibility of this agent, the other player (who is flexible) would respond rationally, that is, produce the Stackelberg follower's output. Thus the inflexible player gains because inflexibility is a form of exogenous commitment.

It is exactly this kind of reasoning that goes into principal-agent models in oligopoly (Vickers, 1984; Fershtman and Judd, 1987; Sklivas, 1987). In these models, owners of firms actually pay to hire managers in order to make their own firms less flexible.

This, in turn, relates to the even larger question of flexibility of government policy in devising macroeconomic policy, as addressed in the paper by Kydland and Prescott (1977). Their problem is related to the problem of commitment in game theory. They show that a government which is totally flexible and takes each policy decision optimally may do worse than one which commits itself to some rules. This follows from the fact that citizens are strategic agents who respond actively to government policy choices. A government that credibly commits itself to some rule and does not budge, even on the occasion when it would benefit by doing so, has the advantage that citizens treat its decision as a *fait accompli* and do not try to undo the government's plans by their own behaviour.

From a theorist's point of view, it is important to be aware of this pathological aspect of flexibility – the fact that flexibility can do damage. Yet it is also important to be aware that this is a pathological aspect. The flexibility of human beings *vis-à-vis* animals *may* damage human beings, but it is arguable that thus far humans have done better on earth than other creatures.

In the end this is an empirical question. Nevertheless, I think we can agree that nations should strive to be flexible, to be able to seize opportunities quickly. A later section of this paper investigates how they can do so. In fact, whether this is ultimately good for a nation or not is not really relevant here. To the extent that most people do want nations to be flexible, the question of how they can be flexible is important.

At this point, however, I want to digress to introduce a rather contentious idea, that of natural flexibility.

IV NATURAL FLEXIBILITY: A DIGRESSION

The above discussion of evolution should make us wonder whether, in situations where flexibility is desirable, it would not emerge and survive naturally. To acknowledge this possibility is to make way for an explanation of some institutions whose existence had earlier appeared puzzling. I shall illustrate this from the example of share tenancy.

The existence of share tenancy in large areas of less developed countries and also in continental Europe in the nineteenth century and earlier has long been a source of puzzlement for the theoretical economist (see, for example, Cheung, 1968; Bardhan, 1983; Basu, 1984, 1990). Not only is share tenancy inefficient, as both Adam Smith (1776) and Alfred Marshall (1920) knew; a landlord who leases out his land on a share tenancy contract also does worse than he would under the fixed rental system. This is so for the obvious reason that a share tenant gets only a fraction of any increase in output brought about by the increased use of fertiliser, labour and other inputs.

Since, on the other hand, the tenant usually incurs the full cost of these inputs, he has a natural tendency to economise excessively on the application of these inputs. Hence, total output is less and so is the landlord's income. Why then does share tenancy exist? The answer to this has turned out to be very difficult and has spawned quite a substantial literature.

It is now evident that there is an intimate connection between what Killick in Chapter 1 calls 'relatively unpredictable and short-term shocks' and systems of land tenure such as *metayage* or share tenancy. To recognise this is an essential step towards understanding the existence of share tenancy. Share tenancy is a market-created shock absorber.

Based on several conversations in a village in Bihar, in eastern India, I had sketched out a theoretical model (Basu, 1992a) showing that, given weather-related uncertainty and limited liability, share tenancy may well be the best tenurial system from the landlord's point of view. I do not want to go into this question here. Instead, I shall demonstrate how share tenancy may be thought of as the market's response to building shock absorbers in the face of relatively unpredictable and short-term disruptions.

To examine this question, let us suppose that agrarian contracts are underwritten by a 'limited liability' clause. In other words, if there is a sufficiently large crop failure, the tenant is allowed to forgo having to pay rent.

Suppose now that the tenant can choose between planting traditional seeds (option T) or some new, more resilient hybrid (option N). The former can yield more output but if there is a drought they fail totally; on the other hand, the new hybrid seeds are more resilient. The chart below sums up the information about the amount of crop yield from the two options in good weather and in bad. Thus, for instance, option T in bad weather yields two units of output.

	Harvest	
	Bad weather	*Good weather*
Option T	2	12
Option N	6	11

Assume that the probability of bad weather is 1/2. By making calculations of the expected yield it becomes clear that option N is the socially more desirable outcome. Note also that expected output is more under N. But now suppose that the limited liability clause is effective and the tenant has the right to an income of 2. Let the rent be 4 units. Then the tenant's consumption under various options and weather conditions as shown below.

Tenant's consumption under fixed-rent tenancy		
	Bad weather	Good weather
Option T	2	8
Option N	2	7

Note that if the harvest yields 2 units, the tenant is exempt from paying any rent and so consumes 2 units. If the yield is 6, the tenant has to pay the rent of 4 units; so he again gets 2 units to consume.

From the above chart it is clear that the tenant will choose the sub-optimal option, namely option T[3] and the newer variety of seed will be rejected. This need not happen under share tenancy. Suppose the same landlord and tenant are bound by a share tenancy contract where half the output has to be given as rent. Then, under limited liability, the tenant's consumption is as shown below.

Tenant's consumption under share tenancy		
	Bad weather	Good weather
Option T	2	6
Option N	3	5.5

In this situation the tenant will choose N, with an expected pay-off of 4.25. This is better for the landlord and for overall efficiency.[4]

Given our present concern, observe that the advantage of share tenancy is that it works as a kind of shock absorber. Compare the bad weather outcomes. From the first chart it is clear that output varies under T and N (being 2 under T and 6 under N). In the case of fixed-rent tenancy, this variation results in no variation in the tenant's income, which remains at 2. Under share tenancy, the variation in yield gets transmitted to a variation in the tenant's consumption.

We could therefore view share tenancy as an institution that emerges naturally in poor regions where output is susceptible to unexpected fluctuations. It is an institution with a certain amount of flexibility. I use the word 'naturally' fully aware that this can be ambiguous. However, in the present context, such ambiguity has useful pedagogic value.

There are two ways in which share tenancy could emerge in situations where it serves the above role of flexibility. First, as in most neoclassical models, it can be a conscious choice on the part of the landlord. However, many authors have argued (and it also seems reasonable to me) that tenure choices are often custom-based. If your ancestors and neighbours chose share tenancy rather than fixed-rental tenancy, you do the same. The pay-offs or utility, at least within a certain range, do not matter.

Interestingly, even if choices are made in this manner (that is, choices are not really choices but are exogenously given), an indirect relation may emerge between pay-offs and the existence of alternative tenurial arrangements. The argument here is founded in evolution and natural selection. If a certain institution is severely sub-optimal, it is possible that it will not survive in the long run because, as discussed in the second section of this paper, its participants will perish through falling living standards and the institution will be replaced by another more optimal one.

Basu *et al.* (1987) dwell at length on how and why customs that have outlived their original purpose can nevertheless continue to survive. This argument goes against functionalism in sociology. But, as seen above, once we bring evolutionary considerations into our analysis, there arises scope for a 'minimal functionalism'.

V ORGANISATIONAL STRUCTURES AND THE FLEXIBILITY OF NATIONS

Moving away from purely theoretical issues, let us now investigate briefly the organisational structures that make for greater flexibility in economies. My arguments here will be based, mainly, on the Indian experience.

One of the causes of the remarkable economic success of South Korea, Taiwan, Japan, Singapore and Hong Kong is believed to be the immense flexibility of these economies. Not only have these countries succeeded in adapting their technologies to the changing world demand, but they also showed great resilience to the two oil shocks of the 1970s.[5] The obverse case is provided by India. The Indian economy has its strengths, but speed of action is not one of them. Hence, an analysis of decision-making in India can provide insights into what makes organisational structures sluggish and how this can be rectified.[6]

On a question as important as this, there are many angles from which one can try to seek answers. India's relative sluggishness may well be rooted in the Hindu philosophy of acceptance, the hot climate, the near 100 per cent humidity in several parts of the country, the reassuring protection from invaders provided by the Himalayas or the hindrance of norms inherited from an end-of-Empire Britain. But I shall focus here on the structures of economic organisations on the ground that, *ceteris paribus* these must be relevant.

Before going into some of the larger issues concerning the organisation of a democracy, let me illustrate how simple policies can be used to inject more flexibility into a real economy. One useful feature of flexibility is elasticity. If demand in an economy is elastic, its control becomes easier because a small rise in price can be used to cut back demand considerably. (Some related ideas are explored by Smith and Ulph in Chapter 8 of this book.) Conversely, lack of elasticity can make economic management that much more difficult. In India, it has often been considered that the demand for petroleum and housing (there are many more such goods but let us focus on these here) is not adequately elastic. Thus housing demand seems to be relatively inflexible and prices move continuously upwards. Similarly, when India's petroleum import costs rise and petroleum prices are raised in the country, demand does not seem to fall sufficiently. Many economists tend to treat these as structural rigidities of the Indian economy, but I believe that a little in-depth analysis will show that policy reforms can remove these rigidities.

In any economy, if the user does not have to pay for the purchase of any particular good, demand is unlikely to be elastic. Thus, if you drive cars but somebody else pays for the petrol, it is unlikely that you will cut back demand much if the price of gasoline rises. This is exactly what has happened in India. Because of a widespread system of perquisites in the form of free petrol and free housing for managers and civil servants, the demand for these goods is less elastic than it would be in the absence of such user–payer bifurcation.

Why, it may be asked, is there such a system of paying salaries in the form of perquisites? The answer to this, in turn, lies in the tax system. Perquisites are virtually tax-free. So people in the income-tax-paying classes prefer to receive a larger part of their income in kind. Hence a change in the taxation system can bring about a greater flexibility in the demand for petrol and housing, thereby making these more manageable.

Let me turn now to the larger subject of the organisation of government decision-making in a democracy. The power of veto, either directly or through intrigue, is far too widely distributed in political systems such as that of India. Too many decision-makers can veto too many decisions. The consequence is that, like the UN Security Council, the government exhibits a natural penchant for maintaining the status quo.

At first sight it may seem that this is an inevitable concomitant of democracy. After all, everybody having a say is what democracy in decision-making is all about. Fortunately, this view is not correct. An organisation – whether it be a firm, a government, or even a nation – can be democratic in at least two different ways. I shall describe an organisation as having *overlapping rights* if everybody has a right to decide on every matter, and as having *partitioned rights* if everyone has a domain over which he or she has the full right to decide. These are, of course, extreme categories, and in reality all democratic organisations will lie along the spectrum between these two poles.

While India is indeed a vibrant democracy, it is arguable that many Indian organisations have a tendency to be too close to the 'overlapping rights' end of the spectrum. This is what has impaired the economy's flexibility and adaptability. A good example of an organisation with an overlapping system of rights is the Indian university system. I know of a leading expatriate Indian neuro-surgeon, who wanted to donate money to Calcutta University so that it could buy some specific medical equipment. He went to Calcutta for a fortnight and for the full fourteen days he went from pillar to post trying to donate the money ('not to take' as he later recounted). But he failed. The reason was simple; no individual or small group was empowered to enter into an agreement to take the money and buy the equipment.

It is important to note that if the Indian economy is to become more efficient and responsive it needs to restructure its organisations and its bureaucracy. In particular, individuals need more room for decision-making without, at every stage, having to get clearance from others including their superiors. Of course, their work can and should be evaluated at intervals, and they can be suitably punished or rewarded. In other words, what is being urged is a push towards a partitioned democracy. It goes without saying that this will not be an easy task, because in an overlapping democracy not only is no one in a position to change the rules but no one may be in a position to change the fact of no one being in a position to change the rules.

Much of this problem has arisen from India's accumulated attempts to build up checks and balances against corruption. What has been achieved is not a reduction in corruption but, instead, sluggishness and a lack of adaptability. It may well be true that having several lateral checks can thwart corruption, since an act of bribery now involves several agencies or individuals whose actions need to be co-ordinated, and one spoil-sport among them can stop the corrupt deal from going through. But before setting up lateral approval organisations one must weigh against this two offsetting arguments. First, over time, as in the case of colluding firms, a group of lateral agents may learn to collude in sharing bribes so that in the long run they may not constitute too much of an impediment to the practice. Secondly, flexibility will tend to decrease as lateral approving agencies multiply. This will happen, in turn, for two reasons: the obvious one of there being more veto power in the system and more approvals to be sought before a project or an action is finally possible and, secondly, the agencies may have a vested interest in holding up approvals because in that way they can raise the 'price' of their approval and encash some of it in the form of bribes.

This suggests that the arguments do not all point in the same direction. We need to scrutinise the structure of organisations to decide whether the system of checks and balances is cutting too much into their flexibility.

VI CONCLUDING REMARKS

The aim of this chapter was to review different ideas of flexibility in organisations and then to assess their utility in the context of macro decision-making and the organisation of governments. The survey had to be a between-the-lines operation because, as the chapter tried to demonstrate in the opening sections, while the importance of flexibility is widely recognised, it does not figure in a systematic and consistent way in any broad school of thought, whether neoclassical or structuralist. It was argued that the idea has cropped up, often under different garbs, in models of industrial organisation, especially in duopoly.

One area which has considerable promise in this regard is evolutionary game theory. Some introductory ideas from this newly emergent branch of economics and biology were presented. The standard thesis was taken a step further by arguing that an essential difference between animal behaviour (for which the original theory was developed) and human behaviour was that human beings could adjust and change their behaviour in response to the context in which they operated. Interestingly enough, flexibility in behaviour does not always turn out to have the greatest survival value and, correspondingly, rigidity is not always detrimental. This idea was picked up later in the context of the organisation of governments.

Before going into the question of 'How much flexibility?', it seemed reasonable to ask if the market did not have some mechanisms to weed out institutions which lacked flexibility. Even if this did not happen directly it ought to happen through the process of evolution. This generated the idea of 'natural flexibility'. It was demonstrated that certain institutions, the existence and, more importantly, the persistence of which were earlier thought baffling may be understood in terms of their having natural flexibility.

While recognising that flexibility can be a disadvantage, one can argue that what is worth having is not inflexibility but what may be called 'strategic inflexibility', that is, the power to appear inflexible whenever that is called for. Hence, overall, flexibility is a trait worth striving for in governments. But why are some governments more flexible than others, even when they are all democratically organised? Using illustrations from India, the chapter tried to argue that this may depend critically on the structure of decision-making and the distribution of veto power among the decision-makers. Two different structures were identified and it was argued that one of them may be superior from the point of view of flexibility. It was also argued that some of the most inflexible structures arose out of piecemeal attempts to plug loopholes which lead to corruption.

The restructuring of organisations is a much harder task than changing actual economic policies. The reason is that with every organisation there emerge systems of vested interest which often have the power to sabotage efforts to bring about the reorganisation. In addition, a change of organisation can be costly and there may be some genuine reasons for looking carefully before one leaps since, reverting back can be costly if not impossible.

NOTES

1 It is relevant here to note that another kind of research provoked by Maynard Smith's work is on how agents 'learn' and change their behaviour in strategic environments (Fudenberg and Kreps, 1993).
2 This is called a civil norm because it is assumed that what is permissible behaviour in a particular society (which determines the bounds of the domain of choice) is determined by the norms of that society.
3 I am assuming risk-neutrality on the part of agents. Hence option T gives the tenant an expected income of 5 and option N gives him an expected income of 4.5.
4 I am overlooking complexities arising out of the reservation incomes of agents. This is worked out in Basu (1992a).
5 In Chapter 7 of this book Chang goes on to argue the need for caution in interpreting the experience of Asian nations which actually exhibit 'flexible rigidities'.
6 Parts of this section are drawn from my paper on recent Indian reforms (Basu, 1993).

REFERENCES

Banerjee, A. and J.W. Weibull (1991) 'Evolutionary selection and rational behaviour', in A. Kirman and M. Salmon (eds) *Rationality and Learning in Economics*, Oxford: Basil Blackwell.
—— (1993) 'Evolution and rationality: some recent game-theoretic results', University of Stockholm, mimeo.
Bardhan, P.K. (1983) *Land, Labour and Rural Poverty*, New York: Columbia University Press and Oxford: Oxford University Press.
Basu, K. (1984) *The Less Developed Economy: A Critique of Contemporary Theory*, Oxford: Basil Blackwell.
—— (1990) *Agrarian Structure and Economic Underdevelopment*, London: Harwood Academic Publishers.
—— (1992a) 'Limited liability and the existence of share tenancy', *Journal of Development Economics* 38: 203–20.
—— (1992b) 'Civil institutions and evolution', Institute of International Economic Studies, University of Stockholm, Seminar Paper no. 523.
—— (1993) 'Structural reform in India 1991–1993: experience and agenda', Delhi School of Economics, mimeo.
Basu, K., E.L. Jones and E. Schlicht (1987) 'The growth and decay of custom: the role of the new institutional economics in economic history', *Explorations in Economic History* 24: 1–21.
Cheung, S.N.S. (1968) 'Private property rights and sharecropping', *Journal of Political Economy* 76: 107–22.
Dreze, J. (1975) 'Existence of an exchange equilibrium under price rigidities', *International Economic Review* 16: 301–20.
Fershtman, C. and K.L. Judd (1987) 'Equilibrium incentives in oligopoly', *American Economic Review* 77: 927–40.

Fudenberg, D. and D. Kreps (1993) 'Learning in extensive-form games', Paper presented at the Nobel Symposium on Game Theory, Bjorkborn, 18–20 June.

Klemperer, P.D. and M.A. Meyer (1989) 'Supply functions equilibria in oligopoly under uncertainty', *Econometrica* 57: 1243–77.

Koshy, D. (1993) 'Moving towards instant fashion', *Economic Times*, New Delhi, 8 September.

Kydland, F.E. and E.C. Prescott (1977) 'Rules rather than discretion: the inconsistency of optimal plans', *Journal of Political Economy* 85: 473–91.

Malinvaud, E. (1977) *The Theory of Unemployment Reconsidered*, Oxford: Basil Blackwell.

Marshall, A. (1920) *Principles of Economics*, 8th edition, London: Macmillan.

Maynard Smith, J. (1982) *Evolution and the Theory of Games*, Cambridge: Cambridge University Press.

Maynard Smith, J. and G.R. Price (1973) 'The logic of animal conflict', *Nature* 246: 15–18.

Schlicht, E. (1993) 'On custom', *Journal of Institutional and Theoretical Economics* 149: 178–203.

Sklivas, S.D. (1987) 'The strategic choice of managerial incentives', *Rand Journal of Economics* 18: 452–5.

Smith, A. (1776) *The Wealth of Nations*, Edinburgh: Strahan & Cadell.

Vickers, J. (1984) 'Delegation and the theory of the firm', *Economic Journal* 92, supplement: 138–47.

4

ECONOMIC ADAPTABILITY IN THE LONG TERM

E.L. Jones

I INTRODUCTION

Consider a review of a book entitled *Making Democracy Work: Civic Tradition in Modern Italy*, in that very free market-oriented journal, *The Economist* (6 February 1993). The reviewer brackets the author, Robert Putnam, with de Tocqueville, Pareto and Weber, no less, going on to point out that Putnam has shown how levels of economic development, education or urbanisation do not explain the differences in the recent performance of regional governments in Italy. 'Mr. Putnam's solution to the puzzle is ingenious, and unsettling' – unsettling to economists, that is. Putnam concludes that governments work best in regions with a high level of 'civic community', or trust, social co-operation and active participation by citizens, '. . . and that the distribution of civic community in present-day Italy was *already clearly evident as long ago as the 13th century*' (emphasis added).

The latter point is the relevant one for present purposes. Some outstanding young economists and economic historians are also breaking ranks and finding important features descending imperturbably from (at least) the High Middle Ages, thus rediscovering the path dependence which historians have always asserted. Moreover, the failures of a quick-fix for the economies of the former Soviet Union and much of Eastern Europe have redirected attention to the 'extricability' problem, i.e. the question of how far the achievement of economic growth may be separated from the social and political context of the market – something brushed aside by many first-phase advisers and commentators. Although this renewed anxiety has led to a lot of Western dreaming about the indispensability of democracy for growth, quite disregarding the East Asian experience, it may be a step towards recognising that economic performance and adaptability are not usefully treated in a contextual vacuum. To sustain *growth* democracy may indeed be important. There are many other complex considerations and so the present chapter will range very widely indeed.

A fundamental difficulty is how to allocate behaviours between those that are indeed historical (path-dependent) and those that represent fluent and new adjustments to changing price incentives. There is a difference on this matter between historians, on the one hand, and economists, led by Alfred Marshall, on the other. A resolution is difficult, since while even in the medium term more behaviours are undoubtedly resistant to price incentives than the assumptions of economics allow, others are more malleable than historians imply. The difficulty, as Abramovitz (1986) frankly admits with respect to inter-country differences in productivity levels, is that no one knows what the black box of responses which he calls 'social capability' actually means or how to measure it. Some of the elements may be identified but the calculus which describes their interaction is obscure and lies outside the realms which economists customarily enter.

This chapter's consideration of the problems is divided into four parts: a discussion of adaptability as a quasi-attribute of societies (or of the Great Traditions), seemingly deeper than a process constantly recreated by contingent historical processes; a review of Abramovitz's investigation of adaptability with respect to 'catching-up' in national levels of productivity; some account of the costs of market adaptation and why rational people resist entering the theoretically desirable world of full adaptability in each and every market; and finally further consideration of impediments that would in any case intervene, emphasising features of the firm and society which are too often assumed away as irrelevantly 'sociological'. This final section includes a longer discussion of the role of relative flexibility in the sequence of industrial revolutions and later de-industrialisations.

II ADAPTABILITY AS QUASI-ATTRIBUTE AND AS PROCESS

Adaptability seems to be sometimes wholly or in part an attribute of the economy, or more precisely of the society, in which it is set, although usually it is a historically conditioned by-product of economic, political and social processes and their interactions. Indeed, strictly speaking, adaptability is almost always historically conditioned, since few social attributes are genuinely intrinsic; they tend to be formed by conditioning, group living, peer pressure and other communal influences. In principle they can always be remoulded by the contrary pressures, such as free intellectual competition and different incentive structures.

Yet to reverse society's every habit would involve deconditioning beyond the dreams of social engineers and, given the imprinting of some behaviours in early life, might not be feasible beyond a certain point. It would mean changing the world. For example, few people manage to shift from one of the Great Traditions or dominant religious orientations to another without, as Adam Smith put it with respect to a change of occupation, their hands sauntering a little. The existence of characteristics so deep-seated as to seem permanent parts of social personality and hence of society means that we can at least refer to quasi-attributes.

This sense will not be congenial to the stern, rather caricature, neoclassicist, who sees the world as full of the infinitely malleable – a place where adjustment to changing sets of relative prices is rapid, if not instantaneous and costless; where history does not matter and may be allowed to fall – if it has any real meaning – into someone else's domain. For all that, I shall take here a more latitudinarian view akin to one expressed by Pollak and Watkins:

> if economists stick to economics and sociologists stick to sociology, then neither will do very well in theorizing about phenomena in which both economic and sociological factors play significant roles.
>
> (Pollak and Watkins, 1993)

A world where non-economic factors are subsumed in economic ones no doubt would be a plastic place constantly remodelled by changes in relative prices. But the world of multiple distortions which we observe surely cannot be looked on in this light. A lack of realism was recognised even by such a writer as Bensusan-Butt, who otherwise made the most extreme claims for the power and rightness of economic reasoning (1960: 176). The difficulty begins when one tries to find a literature generalising explicitly about the extent to which economies refuse rapid adjustment. It is necessary to review a range of issues and cases in order to get our bearings, given the dual presence of ancient and recently renegotiated economic features.

Adaptability as quasi-attribute

Let us take adaptability as quasi-attribute first. A reasonable supposition is that the Great Traditions, Christian, Islamic, Hindu and so forth, are so different that for all practical purposes many of the forms of their economic organisation lie permanently apart. This view is most definitely unappealing to many Western social scientists, particularly economists, and is mostly ignored, except by area specialists. The geographer Carl Sauer caught the point in saying that,

> the social scientists do not especially like the idea that there are other civilizations and cultures than our own, that they are likely to remain different, and that the world is more interesting because of the diversity of its peoples.
>
> (Sauer, 1976: 341)

Generalisations continue to be made in social science when they are patently, or at least presumptively, restricted to Western culture. Thus it is implied in economics that price theory is an aspect of a general theory of choice and obtains everywhere, subject to constraints. This approach is certainly powerful. What is not always emphasised is that the generality of price theory is being assumed, so that the main interest shifts to the character of the constraints and why they are not bid away. Ekkehart Schlicht is fond of pointing out that one can always propose a neoclassical explanation for an institutional arrangement, however unpalatable it may seem (widow-burning, female circumcision, slavery, head-hunting) but the real question is, why do arrangements not arise which would produce a surplus for all? The question is seldom tackled in those terms. Most research, then, either concerns societies within one tradition, or is concerned with other traditions viewed from a Western perspective.

While touching on these fundamental preliminaries, this seems a suitable place to insert a brief note about units of study. For practical purposes, economists tend to be concerned with the national economy, with the economy, that is, of the nation-state. There is a problem in this respect since the actors – individuals or firms – within any one nation or country may have considerable latitude in making decisions. They may exhibit very flexible, responsive behaviour. If the 'national will' and central institutions of the state are relatively weak, this may result in a cacophony, not a tune. The adaptability of the whole economy may not be helped by short-run, opportunistic maximising of this kind. We shall note a case of this later, when we discuss the so-called Decline of the Netherlands.

In any case, the nation-state is neither eternal nor the only possible unit. It was an invention of early modern Europe, and is by no means firmly established yet everywhere else in the world. It is and was nested within a wider range of groupings, such as the Great (Cultural) Traditions already mentioned, which very approximately correspond to the World Religions. Until a century or two ago the large polities of the non-European world were empires like those of the Ottomans, Mughals and Qing (Manchu); smaller polities remained the tribes. Both these groupings had a rough equivalence, but only a rough one, with certain types of economic system.

Within most national economies there were and are regional economies with divergences in economic structure so wide that events and policies favouring one type may harm the next. A given region may have more in common, economically speaking, with other regions in different nation-states than it has with the remaining parts of its own country. And various amalgamations of ethnic minorities, regions and nation-states may possess properties in common that override those of the constituent polities. We can see this most clearly with respect to the 'Chinese Economic Area' of Hong Kong, Guangdong and Fujian, and Taiwan. This 'Area' embraces provinces and states within the networked business culture of the mainland and overseas Chinese, in a fast growing composite of geographical and socio-logical regionalism.

Taken together, these points indicate that nations are not the only possible unit for our purposes, while adaptability at one level may contradict adaptability at another. Although in a moment we shall return for a space to the matter of adaptability in cultures, most of the remainder of our discussion will nevertheless deal with nation-states. The subject is unusual enough to engage us at that conventional level, but we should not forget that the other levels exist, even though their respective and maybe cross-cutting degrees of adaptability have so far scarcely attracted literatures to which we can refer.

The view that cultural differences are old, profound and abiding is widely held by non-economists. Most journalists and those who are obliged to deal with international affairs as they find them tend to believe this, and it is openly defended by advocates such as Adda Bozeman (1971), David Pryce-Jones (1990) and Samuel Huntington as expounded in Harries (1993). Are these people simply misled by appearances, have they become bemused by the surface complexities of the societies they study, and have economists succeeded in piercing veils of illusion still opaque to the eyes of others? In any case, what economic difference would separate traditions make?

At its crudest, the assumption of difference is of an indefeasible path dependence, as if the characteristics of economic systems have descended without alteration from the beginning of time. This cannot be so, of course, and a more restricted version would assert only that cultural traditions remain distinct. Despite the diffusionist element in intellectual history, the populations involved have not really been in the same market for their most distinctive ideas. The self-interest of local purveyors of culture has helped to see to that. Societies from different traditions may at times have competed militarily but seldom did so intellectually, except when their missionaries entered third 'markets'. They may have stayed apart, as separate columns, with the widespread modern tendency towards Westernisation merely reducing customary restraints on maximising drives that are common, in fact universal, in the trade of all large societies.

There has been surprisingly little general work on very long-run processes. Stephen Mennell (1989) makes this point in describing the work of Norbert Elias, who did keep the torch of long-run analysis alight in sociology and whose work (Elias having died in 1991 at 90), is now having something of a revival. Thus it is worth mentioning recent work by the economists/economic historians, Greg Clark (1992) and Avner Greif (1992), who have begun to urge hypotheses along the lines that Britain may have had a high work intensity (higher than modern India) at least as long ago as 1300, and that individualistic Western Latin civilisation diverged at least as early as the Middle Ages from collectivist societies elsewhere. It is novel for the research interests of highly trained American economists to be drawn in these directions and to admit the force and persistence of culture. As yet neither the origins of divergence, nor the mechanisms which held vast societies on straight and narrow paths, have been fully explored, but the Marshallian assumption of malleability in response to price incentives is at last being challenged from within economics and not merely from without, from sociology.

The work of Timur Kuran on Islamic economics (1983) also deals with principles espoused ('unchangeably' since the Closure of the Gate of Interpretation in the tenth century AD) which still differ from Western 'capitalistic' modes, for example with respect to the prohibition on charging interest. Islam may be taken as the most unyielding of the Great Traditions, the limiting case. However, Kuran's work shows that in the main Islamic economies, including Islamic banks, are flexible enough to offset the impediments, whatever the terminology they use. This seems to be a case where the differences are less than the rhetoric would lead one to suppose and relate more to form than they do to substance, without being quite extinguished by convergence on market norms. We shall indeed be obliged to sway one way or the other since universal roles for path dependence and malleability have not been, maybe cannot be, completely demarcated. Their relative preponderance within any one tradition, in this case Islam, has altered according to circumstances within particular societies. The special feature of Islam is the fact of the Closure of the Gate of Interpretation. This, although perhaps not slammed completely in practice, remains a touchstone for those who wish to reassert first principles.

Kuran does describe adjustments within Islamic economies of kinds that would have been anticipated by Alfred Marshall, but he by no means sets out to show that Islamic economies have become identical with the Western kind. As to whether the two systems are a match for one another, with various features acting as substitutes, Kuran appears to find Islamic economies the weaker, as indeed figures of GNP per capita would suggest.

The rejoinder tends to be that Western imperialism has delayed the process of catching up, with adherents arguing that in any case the Islamic system ministers better to the whole of society and is more moral, whatever the gap in levels of material income. On the one hand, therefore, an intrinsic economic adaptability may be claimed while denying that it has been permitted to work fully, while, on the other hand, the moral argument implies that, even if there is less adaptability, as seems to some extent to be so, this is an acceptable price to pay for other virtues. A little reflection will show how difficult it is to form judgements about a concept such as flexibility over entire economic and moral systems. There may be offsetting effects and their relative weight may alter from period to period.

Marshallian incrementalism: adaptability as process

To turn to the leading exponent of perpetual, hidden adaptation to price changes, Alfred Marshall (1920) would probably have anticipated the convergence of systems, though he was really thinking about the power of Western, mainly English, markets to subvert custom. He claimed that behind archaic labels the content of customary forms subtly and continually alters to take account of shifts in relative prices; that the gradual shading denotes a flexibility concealed from the casual gaze by the antiquity of institutions; and that veneration for tradition is often little more than the approval of evolved forms which happen to retain old names, meaning that there is, if not permanent revolution, at least ceaseless incremental change. This 'veil-piercing' view is revealing enough to disclose adjustments to changing prices which might otherwise escape notice, and often do escape the notice of historians, anthropologists and others. Marshall's view is perceptive and valuable. But his ultimate vision is of a world in which adjustments are inevitable, though subtle. Market economists may be expected to find such a vision congenial.

The power of institutional factors and political markets to impede market processes does not receive sufficient credit. We do not learn where the market receives a check; it is assumed to grind away at custom without cease. Although institutions within different systems must often be substitutes for one another, and although within antique social forms behaviour often does quietly adjust to fresh relative prices, it remains impossible to believe that the invisible hand can whip the whole world along at the same pace. Indeed, the phrase 'out of step with history' (Heller, 1989–90) is being used of conservative Islamic societies. Some traditions are surely more innovative or imitative, and therefore more adaptable, than others.

The Hartz thesis

A well-known historical theory postulates the creation of a new family of restricted, derivative traditions in the lands of European settlement. This is the Hartz thesis, a general explanation of the way colonial societies diverged from Britain and Europe, as well as from one another, in terms of dominant institutions and persistent attitudes established at some early, formative period (Hartz, 1964). This period need not have been the time of settlement. Thus, in the opinion of one of Hartz's collaborators, Australia is not a 'fragment' of the England of the convicts but the one desired in their day by the Chartists. The Australian colonies legislated, exceptionally early, five of the six Chartist demands.

The central idea is that each new society is formed, not merely by interaction between settlers and the environment newly met, but by social tendencies imported during the formative period. Subsequent developments in the mother country or countries pass the neo-Europes by. Each new society works out little more than the possibilities latent in the Europe of its formative period – and remains forever restricted in its range of options, missing out on further European novelties as Europe's history rolls on regardless.

This 'fragment theory' seems to have something in it. If it did not pick up a perception, at least in a general way, it would probably not have been proposed in the first place. The whole is like the kind of historical science fiction made familiar by Keith Roberts' *Pavane* and Sir Kingsley Amis' *The Alteration*, both of which envision modern England had the Counter-Reformation prevailed. In this genre, history forks differently, or rather fails to fork, at critical moments. A more conservative future descends from that time.

This is all good knock-about stuff, strongly path-dependent, relying on the correctness of the original reading of history and the reader's willingness to accept that the content as well as the form of institutions can be handed on for long periods, as from a single, early throwing of the points. Only discovering a convincing mechanism whereby the past may be transmitted to the present without substantial amendment could justify such an extreme anti-Marshallian view. Has the idea more than heuristic value? It is undoubtedly rendered problematical by the way markets for information have become more open during the last century or two. Declining information costs would certainly seem to increase flexibility but, because they may permit individual agents to respond in contradictory or chaotic ways, it is not certain that national responses become more effective or that national flexibilities may be ranked according to information costs.

Reluctant as believers in the omnipotence of markets may be to agree, there is something to explain. The new lands have gone down their own historical paths and the more distant, smaller ones have done a good job of avoiding, or never absorbing in the first place, key institutional innovations from the originating ones. There is indeed a 'small-country problem' of disjointed institutional imports. Small countries have small markets and tend to protect them. Where the clerisy is small, old boy networks can easily form; the old girl networks which are supplanting and supplementing them change little more than palace coups might do. Thus, where career slots and key positions are numerically few, and held for long spells, it matters desperately who holds them. Interference with competition along these lines happens everywhere; the point is that in small markets the chances of ossification are greater. The USA at one extreme may thus have escaped the cramping in smaller countries of similar origin, such as Australia.

Path-dependence and process

Deservedly famous work by W. Brian Arthur (1988) and Paul David (1986) has urged that path-dependence strongly influences the history of technology. Indeed, path-dependence as a phenomenon is being widely recognised as a significant aspect of economic life; history is brought back in. The central idea is that the path whereby the present has been reached influences the nature of the present, meaning that sunk costs do matter. More sharply, small and even idiosyncratic decisions made in the past have persistent effects which market forces do not automatically wipe out.

In the case of technology, an inferior choice may become locked in, excluding competitors because of its network externalities. The classic case is that of the QWERTY keyboard (see Liebowitz and Margolis, 1990). If adaptability can be compromised so heavily in technology, similar distortions may obviously be countenanced at the whole-society and Great Tradition levels. This need not mean that we should cease to look out for covert Marshallian processes of adjustment, but it may mean that they are less central than market economists assume; maybe we should expect to find them eroding systems mainly at the margin. On this view, any economy will be a compound of influences transmitted from the past and others created by current forces. The task of apportionment between these categories has scarcely begun.

If these comments seem generally Olsonian, so they are likely to do where that thesis has made so much of the running. Olson's (1982) notion is that stable economies permit the emergence of growing numbers of special interest groups, which he refers to as 'distributional coalitions'. Further, he urges that these rent-seeking groups will recognise no limit on the social costs each is prepared to impose on society in order to secure a larger share of the social output for itself. The efforts do not cancel out (though there is presumably some offsetting effect). On balance they will clip a society's efficiency and total income. They will thus, according to Olson (p. 65), slow down the 'capacity to adopt new technologies and to reallocate resources in response to changing conditions, and thereby reduce the rate of economic growth'.

While this does not distinguish degrees of inflexibility among the Great Traditions (Olson confines himself to trying to account for differences among certain developed economies), the aim is to identify a systematic cramping of performance whereby adaptability is reduced and radical counter-efforts become imperative if ever the endo-parasites are to be flushed out. The application is quite general, with individual histories merely taking variant forms.

My hesitation about Olson's approach is that, whether or not growth-impairing coalitions do multiply in times of stability when there is little to dislodge them, they certainly emerge at times of threat, crisis and depression. Perhaps they arise at both types of period, in which case a big task of historical apportionment still awaits. During periods of crisis there is an inducement to hang on to whatever market share one has and to call for subsidies or other favours. This seems detectable in the story of the English guilds and in the extension of conservative institutions in Asia following invasions there: the latter process can be seen as efforts by native groups to safeguard their position when conquerors had sliced off a large proportion of economic opportunities (see, for example, Jones, 1988, 1990). It is seen, too, in the modern economic history of the USA, where to explain the enormous expansion of Big Government, Robert Higgs (1987) plumps for expansion in times of crisis (such as war) or supposed crisis, and a ratchet thereafter.[1] In this sense processes of change in adaptability are without doubt historically contingent.

A second issue – that of reversibility – comes to the surface. What has been created can presumably be dissolved, and yet this proves not to be so easy. Just as there are multiple distortions in the world, so there is abundant stickiness. The causes may be divided into endogenous and exogenous. The former include self-reinforcing changes, among which figures the model of a self-destructive value system within capitalism ruefully advanced by Joseph Schumpeter, and by John Wesley before him.

Wesley and Schumpeter both worried that capitalism (and Methodism) must self-destruct because success would bring prosperity, which would reduce the incentive for individuals to work hard and save. They probably thought too much in terms of declining effort by key individuals. From the point of view of the economy this might not matter unless there were barriers to the recruitment of aspiring entrepreneurs willing in their turn to work (and by some Smithian compositional principle make society rich). There seems to have been no such total barrier, even in class-bound Britain; the social barriers may even have spurred economic effort if acquiring wealth offered a young man the prospect of crossing them.

Once one starts to canvas limitations on adaptability they nevertheless seem numerous. Another autonomous effect is commonly said to be the self-reinforcing nature of welfare policies which create poverty traps and expectations of largesse. These things can become locked in through political competition for the votes of the recipients and the activism of a tier of social workers dependent on public spending.

Not only the incentives facing the poor are affected. *Ceteris paribus*, everybody responds to incentives, and in Australia farmers in particular under-insure against bushfire losses in the warranted belief that public funds will be made available to them for restocking after a big fire (see Freebairn, 1977). This kind of behaviour is common with respect to disasters. In the bushfire case it induces stocking levels above those which the market would indicate and the constant expectation that resources will be diverted to canny farmers from better uses. Prior claims of this rent-seeking kind *ipso facto* reduce adaptability. All distortions do.

With respect to the exogenous shocks of disasters in India, Cohen and Raghavulu (1977) show that democratic politics has led to a call for relief which the state simply cannot afford to meet. The British raj drew strict lines round what it thought proper to do, perhaps rationalising what it could and could not afford, but after 1947 democracy put pressure on India in the following way: the 'gentry' ceased to carry out their earlier functions of distributing food, organising rescue and burying the dead, abandoning these tasks to authorities whose limited tax revenues meant they could not shoulder them, and thereby creating a welfare gap. Developing societies are vulnerable to this, as early modern England seems to have been (see Kalland and Pedersen, 1984; and Leftwich and Harvie, 1985). What happened eventually in Europe was a closing of the gap by an increasing and (the Irish Famine apart) increasingly effective reliance on the market, with a growing supplementary role for government (see Post, 1985).

These responses to disaster suggest once more that adaptability is a time-specific process rather than an inalienable characteristic of societies. There is no timeless, anthropologists' past to cite as a reference period. Instead, there may be a kind of Kuznets cycle regarding resilience to shocks, as there is with income inequality, meaning that adaptability may diminish in the early stages of development only to increase again with extended markets, greater wealth and a wider array of competent government agencies.

Note that this seems to differ from the views of Killick (Chapter 12), who postulates not a U-shaped curve of flexibility with the progress of development through time but an inverted U. He adduces three main reasons why flexibility may increase with early development – better data collecting, which improves the allocation of resources (presumably mainly by government or very large firms like multinationals); the weakening of traditions; and the economy becoming more industrial and responding better to changes in relative prices. After a period during which flexibility accordingly improves, Killick takes the Olsonian line in which success breeds failure, and envisages a hardening of the economic arteries, with distributional coalitions arising to curb the mobility of factors, the rate of technological innovation, and the reallocation of resources in general.

My own view refers primarily to flexibility in the face of exogenous shocks, and alludes to the 'welfare gap' associated with the decay of customary social provision in early stages of development. This 'gap' implies that some traditional customs and institutions had evolved to buffer the bulk of the population against shocks. In the past, many rulers seem to have had a social insurance function of that kind, as part of their *raison d'être* in addition to the textbook functions of government in providing defence and law and order. In some such way, Chinese emperors from the Song to the mid-late Qing ran the large and (by European standards) efficient system of 'ever-normal' granaries (see Anderson and Jones, 1988: 12; Goudsblom *et al.*, 1989: 37).

Although on average such rulers no doubt milked tax-payers as far as their primitive bureaucracies permitted, they nevertheless acted to even out peasant income over the years. They did not seize all the surplus of a good year for themselves, nor let their subjects gorge on it. Since it is a maxim of welfare economics that well-being increases not merely as income rises but as it is spread more evenly over time, this was a valuable role, involving a form of forced saving for the mass of the populace. On this reading, traditional institutions tended to increase the economy's room for manoeuvre in a run of bad harvests. Their abandonment would not necessarily lead to an improvement in resilience, at any rate not until the market was functioning freely, or more realistically before the market and extended state provision together replaced traditional modes. The Kuznets curve of first lessening, then increasing, equality of incomes may thus be paralleled by a curve of reduced, then expanded, economic responsiveness. Flexibility is associated with the stage of development.

III SOCIAL CAPABILITY AND ABRAMOVITZ'S DISCUSSION

The case of Japan

The compositional principles within an economy are more complex than the invisible hand; business history has come to incorporate the notion of steering by the visible hand of large corporations. Much of the literature on the 'Japanese Miracle' (as well as on that vast anatopism, the transfer of Japanese recipes to Western countries) expatiates on the actions of businesses and government in tandem. Interest in the Japanese case is so high that this section will start by mentioning its special adaptability.

It has been fashionable to cite striking examples of Japanese flexibility, such as the way output was doubled in the ten years from 1979 with a 25 per cent lower input of energy. This was not achieved in the West, where a weaker performance is surely not to be passed off solely by an appeal to the dictates of relative prices. The suspicion left after reading about the economic history of Japan is that adaptability there has been great but asymmetrical – that Japan was, and is, often better than its competitors at seizing productive opportunities but is especially ahead in the vital task of letting old industries go.

Yet even Japan suffers losses from external trade and internal financial shocks. Japan moved round the product cycle less smartly than purely market signals might have prompted. Even Japan has had difficulties in closing down inefficient coal mines or stripping protection from rice growers, automobile repairers and corner shopkeepers. The ahistorical nature of Western exhortations to come into line with the (Japanese) strength has been exposed by the coincidence of recession and economic maturation in that country, which has altered some of its supposedly permanent features. The economy of Japan is by no means totally adaptable; the literature may speak more to the perceived weaknesses of Western countries and a naïve sense that they can improve only by copying perceived Japanese success. The Japanese believe that exhortation works. They take good care that they are right by manipulating their consultative culture, something which could not be replicated elsewhere. There can be little doubt that particular cultural and institutional circumstances have eased Japan's responsiveness.

Abramovitz on catching-up

A not dissimilar position on the importance of social arrangements is evident in Moses Abramovitz's (1986) work on technological catching-up. 'Tenacious societal characteristics', he says, normally account for a portion, 'perhaps a substantial portion', of the failure of some countries to attain the productivity levels of more advanced ones. Having termed the sum of these characteristics 'social capability', he straightaway admits 'the trouble . . . is that no one knows what it means or how to measure it'. The main components seem to Abramovitz to be levels of education, the organisation of corporations, and the outlook of managers, as well as degrees of openness to competition and the adoption of new goods and services, the rate of entry of new firms, and the obstacles raised by vested interests. Unsurprisingly, with respect to the last point he alludes to the work of Mancur Olson. But, for all his candour, the element of circularity in Abramovitz's list and the lack of any proposal to measure adaptability except in terms of particular effects are clearly apparent.

Lagging economies are surely not constrained to close on a leader by exploiting some technological gap. They may remain behind. They may, on the other hand, remould themselves so as to overtake the leader, which is certainly consistent with the history of national leadership changes. There seems to be a tendency to place the burden of such changes less on an increased adaptability in the follower than on a sort of 'insult accumulation' in the leader, arising perhaps in Olsonian fashion. I think this is a wrong emphasis, despite the self-reinforcing nature of decline in a number of examples.

My own reading of historical cases is that change is initiated by economies that start to perform better, that is by productivity gains in some upstart country or marginal region; in short, that the main emphasis in economic history on growing rather than declining regions is proper (cf. Dodgshon, 1987; Jones, 1990). A previous leader seems likely, however, to try to maintain its slice of the pie. This it may do by protective devices, while blaming scapegoat minorities, the weather, or almost anything except the true source, with its uncomfortable lessons about effort, innovation and restructuring. These internal struggles exacerbate the leader's decline. Just as the sources of growth are often institutional innovations in formerly peripheral regions, so the needed responses to challenges are institutional ones too, and these are particularly hard and disruptive to make (for some interesting observations, see Kasper, 1993). In other words, typical responses to competition worsen the situation, slowing the movement out of factors while seldom doing enough to meet the challenge (if they did we would not find cases of 'decline').

Evidently we need a better way of discussing the circumstances in which economies 'speed up' and 'slow down'. Abramovitz depends on Olson and mentions the possibility that growth itself operates to reduce effort, enterprise and savings, thus diminishing the innovativeness on which productivity growth depends. As we have noted, the observation that value systems which successfully promote growth undermine themselves because growth encourages slacker effort is one that goes back long before Olson and even before Schumpeter – at least back to Wesley. However, the matter is ambiguous: Olson's emphasis on the rise of rent-seeking coalitions during periods of stability is incomplete, since shocks and depressions also reduce productivity growth by encouraging defensive market-sharing. Cases vary greatly in detail and history matters. As Abramovitz concludes:

> The state of a country's capability to exploit emerging technological opportunity depends on a social history that is particular to itself and that may not be closely bound to its existing level of productivity.
>
> (Abramovitz, 1986: 406)

IV MARKET ADAPTATION AND ITS COSTS

Long ago Walter Bagehot asked why Lombard Street was usually dull but sometimes very excited. Part of the problem is the failure of investment to synchronise with real opportunities in the marketplace. If investment and profitability matched neatly – if economies were perfectly adaptable in this respect – there would be no cyclical losses and no Schumpeterian gales of creative destruction.

Economists are inclined to look on downturns in the market as a necessary way of winnowing excess capacity. They therefore take fluctuations to be evidence of efficiency or adaptability. The economics profession is fascinated by the self-organising properties of markets and generally suspicious of efforts to regulate them. Non-economists are more aware of market failures, real and imaginary.

Markets do deserve to be commended for their effectiveness, as long as the praise is in the spirit of Churchill's appraisal of democracy, that it is the worst system apart from all the others. After all, the market method of equilibrating supply and demand can scarcely be called smooth. Business crashes and Rustbelts are parts of the price of change; as someone said of death, these things exist so that the future shall not be the same as the past. Ignoring the even higher price of adjustment in non-market systems, the jerky functioning of markets is bound to strike one as costly enough.

Without in the least wishing to dismiss the benefits of price signals, a better understanding of adaptability is desirable as a way of reducing the costs levied by the various forms of maladaptation. There are certainly efforts to reduce these costs. Protection may be looked on as a special case of unadaptability, and economists have taken the lead in trying to persuade a reluctant world to reduce tariffs. But more fundamental rigidities than those created by policy are not so often tackled; it seems to be believed that individual maximising will bid away the problems, though clearly it does not do so readily. The notion that individuals maximise in a simple sense is anyway quite crude, even disregarding the imperfections of any compositional principle (see Frank, 1988). The usual approach is to speak of maximising 'subject to constraints' and to take the constraints as given. There is a case for regarding all constraints as sources of unadaptability which are worth investigating in their own right.

No one should pass off unemployment, recessions, and Rustbelts as little local difficulties. They are testimony to what are too benignly called lags. While markets must be permitted to recombine resources and dispose of redundant ones, these rather more than epiphenomena – the waste products and exhaust gases of the economic system – show that economies are adaptable only in a lumbering way. In aggregate they are also blind, meaning blind to the human costs. Lags are periods of time, and time is irreplaceable for all of us. Transition costs signify real-time disequilibria. Economics has a label for everything.[2] Although a new equilibrium may be superior to the one abandoned, the time spent getting there cannot in itself be requited by adding up the income gained over some (unspecified) future period. The dubious argument has to be made that people will be better-off 'in the long run', yet the fact that time can be valued in terms of income equivalents, or income forgone, and lifetimes are sometimes treated actuarily in a similar way, is unpersuasive in the absence of markets in whole lifetimes.

Thus those who talk about market efficiency should be candid about for whom and over what period they intend returns to be maximised. Differential rates of factor mobility take a heavy toll from those least able on any humanly reasonable timescale to shift their assets or remove themselves in search of work, or yet again to come to terms with their assigned roles as atoms which impersonal forces shunt about the world or leave stuck. In a seminar on enlarging the European Community reported in *IMF Survey* of 8 March 1993, Richard Portes actually recommended that a 'European economic space' be created, a sort of umbrella held out over the aspirant countries of Central and Eastern Europe (p. 70). Beneath this there should be free trade in goods, services and capital, but not in labour. This, he claimed, would 'encourage' (oblige?) these countries to make the structural reforms needed if they are ever to qualify for membership of the Community. Maybe it would, but manoeuvring to prevent people migrating is social engineering on the grand scale, while, given that free trade in capital is often extolled, it is not clear why labour should be excluded. The Managing Director of the IMF, Michel Camdessus, admitted in the same issue of *IMF Survey* that no one has managed to protect the poorest from the costs of first-stage structural adjustment (p. 73).

We can discount the protectionist bleat that people have a 'right' of some kind to industrial employment wherever they currently happen to live. The distribution of population at any one moment is a historical artefact with no obvious celestial warrant. From the points of view of both efficiency and equity, it would certainly be more appropriate in theory to maximise world-wide opportunities to compete. The costs of moving from the present motley economic scene to an ideal economic geography based on some final comparative advantage and a full mobilisation of resources would, however, be more staggering to contemplate than the costs of the present asymmetrical situation.

The fallacy is to think that there can be any final resting-point, that flows of migrants are adjusting to a new equilibrium. There is no reason to suppose that there can be a unique equilibrium, except in an unimaginably stagnant world. In reality, there *is* no global level playing field, no automatic freedom to migrate whither one can earn the highest marginal return, and no chance that there ever will be. Rather the opposite, a closing of more borders, seems likely, while capital remains free to move and trade in goods and services increases, at least within and so far among major trading blocs.

With the international division of labour in manufacturing currently re-arranging itself and structural change taking place which erodes the demand for blue-collar work, one can retort that no more labour is needed in the developed world. There is too much unemployment already. Nevertheless, the world labour market is nowhere near clearing. The price of labour in developed countries is held up by all sorts of devices at the expense of both the domestic unemployed and migrant workers who would offer to work for less. Possibly this labour would not work at the same intensity as existing workforces, for cultural reasons, but at the world level it is evident that there are much higher barriers to adaptability in labour markets than in other markets.

Although early examples can be found of vast movements of population (55 million Europeans left that continent between 1861 and 1960) and of early commuting (the *golondrinas* sailed annually from Italy to take the harvest in Argentina), completely free trade in labour is not much thought about, because it seems unthinkable. Yet any restriction on factor mobility must in principle reduce adaptability in the oddly volatile, oddly sluggish, global economy. Maintenance charges on fixed capital in the developed countries may often be lower than the cost of investing in new capital works and infrastructure in less developed ones. Constructing social infrastructure ought to be easier in developed countries than on 'green-field sites' in the bush. Demand for capital in the developing countries is thus partly an artefact of restrictions on movements of labour towards the infrastructure and equipment already in existence in the developed world. The reason this is not seen is because the modern, historically contingent, extra-economic restrictions on labour mobility are being taken as given, even by those who most ardently advocate 'globalisation'.

The North American Free Trade Association (NAFTA) may be considered in the light of this. While its purpose is higher growth rates, the means is greater trade and capital flows. A *reduction* of 200,000 persons per year is expected in the flow of labour from Mexico to the USA and is semi-explicitly counted as a gain. However much Mexico gains, on the other hand, in terms of growth rates, this will not translate immediately into a greater provision of public goods of the types that already exist in the USA, which could be incrementally improved there with better systems of taxation and investment (*IMF Survey*, 25 January 1993). There may be new jobs in Mexico but there will not quickly be American conditions of life. Note, too, the nature of the gain. After five years NAFTA may have created 325,000 new American jobs and destroyed 150,000, a net gain of 175,000 (*The Economist*, 15 August 1992). While *The Economist* understandably comments that this gain is welcome, small though it is relative to the size of the American economy, it is only a net gain: no gain without pain, at least for industry-specific workers.

One can go further: the terminology of economics is analytical in intent and simply does not dwell on the human costs exacted by the creaking of its gigantic, impersonal machinery. Remember that these costs are not 'merely' income forgone, unemployment experienced, hopes blighted and the personal plans of finite lifespans indefinitely if not forever deferred. They invariably include elevated mortality and morbidity rates.

Thus, while it is intellectually helpful (say) to conceptualise people as the factor of production, labour, there are those who protest that the very use of the term dehumanises.[3] It was Metternich, contrary to his reputation, who at an international conference held up his hands in horror when the word 'war' was used and exclaimed, 'Hush! War is an obscene word; never to be used, lest using it one makes the idea of it more possible.' The objection will seem childish to economists, but it does seem possible that reiterations of this kind may subtly incline the user to demote social costs from the front-rank position they should hold. The force of the statisticians' defence – that social statistics are 'frozen tears' – depends on whether the tears or the icicles are being emphasised.

The cost of protectionism is evident. It is the classic instance and reinforcement of unadaptability. In principle the ideal would be the opposite – completely open, undistorted markets in both goods and factors of production; they may be substitutes but choice would be maximised by freeing both. Merely by considering this we can tell what the agenda would have to be for some hypothetical global policing agency: universal free trade would require all property rights to be enforced, markets to be contestable, contracts to be upheld in the courts, freedom to prevail for movement, occupation and association (which surely implies mass migrations), the macro and money environments to be kept stable, and governments to keep their hands off specific production processes.

These brave – limiting – conditions are everywhere violated, which denotes the world's distance from total adaptability, from automatically clearing markets always moving (instantaneously?) towards (an illusory) perfect equilibrium. The state of the world economy might indeed be portrayed as a great global struggle between Olsonian (1982) and Kasperian (1990, 1992) tendencies, by which I mean the opposed tendencies described by these authors towards the emergence of rent-seeking coalitions, on the one hand, and fierce competition to attract internationally mobile factors of production, on the other.

Whether a world of completely open markets would be habitable or would become an insecure, scrabbling place beset by permanent economic revolution – whether excessive adjustment costs might not replace high transaction costs as the bane of humanity – is another matter. We are talking of a utopian equilibrium, a nirvana that not only is never likely to be attained but would slide out of reach the instant it was gained. Presumably the purpose of conceiving it is as stated – to urge that movements should always be made in the direction of totally free global markets, for fear that weak humanity will constantly slip back. This can mean only that it is the journey, not the arrival, that is desired. Moreover, the closer the approach, the greater the incentive to press for derestriction in other areas, other sovereignties. This is bound to promote countervailing power. A world of never-ending populist resistance and localised social costs is being courted, for the sake of larger, more diffuse, if undoubted, gains elsewhere. We cannot hope to resolve the dilemma here, only to point out that the inability of labour to move is often covertly being assumed.

Presumably the free traders' position is that we should always try to move towards the optimum, since frail humanity will never cease to create obstacles. But the maximal productivity sought brings with it specialisation and risk. The costs of movement are so immediate that resistance to total adaptation is hardly surprising. It is a chimera and offers in reality eternal turbulence. The world would be chaotic if there were complete freedom to move, though standards vary: India twice in a few years had refugee movements across its frontiers larger than the entire population of Australia. Pakistan and Bangladesh took infinitely more refugees during the war in Afghanistan than the 700,000 or so incomers in 1992 who frightened the Central European countries into holding a (futile) meeting.

In countries with a high and mixed immigrant population 'constitutional commitment' may be hard to maintain, and with it the trust that is absolutely vital for the full working of markets. In such circumstances, impersonal institutions are not easy to keep free from segmentation and corruption. Institutions may anyway be less effective instruments than the trust that comes with genuine community feeling. The largest immigrant society, the USA, for a long time manufactured the feeling of belonging, but latterly its central institutions have been under fire, as if 'assimilation' were a plot by WASPs to dominate other groups rather than a programme to invite them to join the common table. This is a poor return for the generosity permitting recent levels (and sources) of immigration and a worrying development in one of the societies most likely, *a priori*, to solve its problems.

As Robert Frank points out (1988: 247), being rooted in a location produces the benefits of trust and personal ties. These benefits include economic ones. The notion is profoundly at odds with the view of both Americans and economists, not to mention American economists, that incomes will be maximised if resources move to their highest-valued uses. To hold a positive opinion of stable societies is also profoundly non-Olsonian. Whereas a stagnant society will miss some advantages, a society in a perpetual state of rapid factor mobility runs a risk of trading-off stability for the sake of febrile adaptability. The 'optimality band' within which it may be desirable to operate has scarcely been located, but the political disinclination to open all borders to all goods, services and factors of production seems more than the result of compounding sectional interests. It is the understandable reaction of people who are being urged to hurry towards a goal the posts of which are always moving.

The abstractions of GATT thus tend to paper over the upheavals that would be needed to achieve them fully. They would require astounding redistributions in manufacturing, the provision of services, and trade flows. They would make the foreseeable future a boiling metabolism. The task of turning some of our gaze from maladaptability to the costs of hyper-flexibility seems important.

To conclude, restrictions on the mobility of labour raise the costs of adjusting to new patterns of trade; essentially they protect the incomes of those who are currently employed in the protected markets. On the other hand, total freedom of movement would cause global chaos. Discussion of these matters seldom specifies just what pattern of adaptability (in the sense of market freedoms) is appropriate at the global level.

V FURTHER HISTORICAL AND METHODOLOGICAL CONSIDERATIONS

General matters

Over what length of time is adaptability to be measured? At one stage an economy may appear to be healthy or arthritic, only to present the opposite face if conditions change. This makes it tempting to compare the study of adaptability with the study of disasters. Just as disasters do not exist in a free-floating way or hold much interest, other than for natural scientists, unless they reveal themselves in terms of the damage they do and by the capacity to respond and recover from them, so with adaptability. It is scarcely there until it is challenged. So to speak, it is the ghost in the machine. Smooth functioning under incrementally changing circumstances may mislead us as to the response likely to be forthcoming when there is a severe price shock or a radically altered commercial context. Only a serious need for adjustment tells us whether or not an economy is adaptable.

The impact of shocks may or may not wash out; it depends what one expects. Take, for example, Colin Clark's statement (in *The Economics of 1960*) that 'political and social upheavals, however violent, have surprisingly little effect on the long-term trend of economic events' (Clark, 1942: 2). The train is hard to derail. But Clark measures this propensity in terms of proportionate changes in real income (aggregate output) per occupied person, adjusted for changes in working hours. In other words, he biases the result downwards and dampens such minor fluctuations as the First World War and the interwar depression. He measures changes in output per unit of time committed. He does not do so in terms of the whole economy, which experiences changing levels of unemployed resources (unworked hours and unemployed people, such as a decidedly non-trivial 22 per cent of the workforce in Britain in 1932).

By this means Clark can assert that the war of 1914–18 had a 'slight and temporary effect', lasting only until the early 1920s when the pre-war trend was resumed. His measure does, admittedly, minimise the amplitude of fluctuations rather than their duration. We should, however, reiterate that unless we specify in advance how soon after a big shock we expect an economy to display the adaptability needed to return it to its prior performance level, we shall not have any unequivocal measure of adaptability. Chronology matters.

Equally to the point is what we mean by performance. Do we, should we, mean only a smooth trend in the rate of economic growth or in some approximation like Clark's measure of real income per hour worked? Do we not need a means of identifying and therefore projecting adaptability which is independent of the growth rate? Grounds for suspecting this have already been mentioned. The performance of a stable period may have been achieved by squeezing output from conventional inputs without the regular spirit of innovation needed to cope with a shock lying in wait, like a robber with a cosh, somewhere down the track.

Consider the seven heads under which economic systems are usually appraised. These are: static and dynamic allocative efficiency, static and dynamic technical efficiency, full resource mobilisation, the degree of equality of income distribution, and resilience to shocks. Some of these are more to the point than others, notably dynamic allocative and technical efficiencies and resilience to shocks. The last is a partial definition of adaptability, whereas absolute income equality, or at any rate the kind of society capable of trying to enforce it, would in my view reduce adaptability. (But this is contentious: the relative income equality of Japan and the Little Dragons is often praised as one means whereby changes needed for the common good were rendered acceptable.) Societies at the other extreme, with highly unequal distributions, will tend to lose adaptability through weaknesses in human capital formation, continual political dissatisfaction, and so on. The 'optimality band' lies somewhere in between.

European industrialisation

The 'tests' that we can administer to judge how economies rate can only be informal and are likely to be what I have called elsewhere 'theorists' history' (Jones, 1984). An essay is not long enough to do what is ultimately needed, which is to write the history of whole economies, in the hope of confronting one's interpretation with things unsuspected. There is, it turns out, some point to the redundancy prevalent in general histories.[4] The alternative is to test hypotheses drawn from existing theory, in the scientist fashion, where the episodes chosen to confront or expound the theory may, consciously or not, confirm what one has in mind already.

Despite this risk, it is interesting to confront the differences in continental, national and regional flexibility revealed by one of history's greatest cases of disequilibrium, the onset of industrialisation in Europe. Standard accounts of this concentrate on the British Industrial Revolution. I shall argue here that this approach is too restricted, both for understanding the underlying forces permitting industrial growth to emerge and for pinpointing the role of relative flexibilities among those forces.

Standard accounts commonly portray some signal event, or sequence of events, as loosening constrictions in the politics, religious life, society and economy of Britain, or England, thus permitting that country to become preternaturally inventive and innovative. As a result Britain, or England, is seen as getting a big jump ahead of more arthritic competitors such as France. Nevertheless, industrialisation is further seen as able rather soon (historically speaking) to burn its way across Europe, while not (until much later) catching fire beyond what I have called the continent's 'asbestos edge' – notably the Ottoman empire (Jones, 1987: 45).

Earlier generations of economic historians were more interested in comparisons between Britain and its near neighbours. They spoke sometimes of 'Popery and wooden shoes' beginning at Calais and imputed a unique accumulation of flexibility, or flexibilities, to the British economy, through the removal of impediments to growth. These impediments were seen as a conservative aristocracy, self-liquidated in the fifteenth-century Wars of the Roses, the monastic system dissolved in the sixteenth century, and laws restricting enterprise which were swept away successively during the Commonwealth period, after the Restoration in 1660, and after the Glorious Revolution of 1688. Like much history, this factual record is not so much incorrect as incapable of revealing the wider processes at work. Note what is presented as first constrained and then freed. It was not some grand abstraction called 'the market', since product markets were relatively free. Rather, it was factor markets, notably those for land and labour.

Modern treatments are more circumspect about British uniqueness, partly in tune with the historiographic revisionism limping into the light after Britain's entry to the European Community, partly (in specialist circles) as a result of a challenging paper by Crafts in 1977 which labelled the Industrial Revolution a stochastic event, with equal *ex ante* probabilities of occurring in France and Britain (see also Pocock, 1991). Later work has indeed emphasised that much of such scientific theory as there was behind key British inventions was in origin French, though the implication once more is that the peculiarly responsive British sociology of an independent craftsman class was needed to embody this science in hardware (Mokyr, 1990).

Accordingly one might wish to say that French society was not 'flexible' enough to capitalise on its own ratiocination, whereas British society was. Obviously Britain did industrialise first and came to act as a source of inspiration and *matériel* for continental European industrialisations, which tends to occlude independent mainland developments. Yet Britain had not been 'flexible' enough intellectually to convert the common European heritage of ideas into relevant scientific propositions in the first place. It may be better, therefore, to start by turning back from these issues of the relative industrial performance of Britain and her neighbours. The differential performance of national and regional units was a lesser matter than the stimulus which the entire European system gave to individual units, the growth and industrialisation of which could scarcely have happened (at any rate when it did) outside this supportive milieu.

Set against the centralised empire, which was the political form prevalent where there were large populations elsewhere, Europe's mosaic of little polities, its emergent system of nation-states, was immensely interconnected and competitive. By later standards its many units had started small but tended to amalgamate as time went by. Moreover, they belonged to a compatible culture, surprisingly given the concern of so much European history with internal rifts. The culture faded eastwards, it is true, into the autocracy of Tsarist Russia but was sharply distinguished only from the lumbering systems of the Ottomans, Mughals, Manchu (Qing) and other non-European dynasties.

The polities of Europe were separately ruled but leaky: capital, entrepreneurship, technology and labour circulated among them. These productive factors did not, however, need to shift *en masse*. Shifts at the margin were all that were required to nudge most rulers away from damaging acts of expropriation. It takes only a latent tendency to create a mood and encourage or discourage factor mobility.

Policy choices in any one part of Europe might be positive, negative or neutral in the eyes of another part, but they would seldom remain unknown for long. There was in effect a single market for information, sluggish only by modern standards. When a policy was deemed ineffective or worse, it could be avoided. When it was thought good, it could be copied. The ebb and flow of factors around the European-cum-Atlantic world had some of the consequences loved or loathed in the globalised market of today: international rivalry to retain or attract them tamed governments, curbed their taxing power, and infringed their sovereignty, although they scarcely knew it and had to pretend otherwise.

How Europe's governments reasserted a considerable part of their sovereignty during the nineteenth century is another story. They went on straining to create nationhood out of ethnic and linguistic fragments (at unification in 1861 few Italians spoke Italian and thereafter the slogan was, 'we have built Italy, now we have to build Italians'), they held on to the initiative with respect to policy, and finally went to war in 1914. But never in peacetime did they achieve the degree of economic isolation typical elsewhere in the world.

Within the competitive arena of the states system, unrequited taxation ceased. Unlike the empires elsewhere in the world, where taxes went frankly to support the élite and little was returned to the ordinary taxpayer, European rulers began tentatively to offer services paid for out of general tax revenues. They also began to set about hiring or attracting entrepreneurs and equipment in order to bring their economies up to the level of the most advanced parts of the continent. Here the most spectacular example was Peter the Great, who spent very heavily and hired hundreds of artisans from the German states, Holland and England during his Grand Embassy tour in 1697–8, to help Russia catch up with the West. Governments were thus pulled and entrepreneurs drawn willy-nilly into converging on best practice. All in all there was a ladder of convergence across Europe for fashions, products, levels of technology, and ultimately rates of growth and levels of income.

The presence of this measure of flexibility across an entire civilisation dwarfs the question of leadership by any single country or region. Between 1600 and 1900 leadership changed anyhow, whereas the system as a whole continued to grow: Britain had been preceded by Venice and the Netherlands and was to be overtaken by Germany, while there were serial rises and declines on the part of proto-industrial and industrial regions.

A further unintended consequence of the arena of multiple competing polities (itself unintended, of course, though subsequently bolstered by diplomacy meant to ensure the 'Balance of Power') was the freeing of thought. This was reinforced by the splitting of Catholic Christendom into halves that were in turn geographically intermingled. Scholars found inspiration and audiences outside their native lands, just as merchants found markets. Intellectuals were often co-opted into the service of the Cold War between Reformation and Counter-Reformation states, but they could not finally be overawed, since they too might hope, as it were, to set up shop elsewhere. This is the competitive background, the metaprocess, beneath the 'factual record' of the history of science. It goes a long way towards explaining its cumulative nature.

We are listening to variations played on a basic melody. Two points are noteworthy: the melody is not 'God Save the King', and some of the early apparatus of economic life had earlier drifted in from as far away as China. This emphasis on the system rather than its parts, on the long run, and on the external context differs from the emphasis in deterministic histories of European countries, especially of Britain, which stress the particularity of genius. The Industrial Revolution did not, however, arise *ex nihil*. We can assert this not merely because we can trace widespread precursors of some of its elements, but because it was clearly the outcome of interaction. Had the Industrial Revolution not occurred in Britain it stood a good chance of popping up in the next most suitable cell of the matrix.[5] In this regard the failure of Tokugawa Japan to generate industrialisation spontaneously, despite its remarkable growth performance, is instructive. Japan was not so isolated politically as appears but in the economic sphere it was effectively solitary, a member of no system to match that of Europe, neither adequately goaded nor stimulated by competition from outside. Internally flexible, as its remarkable structural change from agriculture to proto-industry shows, Japan could not quite go it alone.

Within Europe the responsiveness of the units varied. Crafts (1977) treats the process as stochastic rather than deterministic, though he does so by restricting his analysis to a final stage of iron and textile inventiveness and excluding the wider processes of economic growth. To him, then, either France or Britain might have industrialised first, depending on the luck of making a few key inventions. Be this as it may, in a broader context it is hard to believe that relative adaptability did not weigh in the outcome. But industrialisation came in the most suitable, and not necessarily the most flexible, cell.

Some cells, at least, were probably what the Marxists call precocious. The Netherlands, with the most developed commercial, agricultural and industrial sectors in the world around 1600, may well have been 'too flexible', and indeed industrialised only as a late-comer at the end of the nineteenth century. It was a decentralised country (the Seven Provinces). To be decentralised may have been an advantageous property of the system at large, but tended to disarm any single country in the violently competitive mercantilist arena of eighteenth-century Europe. Non-market elements could overwhelm market flexibility.

Separate agents – the Amsterdam merchants, the individual provinces – pursued their self-interest without enough consideration for the common weal and without the kind of co-ordinating agency that could express their individual actions in the form of common security. Two examples: first, so free-wheeling were members of the *Regentiepatriciaat* that some of them actually invested in the Dunkirk privateers which preyed on the convoys of

Dutch *fluit* ships making up the Channel to Amsterdam. Second, the Netherlands was exceptional for so 'advanced' a country in being unable to institute a government-funded scheme of compensated slaughter during devastating cattle plagues, right up to the establishment of a unitary state in 1799 (see Jones, 1978: 116–18).

For a long time the Dutch prospered but they were unable to go on growing fast against the tariffs and subsidies with which other countries sought to catch up, nor to prevail against European war. The Dutch Republic remained commercial but while, as in Venice before it, total income did not fall, the economy failed to lift along the new trajectory of industrial techniques. They were rich, yes, but not wholly safe. Even Adam Smith thought that defence was of greater importance than opulence and he knew full well about the Netherlands.

Too 'rational' a pursuit of disparate interests and short-run profits risked confining an economy to trading ventures and *rentier* exploits. Without coherent central institutions, the interests of the whole are not easy to defend. Private interests are not required to internalise social costs. Consider more closely the earlier case of Venetian industrial and commercial contraction, which provoked a shift of resources into the service sector over several decades of the seventeenth century. There was no apparent fall in employment or GNP overall, but services, though a rational immediate resort for individual investors and workers, offered no base from which to share in the gains of subsequent industrial development (see Rapp, 1975).

At the less flexible end of the spectrum, autocratic regimes could override some of the conflicting interests evident in Venice or the Netherlands. Brandenburg–Prussia, for example, was far better at providing public goods, priming the pump, and substituting government action for market initiative. Such states were adept at the disaster management which, with varying degrees of effectiveness, was being developed in the eighteenth century (cf. Post, 1985).

However, autocracy could be too extreme and thus too inflexible and unable to substitute for an under-developed private sector. Despite Peter the Great's superhumanly vigorous supervision of the Russian economy, a later ruler, Catherine the Great, succumbed to the blandishments of the landed nobility and reversed the capstone Petrine reform. In 1762 she issued a decree that halted the purchase of villages, which meant that manufacturers could no longer acquire additional labour. Given the limited possibilities of substituting capital for labour at that date, industrial expansion was essentially blocked. In this case, as in modern examples, 'inflexibility' manifested itself as a conservative reaction.

Most European states lay between these two poles and it is possible to make the claim that particular historical sequences of political and economic change had produced enough, but not too much, flexibility in them. Britain's position was privileged because it was there that machines and factories first emerged, in powerful combination. The country had moved to dissolve successive rigidities, seemingly because the legal and political authorities came to recognise the resultant growth as in the national interest. There is space here for only two illustrations – in agriculture, legislative attempts were not permitted to suppress the spread of an important productivity-raising crop, clover; in industry, the law turned against guild restrictions from as early as the end of the sixteenth century (Jones, 1970: 65–6; 1987: 99–100).

Yet the historical compression of the timing and similarity of outcome among many European states, whether they are tagged Britain's 'followers' or not, once again suggests that we should pay more attention to the commonalities of Europe's competitive economic system than to the particularities. The decades when the various instruments joined in (to vary the musical metaphor slightly) necessarily reflect the individual webs of influences within them. But it is easier to describe these influences than to weight them, and more fruitful to watch the conducting of the whole orchestra.

Later history

People have responded at all times to changes in relative prices, but neither instantaneously nor costlessly. There is a sociology as well as an economics. The Jesuits said give them a boy before he is seven and they would have him for life. Schumpeter noted that people form their ideas before they are twenty-five and spend the rest of their lives working them out. And we can observe that environmentalists often yearn to conserve the world as it was when they were young, not the world of some earlier epoch nor yet that of the degenerate present.

The individualist model should not be disregarded. On the other hand, it should not be permitted to obscure the lags in a society's response which arise from the early conditioning of some of its age cohorts, nor again behaviour attributable to the membership of groups. Group behaviour is co-ordinated by pressures from other members and may override individual tendencies.

One way in which social rigidities may dull responses to movements of relative prices is by reducing the supply elasticity of entrepreneurship among individuals who become businessmen but, having social prestige in the back of their minds, opt out early. This attitude seems to mark the classic cases of so-called economic decline – in the Venetian Republic, the Dutch Republic, Britain during the climacteric of the late nineteenth century, and the English-speaking countries today.

Take the 'decline of the Netherlands'. The great-grandsons of men who had expanded its trading economy while struggling to be free from Spain in the sixteenth century became within three or four generations the *Regentiepatriciaat*, city fathers of Amsterdam with proclivities towards law and the church, and increasingly towards the role of *rentier*. This is consistent with the Allocation of Talent model, which sees the relative rewards from entrepreneurship and rent-seeking as crucial, in this case implying a tilt towards the latter.

For the shift in the interests of such a group to have reduced the whole economy's adaptability, a further condition would have had to be satisfied. There would have needed to be a barrier confronting new entrants to business. The élite in eighteenth-century Amsterdam did come to look down on 'trade', but there is no sign that becoming rich had really lost its attraction or been blocked. Even if the aim was to insert one's children into the higher reaches of society, the result could have been a metabolism in which few families stayed long in trade but many passed through its ranks. However, it is possible that if rent-seeking occupations did become the more attractive, young hopefuls might aspire to put their energies into them without passing through the entrepreneurial stage.

Consider, next, England from the late nineteenth century to the present doldrums. Here more than anywhere the case can be made that loss of adaptability was and is social in origin.[6] The more privileged the institution, say the older universities or the commissioned ranks of the armed forces, the more disproportionate the entry from a group chosen because parental incomes were sufficient to pass it through the public, i.e. private, schools, where the stamp of a lifetime's castemark is given (not on the forehead but on the tongue). This policy remains virtually unamended, despite the severity of the external competition faced by Britain and a thousand surveys showing that ability is poorly predicted by social class. (The ability to shine at an early age in educational and military institutions where the informal rules are those of one class may well be predicted by class, but that is not the same thing.)

These reflections come close to the heart of a major division among economic historians, conveniently exemplified by the debate about the climacteric. The split is between those (the more historically- and institutionally-minded) who believe that British entrepreneurs failed to adjust, to seize their chances, to compete successfully with the rising stars of the USA, Germany and eventually Japan, and those (more theoretical and quantitative) who believe that these men did all they could, subject to the constraints under which they found themselves operating. If the latter group of scholars is correct, questions of adaptability or unadaptability do not arise. What a man did was all that he could do. Such a belief is, however, fairly easily guyed as proving its own assumptions, in the sense that it treats entrepreneurs as rational maximisers who must, by assumption, maximise rationally, accept hard constraints but not soft limitations, always adjust, and be unable to fail except as is written in their stars. On this view any 'failure' of the economy as a whole (say a slowing growth rate) must stem from externally imposed conditions of markets and resources.

Apart from anything else, the interpretation sits oddly with the history of the firm. Very few English firms, except in the agricultural sector, have survived under family control for more than three generations. Does this mean that suddenly the fourth generation consists of people who are not rational maximisers? Do they – evidently they do – try to maximise something else? If so, this points to the ambiguity of the maximising postulate. The macro escape clause, that individual firms do not matter if entry to and exit from industries is fluid, cannot rescue the behaviourial postulate in the face of synchronised behaviour by the fourth generation of family businessmen. That behaviour seems after all to be social, influenced by acquired tastes for more genteel occupations.

Differences did exist between American and British behaviour. Chandler's interpretation of the situation in the late nineteenth-century USA is Olsonian: in a relatively new economy, men and institutions had been less able to entrench themselves.[7] Income distribution was less skewed than in Britain, where a labour market segmented by class gave skilled craft workers the impetus to become defensive and impeded overall social mobility, i.e. adaptability in one of its guises. Both the American and British conditions, though arguably adaptations to different sets of factor prices (with lower resource prices and higher wages in the USA), probably reinforced themselves in opposite directions.

All in all, ascriptive, culturally-determined behaviour, rigid legal systems, and political markets will impede adaptability. They will produce *Queen Mary* effects whereby the economy cannot change course quickly, however transparent the signals that it should do so.[8] The world is one of multiple ascriptive features, some of which are enormously ancient. Remember Robert Putnam's thesis, with which we started, that regional government in Italy in the late twentieth century works best where there is most 'civic community' – the differential distribution of which 'was already clearly evident as long ago as the 13th century'.

VI CONCLUDING REMARKS

To repeat an earlier remark, economic flexibility or inflexibility is like a ghost in the machine. We know it is there, a property of social machinery, but find it hard to spot. The procedure here has been to make a survey from as many angles as possible, often alluding to the market purist's assumption that economies do adapt, silently and fast, only to counter with the historian's insistence that societies are not plastic after all, but cling to ancient features, changing, when they do change, only after a lag. Thus we began by considering the role of the Great Traditions, which are so old and deep-seated as to modify the force of the market in innumerable ways, though seldom to the extent that students of culture claim. The truth lies in between, which is one reason that adaptability is so hard to pin down.

We looked next at certain historical stories, such as the Hartz thesis in which the case for large constraints on colonial economic systems is forcefully put, and discussed other cases in which flexibility was similarly compromised. This led to the question of change through time, and the view was expressed that during the early stages of development, when customary means of social insurance were eroded, flexibility was reduced, only to increase again once the economy produced greater resources.

The case was also made, with greater confidence, that degrees of flexibility are in general historically contingent. They arise from particular circumstances and are often handed down through time (i.e. they are path-dependent). The difficult problem of generalising about when new forces will upset old equilibria has not been solved, here or elsewhere. The inconclusiveness of much debate was illustrated by noting Abramovitz's work (1986) on technological catching-up, in which he states that national productivity levels depend on a quality which he labels 'social capability' but freely admits that no one knows what this means. The ghost in the machine again.

In a third section the theme of adaptability is left a little to the side in favour of discussing the costs of market adaptation. The inconsistency of treatments of these costs is pointed out, notably calls for free international mobility of factors which embrace capital but tacitly exclude labour, meaning that theoretical income gains are lost. On the other hand, it is certain that full freedom of labour mobility would create global chaos. No solution is offered here, but the first step is taken of indicating the need to specify what market freedoms and hence degrees of adaptability are appropriate today.

The fourth section returns to historical substance. The main theme dealt with is the explanation of European industrialisation, which is given primarily in terms of the responsiveness of the entire states system. Within this the performance of national economies is similarly attributed to their relative flexibility, such as why Russia's early developmental spurt was aborted and Dutch industrialisation lagged so long, but Britain achieved the Industrial Revolution. Finally, some cases of decline are mentioned, especially the 'climacteric' in late nineteenth-century Britain. Once again, arguments that what happened were really adjustments to current market conditions are permitted to jostle with others to the effect that social rigidities interfered. The balance is tentatively allowed to fall, as throughout the chapter, on the side of historical inflexibilities, of fetters on the ghost in the machine.

NOTES

I am most happy to acknowledge helpful comments by John Anderson, Timur Kuran, Ekkehart Schlicht and Colin White.

1 Higgs (1987) does note underlying trends in the same direction.
2 For some critical remarks on the neglected study of the duration of lags between equilibria, see Engerman, 1993.

3 An instance discovered after this was written in Howkins, 1992. Becker (1993: 392) notes a similar difficulty with introducing the term 'human capital'.
4 On the value of redundancy for performance, see Nonaka, 1991: 102.
5 Somewhat similar points are made in Jerome Blum *et al.*, 1970: 579–80, and Rostow, 1975: 222.
6 Paxman (1991) is a tract on the extent and success of rent-seeking in the British case. See especially Chapter 9 on the military.
7 See the discussion in Kirby, 1992. The thesis of David Hackett Fisher (1989) that British regionalism, community separateness and modal behaviour were transplanted in the USA and persisted in a strongly path-dependent fashion shows that observations about these matters can rarely be categorical. American society was far from exempt from ascriptive features. The point is that it was much freer than British or European equivalents. Casual observation suggests that Australia, and to a surprisingly greater extent Canada, remain closer to Britain than they are to the USA.
8 Frank (1988) gives an unflattering account of why economists do not believe such things happen. For the 'Queen Mary effect', see Browning, 1981: 129.

REFERENCES

Abramovitz, Moses (1986) 'Catching-up, forging ahead, and falling behind', *Journal of Economic History* 46: 385–406.
Anderson, J.L. and E.L. Jones (1988) 'Natural disasters and the historical response', *Australian Economic History Review* XXVIII: 12.
Arthur, W. Brian (1988) 'Self-reinforcing mechanisms in economics', in P.W. Anderson, K.J. Arrow and D. Pines (eds) *The Economy as an Evolving Complex System*, New York: Addison-Wesley.
Becker, Gary (1993) 'Nobel Lecture: The economic way of looking at behaviour', *Journal of Political Economy* 101: 392.
Bensusan-Butt, D.M. (1960) *On Economic Growth: An Essay in Pure Theory*, Oxford: Clarendon Press.
Blum, Jerome *et al.* (1970) *The European World: a History*, Boston, MA: Little, Brown.
Bozeman, Adda B. (1971) *The Future of Law in a Multicultural World*, Princeton, NJ: Princeton University Press.
Browning, E.S. (1981) 'East Asia: in search of a second economic miracle', *Foreign Affairs* 60: 129.
Clark, Colin (1942) *The Economics of 1960*, London: Macmillan.
Clark, Gregory (1992) 'Textile history as world history', Davis, CA: University of California, mimeo.
Cohen, Stephen P. and C.V. Raghavulu (1977) *The Andhra Cyclone of 1977: Individual and Institutional Responses to Mass Death*, New Delhi: Vikas Publishing House.
Crafts, N.F.R. (1977) 'Industrial Revolution in England and France: some thoughts on the question, "Why was England first?"', *Economic History Review*, 2nd series 30: 429–41.
David, Paul (1986) 'Understanding the economics of QWERTY: the necessity of history', in W.N. Parker (ed.) *Economic History and the Modern Economist*, Oxford: Basil Blackwell.
Dodgshon, Robert (1987) *The European Past: Social Evolution and Spatial Order*, London and Basingstoke: Macmillan.
Engerman, Stanley L. (1993) 'Chicken Little, Anna Karenina, and the economics of

slavery', *Social Science History* 17: 161–71, Presidential address to the Social Science History Association.

Fisher, David Hackett (1989) *Albion's Seed*, Oxford: Oxford University Press.

Frank, Robert H. (1988) *Passions Within Reasons: The Strategic Role of the Emotions*, New York: W.W. Norton.

Freebairn, J.W. (1977) 'Temporary assistance for industries', Bundoora: La Trobe University, mimeo.

Goudsblom, Johan, E.L. Jones and Stephen Mennell (1989) *Human History and Social Process*, Exeter: University of Exeter Press.

Greif, Avner (1992) 'Contract enforceability and economic institutions in early trade: the Maghribi traders' coalition', Stanford, CA: Stanford University, mimeo.

Harries, Owen (1993) 'Clash of civilisations', *The Weekend Australian*, 3–4 April.

Hartz, Louis (ed.) (1964) *The Founding of New Societies*, New York: Harcourt, Brace & World.

Heller, M.A. (1989–90) 'The Middle East: out of step with history', *Foreign Affairs* 69: 153–71.

Higgs, Robert (1987) *Crisis and Leviathan: Critical Episodes in the Growth of American Government*, New York: Oxford University Press.

Howkins, Alun (1992) 'Social history and agricultural history', *Agricultural History Review* 40: 161.

International Monetary Fund (1993) *IMF Survey, 8 March*, Washington, DC: IMF.

Jones, E.L. (1970) 'English and European agricultural development 1650–1750', in R.M. Hartwell (ed.) *The Industrial Revolution*, Oxford: Basil Blackwell.

—— (1978) 'Disaster management and resource saving in Europe', in Antoni Maczak and William N. Parker (eds) *Natural Resources in European History*, Washington, DC: Resources for the Future.

—— (1984) Review of Ashok Guha, *An Evolutionary View of Economic Growth*, *Journal of Economic History* XLIV: 1152–3.

—— (1987) *The European Miracle*, 2nd edition, Cambridge: Cambridge University Press.

—— (1988) *Growth Recurring: Economic Change in World History*, Oxford: Clarendon Press.

—— (1990) 'La deindustrializzazione come forma di aggiustamento economico: il caso dell' Inghilterra sud-occidentale', *Quaderni storici* 73: 247–68.

Kalland, Arne and Jon Pedersen (1984) 'Famine and population in Fukuoka domain during the Tokugawa period', *Journal of Japenese Studies* 10: 31–72.

Kasper, Wolfgang (1990) 'The defeat of political power', *Economic Witness*, 28 June: 1–6.

—— (1992) 'Advancing into the 21st century: visions and challenges facing the Downunder economy', *Australian Economic Review* 100: 51–64.

—— (1993) 'Institutional innovation to enhance international attractiveness', Australian Defence Force Academy, Economics and Management Discussion Paper no. 1, August.

Kirby, M.W. (1992) 'Institutional rigidities and economic decline: reflections on the British experience', *Economic History Review*, 2nd series, XLV: 637–60.

Kuran, Timur (1983) 'Behavioural norms in the Islamic doctrine of economics: a critique', *Journal of Economic Behaviour and Organisation* 4: 353–79.

Leftwich, Adrian and Dominique Harvie (1985) 'The political economy of famine', University of York, Institute for Research in the Social Sciences Discussion Paper no. 116.

Liebowitz, S.J. and Stephen E. Margolis (1990) 'The fable of the keys', *Journal of Law and Economics* XXXIII: 1–25.

Marshall, Alfred (1920) *Principles of Economics*, 8th edition, London: Macmillan.

Mennell, Stephen (1989) *Norbert Elias: Civilization and the Human Self-image*, Oxford: Basil Blackwell.

Mokyr, Joel (1990) *The Lever of Riches*, New York: Oxford University Press.

Nonaka, Ikujiro (1991) 'The knowledge-creating company', *Harvard Business Review*, November–December: 102.

Olson, Mancur (1982) *The Rise and Decline of Nations*, New Haven, CT: Yale University Press.

Paxman, Jeremy (1991) *Friends in High Places: Who Runs Britain?*, London: Penguin.

Pocock, J.G.A. (1991) 'Deconstructing Europe', *London Review of Books*, 19 December.

Pollak, Robert A. and Susan Cotts Watkins (1993) 'Cultural and economic approaches to fertility: a proper marriage or a mésalliance?', *Population and Development Review* 19(3), September: 467–96.

Post, John D. (1985) *Food Shortage, Climatic Variability, and Epidemic Disease in Preindustrial Europe*, Ithaca, NY: Cornell University Press.

Pryce-Jones, David (1990) *The Closed Circle: An Interpretation of the Arabs*, London: Paladin Books.

Rapp, R.T. (1975) 'The unmaking of the Mediterranean trade hegemony: international trade rivalry and the commercial revolution', *Journal of Economic History* XXXV: 499–525.

Rostow, W.W. (1975) *How It All Began: Origins of the Modern Economy*, New York: McGraw-Hill.

Sauer, Carl O. (1976) in *Annals of the American Association of Geographers* 66: 341.

5

ADAPTING THE ECONOMIES OF EASTERN EUROPE

Behavioural and institutional aspects of flexibility

Alexander Neuber

If we can agree that the economic problem of society is mainly one of rapid adaptation to changes in particular circumstances of time and place, it would seem to follow that the ultimate decisions must be left to the people who are familiar with these circumstances. . . . We cannot expect that this problem will be solved by first communicating all this knowledge to a central board which, after integrating all knowledge, issues its orders . . . this problem can be solved, and in fact is being solved, by the price system.

(Hayek, 1945: 524–5)

In the real world, to influence economic policy, we set up or abolish an agency, amend the law, change the personnel and so on: we work through institutions. And what really matters is the effects that a modification in these institutions will actually make in the real world.

(Coase, 1984)

I INTRODUCTION

The transformations in Eastern Europe (EE) and the former Soviet Union (FSU) afford not only a great challenge to social science, but also the opportunity to analyse which institutions and behavioural traits determine the essence of an economic system. Flexibility and its determinants are important implicit categories in the reform discussions in these countries. This chapter will attempt to make the assumptions underlying these discussions more explicit, by focusing on the constituent parts of flexibility, namely the nature and determinants of behavioural and institutional flexibility.

In doing so, it will take up some of the questions raised in an earlier paper (Neuber, 1993). There, I had set out an argument against the feasibility of

111

institutional discontinuity in transition economies, arguing for the predominance of behavioural inertia in transition. This chapter goes beyond that presumption to analyse the determinants of behavioural inertia, in order to determine to what extent they may be amenable to decisive policy changes. To my surprise, since I am an institutionalist at heart, the earlier conclusion is found to be hardly tenable, and I have come to the conclusion that policy is an endogenous factor in behavioural change, thereby increasing the possibility of success even of radical departures in economic policy.

In Part II, the structural and behavioural properties of planned economies, and the legacy that they present for reforms, will be analysed. Part III is the core of the chapter, and develops a conceptual framework about the interrelationship of institutionalisation and flexibility of economic activity, as well as the transition outcomes associated with differing assumptions about the feasibility of behavioural and institutional change. Within that framework, the behavioural assumptions underlying the two rival reform agendas, gradualist/institutionalist versus 'big bang'/radical, are examined. In particular, the interaction between institutional (formal) change and behavioural change (norms, values), and the impact of differential speeds of adjustment on transition outcomes, will be analysed. Part IV sums up the analysis.

Throughout, the primary focus is on the generic 'supply-side' adaptability of man as *homo economicus* rather than on the tactical vagaries forced on to the reform process in order to deal with the *politikon zoon* in man; thus the political economy of reform is less emphasised, and the reader is referred to my earlier paper (Neuber, 1993) for a fuller discussion of the implications of political uncertainty for the reform process. Given the embeddedness of economic reform in a process of both democratisation and constitutional reform, the political sustainability of economic reforms does, however, provide an important upper and lower bound on the feasible set of economic policies.

II RIGIDITIES AND FLEXIBILITIES AT THE OUTSET OF REFORM

Some salient structural and behavioural features of planned economies

The inability of planned economies, both centrally planned economies (CPEs) and modified planned economies (MPEs), to adapt successfully over time, has become a major explanation of their demise.[1] While this will not be disputed here, the stereotypical understanding of planned economies fails to recognise that much of the behavioural, and consequently structural, rigidity that could be observed was in itself the result of rational adaptation by economic agents to the prevailing structure. This section will therefore set out some of the salient features of planning, in order to analyse some of the resultant 'dysfunctional' behavioural patterns that have resulted. These, in turn, will play an important role in assessing the ability of agents and structures to adjust as transition gets under way.

The classical command economy relied on material balances planning, based on input-output matrices, to match available resources and the desired supply of final goods; demand was a marginal, and imputed, category in that framework. Overwhelming emphasis was on quantitative parameters and indicators, to the detriment of all other considerations, particularly cost effectiveness and quality.[2] The crucial difference arising *vis-à-vis* market-based enterprises was the orientation of producers on two features: securing sufficient inputs and fulfilling quantitative plan indicators. State-owned enterprises (SOEs) were not, usually, constrained by demand, and hence by definition not responsive to consumer preferences, but more so by resources, which were in perennial shortage due to the inconsistencies of the plan and the insatiable demand by SOEs for inputs in order to secure some slack for plan fulfilment (Kornai, 1979, 1980).

Lack of signalling

The organisational focus on quantities was, of course, due to the fact that prices were reduced to mere accounting units, with often very tenuous links between scarcity values and actual prices. This was also true for foreign trade, where a variable tax-subsidy process severed the link between foreign currency prices and domestic wholesale prices (Wolf, 1988: 216). In seeking to effect allocation in the absence of price signals, Soviet planners faced an economy producing 24 million goods. Although *Gosplan* and *Gossnab*, the central planning agencies, produced plans for only 15,000–25,000 key commodities, this was still a daunting, and ultimately impossible, task (Hewett, 1988: 185).

Adjustments and flexibility, to the degree that they existed, manifested themselves in quantitative parameters: 'In other words, the system of official prices in the CPE does not serve as a transmission belt for economic disturbances or as a signalling device for adjustment to such disturbances' (Wolf, 1988: 10). Enterprises adjusted only quantities (factor inputs, output targets, imaginative accounting, etc.), but not production techniques or factor payments; economising was not part of the framework, and adaptability in that respect, while sought after by planners, did not materialise.

The static inefficiencies that resulted from the absence of price signalling and the impossibility of perfect planning, are proverbial.[3] More interestingly, the process of planning created dynamics of behaviour and adjustment that exacerbated these static inefficiencies. Given the complexity of the information problem, plans were formulated in incremental and marginal terms, based on the preceding plans, thereby introducing a considerable degree of hysteresis into the process. This pre-empted, organisationally, the

113

possibility of making repeated top-down adjustments in the planning process, thus exacerbating the dynamic deficiency of the system.[4]

This organisational infeasibility of flexibility is compounded by the pervasiveness of perverse incentives and principal–agent problems in the planner–enterprise relationship. Taut planning, plan revisions, re-ordering of plan priorities and realignments of bonus schemes never resolved the basic informational asymmetry, or the resultant patterns of dysfunctional behaviour. The lack of exit, of proper signalling, and of instruments that might have induced non-measurable effort, effectively made intra-hierarchy adjustments the only area where responsiveness was crucial. Given the incentive structure, however, adjustments in this sphere had a spurious relationship, if any, to economic efficiency.[5] In order to minimise the principal–agent problems (and in view of their faith in economies of scale), socialist planners had a decided preference for the 'rationalisation' of production in very large units; the industrial structure was therefore characterised by a far higher degree of concentration than in market economies, a legacy that has proved to be a formidable obstacle to adjustment in transition.

Adjustment patterns of state-owned enterprises with soft-budget constraints

Apart from the aforementioned functional characteristics exhibited by (SOEs) in planned economies, there are behavioural implications of SOEs' *ex ante* knowledge that the government will, in all likelihood, bail out loss-making enterprises. This is, of course, Kornai's (in-)famous soft-budget constraint (SBC), which was the single most important cause of the shortage economy, as manifest in 'investment hunger' and perennial excess demand and hoarding of inputs. Moreover, it became an important behavioural parameter, as it affected not only the financial side of SOEs' activities, but became integrated into expectations, and consequently behaviour.[6] As such, it further reduced the effect that prices might have had on SOE behaviour: the SBC 'decreases the elasticity of demand for all alternative inputs, of all factors; diminishes the firm's sensitivity toward the interest rate, exchange rate, and so on. Similarly, the multiproduct firm will be less sensitive to changes in relative output prices. Summing up: the general price responsiveness of the firm declines' (Kornai, 1986a: 10). On a macro level, the SBC implies the absence of exit, and by protecting 'the inefficient firm against constructive destruction . . . impedes innovation and development' (Kornai, 1986a: 11). On a micro-level, it entails the lack of adjustment in the productive sphere, and the concentration on intra-hierarchical adjustment and bargaining instead. To the extent that the SBC is a psychological phenomenon that is highly correlated with the credibility, or otherwise, of the government's threat of no bail-out, SBCs have persisted in most economies in transition, since the credibility of sustained reforms was initially very low. Thus, SOE adjustment in transition becomes a function both of credible reform commitments and credible enforcement of hard budget constraints.

Lack of dynamic development

Until the early 1970s, socialist economies achieved respectable growth rates of GDP, and, to a lesser extent, of total factor productivity (Kornai, 1992: 187; Gregory and Stuart, 1986: 333–4). This performance was, in large measure, due to extensive growth that relied on increased inputs rather than on improvements in the productivity of existing factor stocks. Growth was of the 'high cost' variety, in that it implied considerable sacrifice in terms of lower consumption and leisure. However, after 1970 a notable stagnation occurred, with total factor productivity growth converging on zero. Gomulka (1990: 111) has argued that the relative dearth of endogenous technological innovation did not affect economic performance until the early 1970s, because the socialist economies were able to diffuse basic technological advances from advanced to backward sectors and could rely, to some degree, on the import of technology. As the opportunities for internal diffusion were exhausted, and as technological developments made a quantum leap with the widespread introduction of information technology into production and organisation, the innovative deficit of the socialist economies was clearly revealed in dropping productivity and growth rates.

The failure of socialist economies to innovate has been linked to many factors: risk-aversion of managers in an environment of 'taut planning'; inadequate rewards and incentives, in particular the arbitrary appropriation of returns by the centre; absence of an exit threat; and insufficient ability to screen innovative projects in a centralised economy, resulting in fewer trials (Qian and Xu, 1992: 2). The last factor appears to be the crucial distinguishing factor between market economies and planned economies: innovation is a decentralised process, requiring an adequate 'selection environment' (Nelson and Winter, 1982). In order to induce a lot of innovative activity, its rewards must be recoverable, and known to be so. It is the ability of market economies to change the institutional framework in response to innovative pressures that arguably provides dynamic potential. Institutional economists have focused for some time on this factor as the actual strength of the market system, rather than on static Pareto-optimal allocative efficiency.[7]

Modified central planning as an attempt to introduce flexibility

Three countries in Eastern Europe experimented with more decentralised systems to overcome some of the aforementioned problems: the former Yugoslavia, which had a system of labour self-management since the early 1950s, Hungary, which embarked on gradual, piecemeal reforms in the late

1960s, and Poland after the Solidarity interlude in 1981. These MPEs decentralised decision-making to the firm level, and replaced detailed quantitative planning by indicative planning. However, their attitude towards allocation through the market (or a semblance of price-related signals) was equivocal. Partial liberalisation of prices therefore created new distortions, and incentives were still misaligned owing to the absence of clear property rights.[8]

Moreover, state ownership and the paternalistic attitude at the heart of the SBC remained. In effect, 'plan bargaining' over quantities was merely replaced by a more pervasive 'regulator bargaining', encompassing credits, tax relief and subsidies. Thus, direct bureaucratic control was replaced by indirect bureaucratic control, but the supply responsiveness of the state sector, while better than in CPEs, was still disappointing (Kornai, 1986b; Wolf, 1991). A similar tendency took hold in the Soviet Union in the late 1980s, and here as in Hungary efforts at adjustment were not focused on the productive sphere but on the negotiating table, as a direct result of over-rigid planning.[9] By and large, therefore, decentralisation failed to induce the flexibility and responsiveness in the productive sphere that it was supposed to achieve.

Adaptability of economic agents in rigid structures

Having outlined that CPEs and MPEs were both characterised by a significant degree of systemic and behavioural rigidity, it is necessary to point out that beneath the general structure significant behavioural flexibility was being displayed by economic agents attempting to overcome the rigidities of the formal framework. For the purposes of the analysis, it is important to identify to what extent adaptability was a function of the environment. The possibly dysfunctional characteristics of the responsiveness, insofar as they are a rational response to the rigidities of the official system, are of less concern, since it can be presumed that, given a sustained and credible shift in that system, the degree of adaptability will remain but will no longer lead to dysfunctional outcomes. Several instances of flexibility will underscore the high degree of responsiveness of a subset of economic agents.

"Exit', in the sense of joining the shadow economy, was, of course, another pervasive form of adaptation. Here we are more concerned with intra-system adaptation. However, the second economy did play an important role in providing a learning environment for entrepreneurs. Furthermore, it reduced the need of the formal system to adapt, as it could draw on the flexibility inherent in the second economy:

> In the de facto system persistent shortages trigger the second economy into action as individuals seek to fill the gaps in the supply of goods and services in contravention of the law. The result is an essentially illegal, highly flexible system that identifies changes in demand and

responds to them. It is primarily in the business of supplying services, but also some goods. This is a clear example of a way in which the de facto system is far more adroit at responding to changes in demand than the formal system would suggest.

(Hewett, 1988: 213)

Managers of SOEs also adopted a variety of responses to deal with the arbitrariness and rigidity of the planning mechanism. In the absence of price signals, they relied on a wide array of indicators from both the shadow economy and the official economy, exhibiting a considerable degree of sensitivity to those developments that might endanger their supply of vital inputs. On the basis of these signals, managers employed various techniques, such as informal barter deals or the use of expediters or procurement scouts (*tolkachi*) in order to obtain scarce inputs. These actions entailed high, often non-monetary transaction costs.[10] In order to minimise these costs, enterprises sought to hoard all kinds of material supplies and tradable barter products, thereby exacerbating the shortages. These 'safety factors' allowed SOEs considerable organisational slack; flexibility was thus applied only to the extent that it provided a safeguard against unforeseen shocks.[11]

The 'quasi-market' that developed was characterised by widespread horizontal and vertical bargaining, as well as the necessary conduits such as 'side-payments' (Pejovich, 1989: 70). Again, the question arises as to whether these patterns of interaction might serve a purpose during transition, or whether they merely indicate the existence of flexibility *per se*. Sociologists have argued that 'the existence of parallel structures in the informal and interfirm networks means that instead of an institutional vacuum we find routines and practices, organisational forms and social ties, that can become assets, resources, and the basis for credible commitments and co-ordinated actions' (Stark, 1992b: 300). The downside of these managerial networks has been their asymmetric access to state property during transition.

Industrial relations was another area where flexibility was introduced in order to cope with the rigidity of the formal system. Thus throughout the region, in varying degrees the co-optation of labour became necessary to solve the increasing inconsistencies of planning. In Hungary and Poland, workers' councils were given a formal role in the governance of SOEs, thereby raising their stake in its performance and securing necessary co-operation.[12] Apart from these formal attempts to introduce flexibility into industrial relations, there was a lot of adjustment at the shop-floor level. In East Germany, management was obliged to compromise with employees in informal 'plan-fulfilment pacts', in order to secure the necessary co-operation and flexibility (Voskamp and Witte, 1991: 360). Similarly, sociological studies of Hungarian shop-floor practices come to the conclusion that 'not as a virtue but as a necessity in response to often occurring "crises", the production process in state socialist economies requires a flexible allocation of labour on the shop floor' (Stark, 1986: 494).[13] The ad hoc nature of many of these arrangements, as well as the uncertainties regarding fulfilment of the implicit contracts, entailed a significant degree of mutual suspicion and uncertainty, making this a second-best mechanism of adaptation at best.

Planned economies thus demonstrated the deleterious effects of seeking to over-institutionalise economic activity. The pervasiveness of planning resulted in large systemic rigidities; in the words of Oliver Williamson (1991: 35), 'the stability value of socialism turned out to be an immobility burden in the end'. As a result, the traditional CPE, as well as the modified versions, exhibited many salient characteristics of an inflexible economy, such as low supply elasticities, low degrees of innovation, high degrees of structural and behavioural inertia (due to the planning system), as well as highly imperfect information and incentive systems (due to the structure of property rights and the manipulation of relative prices). At the same time, the flexibility of many agents in trying to cope with the constraints imposed by these structural rigidities of the shortage economy must be emphasised, such as the emergence of entrepreneurship in parallel markets or the ingenuity of managers of SOEs in securing scarce inputs. Adaptability was limited, but well focused (on intra-hierarchical bargaining), given the unique constraints and distorted incentives of the system. While agents were used to low-adaptation equilibria, this evidence does not generically preclude the emergence of more pervasive behavioural flexibility, if constraints were to change.

III BEHAVIOURAL AND INSTITUTIONAL ASPECTS OF FLEXIBILITY IN TRANSITION

An economic epoch implies an interplay of technological and economic changes not only with institutional modifications but also with shifts in beliefs entertained by the societies that participate in it; and the time and effort required to overcome the resistance of old beliefs and to evolve the new and more appropriate spiritual framework may partially account for the length of epochs.

(Kuznets, 1966: 7)

A framework for analysis

Given the legacy of planning, Eastern Europe and the former Soviet Union are embarked on a systemic transformation that is, for the most part, inspired by the perception of the market economy as the superior framework for economic activity. Significantly, most attention has focused on the comparative advantage of market economies in static efficiency terms, and much less on how the institutional set-up facilitates dynamic efficiency. To the extent that these countries desire the performance properties of market economies, they must determine what factors determine the superior dynamic abilities, and by which means these can best be introduced into their economies. In particular, are secure (private) property rights and free price formation sufficient to obtain Schumpeterian competition, or does the market entail further institutions, norms and state-sponsored conduits, without which it cannot fulfil its static and dynamic signalling functions? Is there hysteresis in behaviour, and path dependence in institutions? If so, what are the implications of existing behavioural norms, values, and institutions for transition policy?

A great deal of the debate about appropriate transition policies in EE and the FSU is centred around these questions. The principal debate about the appropriate speed and sequencing of reform policies, often couched in the none too helpful dichotomy of gradualism versus 'big-bang', is based on different assumptions about the relative ease with which behavioural patterns and institutions in emerging market economies (EMEs) can, and ought to, be changed as a result of policy. There is little disagreement about the complementarity of markets and institutions, and the embeddedness of modern market economies in complex institutional frameworks, encompassing widespread state regulation and delineation of market boundaries (e.g. anti-trust regulations, social security and welfare provisions, depositor insurance and banking supervision, environmental regulation, sophisticated state administration, provision of a legal framework, etc.). However, there is much less agreement about the feasibility, and desirability, of policy-induced discontinuity in the institutional framework, nor is there agreement about the optimal intertemporal distribution of the transition costs that are associated with the systemic change.

Although flexibility (of agents, values, behaviour, and institutions) is not an explicit term of reference in this debate, it is an important underlying concept, the assumptions about which are, however, not usually spelt out. Prior to discussing the flexibility properties of transition policies and paths, blueprints and actual ones, this chapter will set out an analytical framework of behavioural and institutional flexibility in which to structure that discussion. In particular, it will be helpful to identify the potential trade-offs that exist between the degree of institutionalisation of economic activity, on the one hand, and the extent of uncertainty and flexibility, on the other. To the extent that institutions reduce uncertainty, they are also likely to reduce flexibility.[14] To the extent that they constrain, or enable, behavioural changes, the differential speed of adjustment of culturally and systematically derived norms of behaviour, on the one hand, and formal institutions, on the other, will lead to different outcomes in transition, and thus to varying transition paths in terms of flexibility and associated benefits and costs.

For the purpose of this chapter we shall adopt Douglass North's definition of institutions:

Institutions are the constraints that human beings impose upon themselves to structure human interaction. They consist of formal rules and informal standards of behavior and of their enforcement characteristics. Formal rules include political (and juridical) rules, economic rules, and contracts. . . . Given the bargaining strength and interests of the decision making parties, the function of the rules is to facilitate exchange, political or economic. Informal constraints include conventions that evolve as solutions to coordination problems and that all parties are interested in having maintained; norms of behaviour that are recognized standards of conduct; and self-imposed codes of conduct such as personal standards of honesty and integrity. Conventions are self-enforcing. Norms of behavior are enforced by the second party (the threat of retaliation for contract violation) or by a third party (societal sanctions).

(North, 1992: 4–5)

Institutions arise in societies due to the pervasiveness of uncertainty, the imperfect delineation of property rights, and the bounded rationality of agents, all of which raise transaction costs in the absence of constraining institutions.[15] Clearly, however, institutions also fulfil enabling functions, by stabilising the environment for economic activity and by reducing uncertainty.[16] For the purposes of the analysis, it is necessary to distinguish norms and patterns of behaviour, also referred to as organisational norms, from formal institutions.

The trade-offs between the degree to which formal institutions are developed in an economy and the degree to which that economy is characterised by flexibility, uncertainty, and transaction costs, can be represented by a simple diagram as in Figure 5.1.

Thus, the formal sector in CPEs was characterised by a highly elaborated institutional framework, with very little flexibility (in the official plan), little uncertainty (under the assumption of plan consistency and fulfilment), and low transaction costs (as all flows of goods and services were centrally directed and enforced). Given the inflexibility of this system, the secondary economy developed, mostly illegally; while it was much more responsive and flexible than the formal system, it was characterised by high uncertainty (given its illegal status) and high transaction costs (due to highly imperfect information and the need for self-enforcement of contracts).

Similarly, one could argue that the US economy is more flexible and institutionalised to a lesser degree than, say, that of Germany. The state presence in the economy is lower, regulation is less pervasive, and contracts are more flexible, particularly in the labour market. The inherent flexibility is bought at the cost of more uncertainty (lesser welfare state, more open competition, fewer institutional safeguards). The difference in transaction costs is not easily observable, but the high lawyer per capita ratio in the

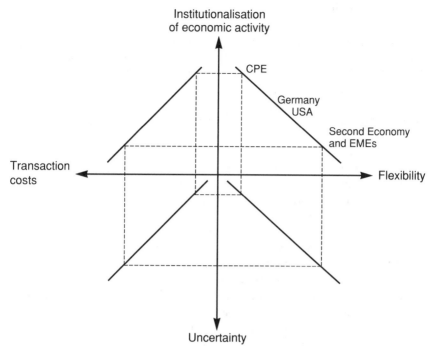

Figure 5.1 The institutionalisation–flexibility schedule

USA, as well as the reliance on hostile takeovers rather than on corporate governance through banks, can be interpreted as pieces of circumstantial evidence.

Transition economies are initially characterised by much uncertainty, as the planning apparatus is dismantled and not immediately replaced by new market institutions. The 'institutional meltdown'[17] of the formal system shifts the formal sector into conditions similar to those prevalent in the parallel economy prior to reform. This situation is characterised by flexibility, which under these circumstances is identified with the absence of stability rather than a desirable attribute of the system. Moreover, as this process of economic change is often embedded in a political and constitutional transition (Offe, 1991), with high correlation between the respective uncertainties, the creation of economic institutions is merely a necessary condition for more stability.

As institutions evolve, they will constrain agents' actions and provide for a more stable, if less flexible, environment.[18] In terms of the reform debate, the question arises whether it is possible to move from the rigidity and certainty of planning to a midpoint on the institution–flexibility schedule while avoiding the transitional low institutionalisation/high flexibility/high uncertainty equilibrium characteristic of the second economy. This, essentially, is the agenda of the gradualists.

More important than this primary aim of establishing an equilibrium in institution–flexibility space that is commensurate with the values and risk preferences of society, however, is the degree to which the new institutions will be able to adapt over time, to provide the dynamic flexibility required. At a general level, the adaptability of institutions has been identified by many authors as a major determinant of sustained economic development.[19] However, the evolutionary nature of modern capitalist economies makes it difficult to pinpoint the decisive factors or driving forces.[20]

Clearly, countries seeking to emulate market economies face an 'institutional indeterminacy' problem in that there is a wide range of economies with very different institutional characteristics which appear to be successful. North, whose research has focused most decisively on the requirements for 'adaptive efficiency', suggests that two broad factors are important: 'aligning the informal constraints with the formal rules and creating and maintaining a polity that will support adaptively efficient institutions' (North, 1992: 11). The institutionalisation of self-correcting mechanisms and an organisational culture that promotes multiple trials would appear to offer the best possibilities in this regard.[21] The new institutional economics, for one, is far from offering a satisfactory answer to this central question, as Furubotn readily admits:

> At present, it seems true that the best advice economists can give Eastern European societies is to proceed with free market reforms. What is generally needed, however, is a theory of development that is capable of dealing, in some depth, with the interrelations between institutional change and growth. The fact that the profession has no generally accepted theory of this type to offer suggests how much work is yet to be done in adapting political economy and the analysis of institutions to the problems of reconstruction.
>
> (Furubotn, 1992: 206)

Eastern Europe provides not only difficult questions in this regard, but also a testing ground that may actually contribute towards the development of such a theory. A first step in that direction would be a clarification of the effects of differential rates of change in informal and formal institutions. This is attempted in the matrix in Figure 5.2.

There are several issues here that require analysis. One concerns the feasibility of effecting comprehensive change of formal institutions in a discontinuous and rapid manner. If that were possible, and if economic agents exhibited values and behavioural traits that did not differ significantly from those found in market economies, a sustained systemic transformation could result quickly. EMEs could thereby secure an environment where private and social returns did not differ significantly, and the adaptive

		Adjustment of beliefs and behaviour	
		slow (Homo-sovieticus)	*fast* (Homo economicus)
Changes in the institutional framework	*slow*	**Dominance of inertia and path dependence** **Entropy** • insufficient, non-credible reforms • insufficient signalling of regime change • persistence of soft budget constraints	**Unbridled capitalism** • spontaneous privatisation (lack of clear property rights) • short-term 'mercantilism' and arbitrage (lack of institutional stability) • myopia and decapitalisation of labour-managed SOEs (lack or corporate governance and privatisation) • monopoly pricing (lack of regulation and restructuring) • fraud (lack of oversight and administrative and legal capacity)
	fast	**Exit** • bankruptcy • unemployment • dysfunctionality	**Sustained systemic transformation** • private sector dynamism • embeddedness of market activity in stable institutional framework • successful privatisation • better supply responsiveness of SOEs

Figure 5.2 Behavioural and institutional change in transition economies

efficiency properties commonly attributed to market economies would obtain. If agents' behaviour did not shift significantly under such a regime change, however, they would soon become dysfunctional

If one posits, however, that the institutional framework, and its stability, will only evolve over time, no matter what the degree of social engineering, then the matrix reduces to a 1 × 2 in the transition phase. Determining the character of transition economies under these circumstances depends to a significant degree on one's assumptions about the utility function of economic agents in planned economies, and about their ability, or otherwise, to react to market-based signals. In other words, are the societies of EE and the FSU dominated by the *homo sovieticus* species, which has become accustomed to minimal responsiveness, exhibits no initiative, and favours stability and low-level certainty above all? Or was *homo sovieticus* merely an adaptation of *homo economicus* to the incentives and institutional constraints of planned economies, who will now exhibit his/her full potential as institutional constraints and incentives change? If it is the former, and we assume that behavioural change proceeds as slowly as institutional change, i.e. path dependence is the dominant feature, then reforms will not succeed to effect a credible departure from the present framework.[22] Unfulfilled expectations would reinforce behavioural inertia, and a low-level equilibrium of entropy would result.[23]

If, however, economic agents in EE and the FSU are assumed to respond to incentives in much the same way as agents in the West, then the new possibilities afforded by these incentives will induce significant changes in behaviour, which initially will be fairly unconstrained by market-framing institutions. Hence, unbridled capitalism would emerge, with scope for personal initiative and significant divergence between private and social returns to activity. These discrepancies might be interpreted as learning or set-up costs. If one assumes that future returns to learning will be significant, and that excessive private returns reinforce the signalling of incentives to agents and thereby accelerate behavioural adaptation, then the net present value, both private and social, of this transition path may well still be positive.

The remainder of this section will seek to determine the likely outcome in EMEs, and will assess the implications of gradual and radical reform agendas in this framework. To that end, we first analyse some behavioural and attitudinal properties of societies in EMEs, and the extent to which path dependence is present in behavioural patterns. On that basis, we shall analyse the institutionalist critique by gradualists of the radical agenda, and then present the case for big-bang reforms in the light of that critique

Adaptability of preferences and behaviour in transition

Behaviour is not only a function of the environment, but also a reflection of the values and preferences held by individuals. Changes in the environment will only elicit behavioural responses, and changes, if the set of preferences is conducive to such adaptation, and itself endogenous to the changing environment. Therefore, it is important to establish whether the preferences of societies in EMEs are amenable to behavioural adaptation, which is a *sine qua non* if the systemic transformation is to take hold.

Planned economies provided a high degree of economic security, if at a low welfare level, as well as an egalitarian bias, qualities that were valued by their societies. However, they were also at the root of the aforementioned dynamic deficiencies. For flexibility in behaviour to obtain, agents must be willing to assume risk and to tolerate income inequalities, both of which arise from private property and initiative. Given the oversimplified dichotomy of socialism and capitalism, however, societies in EMEs are not aware that the market entails not only higher levels of welfare but also higher degrees of uncertainty. This cognition problem (Schopflin, 1992: 9) arises from a low level of economic literacy and results in the desire for a market system that provides both the level of economic security afforded by the

Swedish welfare state and the allocative and dynamic efficiency of the unregulated US economy.[24] Expectations are therefore bound to be disappointed. While societies in market economies similarly desire both security and high standards of living, they are usually aware that there is a partial trade-off, and their preferences will guide their choice of institutions accordingly. East Europeans, and more so inhabitants of the FSU, are often not aware that there is no value-independent 'international best practice' of market capitalism.

The evidence on preference changes is not uniform. A survey conducted in the Russian Republic in 1990 found very low levels of support for privatisation (26 per cent), and private hiring of employees (27 per cent), as well as little willingness to open one's own business (23 per cent).[25] However, the level of indecisiveness was even greater (39 per cent, 50 per cent, and 52 per cent, respectively).[26] The rapid change in preferences, arguably as a function of the changing ideological environment, can be seen from the fact that in November 1991, after the failed coup, 70 per cent of respondents in a survey conducted throughout the FSU were in favour of the creation of private enterprises (see Vainshtein, 1992: 365). Thus there appears to be a process of 'social osmosis' (Shiller et al., 1992: 181) at work, in that preferences converge towards a set that is more compatible with the new system.[27]

Survey evidence comparing Soviet and US economic attitudes thus finds little evidence of significant differences (Shiller et al., 1991). On the contrary, agents in Western economies are found to be more risk-averse than their Eastern counterparts (Shiller et al., 1992: 166).[28] Nonetheless, some have argued that the Russian tradition has created a community-based rationality which dominates individual behaviour and makes it unreceptive to neoclassical incentives of individual wealth maximisation.[29] However, the fact that in the 1980s private peasant plots, accounting for merely 3 per cent of land, produced over half of the country's potato crop would seem to contradict that presumption (Tidmarsh, 1993: 71–2). The real question is how much observed behaviour was due to the structural environment, and how much reflects genuine preferences.

The tolerance of inequality is changing to a far lesser degree, in part due to the highly publicised abuses of positional asymmetries by SOE insiders and the wealth accumulated in 'unproductive' arbitrage activities.[30] On the other hand, it has been suggested that 'people have conceptions of justice which lead them to have preferences over mechanisms of distribution independently of their outcomes: . . . recent Polish survey data confirm that people may be more tolerant of inequalities engendered by markets than by administrative decisions' (Przeworski, 1991: 6). The longevity of cultural stereotypes about 'undue gains' might make this a more protracted process in the FSU than in EE.

In view of the pace of change, and the level of associated uncertainty, it is not surprising that preferences and expectations are characterised by considerable volatility. Expectations, in particular, tend to be very short-term, such that their near-certain frustration creates an impetus for alterations of attitudes (see Schopflin, 1991: 248; Vainshtein, 1992: 365). This would suggest that preferences are endogenous to such a degree that they themselves will not be a catalyst of, but rather a reactant to, change. There may be a 'window of opportunity' to reinforce adaptability of values conducive to market activity, but the change in values will only become non-transient if the systemic change will be perceived as such.

The critiques levelled by sociologists, evolutionary economists, and institutional economists against radical reform blueprints focus on three (mutually non-exclusive) factors:

- the *homo sovieticus* argument: agents do not adjust their behaviour instantly, and altered incentives will therefore not lead to immediate improvements in economic efficiency;
- if behaviour adjusts, it will exhibit a bias toward the short-term and a strong divergence between private and social returns; in Max Weber's terms, mercantilism and not 'rational capitalism' will result;
- markets are themselves institutional constructs, requiring the creation of state-sponsored constitutive institutions, without which markets will not perform socially optimal allocative functions.

In sum, they suggest that the lack of short-term adaptability, both of informal and formal institutions, creates significant transition costs and deadweight losses.[31] In order to evaluate this argument, it is necessary to analyse the extent to which it is borne out by actual events, and the extent to which observed transition costs are counterbalanced by the public good benefits of the sustained integration into the economy of mechanisms facilitating allocative and adaptive efficiency.

Homo sovieticus or homo economicus?

The *homo sovieticus* assumption is frequently made, both implicitly and explicitly, by proponents of gradualist agendas.[32] And while it is recognised that these behavioural attributes have arisen in response to the systemic environment of planning, their non-adaptability in transition is posited nonetheless. However, insofar as behaviour under planning was conditioned by situational rather than attitudinal factors, it is incorrect to presume that a new environment will not evoke different, more suitable patterns of behaviour within a reasonably short time-span.[33] The comprehensive study by Shiller *et al.* (1992), which compares attitudes in Russia, Ukraine and East Germany with those in the USA, Japan and West Germany, comes to the conclusion that there is much more evidence of situational differences in attitudes than in underlying attitude.[34] Respondents in ex-communist

126

countries are not found to exhibit different attitudes to risk, labour market incentives, or entrepreneurial activity.[35] This evidence, in conjunction with the aforementioned endogeneity of attitudes, which suggests a quick adaptation by sizeable sectors of the population in response to systemic shifts, thus casts considerable doubt about the contention that 'Soviet-type' individuals are less responsive to market incentives. At an empirical level (see below), it appears to be even less tenable.

Mercantilism versus capitalism

In fact, another strand of the gradualist critique concedes adjustments in behaviour, but criticises the unsuitability of the resultant behaviour for 'rational capitalism'.[36] Thus the street vendors swarming in public places in EE, the individuals that operated under near-market conditions in the parallel economies of planned economies and have now moved to the informal economy, as well as the co-operatives and *spekulanty* that are despised throughout the FSU, are seen as not qualified for entrepreneurial activities: 'Hopes that people active in the black market will turn overnight into industrial entrepreneurs are misguided. Speculators have no experience with production, since they have made their fortunes by parasitizing the public distribution system' (Zhukov and Vorobyov, 1991: 50–1).[37] These activities do not constitute the beginnings of a market economy, it is argued, since they exhibit a decisive short-term, 'quick-buck' profiteering bias; supply elasticities of the economy are hence not improved by these predominantly trading activities (Zhukov and Vorobyov, 1991:3). Thus, they ought not to be interpreted as a positive return to reforms, and the behavioural constraint or *homo sovieticus* argument is taken to hold in modified form.[38]

As a factual observation, the predominance of trading activities in the initial reform phase is entirely correct. Even when one abstracts from the fact that in the short run the capital stock is fixed, and activity with short-term focus would dominate market interactions, the evidence accords entirely with this myopic bias. Sztompka (1991: 301–3) identifies several practices in Poland that exhibit a high divergence between private and social returns: 'parasitic innovativeness'[39] and 'institutional evasion' refer to the high skill levels developed by economic agents in coping with the short-comings of the planning system, confirming behavioural persistence of sorts. Similarly, a pervasive 'grab and run attitude' is reflective of the inherent short-termism of economic activity in transition. Many of the new millionaires in EE and the FSU started out as money changers. Similarly, an analysis of structural change in 1990–1 in the Polish economy concludes that while 'the overall pattern of adaptation in the economy is rapid and in the right direction, . . . growth is mostly in very small firms, mostly in non tradables, and mostly outside of manufacturing' (Berg and Blanchard, 1992: 28).[40]

However, casual empiricism entirely misses the rationality of this activity at the present point in time. Formal economic institutions are uncertain, and in a process of reconfiguration. Political and constitutional institutions are still oscillating around a medium-term equilibrium. Similarly, informal institutions such as general routines of conduct, which provide the most important safeguard against uncertainty, are in a state of flux. Thus, uncertainty is the defining characteristic of initial transition phases, as theorised above.[41] In such an environment, incremental adaptation by trial and error of agents with bounded rationality is a logical outcome (Alchian, 1950). It is a standard tenet of transaction-cost economics that in the presence of bounded rationality and opportunistic behaviour, information costs, governance costs, and enforcement costs of market transactions are prohibitively high. Without an institutional framework that provides these services as public goods, market-based transactions will be much reduced in scope (North, 1981, 1990; Williamson, 1985, 1991). Moreover, agents are cognisant of a history of equivocal reform attempts and attitudes towards private activity.[42]

Given, therefore, that economic behaviour is shaped by institutional structures and incentives, as well as its risk properties, transition agents act entirely like prudent *homo economicus*, minimising medium-term exposure and engaging in activities that are commensurate with the given environment.[43] In fact, it would be entirely irrational to engage in long-term projects under these circumstances, or to believe that the systemic reforms could not be revoked tomorrow.[44] By building on the abilities developed to deal with the arbitrariness and uncertainty of planning,[45] economic agents are therefore adapting as much as necessary; the sophistication of their measured responsiveness thus defies simple interpretations of myopia or profiteering.

Markets without an adequate institutional frame

This is arguably the most pertinent and apposite set of objections that can be made against the radical agenda. While price liberalisation ('the commercialisation of economic life' and the 'absence of irrational limitations on trading in the market') can be decreed overnight, and private property can be introduced rapidly *de jure*, many other institutions characteristic of market economies cannot achieve:

- secure *de facto* property rights ('the appropriation of physical means of production as disposable property'),
- the credible and autonomous establishment of the rule of law ('rational and calculable law', resulting in 'calculable adjudication and administration'),
- efficient factor markets ('free labour' and 'speculation, i.e. when property can be represented by negotiable paper'), and

128

- sophisticated public administration and anti-trust and banking regulation ('expert officialdom').[46]

It is but to state the obvious to say that the establishment of these institutions, while desirable as quickly as possible, will take considerable time. Furthermore, it is also evident that their initial absence or imperfect set-up will entail significant distortions and costs.[47] Critiques to that extent verge on tautology, and miss the underlying questions and trade-offs: Are the costs associated with the imperfect institutional framework in transition balanced by subsequent gains arising from the sustained introduction of systemic change?[48] And is there a coherent alternative framework, that will economise on these distortions and transition costs (presumably by a simultaneous gradual evolution of formal and informal institutions), which also has equal or more probability of attaining the systemic change and generating the benefits of superior allocative and adaptive efficiency? In this context it is entirely unhelpful to posit an absolute benchmark (no distortions and transition costs, but guaranteed attainment of the endpoint in a reasonable time horizon), in order to evaluate the deficiencies of radical transition paths thereby.[49]

Institutionalists perceive the market to be predominantly a construct, arising from 'conscious public or, if necessary, state action' (Kregel et al., 1992: 112), rather than a natural occurrence of agents seeking exchange. Thus it is argued that radical reforms, by relying on price liberalisation and property reform as principal measures, are characterised by the 'error of spontaneity', as entrepreneurial action will often fail to constitute markets. Moreover, 'capitalism by design', to the degree that it entails a conscious effort at institution-building as part of the radical blueprint, is doomed to fail as it ignores the considerable degree of path dependence inherent in institutional frameworks.[50] The erroneous presumption of an 'institutional void' is imputed to underlie the radical conceptualisation, which will therefore 'fail because the clash of holistic reforms with existing and surviving institutions, practices, and attitudes which are "alien" to the new system will produce unexpected results' (Pickel, 1992: 190).

However, the 'institutional naïveté' of radical blueprints is more often than not a false presumption.[51] De facto, it is quite impossible to alter many institutional structures and practices overnight; institutional inertia is prevalent in all economies. The real question, again, concerns the extent to which the radical agenda is able to minimise institutional inertia and induce flexible adaptation, both by giving correct and consistent signals to agents and by seeking to construct a new institutional framework that is conducive to market-based exchange. The likelihood of that success, and the resultant pay-offs, must be taken into account when exposing the costs and distortions that arise as institutional development lags behind the initial creation of the market. It is beyond the scope of this paper to deal adequately with all aspects of the institutionalist critique. Therefore, we shall limit the analysis to a brief overview of the most important institutional deficiencies of the radical transition path. In doing so, we shall outline the essential shortcomings and attempt to put the associated costs and distortions into context.

Rational and calculable law

Due to the instrumental character of the law under communist regimes and its subordination to political ends, the legal system will require both time and new human capital in order to regain any legitimacy. Given the widespread uncertainty in transition, the judiciary could play an important role in safeguarding the rules of the game and signalling the change from a discretionary to a rules-based system, thereby adding to the credibility of the change of regime. The attainment of legality, both objectively and subjectively, depends in large measure on the credibility and legality of policy-makers in transition.[52] While it is true that 'law partially constitutes the social order' (Klare, 1991: 74), its imperfect state may impinge more on those transitions which are undertaken in an environment without defined (constitutional) boundaries.[53] Thus, the lack of a generally agreed constitutional order in Russia, as well as the low legitimacy accorded to wide sections of the executive and legislative, have raised the importance of judicial impartiality and legitimacy as a safeguard.[54] In those economies where the political break with the past has been clearer, and the legitimacy of new élites higher, juridical imperfections have had less of an impact on the course of transition.

Factor market imperfections

The lack of credit market reforms in the initial stage of transition is proving to be a considerable obstacle to the responsiveness of industrial SOEs. As many of the new commercial banks were spun off the monolithic central banks, which issued loans as part of the planning process, they are burdened with considerable stocks of non-performing loans.[55] This has resulted in considerable hysteresis in bank lending behaviour. In the absence of a restructuring of bank portfolios at the outset of reform,[56] they have neither significant incentives to change their lending behaviour, nor initially the capacity to differentiate between debtors. Therefore they tend to roll over old bad debts, and issue new ones to old dubious debtors.

This behaviour rests in part on the awareness of banks that financial markets in all types of economies have a negative 'network externality', in that the bankruptcy of an important financial institution creates uncertainty for the whole financial sector and beyond. Since 1929, therefore, depositor insurance and government regulators in market economies effectively prevent this externality from affecting the non-financial sectors of the economy

(Cui, 1992). The implicit government insurance, however, again creates a certain moral hazard.[57] The expectancy of bail-out, coupled with continued state ownership, and even cross-ownership by banks,[58] provides another component of inertia in bank lending. Their portfolio concentration, in terms of both sectors and single debtors, and the fact that the initiation of bankruptcy proceedings against defaulting debtors would expose their own untenable balance sheets, has generally provided a disincentive to enforce tight credit constraints.[59]

Moreover, their attempts to recapitalise have resulted in large interest margins, making credit very expensive. Consequently, profitable firms have sought to reduce their lending, while most borrowing is done by SOEs in distress, whose performance is below average, but who are still able to obtain credit to maintain liquidity and working capital in the face of falling sales.[60] This adverse selection problem exacerbates the portfolio problems of banks, and reinforces their passivity as creditors. Banks are therefore maintaining the credit component of the soft-budget constraint, leaving a partial loophole to those SOEs that are unable or unwilling to embark on the difficult adjustment process. The signalling reinforces a 'wait-and-see' attitude on the part of SOEs, as the credibility of the systemic change is undermined due to the lack of financial restructuring. Governments, which have so far been reluctant to socialise the debt and acknowledge the latent fiscal burden, are addressing this issue as one of the important 'second-round' problems. To the extent that an immediate assumption of most of the debt overhang by the national governments would have created large fiscal deficits and thus failed the stabilisation efforts, this delay was inevitable.

The labour markets of EE were one of the few functional markets under planning, albeit with significant rigidities; labour turnover was considerable in CPEs.[61] And although labour market institutions and labour relations are found to exhibit considerable inertia in transition (Freeman, 1992), an analysis of the factors underlying the emergence of sizeable unemployment in the former Czechoslovakia, Hungary and Poland comes to the conclusion that 'despite the severity of the shocks experienced, market forces appear to be working very effectively to restore equilibrium' (Jackman et al., 1992: 36). The lagged emergence of structural unemployment, due to the slow attrition of surplus employees by SOEs, as well as the rapid increase in private sector employment, has helped to mitigate labour market imperfections. In the medium run, however, the acute housing shortage might pose a considerable constraint to mobility, and hence flexibility, of labour allocation.

'Expert officialdom'

Widespread regulation of economic activity is an integral part of modern market economies, which safeguards against socially undesirable outcomes and instances of market failure (Koslowski, 1992: 689; Taylor, 1991, 36).

Thus it has been argued that a market cannot fulfil social objectives in the absence of such regulation, e.g. without anti-trust and banking regulations.[62] Similarly, the lack of a capable administration is said to have slowed privatisation efforts (Berg, 1992) and to have hampered tax collection (Tanzi, 1992), thus providing a considerable drag on important reform elements. However, it would have been quite impossible to rely on the old state apparatus, used to perpetual micro-interventions in the running of enterprises, to execute a sophisticated regulatory or industrial policy, as Lipton and Sachs (1990a) have emphasised; in fact, its inadequacy strengthens the case for radical reforms.[63]

Delaying reforms in order to ameliorate this situation was never a feasible option. In particular, the danger of monopoly pricing after price liberalisation in the absence of adequate regulation has been overstated in many reform debates. The evidence, *ex post facto*, shows many of these concerns to be exaggerated. In Poland, for example, mark-ups in the year after the big bang were of roughly the same level as before reform (Schaffer, 1992: 81). And even where monopoly power may be exerted because of a lack of domestic or import competition, the resource misallocation costs may be much less than commonly asserted.[64] Short-term supply elasticities in those sectors where monopolisation is particularly severe, such as consumer goods in the FSU, will initially lag behind those in more competitive sectors, following price liberalisation (Zhukov and Vorobyov, 1991: 7). Nonetheless, policy prescriptions that are excessively focused on the monopolistic structure of Soviet industry are liable to be a pretext not to introduce market forces (Kroll, 1991: 170).

The gradualist agenda

What unites all these criticisms is their partial character. They are justifiably focused on imperfections and deficiencies in parts of the radical agenda. Institutions evolve only over time, and so will effective governance and the enforcement mechanisms needed to provide certainty for market-based exchange. If one draws the conclusion that this path dependence of institutions is likely to lead to the failure, or excessively costly nature, of radical reforms, then a credible and consistent alternative must be developed which is likely to induce the necessary adaptation of agents while lowering transition costs.[65] An ideal gradualist scenario would thus need:

- to arrest the fall in output and social welfare experienced by socialist economies prior to reforms, i.e. to stimulate new private production and to maintain state production levels;
- to provide credible and consistent signals to agents, public and private, that they will henceforth be able to appropriate the returns to effort; and

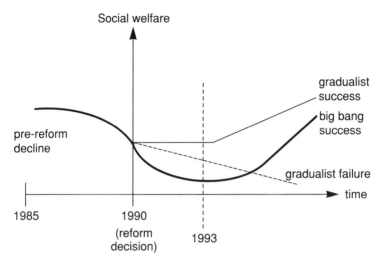

Figure 5.3 Alternative transition paths

- to create the institutions and promote the structural reforms needed to effect the transformation.

The optimal outcome (depicted in Figure 5.3) would therefore economise on the transition costs of the radical reform while securing its success in terms of credibility and attainment of the transformation of the system. Often, however, the former (minimisation of costs) is considered not only a necessary, but also a sufficient, condition for a 'successful' gradualist strategy. Any further loss in output as a result of the reform process is postulated as unacceptable,[66] despite the fact that these costs might be associated with positive restructuring and adaptation.[67] Moreover, to the extent that deficiencies arise from the need for a far-reaching reconfiguration of the institutional infrastructure and the necessity of structural adjustment in order to reduce the biases in resource allocation and industrial structure induced by planning, they are inevitable, no matter what transition regime is adopted.[68]

The optimal gradualist path would imply a successful stabilisation (in order to provide certainty for agents), at least partial price liberalisation (in order to provide signals to direct economic activity), a credible commitment to private enterprise and privatisation (in order to provide long-term incentives rather than arbitrage and decapitalisation incentives), and a political order that differed sufficiently from the old to reassure agents that arbitrariness, instrumentalisation of the judiciary, and periodic interference in activity by the authorities were matters of the past – hardly an easy task.[69] Furthermore, the lack of consistency might lead to conflicting and/or non-credible signals, so that gradual paths are liable to entail slow decay rather than the optimal path (see Figure 5.3).

133

Often, the critiques of institutionalists and gradualists are as partial as their policy prescriptions. By focusing on the structural impediments to desired supply responses in particular areas, such as monopolistic production structures (Zhukov and Vorobyov, 1991: 31–4) or debt-laden commercial banks (Brainard, 1991: 57), and by suggesting only partial remedies to these partial problems, they simply ignore any inconsistencies that their recommendations may have in the design of a comprehensive reform programme.[70] More often than not, gradualist agendas are scant on detail and large on vague prescriptions, such as 'growing out of the market' (Murrell, 1992b), or relying on a 'pull rather than a push strategy'.[71] Moreover, the lessons of political choice theory are usually entirely disregarded in their conceptualisation.[72]

Some observers have suggested that one important emphasis of reform ought to be the substitution of discretion with rules, in order to establish political credibility and minimise time inconsistencies in agents' behavioural responses to policy changes (Calvo and Frenkel, 1991: 143–4). As hypothesised in Figure 5.1, this reduction of flexibility may be associated with credibility gains, which in turn facilitate long-term adaptiveness on the part of agents. Institutions do play an important role in constraining the authorities' ability arbitrarily to change the course of reforms, or to reverse elements of it.[73] Therefore, their speedy creation is an important factor in lengthening agents' horizons and facilitating their responsiveness to the new environment. While institutionalists focus on many market-framing institutions in this context (Williamson, 1991: 27), they forget that the market is in many ways the most important, and least easily reversible institution, that can provide a safeguard against the reversibility of reforms.

The upshot of this discussion is that gradualism, due to its inherent credibility deficiency, is unlikely to induce the desired changes in behaviour needed to transform the economic system. In the absence of other consistent plans, radical reforms may therefore still present the best option, notwithstanding the second-best nature of the institutional framework in the initial phases.[74] Moreover, an endpoint-driven strategy of reform is desirable if the reformers are confident that they are able to identify the institutional and other parametric characteristics that make for the superior static and adaptive efficiency of market economies. Basing himself on Weber and North,[75] the adviser most closely associated with the radical reforms in Poland and Russia, Jeffrey Sachs, is clear on the essentials:

> Modern capitalism and modern economic growth emerged in Western Europe in large measure as the result of key institutional and political innovations that established clear property rights and a separation of the state from commercial and industrial activities. The wave of reforms between 1750 and 1870 included: the abolition of servile obligations and other feudal remnants throughout Europe; the codifi-

cation of commercial and civil law; the introduction of modern company law; and the institutions of a modern fiscal system, in which statutory tax obligations replaced tax farming, the 'squeeze' of local bureaucrats, payment in kind rather than money, arbitrary confiscations, and tax exemptions of the nobility. While these liberalizing reforms evolved gradually in the United Kingdom, they were imposed from above in many other countries, as the result of war, revolution, or enlightened authoritarian rule. . . . After decades of economic debacle, the long-delayed incorporation of 'international best practices' is once again on the agenda. But after 135 years of debating whether peasants should own land in Russia . . . it is a little silly to talk about 'rapid' versus 'slow' privatization.

(Sachs, 1993b: 1–3)

The radical agenda

A good case for comprehensive, fast reforms has been made elsewhere.[76] Our concern here is to understand why, given its assumptions about the pace of behavioural and institutional change, the recommendations of the radical agenda are likely to elicit a faster supply response on the part of economies in transition. The radical agenda is based on the understanding that the two decisive failings of planned economies were their lack of price signals to direct economic activity, and their lack of private property rights. Furthermore, it is cognisant of the fact that while many people in Eastern Europe are ill-informed about the nature and consequences of market economies, they nonetheless see 'capitalism' as a desirable system and any reform package that propagates 'capitalism' as its endpoint is likely to find more support and responsiveness than others, *ceteris paribus*. Radicalists are also inclined to view economic agents in planned economies as a distorted version of *homo economicus*, rather than as inertial *homo sovieticus*. Furthermore, despite much alleged criticism to the contrary, the radical agenda is aware of the need for wide-ranging institutional reform to complement the introduction of the market (e.g. Lipton and Sachs, 1990a: 99).

What crucially distinguishes the radical from many gradualist agendas is the assumption that the introduction of the price system and private property rights is a sufficient, rather than merely a necessary, condition, to elicit a general behavioural and supply response from agents in transition economies even in the (initial) absence of market-framing institutions.[77] The implicit costs associated with market failures and second-best outcomes, however, are the price to be paid for establishing the perception of a credible reform. Agents will only adapt their behaviour from myopic profiteering to desired medium-term investments in effort and productive capacity, if they have good reason to believe that the reforms will be sustained, a point also emphasised by Boycko:

The credibility problem is particularly severe because in the chaotic pre-reform economic conditions even a hard-line communist government might temporarily consider some pro-market measures, like a price increase, to stabilize the situation. The success of the reform will depend critically upon the public's perception of its credibility.

(Boycko, 1991: 43)

Unless reforms succeed in breaking the inertia in expectations of agents accustomed to undergo repeated reform failures, adaptation will not take place, and these expectations will become self-fulfilling. By projecting a radical systemic change, and by providing visible signs of that change (e.g. currency convertibility, elimination of shortages, potential for legal *enrichessez-vous*), radical reforms have the highest potential for breaking behavioural inertia and eliciting the desired supply responses. Since long-run supply elasticities are closely matched to long-run expectations, only teleological reforms that entail the credible vision of an endpoint consistent with present developments will induce agents to invest in long-run capacity, despite the presence of uncertainty about the likelihood of attainment of that endpoint. Gradualist agendas, by neglecting the importance of credible signalling for changes in expectations and behaviour, are less likely to secure the same level of responsiveness unless the endpoint vision is as strong, and the likelihood of its attainment as high.[78]

To the extent, however, that excessive politicisation of economic reforms is more likely to occur with radical shifts in economic policy, the intrinsic credibility of these reforms may be undermined by a lack of confidence in their political sustainability. In other words, changing the pay-offs in a game may not alter the dominant strategy of the players, if there is a sufficiently large probability of a change in the rules of that game. Therefore, an advocacy of bold reforms must go hand in hand with the recognition that coalition-building, support-building tactical measures and sub-optimal reform measures may be compromises inherent in that economic reform path. While Poland has managed this balancing act remarkably well, instituting a new economic system while at the same time successfully managing the transition to democracy, Russia's reformers have had to compromise more often, both by sacrificing consistency in economic reforms, and by undermining the democratisation process and the constitutional order.[79]

The record of radical reforms has also been much better, both in terms of supply responsiveness and of costs, than frequently assumed. Thus Bruno (1992: 5), after surveying the initial results in five East European economies, surmises that 'the main surprise from the point of view of both policy makers and the [International Monetary] Fund initial forecasts, however, turns on the estimated speed of response of the productive system to the new price and incentive signals'. Similarly, while much attention has been paid to the decline in officially measured GDP in transition economies, which arguably overstates the real decline in both GDP and living standards considerably,[80] the welfare gains of consumers due to the elimination of the shortage economy are not usually taken into account when evaluating radical reforms.[81]

Hence, there can be little doubt that a functioning market requires, for both efficiency and equity reasons, a comprehensive institutional framework. Its rapid establishment is necessary not only to reduce the divergence between private and social returns to economic activity, but also to reduce transaction costs and uncertainty, thereby lengthening the horizons of economic agents and channelling their adaptive characteristics into less myopic areas of activity. However, without credible signalling of the change of regime *ab initio*, including a commitment to establish the market and the principle of private property, however imperfect, behavioural and structural inertia is likely to be the most rational adaptive strategy of economic agents in an uncertain environment.

IV CONCLUDING REMARKS

This chapter has attempted to outline some pertinent theoretical considerations about the feasibility of, and strategy for, the reintroduction into Eastern Europe and the former Soviet Union of flexible behavioural and institutional frameworks for economic activity. On a conceptual level, however, several important points have been identified.

Despite the structural rigidity and the low levels of behavioural flexibility inherent in planned economies, economic agents in these economies are equipped with a generic ability to adapt to changing circumstances and incentives. While institutional path dependence is unavoidable to some extent, and while behavioural inertia may partially persist, this legacy *per se* is thus not inimical to the speedy establishment of a market economy. The lack of an adequate institutional framework in the initial stages of transition is accompanied by a high degree of uncertainty. The new environment is further shaped by the inertial expectations of agents, who are cognisant of a history of failed reforms. Given, therefore, objective and subjective uncertainty about the persistence and quality of the new environment, agents with bounded rationality will seek to minimise risk and will engage in activities that are commensurate with their expectations and horizons; flexibility hence 'undershoots' its potential. This accounts for the myopic bias in much observed activity in the early stages of transition.

The lagged introduction of market-framing institutions enhances the responsiveness of agents, however, in that returns to initiative are not constrained by societal and legal prescriptions, thereby reinforcing the signals of price liberalisation and property rights reform; flexibility in this instance 'overshoots' its potential. The differential speed of adjustment of behaviour and institutions results in short-term gains in individual responsiveness at the expense of society. These are, however, set-up and learning costs that cannot be avoided if a systemic change is to be credibly signalled to agents. There exists therefore an intertemporal trade-off between the costs to society in the short term and its gains in the long term, when institutions realign private and social benefits so that the returns from the elicited supply response are adequately distributed.

Since long-run supply elasticities are closely matched to long-run expectations, only teleological reforms that entail the credible vision of an endpoint consistent with present developments will induce agents to invest in long-run capacity, despite the presence of uncertainty about the likelihood of attainment of that endpoint. The reliance on price liberalisation and property rights reform as sufficient conditions must therefore be regarded as the strategy most likely to succeed. Gradualism, because of its inherent credibility deficiency, is unlikely to induce the desired changes in behaviour needed to transform the economic system. In the absence of other consistent plans, radical reforms therefore still present the best option, notwithstanding the second-best nature of the institutional framework in the initial phases. Once signalling has induced a basic shift in behaviour, reforms must focus on building the market-framing institutions as quickly as possible in order to reduce uncertainty and the short-term bias in economic activity. To the extent that property rights reform is postponed, that macro signals are inconsistent, that fundamental institutions are not, or are inadequately, introduced, or that the political instability is such as to overshadow economic signals, the likelihood of success of the radical reform agenda is reduced.

NOTES

I am grateful to Beata Bieszke, Nick Braden, and Katharina Pistor for many stimulating discussions, and to Douglass North and to the participants of the ODI Conference for valuable comments, in particular to John Henley and Tony Killick.

1 The CPEs (Bulgaria, CSFR, GDR, Romania, USSR) relied on centralised, detailed quantity-based planning until the regime change, while MPEs (the former Yugoslavia since 1948, Hungary since 1968, Poland since 1981) have used parametric planning (taxes, subsidies, credits, administered prices) in order to direct economic activity.

2 For good analyses of the logic and operation of the classic system, see Gregory and Stuart (1986), Hewett (1988), and Kornai (1992).

3 There is, however, a group of scholars who posit that under certain conditions, 'the socialist economy may be allocatively efficient relative to market economies', albeit 'at the cost of a slow rate of technological innovation'. The argument rests on the fact that 'when qualities of production and input–output relationships are stationary (due to a lack of technological innovation), the central planners' allocation task is not terribly difficult' (Cui, 1991: 61). However, this argument ignores the political impact on plan formulation (e.g. the bias towards military sectors and heavy industry), the ever-presence of (technological) change, as well

138

as the impossibility, even in a static environment, both of computing a general plan and of securing its implementation. For other theoretical arguments on the allocative efficiency of planning, see M. Weitzman (1970, 1977). For attempts to prove the argument empirically, see R. Whitesell (1990) and P. Murrell (1990a).

4 Kornai (1992: 128) emphasises the implicit rigidity: 'Technical difficulties with modifying the plan are one factor arousing opposition to the making of suitable adjustments by the bureaucracy to events unforeseen in the plan. This applies not just to unplanned-for problems but to favorable developments as well. It is hard to get any new invention applied or new products introduced if it did not feature in the original plan. The plan directs its implementers, but it also ties their hands, making it one of the sources of economic rigidity and lack of flexible adaptation.'

5 Douglass North (1992: 10) has recently reiterated this lesson in a general context: 'The development of large-scale hierarchies produces the familiar problems of bureaucracy. The multiplication of rules and regulations inside large organiz- ations to control shirking and principal–agent problems results in rigidities, income dissipation, and the loss of flexibility essential to adaptive efficiency.'

6 'The "softening" of the budget constraint appears when the strict relationship between expenditure and earnings has been relaxed, because excess expenditure over earnings will be paid by some other institution, typically the State. A further condition of "softening" is that the decision-maker *expects* such external financial assistance with high probability and *this probability is firmly built into his behavior*' (Kornai, 1986a: 4; emphasis added).

7 Thus Pejovich (1989: 59–60) argues that 'one set of institutions may be superior to another set not because it happens to be more technically efficient in terms of the standard maximization paradigm, but because it encourages the flow of innovation with the expansion of the opportunity set. . . . The issue of economic progress boils down to the problem of finding a set of institutions that will maximize the flow of innovation.' Similarly, arguing in the Schumpeterian tradition, Nelson and Winter (1982: 277) opine that 'the market system is (in part) a device for conducting and evaluating experiments in economic behavior and organization.' On this basis Cui (1991: 63) surmises that 'the philosophy of existing socialism is a kind of intellectual hubris because it assumes that mankind can find an efficient organizational form once and for all and thus no continuous social experiment is necessary.'

8 Analysing the Hungarian situation after two decades of reform, Kornai (1986b: 1698) concluded that there exists a 'vicious circle between the arbitrariness and irrationalities of the relative price system on the one hand and the soft budget constraint syndrome on the other . . .' Nonetheless, Hungary's attempts at reform, which brought into existence a large parallel (private) sector, proved very valuable in its transition.

9 'When the production program is conveyed on a mandatory basis [to the enter- prise], the excessively rigid norms preclude any changes in the plan, and hence the burden of excessive rigidity lies entirely on the enterprise's shoulders. Under these conditions (and also under the ordinary conditions of indeterminacy regarding the quality of the norms) "bargaining" for the parameters of the normative mechanism and their individualization become inevitable. [Thus,] the command economy is gradually being replaced by the "consensus economy" ("bargaining economy") in which the relations of higher and lower are not only (and not so much) the relations of subordination as the relations of exchange. Material-technical resources, money, norms, various incentives for managers, etc., are the resources (arguments) of the higher-situated participants in this "bargaining"; the fulfillment of production targets (or promises to do so),

participation in periodic campaigns (especially in agriculture), etc., are the resources of the lower-ranking participants' (Aven and Shironin, 1987: 33).

10 'Barter makes it possible for many companies to survive difficult periods. The sheer effort necessary to obtain scarce goods channelled them to those who needed them most (and could afford the non-monetary markups). . . . Basic information about from whom and for how much the desired product can be obtained is gathered with great effort, through endless trips, talks, and contacts with mutual friends. The high cost of acquiring information means that the participants in this market make decisions and sign contracts on the basis of fragmentary knowledge, without a broad view of the options' (Kawalec, 1992: 140–1).

11 Excessive vertical integration of economic units was another dysfunctional result of the attempt to overcome the uncertainties of supply under planning. Voskamp and Witte (1991: 348f) show how 'rationalisation workshops', which were initially intended as stop-gap measures to provide additional flexibility, became rapidly integrated into the structures of the East German *Kombinate*.

12 See Federowicz and Levitas (1992) for an interpretation of the rise of Polish workers' councils due to, *inter alia*, economic pressures for greater flexibility at the point of production. In Hungary, as in Russia under *perestroika*, managers were given a greater degree of power than workers' councils, with the result that the major SOE stakeholders in those two countries at the outset of reform were managers rather than employees, as in Poland and the former Yugoslavia.

13 For interesting sociological accounts of the various levels at which such informal networks and bargaining introduced flexibility into the system, see M. Burawoy and J. Lukács (1992) as well as D. Stark and V. Nee (eds) (1989).

14 Malinvaud (1992: 20) has also recently emphasised this dilemma: 'Good economic performance requires both stability and flexibility, which may not be easy to achieve simultaneously, or to reconcile after a strong shock.'

15 There is a growing literature in the fields of institutional economics, organisational economics and transaction cost economics on these issues. For a discussion of bounded, or procedural, rationality, see Simon (1985), and North (1992: 14) for its instrumentality in the formation of institutions. For stimulating analyses of the nature of institutional change, see North (1981, 1990, 1992). For a property rights approach, see Barzel (1989). For a transaction cost approach, see Williamson (1985). For an overview over this literature, see Furubotn and Richter (1991), Eggertson (1990) and the contributions to the March 1993 issue of the *Journal of Institutional and Theoretical Economics* 149(1).

16 Soskice *et al.* (1992) review the sociological evidence on this and suggest it as a field of further study for economists. See also Stark (1992a: 5) and Kregel *et al.* (1992: 29).

17 The term is due to Thurow (1992), p. 110.

18 Note that stability *per se* does not imply that the institutional set-up is efficient. Stability as such is therefore merely a necessary condition. The elusive element is the sufficient condition for flexibility to obtain in the presence of stable institutions.

19 See Morris and Adelman (1988: 212f), Galbraith (1990: 7), and particularly North (1992) on the importance of the adaptability of institutions.

20 Economists, in particular, have misgivings about the lack of concrete analytical levers in this regard, as Malinvaud (1992: 19) makes abundantly clear: 'I believe that unfortunately our understanding of how institutions change is still so vague that a scientifically trained economist like me wonders whether this should be called understanding.'

21 See Frydman and Rapaczynski (1992: 268) for a similar point. Arguably, the adaptability properties of a given institutional framework are not constant over time. The structural crises in, e.g. Germany, Italy, the UK and the USA, would suggest that institutions have a life-cycle during which they might not hinder adaptive efficiency sufficiently to be removed, but as petrification and inflexibility reach some trigger threshold, society pushes for a shift in those institutions (e.g. the abolition of proportional representation by referendum in Italy, the movement for a written constitution in the UK, the disdain for congressional politics and ineffectual economic policy in the USA).

22 North (1993: 21) has argued that 'it takes much longer to evolve norms of behavior than it does to create formal rules and for those economies without a heritage of such norms the reconstruction process is necessarily going to be long and the outcome very uncertain'. It would appear necessary to differentiate whether behaviour adapts to incentives, and if that adaptation is detrimental to social welfare due to a lack of self-restraint and communally enforced codes of behaviour, which appears to be North's concern.

23 A public-choice interpretation would see coalitions of losers and non-adaptive fractions of society gain leverage over the political process in order to forestall further systemic change, thus bringing about inconsistencies and compromises that will effectively stop the systemic transformation. For an interpretation of post-war Argentine economic history in this framework, and the lessons that it holds for EE and the FSU, see J. Sachs (1992c). The political context of reform in Russia is a good illustration of this possibility. See also Lipton and Sachs (1990b), Lipton and Sachs (1992) and Sachs (1992a, 1992b) for further discussions of the political context of reform.

24 Galbraith (1990: 4) has pointed out this gap between expectations and reality: 'Let us be clear. What the countries of Eastern Europe see as the alternative to socialism . . . is not capitalism. Were it capitalism in its classical form, they would not for a moment want to change. The alternative they see is the modern state with a large, indispensable, mellowing and stabilising role for government.'

25 See Slider et al. (1991). Among the Soviet republics surveyed, the RSFSR consistently showed one of the lowest willingnesses to tolerate the implications of a market economy, and the Baltic republics, Armenia and Georgia the highest.

26 North (1981: 65) has emphasised the correlation between systemic change and attitudinal changes: 'Just as the rise of a political-economic unit is associated historically with a consensus on values, the decline is associated with a disintegration of a common value system.'

27 See Alchian (1950) for an explanation of the convergence of attitudes and norms in a habitual manner due to procedural rationality. North (1981) has sought to instrumentalise a theory of ideology to explain change that cannot be accounted for by neoclassical conceptualisations. Because *homo economicus* is not characterised by instrumental rationality, his values become an important component of institutional change: 'Procedural rationality, because it means that the subjective model of the actors that are responsible for the way they process information shape the way individuals perceive problems and hence shape the choices they make. In this context the ideas, ideologies, dogmas, myths that people believe in matter, and the successful restructuring of an economy is going to entail restructuring of people's perceptions' (North, 1992: 15).

28 This should not be interpreted to mean that there are not significant sections of society that are less able or willing to assume the attitudes of the new system. A curious example of a shift in the opposite direction, towards more state patronage, comes from unexpected quarters: Polish agriculture, which has been the

only sizeable private sector of any of the former planned economies. According to a November 1992 poll, 51 per cent of the farmers surveyed stated that the future Polish economy should be a mixture of socialism and capitalism, 87 per cent held that the government should take the farmers' entire production, and 89 per cent wanted the government to set guaranteed minimal prices on agricultural products. ('Trzecia droga?', Ekonomia i Rynek VI, *Rzeczpospolita*, 15 January 1993; I am grateful to Maciej Gadamski for this reference.)

29 Malkov (1992: 28) has argued that 'Rationality is not part and parcel of Russian culture. Rather, community-mindedness plays the role of rationality. Community-mindedness . . . denies individual preferences and demands acknowledgement of collective or group preferences.' He concedes, however, that Russian cultural patterns are transforming in the direction of Western patterns.

30 When asked in September 1991 what ought to underlie the economic reform in Russia, (i) stimulation of business and a free market, or (ii) organisation of a fair distribution of food and consumer goods among the people, 60 per cent in small towns and rural areas favoured the latter, and inhabitants of large cities except for Moscow favoured (ii) over (i) by a narrow margin (Vainshtein, 1992: 370).

31 There is, unfortunately, a single-mindedness in evaluating any evidence of costs as an (avoidable) manifestation of policy errors (see, e.g. Etzioni, 1991). Thus the appearance of unemployment levels of around 10 per cent in Poland and Hungary, perfectly in line with those observed in France and the UK, is interpreted in absolute terms, irrespective of its relative level or the fact that it might symbolise desirable restructuring and the introduction of cost-minimising practices in enterprises. An adequate interpretation would supplement information on unemployment levels with information on employment growth in the private sector, real wage developments, consumption levels, and qualitative evidence on restructuring in SOEs, in order to judge both its causes and the benefits that might accrue as a result of it.

32 The most forceful explicit formation is by Zhukov and Vorobyov (1991: 2) 'Entrepreneurial skills, mentalities, and even patterns of social action were irrevocably lost. With the death of the entrepreneurial class, such social phenomena as rational profit-seeking behavior in production simply disappeared. . . . The social basis for a "capitalist spirit" in the Weberian sense has been completely destroyed.' See also Stark (1992a: 4–5), Etzioni (1991: 6), Murrell (1990b: 3), and Tidmarsh (1993).

33 'Situational influences may change quickly. If such situational influences predominate, as policy regimes change, we may hope for quick progress; thus reforms should proceed quickly. On the other hand, if attitudinal factors predominate, then policy makers in ex-communist countries might be advised to be cautious about the transition to a market economy' (Shiller *et al.*, 1992: 128–9).

34 The insight that situational and institutional factors are decisive in directing what are essentially constant human qualities goes back to Max Weber (1927: 335): 'The notion that our rationalistic and capitalist age is characterised by a stronger economic interest than other periods is childish; the moving spirits of modern capitalism are not possessed of a stronger economic impulse than, for example, an oriental trader.'

35 Among the remarkable results of this study was evidence on the distrust of agents towards arbitrary policy changes on the part of the authorities. The fear of appropriation of gains from initiative and entrepreneurial activity was considerable; e.g. 50–60 per cent of respondents in Russia thought nationalisation of private businesses without compensation within the next five years a likely or

possible outcome (Shiller *et al.*, 1992: 159). This points to the importance of credible commitments to systemic change and of unambiguous signalling on the part of the government, as well as to the installation of legal safeguards (which, given the instrumentality of law under these systems, will only become an effective safeguard after a considerable time lag).

36 Max Weber (1927: 334) distinguished between trading, speculating and money lending, and the evolution of 'rational capitalism' after the Middle Ages, which focused on market opportunities in a more consistent, production-oriented manner.

37 For similar views, see Etzioni (1991: 6), Kregel *et al.* (1992: 114) and Piore (1992: 181–2). Note that there appears to be no difference in the judgement of these activities by Russian consumers, or by trained Russian economists. On strict efficiency grounds, the income distribution resulting from these arbitrage activities is irrelevant. Insofar as the allocation of resources is improved by this system of retrading, arbitrageurs fulfil an important economic role, irrespective of the fact that they do not increase the total amount of available goods.

38 Note that arbitrage is the classic example of responsiveness to price signals. The acknowledgement of its widespread existence is therefore difficult to square with the standard interpretation of *homo sovieticus*.

39 New forms of 'parasitic innovativeness' have arisen in the wake of privatisation and emerging capital markets, leading to highly publicised bank frauds in Poland. Smuggling and tax evasion are other symptoms. Spontaneous privatisation, referring to variously engineered theft of state assets by managers and members of the *nomenklatura*, is also a widespread indication of this phenomenon (see Johnson, 1991a, 1991b).

40 Note, however, that activity has shifted from mere trading into labour-intensive services and production. More recent evidence (Berg, 1992; Rostowski, 1993; Schaffer, 1992) shows that private sector activity is also sizeable in manufacturing, thus providing further evidence of the hypothesised correlation between the stability of the institutional framework and the horizons of entrepreneurs.

41 See also Tirole (1991: 16–18) for an analysis of various sources of uncertainty in the 'noisy phase' of transition.

42 This is by no means a new insight. Kornai (1986b: 1706) has described the attitude of agents in the formal private (!) sector in Hungary, four years after its establishment by legal acts: 'many of them are myopic profit maximizers, not much interested in building up lasting goodwill by offering good service, and quick and reliable delivery or by investing in long-lived fixed assets. Encouragement and discouragement alternate; quiet periods are interrupted by orchestrated media campaigns crying out against "speculation" and "profiteering". A confidence-strengthening of many years is needed to extend the restricted horizon.' Williamson (1991: 24–6) describes similar instances of ambiguous pronouncements of Polish, Yugoslav and Soviet authorities, similarly reducing the horizons of economic agents there.

43 North (1992: 7) has stated this unequivocally: 'The institutional constraints together with the traditional constraints of economic theory define the potential wealth maximizing opportunities of entrepreneurs (political or economic). If the constraints result in the highest pay-off in the economy being criminal activity, or the pay-off to the firm is highest from sabotaging or burning down a competitor, or to a union from engaging in slowdowns and make-work, then we can expect that the organization will be shaped to maximize at those margins. On the other hand, if the pay-offs come from productivity-enhancing activities, economic growth will result.'

44 The survey evidence on Ukraine and Russia by Shiller *et al.* (1992: 164, 176) supports this contention fully. Situational features of these economies (rather than attitudinal deficiencies on the part of their would-be entrepreneurs) are found to 'discourage a rational individual in Russia or Ukraine from undertaking entrepreneurial endeavours or long-term investments'.

45 To sociologists, this insight comes easier than to economists: 'Today, institutionalization is undoubtedly low and uncertainty high. But it does not follow that paralysis and disorder are the consequence. Instead, we should expect to see actors, already accustomed to negotiating the ambiguity of contradictory social forms, face new uncertainties by improvising on practiced routines' (Stark, 1992b: 301).

46 Weber's (1927: 276ff) catalogue of the necessary conditions for the rise of modern capitalism in the nineteenth century is still a pertinent guide to the requirements for systemic transformation.

47 For discussions of institution-building and transition costs, see Murrell (1990, 1992a, 1992b), Neuber (1993) and Stark (1992a). See also Freeman (1992: 26ff) for a discussion of the expectations of winners and losers, resulting in a U-shaped support curve for reform. The ramifications are primarily, political: 'The key period for the transition is at the bottom point of the support curve. If 50+ per cent turn against the program, then a democratic government might back away from a valid transition program – though if it "stayed the course", support would rise.' Myopia in expectations is therefore a decisive parameter.

48 In narrow financial terms: is the net present value of the reform project, which by its very nature has a long gestation period and hence significant start-up costs, positive? While it will only be possible to judge that question once the future stream of benefits is actually observable (therefore requiring considerable faith in the eventual occurrence of those benefits), it is conceptually ludicrous to evaluate the project on the basis of the initial investment costs.

49 Curiously, in this respect the institutionalist critique shares the methodology of a great deal of neoclassical analysis, which also normatively posits a non-distortionary first-best world when evaluating the presence of multiple distortions.

50 Zhukov and Vorobyov (1991: 31) argue this very strongly for the FSU: 'The peculiarities of the Soviet socioeconomic and institutional structure are ignored in orthodox proposals; they do not even provide concrete policy designs. The reformers' blind faith in the invisible hand, the instant creation of Soviet Economic Man, and the rationality of utility maximizers reflect a more general shift towards unreason in the nation's mass consciousness in the face of generalized social and ideological crisis.'

51 See North (1993: 12) for a recent restatement of this presumption. Thus the adviser most prominently associated with the radical agenda, Jeffrey Sachs, has made it clear that his conception of reforms also entails a sophisticated institutional framework: 'Capitalism today is a very complex system with a large role for the state, with some state ownership and so forth. Nineteenth-century capitalism is dead. . . . For Poland that means emulating the capitalism existing in the EEC. The EEC has seven thousand codes – industrial and legal standards and so forth. Poland is in the systematic process of adopting all these codes in every area of economic life' (June 1991 interview in *Omni*, as quoted in Koslowski, 1992: 690).

52 Litwack (1991: 78) defines legality by two criteria, one objective and the second subjective in nature: '(1) a mutually consistent set of laws; and (2) a belief by the population in the stability and enforcement of these laws.'

53 See Offe (1991) for a discussion of the difficulties of effecting a transition in a boundless environment.

54 Ackerman (1992: 46–7) has therefore stressed that the legal constituting of state power through a new constitution is a precondition for the successful emergence of a market economy. In that context, the insufficient attention paid to the intrinsic value of the rule of law in the tactically dominated reform struggle in Russia is emerging As a major credibility liability for its further reform efforts.

55 These vary from 15–20 per cent of the portfolio in the CSFR and Hungary, to 30–40 per cent in Bulgaria and Poland (Bruno, 1992: 32).

56 The cancellation of these debts is associated with considerable moral hazard. Romania's actions in this regard hold a lesson, as the problem has re-emerged quickly. Hungary has taken a partial approach, cancelling 50 per cent of the debt and allowing write-offs against profits (i.e. a further loss in corporate income tax of 40 per cent) on the remainder (cf. Bruno, 1992: 33). The recapitalisation through privatisation vouchers, and/or privatisation revenues, advocated by Lipton and Sachs (1990b) and practised in part in Czechoslovakia, appears to be a good solution.

57 And it conceals, *de facto*, an intertemporal fiscal deficit, since no government in EMEs will be able to withstand the repercussions from the negative 'network externality', thus prohibiting actual bankruptcies without bail-out of commercial banks. This self-fulfilling expectation thus undermines the credibility of reforms, and leads to lesser adjustment.

58 Speder (1991: 146) has pointed out the perverse result of such ownership structures for the Hungarian banks, which lend 45 per cent of their loans on preferential access to their own (non-state) shareholders.

59 For a detailed discussion of this problem, and possible solutions, see Corbett and Mayer (1991) as well as Begg and Portes (1992).

60 Similarly, new private enterprises have found it difficult to obtain credit, given their unproven reputation and limited collateral (Gomulka, 1992: 13). Evidence by Johnson (1992) and Rostowski (1993) suggests, however, that this has not inhibited the rapid growth of Polish private enterprise in a notable manner. Speder (1991: 132) cites a trebling of the investment credits going to Hungarian small enterprises, also indicating that this deficiency ought not to be overstated.

61 See Vodopivec (1990).

62 The latter is a particularly acute problem. By one account (Berg, 1992), most of the newly founded private banks in Poland are already insolvent. In Russia, many enterprises are founding their own banks with insufficient supervision (Gelb and Singh, 1992: 5).

63 'The bureaucracy provides an extraordinarily important practical argument for radical free market policies, even in circumstances where "market failures" exist and pure theory might suggest more nuanced policies. It is naive to think of the existing bureaucracy as equipped, professionally or temperamentally, to implement sophisticated policies based on Western-style theories of the welfare economics of the "second-best". The bureaucracy cannot be relied upon for efficiency in regulating monopoly prices, promoting infant industries, or implementing industrial policy' (Lipton and Sachs, 1990a: 88).

64 Boycko (1991: 40) cites studies suggesting that these costs may be 0.1 per cent of GDP in Western economies, and adds: 'Even if, because of higher concentration levels, the monopoly misallocation costs in a socialist economy turn out to be 10 times higher, or 20 times higher, than in a Western economy, they still would not be terribly impressive as compared to the inefficiencies due to fixed prices.'

65 Gradualist criticism is often focused on the second-best nature of the radical agenda. Boycko (1991: 36) has made highly pertinent point about the (often inadequate) benchmarking of reform blueprints for transition economies.

'During the transition period policy-makers have to choose from a very limited set of options all of which may well be highly imperfect and painful. . . . So, to provide an argument for some particular policy measure one need not claim that it is good in some absolute, or "first-best", sense: all one has to demonstrate is that the alternatives to the proposed measure are even worse. Similarly, a measure cannot be rejected on the grounds that it does not lead to the "first-best" outcome; the relevant question is whether measures leading to better outcomes are actually available.'

66 Thus Kregel et al. (1992: 120) state that 'Shock therapy on its own, or other social experiments in the name of a better future, cannot be acceptable, if this brings about present economic disaster and political disorder.' Note that their set of unacceptable outcomes is actually identical with the set of initial conditions in EMEs, and hence quite useless as a criterion for the evaluation of shock therapy. A different proposition has been put forward by Murrell (1992a: 10), who approvingly cites M. Oakeshott (1964) as a criterion: 'First, innovation entails certain loss and possible gain, therefore, the onus of proof, to show that the proposed change may be expected to be on the whole beneficial, rests with the would-be innovator.' In the context of EE, this proposition is absurd for two reasons: first, to almost any observer the question of the desirability of the *status quo ante* is beyond rational discourse. And secondly, the possibility of a J-curve development with uncertain outcome would suggest that, by this criterion, no change might be undertaken.

67 The experience of Latin America in the 1980s suggests that returns to consistent adjustment efforts take time in materialising. Thus Williamson (1992: 11) surmises that 'the "Washington consensus" has further confirmation . . . by the recovery that is now clearly gathering force in Latin America. It took up to five years for these policies to begin to pay off, but they are now doing so. *Adjustment is an investment and not an exercise in self-flagellation*' (emphasis added).

68 On this, see Winiecki (1991). The timing of the gradualist critique also appears to be critical: in 1993, the economies of the most successful reformers, Poland, the Czech lands and Hungary, have bottomed out or shown signs of sustained increases. Thus the recent evaluations of gradualists such as Kregel et al. (1992: 109) entail as much myopia as their assumptions about agents: 'By 1992, the contention that the new "Big Leap Forward" will anew end in disaster has become certainty. The increasing weakness of the economies to be transformed are now apparent. In none of the transformation economies the decline of production, investment and employment has come to a halt or has been reversed.'.

69 J. Williamson (1992: 21), a self-confessed 'instinctive gradualist', in attempting to derive a consistent 'minimum bang' from first principles and the initial conditions of EMEs, found 'that in the specific circumstances of the economies in transition a "minimum bang" is in practice not much different to the sort of "big bang" advocated by Jeffrey Sachs, who is a temperamental advocate of shock treatment.'

70 Murrell (1990b), for example, suggests that 'macroeconomic stringency is disastrously inappropriate at the very earliest stages of reform when entry must be encouraged and when, in the private sector, the disciplinary forces of austerity are perhaps not as valuable as the creative forces of institutional innovation'. However, if inflation is rampant, and subsidies to SOEs are not discontinued, how is entry of private enterprises to be facilitated?

71 Etzioni's (1991: 10) prescription is telling: 'If we are correct that rapid transition *cannot* be accomplished, one must ask under what conditions a more gradual transition could be attained? The answer seems to be: 1. If one could keep expectations low, so that results would be fulfilling rather than frustrating; 2. If

the rewards of the transition could be kept high compared to the pain, which a "pull" strategy seems to offer; 3. If the moral case for the new regime could be strongly made, which is easier to do for the more humane and less brutal transition.' Condition 1 is factually unattainable: expectations are high initially, no matter how unrealistic that may be. Condition 2 is an intertemporal confusion. And condition 3 has been politically appropriated by those (e.g. in the Russian parliament) that seek a less brutal transition for themselves. Etzioni's 'pull' strategy also implies correct signals for those that are supposed to do the pulling, hence stable, liberalised prices, etc.

72 Lipton and Sachs (1990a: 87–8), on the other hand, emphasise the political pitfalls of tempting low-cost transitions: 'These conditions will produce ample opportunities for politicians who promise illusory low-cost paths to reform. In the short term populist pressures will lead to opposition to cuts in subsidies and to calls for "reactivation" of the economy through wage increases and demand expansion. In the longer term, populist politicians will find support among workers in declining industries, who will press for protection, subsidies, and other steps to halt the necessary industrial restructuring.' See also Alesina and Drazen (1991), Fernandez and Rodrik (1991) and Dewatripont and Roland (1992) for political theories of reform resistance based on, respectively, allocation of losses, uncertainty regarding that allocation, and adverse selection and time consistency.

73 On this, see K. Shepsle (1991) and North (1993).

74 'The paradox of transition is thus quite acute: while all "rationally" created institutional structures are imperfect and subject to failure, there is no choice but to proceed with the design. The paradox may be, at least in part, attenuated by the creation of self-corrective mechanisms that might take over at the point beyond which the foresight of the designers cannot reach' (Frydman and Rapaczynski, 1992: 285).

75 North (1992: 11) has recently restated the superiority of market economies in terms of adaptive capacity: 'It has been the relative flexibility of institutions of the western world – both economic and political – that has been the mitigating factor in dealing with these problems. Adaptive efficiency, while far from perfect in the western world, accounts for the degree of success that such institutions have experienced. The basic institutional framework has encouraged the development of political and economic organizations that have replaced (however imperfectly) the traditional functions of the family; mitigated the insecurity associated with a world of specialization; evolved flexible economic organization that has induced low cost transaction; resolved some of the incentive incompatibilities of hierarchies, and encouraged creative entrepreneurial talent; and tackled (again very imperfectly) the external effects that are not only environmental but also social in an urban world.'

76 See Lipton and Sachs (1990a), Blanchard et al. (1991), Aslund (1992), as well as J. Williamson (1992.)

77 However, a certain 'overshooting' due to this assumption has occurred, as some of the costs deriving from slow institution-building were considerably underestimated. For an analysis of policy overshooting on political grounds, see Neuber (1993).

78 The latter is, for example, true of Hungary, which was considerably advanced in gradualist reforms by 1990 and perceived the remaining liberalisations as steps towards a market economy. Its institutional base approximated that of a market economy more than any other planned economy, providing further indicators to its agents that gradualism would not mean eventual reversal or some third way.

79 For an in-depth discussion of the political economy of transition reforms, see Neuber (1993) and Pickel (1993).

80 Berg and Sachs (1992: 139ff) point out some of the statistical inadequacies of measurement, and provide new evidence of the fall in Polish living standards based on household expenditure surveys. They conclude that aggregate food consumption fell by 2.2 per cent between 1989 and 1990, and non-food items by 7 per cent, making for a weighted average of 4.8 per cent, instead of the statistical drop in real wages of 37 per cent.

81 Boycko (1991: 38–9) has attempted to calculate the gains to consumers. Measuring the value of queuing by the ratio of free market food prices to state food prices, adjusted for the proportion of income spent on food, he concludes that 'the amount of effort spent in queues and the search for foodstuffs only was roughly equivalent to . . . almost 75 per cent of personal disposable income.' Thus, the 'huge inefficiencies in the distribution system can be eliminated very quickly, bringing about a tremendous welfare gain even without a (positive) output response.'

REFERENCES

Ackerman, B. (1992) *The Future of Liberal Revolution*, New Haven, CT: Yale University Press.

Alchian, A. (1950) 'Uncertainty, evolution, and economic theory', *Journal of Political Economy* 18(3): 211–21.

Alesina, A. and A. Drazen (1991) 'Why are stabilizations delayed?', *American Economic Review* 81(5): 1170–88.

Aslund, A. (1992) *Post-Communist Economic Revolutions: How Big a Bang?*, Washington, DC: The Center for Strategic and International Studies.

Aven, P.O. and V.M. Shironin (1987) 'The reform of the economic mechanism', *Izvestiia Sibirskogo otdeleniia Akademii nauk SSSR. Seriia ekonomika i prikladnaia sotsiologiia* 13(3): 32–41, reprinted in M. Yanowitch and J. Gillula (eds) (1988) *Problems of Economics: A Journal of Translations*, Armonk, NY: M.E. Sharpe, 33–48.

Barzel, Y. (1989) *Economic Analysis of Property Rights*, Cambridge: Cambridge University Press.

Begg, D. and R. Portes (1992) 'Enterprise debt and economic transformation: financial restructuring of the state sector in Central and Eastern Europe', Discussion Paper no. 695, London: Centre for Economic Policy Research.

Berg, A. (1992) 'Stabilization and liberalization of a reformed Communist economy', unpublished PhD dissertation, Cambridge, MA: MIT Press.

Berg, A. and O. Blanchard (1992) 'Stabilization and transition: Poland 1990–1991', Paper presented at the NBER conference on Transition in Eastern Europe, February.

Berg, A. and J. Sachs (1992) 'Structural adjustment and international trade in Eastern Europe: the case of Poland', *Economic Policy* 14: 118–73.

Blanchard, O., R. Dornbush, P. Krugman, R. Layard and L. Summers (1991) *Reform in Eastern Europe*, Cambridge, MA: MIT Press.

Boycko, M. (1991) 'Price decontrol: the microeconomic case for the "Big Bang" approach', *Oxford Review of Economic Policy* 7(4): 35–45.

Brainard, L. (1991) 'Reform in Eastern Europe: creating a capital market', *Economic Review of the Federal Reserve Bank of Kansas City*, January–February: 49–58.

Bruno, M. (1992) 'Stabilization and reform in Eastern Europe: a preliminary evaluation', IMF internal paper.

Burawoy, M. and J. Lukács (1992) *The Radiant Past: Ideology and Reality in Hungary's Road to Capitalism*, Chicago: University of Chicago Press.

Calvo, G. and J. Frenkel (1991) 'Credit markets, credibility, and economic transformation', *Journal of Economic Perspectives* 5(4): 139–48.

Corbett, J. and C. Mayer (1991) 'Financial reform in Eastern Europe: progress with the wrong model', Discussion paper no. 603, London: Centre for Economic Policy Research.

Cui, Z. (1991) 'Market incompleteness, innovation, and reform: commentary on Adam Przeworski's article', *Politics and Society* 19(1): 59–70.

—— (1992) 'Can privatization solve the problem of soft budget constraint? – "Monetary" vs. "Real" perspectives on East European reforms', Paper presented at the Conference on Privatization in Eastern Europe, Asia and Latin America, Brown University, April.

Dewatripont, R. and G. Roland (1992) 'Economic reform and dynamic political constraints', *Review of Economic Studies* 59: 703–30.

Eggertson, T. (1990) *Economic Behavior and Institutions*, Cambridge: Cambridge University Press.

Etzioni, A. (1991) 'Eastern Europe: the wealth of lessons', *Challenge*, July–August: 4–10.

Federowicz, M. and A. Levitas (1992) 'Works councils in Poland: 1944–1991', forthcoming in J. Rogers and W. Streek, *Contemporary Works Councils*.

Fernandez, R. and D. Rodrik (1991) 'Resistance to reform: status quo bias in the presence of individual-specific uncertainty', *American Economic Review* 81(5): 1146–55.

Freeman, R. (1992) *What Directions for Labor Market Institutions in Eastern and Central Europe?*, Cambridge, MA: National Bureau of Economic Research.

Frydman, R. and A. Rapaczynski (1992) 'Privatization and corporate governance in Eastern Europe: can a market economy be designed?', in G. Winckler (ed.) *Central and Eastern Europe Roads to Growth*, Washington, DC: International Monetary Fund.

Furubotn, E. (1992) 'Eastern European reconstruction problems: some general observations', *Journal of Institutional and Theoretical Economics* 148(1): 201–6.

Furubotn, E. and R. Richter (1991) *The New Institutional Economics*, College Station, TX: Texas A & M University Press.

Galbraith, J. (1990) 'Revolt in our time: the triumph of simplistic ideology', in G. Prins (ed.) *Spring in Winter*, Manchester: Manchester University Press.

Gelb, A. and I. Singh (1992) 'Fact-finding tour at Russia's industrial firms', *Transition* 3(11): 4–5.

Gomulka, S. (1990) *The Theory of Technological Change and Economic Growth*, London: Routledge.

—— (1992) 'On the design of economic policy: the challenge of Eastern Europe', Paper presented at the Kiel Week Conference on Economic Growth in the World Economy, June.

Gregory, P. and R. Stuart (1986) *Soviet Economic Structure and Performance*, New York: Harper & Row.

Hayek, F. von (1945) 'The use of knowledge in society', *American Economic Review* 35(4): 519–30.

Hewett, E. (1988) *Reforming the Soviet Economy*, Washington, DC: The Brookings Institution.

Jackman, R., R. Layard and A. Scott (1992) *Unemployment in Eastern Europe*, Cambridge, MA: National Bureau of Economic Research.

Johnson, S. (1991a) 'Soviet "Privatization" in spring 1991: the grab for property', in *The Social and Political Consequences of Decentralization and Privatization*, Meeting Report, Gdansk, Poland.

—— (1991b) 'Spontaneous privatization in the Soviet Union. How, why and for whom?', Stockholm: WIDER Working Papers no. 91, September.

—— (1992) 'Private business in Eastern Europe', Paper presented at the NBER conference on Transition in Eastern Europe, February.

Kawalec, S. (1992) 'The dictatorial supplier', in J. Wedel (ed.) *The Unplanned Society*, New York: Columbia University Press.

Klare, K. (1991) 'Legal theory and democratic reconstruction: reflections on 1989', *University of British Columbia Law Review* 69: 69–103.

Kornai, J. (1979) 'Resource-constrained versus demand-constrained systems', *Econometrica* 47(4): 801–20.

—— (1980) *Economics of Shortage*, Amsterdam: North Holland.

—— (1986a) 'The soft budget constraint', *Kyklos* 39(1): 3–30.

—— (1986b) 'The Hungarian reform process: visions, hopes, and reality', *Journal of Economic Literature* 24: 1687–737.

—— (1992) *The Socialist System: The Political Economy of Communism*, Princeton, NJ: Princeton University Press.

Koslowski, R. (1992) 'Market institutions, East European reform, and economic theory', *Journal of Economic Issues* 26(3): 673–705.

Kregel, J., E. Matzner, and G. Grabher (1992) *The Market Shock: An Agenda for the Economic and Social Reconstruction of Central and Eastern Europe*, Ann Arbor, MI: University of Michigan Press.

Kroll, H. (1991) 'Monopoly and transition to the market', *Soviet Economy* 7(2): 143–74.

Kuznets, S. (1966) *Modern Economic Growth: Rate, Structure and Spread*, New Haven, CT: Yale University Press.

Lipton, D. and J. Sachs (1990a) 'Creating a market economy in Eastern Europe: the case of Poland', *Brookings Papers on Economic Activity* 1: 75–34.

—— (1990b), 'Privatization in Eastern Europe: the case of Poland', *Brookings Papers on Economic Activity* 2: 293–342.

Lipton, D. and J. Sachs (1992) 'Prospects for Russia's economic reforms', *Brookings Papers on Economic Activity* 2: 213–84.

Litwack, J. (1991) 'Legality and market reforms in Soviet-type economies', *Journal of Economic Perspectives* 5(4): 77–89.

Malinvaud, E. (1992) 'Comment on Douglass C. North "Privatization, incentives, and economic performance"', in H. Siebert (ed.) *Privatization: Symposium in Honour of H. Giersch*, Tubingen: J.C. Mohr.

Malkov, L. (1992) 'How rational is the behavior of economic agents in Russia?', *Comparative Economic Studies* 34(1): 26–40.

Morris, C. and I. Adelman (1988) *Comparative Patterns of Economic Development. 1850–1914*, Baltimore, MD: Johns Hopkins University Press.

Murrell, P. (1990a) *The Nature of Socialist Economies: Lessons from East European Foreign Trade*, Princeton, NJ: Princeton University Press.

—— (1990b) 'An evolutionary perspective on reform of the Eastern European economies', University of Maryland, College Park, MD, May, mimeo.

—— (1992a) 'Conservative political philosophy and the strategy of economic transition', *East European Politics and Societies* 6(1): 3–16.

—— (1992b) 'Evolutionary and radical approaches to economic reform', *Economics of Planning* 25(1): 79–95.

Nelson, R. and S. Winter (1982) *An Evolutionary Theory of Economic Change*, Cambridge, MA: Harvard University Press.

Neuber, A. (1993) 'Toward a political economy of transition in Eastern Europe', *Journal of International Development* 5(5): 511–30.

North, D. (1981) *Structure and Change in Economic History*, New York: Norton.

—— (1990) *Institutions, Institutional Change and Economic Performance*, Cambridge, MA: Cambridge University Press.

—— (1992) 'Privatization, incentives, and economic performance', in H. Siebert (ed.) *Privatization: Symposium in Honour of H. Giersch*, Tubingen: J.C. Mohr.

—— (1993) 'Institutions and credible commitment', *Journal of Institutional and Theoretical Economics* 149(1): 11–23.

Oakeshott, M. (1964) *Rationalism on Politics, and Other Essays*, New York: Basic Books.

Offe, C. (1991) 'Capitalism by democratic design? Democratic theory facing the triple transition', *Social Research* 58(4): 865–92.

Pejovich, S. (1989) 'Liberty, property rights, and innovation in Eastern Europe', *Cato Journal* 9(1): 57–72.

Pickel, A. (1992) 'Jump-starting a market economy: a critique of the radical strategy for economic reform in light of the East German experience', *Studies in Comparative Communism* 25(2): 177–91.

—— (1993) 'Authoritarianism or democracy? Marketization as a political problem', Paper presented at the Fifth Annual Conference of the Society for the Advancement of Socio-Economics, New York, 26–8 March.

Piore, M. (1992) 'The limits of the market and the transformation of Socialism', in B. Silverman, R. Vogt and M. Yanowitch (eds) *Labor and Democracy in the Transition to a Market System*, Armonk, NY: M.E. Sharpe.

Przeworski, A. (1991) 'Could we feed everyone? The irrationality of capitalism and the infeasibility of socialism', *Politics and Society* 19(1): 1–38.

Qian, Y. and C. Xu (1992) 'Innovation and financial constraints in centralized and decentralized economies', Discussion Paper no. 109, Centre for Economic Performance, London School of Economics.

Rostowski, J. (1993) 'The implications of very rapid private sector growth in Poland', School of Slavonic and East European Studies, University of London, mimeo.

Sachs, J. (1992a) 'Accelerating privatization in Eastern Europe: the case of Poland' in L. Summers and S. Shah (eds) *Proceedings of the World Bank Annual Conference on Development Economics 1991*, Washington, DC: World Bank.

—— (1992b) 'Privatization in Russia: some lessons from Eastern Europe', *American Economic Review* 82(2): 43–9.

—— (1992c) 'Building a market economy in Poland', *Scientific American* March: 26.

—— (1993a) 'Achieving monetary stabilization in Russia in 1993', Cambridge, MA: Harvard University, mimeo.

—— (1993b) 'Comments on "The Chinese and Eastern European routes to reform" by Alan Gelb, Gary Jefferson, and Inderjit Singh"', prepared for the Eighth Annual Macroeconomics Conference of the NBER, 12–13 March.

Schaffer, M. (1992) 'The Polish state-owned enterprise sector and the recession in 1990', *Comparative Economic Studies* 34(1): 58–85.

Schopflin, G. (1991) 'Post communism: constructing new democracies in Central Europe', *International Affairs* 67(2): 235–50.

—— (1992) 'Political culture under post-communism', London School of Economics, mimeo.

Shepsle, K. (1991) 'Discretion, institutions and the problem of government commitment', in P. Boudrieu and J. Coleman (eds) *Social Theory for a Changing Society*, Boulder, CO: Western Press.

Shiller, R., M. Boycko and V. Korobov (1991) 'Popular attitudes toward free markets: the Soviet Union and the United States compared', *American Economic Review* 81: 385–400.

—— (1992) 'Hunting for homo sovieticus: situational versus attitudinal factors in economic behaviour', *Brookings Papers on Economic Activity* 1: 127–95.

Simon, H. (1985) 'Human nature in politics: the dialogue of psychology with political science', *American Political Science Review* 79: 293–304.

Slider, D., V. Magun and V. Gimpel'son (1991) 'Public opinion on privatization: republic differences', *Soviet Economy* 7(3): 256–75.

Soskice, D., R. Bates and D. Epstein (1992) 'Ambition and constraint: the stabilizing role of institutions', *Journal of Law, Economics and Organization* 3(3): 547–60.

Speder, Z. (1991) 'The characteristic behaviour of Hungarian commercial banks', *Acta oeconomica* 43(1–2): 131–48.

Stark, D. (1986) 'Rethinking internal labor markets: new insights from a comparative perspective', *American Sociological Review* 51: 492–504.

—— (1992a) 'Path dependency and privatization strategies in East-Central Europe', *Eastern European Politics and Societies* 6(1).

—— (1992b) 'From system identity to organizational diversity: analyzing social change in Eastern Europe', *Contemporary Sociology* 21(3): 299–304.

Stark, D. and V. Nee (eds) (1989) *Remaking the Economic Institutions of Socialism: China and Eastern Europe*, Stanford, CA: Stanford University Press.

Sztompka, P. (1991)'The intangibles and imponderables of the transition to democracy', *Studies in Comparative Communism* 24(3): 295–311.

Tanzi, V. (1992) 'Financial markets and public finance in the transformation process', Working Paper no. 29, Washington, DC: International Monetary Fund.

Taylor, L. (1991) 'The post-socialist transition from a development economics point of view', Cambridge, MA: MIT, mimeo.

Thurow, L. (1992) *Head to Head: The Coming Economic Battle Among Japan, Europe and America*, New York: Morrow.

Tidmarsh, K. (1993) 'Russia's work ethic', *Foreign Affairs*, Spring: 67–77.

Tirole, J. (1991) 'Privatization in Eastern Europe. Incentives and the economics of Transition', Paper presented at the NBER Macroeconomics Meeting, February.

Vainshtein, G. (1992) 'The Socio-psychological aspect of reform of the Soviet economy', *Communist Economies and Economic Transformation* 4(3): 361–72.

Vodopivec, M. (1990) 'The labor market and the transition of socialist economies', Working Paper Series no. 560, Washington, DC: World Bank, December.

Voskamp, U. and V. Witte (1991) 'Industrial restructuring in the former German Democratic Republic (GDR): barriers to adaptive reform become downward development spirals', *Politics and Society* 19(3): 341–71.

Weber, M. (1927 [1950]) *General Economic History*, New York: The Free Press.

Weitzman, M. (1970) 'Iterative multilevel planning with production targets', *Econometrica* 38(1): 50–65.

—— (1977) 'Is the price system on rationing more effective in getting a commodity to those who need it most?', *Bell Journal of Economics* 8(2): 517–24.

Whitesell, R. (1990) 'Why does the Soviet economy appear to be allocatively efficient?', *Soviet Studies* 42(2): 259–68.

Williamson, J. (1992) 'The Eastern transition to a market economy: a global perspective', Occasional Paper no. 3, Centre for Economic Performance, London School of Economics.

Williamson, O. (1985) *The Economic Institutions of Capitalism*, New York: The Free Press.

—— (1991) 'Institutional aspects of economic reform: the transaction cost economics perspective', University of California, Berkeley, CA: mimeo.

Winiecki, J. (1991) 'The inevitability of a fall in output in the early stages of transition to the market: theoretical underpinnings', *Soviet Studies* 43(4): 669–77.

Wolf, T. (1988) *Foreign Trade in the Centrally Planned Economy*, London: Harwood.

—— (1991) 'The lessons of limited market reform', *Journal of Economic Perspectives* 5(4): 45–58.

Zhukov, S. and A. Vorobyov (1991) 'Reforming the Soviet Union: lessons from structural experience', Working Paper no. 96, Stockholm: WIDER.

6

ECONOMIC INFLEXIBILITY
IN AFRICA

Evidence and causes

Tony Killick

I INFLEXIBILITY AMIDST RESPONSIVENESS

Prima facie indicators of inflexibility

It is suggested in Chapter 12 that economic flexibility is a rising function of the level of development, with the least developed being the most inflexible. Since Africa is the least developed of all major regions, if this hypothesis were valid we would predict inflexibility for the economies of sub-Saharan Africa (abbreviated hereafter to 'Africa'). The evidence bearing upon this is considered in Part II but we may already provide some *prima facie* indicators in support.

Some are presented in the statistics relating to structural change in Table 6.1. This shows an, at best, halting progress with economic modernisation. Comparing these trends with observed regularities of structural change during economic development, we see only gradual moves towards industrialisation and away from primary production. We see gross saving and investment rates remaining in 1989 about where they were in 1965 (if we can rely on the statistics), again in contrast to other developing regions. Partly in consequence of low saving rates, we see a far heavier dependence on aid receipts, relative to GNP, than in the rest of the developing world.[1] Perhaps the most significant indicators in the table, however, are those relating to the composition of exports (line 8). Africa's export record will feature prominently later in this chapter, but note now the unchanged reliance on primary product exports, a record which contrasts starkly with the other regions.

A further indication of Africa's comparative inflexibility can be obtained by examining its record with the 'structural adjustment' programmes of the World Bank, that have been so widely adopted since the early 1980s. This is highly pertinent information because it relates specifically to progress with strengthening economic structures and institutions, and with reforming policies to these ends. The most relevant evidence is contained in the latest World Bank report on the Bank's experiences with lending in support of structural adjustment programmes (World Bank, 1992c). Overall, this gives a rather up-beat evaluation, but it differentiates sharply between the results obtained in middle-income and low-income (including African) countries. In general, it found its programmes were associated with a recovery in growth; improvements in various policy indicators; a recovery, after a lag, in private saving and investment; reductions in inflation; and improvements in export performance.

However, in respect of each of these except the last the response was far weaker in African (and other low-income) countries: only slight recovery of growth; smaller improvements in policy (and lower programme implementation rates); stagnation at low levels of private saving and investment; no reduction in inflation. Moreover, the differences in outcome can only partly be explained in terms of the superior policy and implementation record of the middle-income adjusting countries. More fundamental structural obstacles stand in the way of improved performance so that (with apologies for the Bank-speak), 'The evidence to date for low-income countries suggests that adjustment lending is a necessary – but not sufficient – condition for transition to a sustainable growth path'.[2]

Other econometric tests point to similar conclusions, with Elbadawi (1992: 45) finding substantially weaker results from Bank adjustment programmes in Africa than for other developing countries. In a separate paper, Elbadawi and colleagues (1992) take the analysis further to compare the results of adjustment programmes in Africa with those in other low-income countries, producing results strongly adverse to Africa. With export performance again an important exception, results with respect to growth, saving, investment and inflation were a good deal worse for Africa, where programmes were associated with deteriorations in these variables (see Elbadawi et al. 1992: 28–9 and Table 5.8). Programme execution was worse too.

A *prima facie* case therefore exists. So does a presumption that this revealed inflexibility has contributed importantly to the well-known relative economic decline of Africa in recent decades, which has left it, alone among the major developing regions, largely outside the remarkable economic growth and development of the past four decades.[3]

The paradox of responsiveness

At the same time, this evident inflexibility appears to be contradicted by the well-established responsiveness to pecuniary incentives of Africans as consumers and producers. The colonial view of the prevalence of a backward-bending supply curve of labour, with 'target' workers reducing their hours of work in response to higher wages, has long been abandoned, to be replaced by Harris–Todaro or job-search models based on the postulate of maximising behaviour, subject to constraints.[4]

Similarly in agriculture, the notion that Africa's traditional smallholder

155

farmers do not respond 'normally' to price incentives has been rejected in the face of overwhelming evidence to the contrary.[5] There have been episodes of what looked like a perverse agricultural supply response in African countries experiencing acute shortages of imported goods. Upon analysis, however, this can be explained as an optimising response to the rationing of imported incentive goods.[6]

The responsiveness of Africans as consumers and producers has been more dramatically demonstrated by their resourcefulness in the periods of economic decline and hardship that many of them have experienced. MacGaffey and her associates (1991) have shown this for Zaïre – a country whose economy has been systematically pillaged by a kleptocratic regime and whose citizens have responded by creating, as a means of survival, a 'second' or parallel economy they estimate to be twice as large as the officially recorded one (p. 11). Fuel stolen from the copper industry keeps food supplies open to the towns. Roadside workshops keep vehicles on the road against all the odds. The profits of the second economy are used to finance the provision of public goods that the state fails to provide: health facilities, schools, road maintenance. Or take the following account by Mukohya in the same study:

> the expansion of the second economy and the rush into its activities is a spectacular phenomenon which shocks and amazes the observer. Rural and urban marketplaces are inundated daily with persons of both sexes who buy and sell at prices arrived at by haggling and impossible to control. In Butembo, a rough census of households in the center of town reveals that at least 132 out of 200 sell goods from their houses, in the street, or in one of the eight markets. . . . A significant number of the young, most of them illiterate, have left their villages to establish themselves permanently in the forest and dig for gold. Poachers, usually young and better armed than the rangers, ravage the national park of Virunga.
>
> (Mukohya, 1991: 65–6)

We may also cite the vigour of the smuggling trade in much of Africa, in response not merely to the usual trade barriers but to distortions in exchange rates and in administered producer prices. There may be a well-established smuggling of cash crops from A to B (say of cocoa from Ghana to Côte d'Ivoire) but that will quickly be reversed (as it has been with these countries) if movements in relative prices make it favourable to do so.

People all over Africa have responded no less vigorously to other opportunities for capturing rents created by import restrictions, price controls and other forms of market restrictions – contributing to the widespread corruption so widely complained of. In fact, the response has been so vigorous that in some countries the state is in crisis, with only the most tenuous hold on economic life and forced, by its scale and superior efficiency, to tolerate a parallel economy which decimates the tax base.

So there is a paradox. How can it be that the economies of Africa collectively display the symptoms of inflexibility while their peoples are so resourceful, responsive and enterprising? The answer must lie in the constraints on these peoples, so that the results of their efforts do not result in flexible national economies. These constraints are explored in Part III. The next step, however, is to examine in more detail the evidence relating to flexibility. We marshal evidence on three aspects: the revealed ability to take advantage of both trading opportunities and modern technologies, and elasticities of supply in agriculture.

II EVIDENCE OF INFLEXIBILITY

The ability to take advantage of trading opportunities

With the partial exception of Nigeria, the economies of Africa are small.[7] This means that they are heavily reliant on trade with the rest of the world – and, therefore, that welfare is highly sensitive to their ability to take advantage of newly developing trading opportunities.[8] However, of all the developing regions, Africa suffers most from a chronic tendency for unviable balance-of-payments deficits. This cannot be reduced to any single statistical demonstration but note the following:

- It was necessary to resort to large cuts in imports during the 1980s, with volumes falling by an average of 37 per cent in 1980–90, or 21 per cent if major oil exporters are excluded (Baban and Greene, 1992: 1).
- Its African members have had frequent recourse to IMF assistance, with no less than thirty-three African countries having had Fund programmes during FY1991/92 alone, with a further three ineligible because they were in arrears with repayment of earlier credits (IMF, 1992a, Tables 5 and II.3, 4 and 5).
- Despite the import cuts, Africa's current account deficit in 1973–92 averaged 23 per cent of export earnings – a proportion far higher than for any other developing region – and ended the period higher than it began.[9]
- Africa was far more reliant on aid receipts than other developing regions, with receipts in 1991 equivalent to nearly 10 per cent of GNP, against 0.7 per cent and 2.1 per cent respectively for eastern and southern Asia and 1.5 per cent for all developing countries taken together (Table 6.1, line 6).
- Even though the average interest and maturity terms on which they had borrowed were relatively favourable, and despite substantial debt write-offs, many African countries have large debts relative to GNP and, with few exceptions, have been unable to maintain scheduled service payments.[10]
- Africa's international reserves are far lower than for any other region, averaging only 13 per cent of annual imports in the period 1983–91.[11]

Table 6.1 Comparative economic structures, 1965 and 1991

	Sub-Saharan Africa		East Asia		South Asia		Latin America and Caribbean		All low- and middle-income countries	
	1965	1991	1965	1991	1965	1991	1965	1991	1965	1991
1 Average GDP ($ billion)	0.8	5.5	–	–	–	–	–	–	4.6	41.0
2 Agriculture as % GDP	41	31	42	19	44	31	16	–	30	19[a]
3 Manufacturing as % GDP	8	12[b]	27	33	15	17	23	–	21	–
4 Gross domestic investment as % GDP	14	16	22	35	17	19	20	19	20	24
5 Gross domestic saving as % GDP	14	14	23	36	14	17	21	24[a]	20	27[a]
6 Aid receipts as % GNP	–	10.0	–	0.7	–	2.1	–	0.5	–1.1	1.5
7 Total external debt as % GNP	–	108	–	28	–	36	–	41	–	42
8 Share of primary products in exports	92	92	89	28	63	28	93	66	74	52
9 Urban population as % of total	14	29	19	52	18	26	53	72	24	46

Notes: [a] 1989 figure. [b] Unweighted mean.

Source: World Bank 1991 and World Bank 1993a.

Underlying these symptoms of distress is an exceptionally weak export performance. The growth of export earnings has been very slow by comparison with other developing countries, increasing by only 13 per cent in 1980–90, against 92 per cent for all developing countries together (Baban and Greene, 1992: 1). In consequence, Africa's importance in world trade, as measured by market share, has declined steadily, from 4.7 per cent of world exports in 1980 to 1.9 per cent in 1991 (UN, 1993, Table A.16). Over the same period, its share in developing country exports went down from 16 per cent to 8 per cent (UN, 1993: Table A. 16).

Although, in common with other developing countries, Africa suffered from worsening world prices for its traditional exports in this period, poor volume performance has been the chief source of the relative decline just described. Thus, while developing countries as a whole expanded their export volumes at an annual rate of 4.1 per cent in 1980–90, African export volumes expanded at only 2.7 per cent (World Bank, 1993a: Table 14; see also Svedberg, 1991: 20–2).

While a host of factors contributed to the outcomes just described, we shall for the moment confine ourselves to one aspect which relates to the relative inflexibility of the economies of Africa, namely their revealed inability to take advantage of trading opportunities arising from changes in the composition and geography of world trade. (We shall take up two further aspects later, relating to responsiveness to devaluations and technological advances.)

There is a well-known trend in world trade in favour of manufactures at the expense of primary products. During the period 1965–90 world trade in manufactures grew three times as fast as trade in raw materials and more than two-thirds faster than trade in food, accounting for three-quarters of total world exports by the end of the period (World Bank, 1992b: 13–14). Moreover, this change has been amply signalled by the movement of relative prices, with particularly large falls in world commodity prices relative to those of manufactures since the late 1970s.

Developing countries as a group have responded to this change and, indeed, have played a prominent part in it, with the East Asian 'Tigers' being particularly vigorous. Africa, however, has been almost entirely left out. As much is indicated by the statistics in Table 6.1 which show an unchanged predominance of primary products in total exports (at 92 per cent in 1991, in sharp contrast with all developing countries taken together). Moreover, the commodity concentration of exports remains extraordinarily high in most African countries. From data on forty-three African countries, in only seven did the two most important export commodities make up less than half of total earnings in 1987–9 (Baban and Greene, 1992: Table 10). The top two exports made up an average of 73 per cent of total exports for African countries taken together.

Of course, diversification is not desirable for its own sake – it all depends

159

in which directions the diversification occurs.[12] No doubt the most significant feature of Africa's trading record is its failure to participate in the relative growth of trade in manufactures, and developing country participation in this. This is shown by the estimate that between 1960 and 1985 Africa's share of total developing country manufactured exports fell from 9.3 per cent to 0.4 per cent (Riddell, 1990b: Table 2A.3). Some African countries have achieved a degree of success with manufactured and other 'non-traditional' exports, with signs of accelerating progress in the most recent years.[13] Overall, however, Africa's failure to participate in the great expansion in trade in manufactures has been so complete that it has virtually fallen off the statistical screen.

A similar story of inflexibility emerges when we examine the destination of Africa's exports. This too must be viewed against the background of global change, with developing countries constituting a quarter of total world demand for manufactured exports and the countries of Eastern and Southern Asia offering markets of rapidly growing importance (see World Bank, 1993b: Tables 12 and 13). However, the European Community and other OECD countries remain overwhelmingly Africa's most important markets, comprising in 1987 an estimated 69 per cent of the markets for its major exports (the same proportion as ten years earlier).[14] Although the data base for generalising about this is weak, it appears that African exporters have failed to take full advantage of major new markets.

This failure to respond to emerging trading opportunities has contributed in a major way to the region's balance-of-payments difficulties. In turn, the payments difficulties have imposed a major constraint on growth and development, with the resulting poor import capacity leading to shortages of capital goods and producer materials. In consequence, both investment and capacity utilisation have declined, further reducing the continent's international competitiveness and ability to respond to new opportunities.[15] As already mentioned, it also seems likely that shortages of imported goods have had adverse effects on output as well as living standards in some African countries, by blunting incentives (see Killick, 1993: 38–9). Its revealed inflexibility in trade has cost Africa dear.

The ability to take advantage of modern technologies

In manufacturing, the importance for international competitiveness of keeping abreast of modern technological advances scarcely needs stating. Electronic and information technologies have revolutionised many production and inventory control processes. They have made possible a proliferation of product varieties and large improvements in quality. They have speeded up the generation of new designs – and the obsolescence of old ones – and have permitted more differentiated products and shorter product cycles. Moreover, access to up-to-date technologies is by no means an exclusive preserve of advanced industrial countries, as witness the success of several Asian countries in industries utilising relatively high-tech processes.

When we turn to agriculture the case is a little less axiomatic in the African context. It is widely noted that Africa has been little affected by the 'green revolution' technologies widely adopted in the Punjab and elsewhere in southern Asia in the 1960s; nor has it enjoyed any other comparable breakthrough in cultivation techniques. In much of the continent cultivation techniques today differ little from those that have been in use for many decades,[16] although there is increased use of improved hybrid varieties such as maize.

On the other hand, most of Africa is still free of the high population densities which mark much of Asia. There is a case to be made that improvements developed and introduced by farmers under the spur of rapid population growth may be sufficient to keep abreast of needs in the low densities and extensive cultivation typical of Africa.

However, this is not an argument that stands up well to scrutiny. First, urbanisation is proceeding apace and this increases the rate at which it is necessary to increase agricultural output to keep pace with demand. Urbanisation also makes the acceleration more difficult because a disproportionate part of the growth of urban populations is of young men from rural communities. Second, Africa's heavy reliance on agricultural exports means that it cannot turn its back on technological advances in the rest of the world if its cash crops are to remain competitive and profitable. Nor can it afford large food imports resulting from lagging agricultural performance at home.

Third, country- or continent-wide statistics of low population densities can give an impression of land abundance which is highly misleading once cultivability is taken into account. The UN Economic Commission for Africa estimates that population densities on arable land in Africa are nearly twenty times the overall average,[17] and on the best land there can be very high densities indeed. In much of the forested area of West and Central Africa there is still an abundance of cultivable land but elsewhere on the continent land is emerging as a scarce resource – to be augmented, therefore, through improved methods of husbandry. Even where land is not a binding constraint agricultural labour often is, particularly at times of peak seasonal demand, so that departures from traditional labour-intensive methods are necessary to raise productivities. Finally, the accelerating development of biotechnology looks set to revolutionise much of agriculture and the continent which relies most heavily upon this sector cannot afford to be left behind in taking advantage of this development, nor to leave it all to Western-based multinationals pursuing their own interests.

In short, in both the industrial and the agricultural realms that aspect of economic flexibility which relates to the ability to absorb and adapt modern technology is of great importance to Africa. Although the evidence is

Table 6.2 The productivity of arable land and agricultural labour, 1975–90
(measured in international dollars)

	1975	1990	Growth rate 1975–90 (% p.a.)
A Median yield per hectare			
Africa	267	390	2.5
Asia	412	716	3.7
Europe	783	1,297	3.4
South America	480	810	3.5
B Median output value per person			
Africa	328	410	1.5
Asia	442	779	3.8
Europe	3,631	10,665	7.3
South America	1,477	3,172	5.1

Source: Median values of country data, computed from FAO, 1993.

scrappy and unreliable, it points to only slow rates of technological advance in Africa by comparison with other regions. We can present only parts of the jigsaw but the results are quite persuasive.

First, FAO estimates presented in Table 6.2 indicate both for the value of yields per hectare and of output per person (a) that the African averages are far below those of other regions and (b) that they are rising more slowly. Given the notorious unreliability of African agricultural data, such estimates need to be treated with caution but they are broadly consistent with other information about the agricultural situation in Africa.

A similar story emerges from (rather more firmly-based) data on selected export crops. Table 6.3 sets out average physical yields 1970–71 and 1985–86 for coffee, cocoa and cotton – three of the continent's most important agricultural exports – comparing African values with those of the other chief developing country exporters of the same products. Here too yields are well below those of competing exporters, with African yields in the later period typically only a half to two-thirds of other producing countries. For cotton and coffee the absolute size of the yield gap increased over the fifteen years, and also relatively in the case of coffee. There is a sizeable spread in the yield figures for individual countries but Table 6.3 also shows that the results of the highest-yielding African exporting countries were consistently below the best-performing of their competitors, again with an apparent tendency for the gap to widen.

While it is true that statistics of yields and productivities can provide only indirect evidence on technological progress, Tables 6.2 and 6.3 nevertheless suggest a lagging pace of change, and there is a certain amount of more direct

Table 6.3 Comparative average yields for selected export crops
(major African and other producers)

		Coffee		Cocoa	Cotton	
		1970–1	1985–6	1985–6	1970–1	1985–6
Average yields per hectare (kilogrammes)						
Means	Africa	506	544	378	286	416
	Others	671	849	690	562	757
Medians	Africa	409	461	–	270	459
	Others	564	722	–	614	835
African yields as % of others						
	Means	75	64	55	51	55
	Medians	73	64	–	44	55
Highest-yielding African country as % of highest yielding 'other' country		72	67	74	62	59

Source: Computed from Akiyama and Larson (1989) cited in Baban and Greene (1992, Table 9).

evidence of this. For example, evidence on fertiliser use points in the same direction, as indicated by the following estimates of kilograms of plant nutrient per hectare of arable land (World Bank, 1992a: Table 4; 1993a: Table 4):

	1970–71	1990–91	growth rate
sub-Saharan Africa	33	90	5.1
South Asia	135	740	8.9
all developing countries	256	867	6.3

On this evidence too the gap between Africa and other developing regions is enormous, and widening absolutely and relatively.

Binswanger and Pingali similarly note little progress with mechanisation:

Generally speaking, tractors have been cost-effective where land is abundant and labor scarce (as in North America). Following that logic, many agricultural experts once thought tractors would be appropriate for Africa, too. But many tractorization projects failed, and Africa today is less mechanised than even the land-scarce, labour-abundant countries of South Asia.

(Binswanger and Pingali, 1988: 90)

They go on to cite a study showing that ten out of fourteen tractorisation projects in Africa had failed to raise yields. Ruttan and Thirtle's 1989 study of technological and institutional change in African agriculture expresses concern that the new seed-fertiliser technology which has made so much difference in Asia has had much less impact in Africa and notes (p. 34) a 'gross underinvestment in the human capital needed to invent, diffuse and effectively utilize new agricultural technology'.

Evidence relating to trends in industrial technology in Africa is even more patchy but also points towards lagging progress. The most general (indirect) evidence is summarised in the following statistics of mean labour productivity in African manufacturing as a percentage of the North American average: 1970, 15.7 per cent; 1980, 12.6 per cent; 1990, 10.0 per cent (UNIDO, 1993: Table II.42).

(The figures for average wages given in the same source show a slower relative decline and imply a 30 per cent increase in unit labour costs in African manufacturing over these twenty years.) In only three of the 28 specific manufacturing industries covered by the UNIDO data did Africa's relative productivity improve between 1970 and 1990, with wood and rubber products the most important. Some industries experienced calamitous declines: petroleum refining (−82 per cent); tobacco products (−75 per cent); paper (−62 per cent).

Although there is no systematic evidence to demonstrate this, it is probably accurate to characterise a high proportion of existing manufacturing firms in Africa as based on long-outdated technologies, struggling (often with great ingenuity in the face of shortages of imported spares) to keep obsolete machinery going, unable or unwilling to invest adequately in needed new plant, confined by their own uncompetitiveness to producing for the local market and able to compete even on this market only as a result of high protective barriers (DeRosa, 1990, 1991). Sanjaya Lall's Chapter 9 in this volume appears to take a similar view, drawing attention to the minuscule base of industrial skills in Africa and the extremely low levels of industrial R&D.[18]

If this characterises the general case, there are best-case exceptions. The results of Mbelle and Sterner's (1991) research on two Tanzanian manufacturing industries are probably quite widely valid: that best-practice African manufacturers are efficient by international standards, but that many other firms in the same industries fall far short of the standards of the best-practice firms. If this is so, competition must be highly imperfect for such a situation to persist.

To provide a few more pieces of the jigsaw, a slow pace of technological progress is implicit in estimates which show no improvement at all in total factor productivity in Africa during the period 1960–87, against a trend increase of 0.6 per cent p.a. for all developing countries, and a substantial decline in Africa in 1973–87 (Boskin and Lau, 1990). Finally, there are the

Table 6.4 Summary of agricultural supply elasticities

Crop	Africa	Other developing countries
Wheat	0.31–0.65	0.10–1.00
Maize	0.23–2.43	0.10–0.30
Sorghum	0.10–0.70	0.10–0.36
Groundnuts	0.24–1.62	0.10–4.05
Cotton	0.23–0.67	0.10–1.62
Tobacco	0.48–0.82	0.05–1.00
Cocoa	0.15–1.80	0.12–0.95
Coffee	0.14–1.55	0.08–1.00
Rubber	0.14–0.94	0.04–0.40
Palm oil	0.20–0.81	–

Source: World Bank (1986: Table 4.4). Based on Askari and Cummings (1976); Scandizzo and Bruce (1980).

following suggestive figures on patenting for the period 1962–87:[19] Asia, 18.17; Latin America, 9.59; sub-Saharan Africa, 0.91.

Elasticities of supply in agriculture

The concept of the price elasticity of supply is the dimension of economic flexibility which is most familiar in economics and the easiest to measure. So far as Africa is concerned, most of the information relates to agriculture. There is a substantial literature investigating the influence of prices on agricultural output, and also non-price influences.

Much of this research has been conducted at the level of agricultural supply aggregates, but Table 6.4 brings together average elasticities from surveys of specific crops. The lower end of each entry represents the average short-term response and the upper end gives the long-run average (although there are special doubts about the reliability of the latter). We see that all the results are positive and that the values for Africa tend to be larger than for other developing countries, further attesting to the responsiveness of African producers described earlier.[20] However, most of the values are below 1.0. Also, the time-lags before the elasticities take on their maximum values can be long, particularly for tree crops.

Lower supply elasticities can be predicted when we turn to the responsiveness of the agricultural sector as a whole, for the option of increasing output by switching resources between crops is largely ruled out. Some increases in total output can be won by greater applications of fertilisers, insecticides and the like, but if we see the output of a sector as fundamentally determined by factor inputs and technologies, then agriculture can increase output in response to an improvement in its terms of trade chiefly by raising the utilisation of previously under-employed land and labour, by attracting

Table 6.5 Some econometric estimates of agricultural sector price response, 1963–81

Country or region	Short-run estimate	Long-run estimate
Burkina Faso	0.22	0.24
Côte d'Ivoire	0.13	0.13
Ghana	0.20	0.34
Kenya	0.10	0.16
Liberia	0.10	0.11
Madagascar	0.10	0.14
Senegal	0.54	0.54
Tanzania	0.15	0.15
Uganda	0.05	0.07
SSA average	0.18	0.21

Source: Binswanger (1990: Table 2).

factors from other sectors and/or by improving cultivation techniques. In the short run both techniques and factor supplies will be relatively immutable; it is only after a period of years that much can be done about these things.

Table 6.5 reproduces the results of Binswanger's (1990) survey of estimates of sectoral supply elasticities for African countries by various authors, showing positive but generally low values. Cleaver (1985) has studied the influence of policy interventions on aggregate agricultural supply in Africa. He concludes that policies depressing producer prices reduced output – but that the influence of these price-depressing policies was 'considerably less than is generally thought' (with a coefficient value of only 0.2) and that non-price factors were 'much more important'.

A related area which has been the subject of a good deal of empirical research is the supply responsiveness of agriculture to exchange-rate depreciations. Perhaps the most useful study for our purposes is that undertaken by Faini and de Melo (1990), because it contrasts the responses of countries exporting manufactures with (mainly African) exporters of non-oil primary products. Although a positive response to devaluation was found in both groups, the observed improvement was considerably larger for the manufacturing countries, where a given depreciation resulted in a 2.1 percentage point improvement in the trade balance, against only 0.8 among the primary producers (pp. 13–14). The authors also found substantial short-term losses of output following devaluation and concluded that use of this instrument 'appears to be ineffective' in commodity-exporting countries.

Other research on the effects of exchange-rate changes focuses more specifically on African agriculture. This too tends to find limited supply responses to devaluations, although results vary according to whether the products are annual or tree crops. Jaeger's (1991) research suggested that the real exchange rate does have a significant effect on total agricultural supply in Africa but that short-run elasticities are often small and occasionally perverse, while data problems prevent reliable estimation of longer-run elasticities.

Cleaver (1985) also investigates the influence of the exchange rate on the growth of agricultural output in Africa, concluding that 'currency over-valuation does agriculture no good. Currency depreciation will have a significant, but not very large, impact on agricultural growth' (p. 20). Diakosavvas and Kirkpatrick (1990) take agricultural exports as their dependent variable. They group African countries according to their exchange-rate histories and agricultural export trends, as well as undertaking regression tests, with results similar to those of Jaeger and Cleaver: there is evidence of the expected association but it is generally not large and there are various exceptions to the general relationship.

In fact, of the researchers surveyed, only Balassa (1990) finds a strong agricultural response to the exchange rate. He tests for the effects of currency over-valuations in 1965–82, obtaining coefficient values of >1.0, significant at the 1 per cent level, with particularly strong results for 1974–82. It is possible, however, that this outrider result is due to a regression equation which includes only one other explanatory variable (foreign income), so that his exchange rate variable may be picking up the results of other influences. His R^2s are very small.

One other noteworthy piece of evidence should be mentioned. We reported above Faini and de Melo's contrasting results for exporters of manufactures and (non-oil) primary products. Unfortunately, there is not enough of a history of African manufacturing exports to be able to test this at the regional level, but we may report the findings of Newman et al.'s (1990) investigation of the export price responsiveness of manufacturers in Côte d'Ivoire. They found these to be highly sensitive to relative prices, and also to changing levels of domestic demand, with exports responding positively to improved export prices, negatively to higher import prices and negatively to increases in domestic demand.

This result is in line with the suggestion in Chapter 1 of this book that one of the determinants of the responsiveness of the productive system is the ease with which it is possible to switch between production for home and foreign markets. This is a greater possibility for manufacturing firms than for most agricultural exporters, and even less so for most mining concerns. With only a few exceptions (e.g. coffee in Ethiopia), there is typically little home demand for Africa's primary product exports. In principle, cash crop farmers have the option of switching their land to the cultivation of food-stuffs but it is easy to exaggerate the ease with which this can be done.[21] Even where the land is suitable for such conversions, there are usually substantial costs involved and the change is only likely to occur over a period of years and in response to strong, persistent signals.

In brief, this survey again draws attention to the relative inflexibility of Africa's agricultural and export sectors. While producers do generally respond positively to improved relative prices, the magnitude and speed of their response are muted. Part of the problem, just mentioned, is the difficulty of switching between the satisfaction of home and foreign demand, which is typical of early-stage developing countries reliant upon primary production. Virtually all the commentators surveyed above mention the importance of non-price influences too, and we shall discuss these shortly.

Interactions

We have now reviewed three major aspects of inflexibility in African economies: limited ability to take advantage of opportunities created by the changing structure of demand in international trade; limited ability to incorporate the fruits of modern knowledge in productive systems; and low supply elasticities. We should now note interactions between these.

It seems highly probable, for example, that technological obsolescence in much of African manufacturing is closely related to the continent's exceptionally poor export record, by comparison with other developing regions. Similarly, the difficulties which Africa has had in applying modern knowledge to agriculture contribute to the modest supply elasticities just reported. The data in Table 6.3 suggest further that the lagging rate of change in agriculture is tending to undermine the competitiveness, or profitability, of the continent's agricultural exports – a particularly large problem for countries, like those of the Franc Zone, with fixed exchange rates. This too helps to explain low supply elasticities, as well as drawing attention to a disturbing long-term trend.

Agricultural backwardness has also reduced the continent's ability to feed itself, with food imports creating additional large claims on scarce foreign exchange. Thus, per capita food production is estimated by the World Bank to have declined at −1.0 per cent p.a. over the period 1979–91 (contrasting with increases in all other developing regions) with deteriorations in twenty-three out of thirty-three African countries, while recourse to food aid and commercial imports of cereals had considerably increased (World Bank, 1993a: Table 4).[22] Moreover, the situation appears likely to worsen. Von Braun and Paulino conclude their survey of the food situation in Africa thus:

> The food situation in sub-Saharan Africa can be expected to become increasingly serious as the end of the century approaches. Data re-inforce earlier findings of the slowdown of the region's food production growth under conditions of fast-rising food demand that is largely driven by population increase. The rapid decline of non-cereal [food] exports and rapid increase of cereal imports in sub-Saharan Africa can combine to expand the region's net imports of basic food

staples by the year 2000 to seven times the average yearly level in 1979–83.

(Von Braun and Paulino, 1990: 516)

At the same time, low export responsiveness and balance-of-payments weaknesses have held back technological progress. This has happened as a result of shortages of imported capital goods and other inputs embodying productive improvements. But it has also occurred as a consequence of the poor climate created for innovation and new investment by the all-pervasive shortages of foreign exchange and the resulting uncertainties about domestic economic performance and policies.

Finally, we should note that the often-stated advantage of exposure to international trade as facilitating technology transfer appears not to have had a powerful effect, even though African countries are among the most trade-dependent in the world. Part of the explanation may be that the type of trade is at least as important as the volume for technology transfer. Also pertinent is the fact that Africa has in recent decades attracted little direct foreign investment by comparison with other developing regions.

III CONSTRAINTS ON FLEXIBILITY

Part II was largely taken up with a factual presentation of evidence on inflexibility and had little to say about the sources of the phenomenon. In approaching this task now, we will adopt a framework developed elsewhere that the flexibility of an economy is a function of (a) its informational and incentive systems and (b) the factors bearing upon the responsiveness of economic agents to the information and incentives. In what follows we shall follow this general scheme but concentrate on those aspects which appear to bear most crucially on the inflexibility of African national economies. We start with information flows, move on to incentive systems and then proceed to examine various constraints upon the responsiveness of African producers and consumers.

Information flows

The standard of information available to producers and consumers is not readily amenable to measurement but one important aspect is the quality of government statistical services. On this we can do no better than to quote a late 1980s report by the UN Economic Commission for Africa. This complained of the failure of statistical systems in Africa to respond to data needs:

> Data gaps affect every sector and every aspect of the African situation. In the field of demography, even the size and growth rate of population in some of the African countries cannot be unambiguously determined. In the field of social statistics, there are gaps relating to

169

Table 6.6 Comparative indicators relating to dissemination of information

		Sub-Saharan Africa	South Asia[a]	Latin America	Industrial countries
1	Adult literacy rate, 1990 (%)	47	42	85	96[a]
2	Radios per 1,000 people, 1990	150	90	340	1,130
3	Televisions per 1,000 people, 1990	23	29	164	545
4	Newspaper circulation per 1,000 people, 1988–90	11	14	94	304
5	Telephones per 1,000 people, 1986–8	18	8	84	590

Note: [a] From World Bank (1992a: Table 1).

Source: UNDP (1993: Table 52).

literacy, school enrolment ratios, the institutional status of the child and poverty levels. And in the field of economic statistics, basic economic series like GDP and resource flows are sometimes lacking. Data on natural resources and the environment are, if available, in a very rudimentary state.

(Chander, 1990: 1)

Given the burden on UN agencies to be diplomatic, this report can scarcely be overstating the position. That it is not is suggested by the results of a detailed comparison of import and export statistics by Yeats (1990). From this he concluded that official data on inter-African trade are useless for the assessment of either the level or the direction of trade, and of limited use on the composition of such trade and trends in it.

A further illustration of poor economic intelligence is provided in an account by Klitgaard (1991: 38–9) of how, following the decontrol of prices, the Zambian authorities found themselves without information on what was happening. They therefore conducted a special survey within Lusaka, discovering, *inter alia*, that within this rather small city there were cases of three-fold differences in the final prices of identical items – suggesting that traders and consumers were at least as ill-informed as the government.

The unavailability or unreliability of basic statistics is compounded by difficulties of dissemination. Table 6.6 pulls together some suggestive illustrations. In respect of each of the five indicators in the table Africa is at a large disadvantage relative to Latin America, although its position *vis-à-vis* Southern Asia is mixed. The contrast with the developed countries is, of course, stark.

Arguably the most important are the figures relating to adult literacy, where it can be seen that even now, a full three decades after independence in most countries, more than half the adult population remains illiterate – and unable, therefore, to receive information through the printed word. Proportionately, the newspaper readership figures are even more to Africa's disadvantage (to say nothing of the appalling quality of many of its news-papers), although this is partly compensated by a relatively high ownership of radios. The figures on telephone densities also point to poor communi-cations and this is made worse by a generally poor quality of service, with average local call completion rates of under 30 per cent (Moussa and Schware, 1992: 1738–9).

In short, there seem strong grounds for believing that the availability and dissemination of economic information are very poor in Africa, a condition which can only impede the responsiveness of economic agents to changing conditions and opportunities.

Inadequate incentives

Since the earlier discussion of supply elasticities concentrated on the respon-siveness of Africa's export and agricultural sectors – and because most available evidence pertains to these sectors – we shall retain this focus in what follows. The task here is to elucidate factors bearing upon the pecuni-ary incentives faced by Africa's exporters and farmers.

World prices

It is well known that, for reasons deeply embedded in the changing struc-tures of world supply and demand, world price trends have been strongly adverse to exporters of primary products. This is clearly shown in Figure 6.1, which indicates a negative trend in real non-oil commodity prices since 1948. Indeed, there is accumulating evidence of an even longer-term deterio-ration.[23] At least since the early 1980s, the trend has been particularly adverse for food, tropical beverages and vegetable oils.[24]

With deteriorations of this severity, it is difficult for even the most effective governments to protect producers from these trends (even if it were desirable to do so). For an analysis of the long run, it is, in any case, open to question whether we should regard African countries as merely passive recipients of world prices. In the short run the small-country assumption is appropriate but over twenty to thirty years the question becomes, why have those confronting long-run downward trends in the real prices of their traditional exports not responded by diversifying? The adverse terms-of-trade experience of low-income Africa is more a symptom of the inflexibility we are investigating than a cause of it. To put it another way, if many Asian countries had a better terms-of-trade experience over the same period this was because they reduced their dependence on commodity exports facing

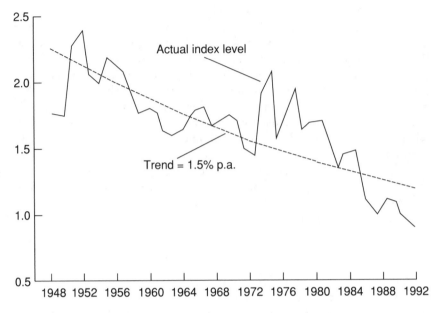

Figure 6.1 Real non-oil commodity prices, 1948–92 (index 1987 = 1)

Source: World Bank, 1993b: Figure 6.1.

weak global demand. Thirty years later Kindleberger's (1962: 103) comment on countries which complain about adverse terms of trade seems highly pertinent: 'The complaint will be true, but the difficulty will lie not in the manipulation of its terms of trade by the world beyond its frontiers, but in its incapacity to transform.'

Domestic impairments of producer incentives

If, instead, we search for domestic factors which dampen producer incentives, the conventional consensus lays much of the blame on past policy interventions by African governments which reduced the prices received by producers. Exchange-rate policies deserve particular mention. The extreme case is represented by Francophone West and Central African countries which are members of the Franc Zone and had an unchanged nominal exchange rate against the French franc from 1948 until a belated devaluation early in 1994. While not going to this extreme, most other African countries maintained 'adjustable-peg' policies, a practice which resulted in rather inflexible nominal rates during the 1960s and 1970s. At the same time (outside the Franc Zone) inflation was more rapid than in the rest of the world. This combination led to a major real exchange-rate appreciation in most African countries during the 1970s.[25]

The disincentive effect of exchange-rate overvaluation for exporters (and import substituters) was often compounded by other factors. The narrowness of the tax base and the difficulties of enforcing direct taxes led many African governments to rely upon taxes on international trade. Some taxed exports heavily, either overtly or covertly through state marketing monopolies offering producer prices far below the local-currency equivalent of world market levels. A World Bank report (1981: 56, Box D) studied the extent to which export crops were being taxed or subsidised by African governments in 1976–80. All but four of twenty-nine separate estimates were negative, i.e. showed net taxation, with an estimated average tax rate of 35 per cent. Other studies have produced comparable results. To take a recent example, Lele (1992: Tables 2.10 and 2.12) produces data relating to six countries in East and West Africa and finds for the sixteen crops studied that, after adjusting for currency overvaluation, farmers in 1984 (the latest year for which complete data were available) received a mere 36 per cent of the international value of their crops.[26]

Quite apart from revenues accruing to the state through these means, there was additional 'taxation' in the form of excessively high marketing costs on the part of the marketing monopolies.[27] There was also implicit taxation of exporters resulting from high protection levels afforded to local industry. DeRosa (1990 and 1991) shows low-income African countries to be exceptionally heavy protectors and estimates that liberalisation would, on average, raise the price of exports relative to non-traded goods by 15–34 per cent (although he also found large inter-country variations). He estimates that the effects of this 'taxation' were to reduce exports by similar proportions and to discourage diversification.

With overvalued exchange rates, fiscal taxation, inefficiency on the part of state marketing boards and price biases induced by protectionism, the disincentives against cash crops were severe. This helps to explain the poor African record with regard to agricultural production and exportation, and the low rates of investment in, and adoption of, improved cultivation methods reported earlier.

At the same time, we should not exaggerate the quantitative importance of interventions which impaired price incentives, for we saw in the previous section that supply elasticities with respect to price are commonly quite low. Moreover, not all the policy-induced price distortions work to the disadvantage of farmers, e.g. explicit or implicit subsidies on fertilisers, insecticides, farm equipment and other inputs. Overall, Cleaver (1985: 16) found that policy interventions had commonly depressed producer prices but that the negative impact of these on output 'is considerably less than is generally thought', with other factors 'much more important'. We should also recall his conclusion, reported above, that devaluations were unlikely to make more than a small contribution to agricultural growth.

To put it another way, it is not only to price that output can respond. It is interesting to compare the price elasticities reviewed earlier with output responsiveness to non-price, or structural, variables, although only a little evidence is available on Africa. Work on India by Chhibber (1989: 65–6) found some tendency for responses to improved irrigation facilities to be larger than to improved prices in the short run, but there was a much stronger result from long-run elasticities: '. . . in India in the period 1954–5 to 1977–8 the elasticity of aggregate output with respect to non-price factors, was approximately three times the elasticity with respect to inter-sectoral prices'.

This result is consistent with others surveyed by Binswanger (1990). He concludes that it is easier to show that structural variables have a positive impact on aggregate output than it is to show price effects. Access to irrigation again emerges as highly influential. So do education and health, and the quality and density of the rural roads network. Public research and extension services can have a powerful influence on the output of particular crops but much less on total agricultural output.

Further support is provided by Diakosavvas (1989). He investigates, for thirty-five developing countries in 1974–84, the impact on output of chang-ing levels of government expenditures on agricultural services and infra-structure, and concludes that, on average, a 10 per cent increase in government spending will induce an approximately 3 per cent increase in output.[28] The more common case of declining government expenditures was associated with reducing agricultural output, which also reacted ad-versely to instability in the provision of government services.

Responsiveness to price and non-price variables are not independent of each other, however. For farmers to be fully responsive to price movements other conditions must be satisfied: supporting institutions and the basic infrastructure should be adequate; markets should be reasonably competi-tive and efficient; there should be ready supplies of raw materials and other inputs. In Africa all these probably deteriorated in the 1960s and 1970s (and in some cases, through the 1980s). Export promotion services were weak, as was technology policy. There was a widely observed deterioration in the systems of transportation (particularly in road networks), communi-cations and marketing.

The severe effects of the under-development of the rural infrastructure are well illustrated in a study by Ahmed and Rustagi (1987: 114). They compared the proportion of the final price of local food grains reflected in farm-gate prices in African and Asian countries, finding that in the African countries farmers received only about 40–60 per cent of the final price, against around 80 per cent in each of the Asian countries. Decomposition of these differences suggested that about two-fifths were the result of higher transportation costs in Africa, with much of the rest attributed to higher taxation and lower efficiency in marketing agencies. Part of the difficulty with transport costs, they pointed out, lay with the lesser extent of rural electrification in Africa, resulting in a concentration of grain milling in the towns, compared with more local processing in Asian countries.

The poor and deteriorating state of rural infrastructure in Africa almost certainly reduced market efficiencies, a decline further fostered by the protectionism just described, by financial sector repression, and by price controls and other interventions fostered by a general distrust of market forces.

The problem, then, has not so much been too much state interventionism but the wrong kinds of intervention. Many of the most common interventions had the effect of blunting incentives, through taxation, ill-chosen experiments with state farms, the domination of marketing and distribution by state-owned monopoly corporations, the mis-direction of research and extension services, and the like. It is therefore not surprising that Balassa (1990) should find evidence of negative correlation between state interventionism and agricultural export performance. At the same time, there has by common consent been too little intervention by way of investments in, and maintenance of, rural roads and other infrastructure; or in the improved provision of agricultural research and extension services; or in spending on education, training and health.

Quite apart from specific measures and neglects, the overall policy environment has also often had the effect of dampening incentives. Of particular importance here are questions like whether the general orientation of policy encourages private enterprise and investment (e.g. by recognising the positive role of profits, or by the creation of an 'enabling' legal framework, or by policies which encourage the growth of efficient rural capital markets and credit institutions); whether the quality of macroeconomic management is sufficient to provide the stability of price signals which is so important if risk-averse smallholder farmers are to respond; and whether the government's own policy signals will have sufficient credibility to evoke strong responses. In too many countries the answers to these questions have been negative. There has been insufficient fiscal and monetary control for producers to regard improved nominal prices as having more than a transitory effect on their real returns; laws and policies have sometimes been tilted in favour of the state, or erratically enforced; the supply of imported inputs and incentive goods has been undependable.[29]

It is evident, then, that there is a wide range of ways in which policy interventions – and neglects – have adversely affected farmer incentives, reducing the value and dependability of the prices they receive, increasing their transactions costs, discouraging investment and innovation. However, it would be a mistake to put it all down to the failings of governments, for not all governments have fallen into these errors, or have persisted with them. Beynon (1989) has suggested that the degree of taxation (broadly understood) of African agriculture has been gradually decreasing over time, so that this cannot easily explain continuing weak agricultural performance.

A number of other factors are discussed a little later, but we should remember here that market failures can also reduce producer incentives. We are well advised not to take an idealised view of the efficiency of markets in the rural economy. Thus Lele (1988: 199) writes of an 'absence of capital markets' as a major constraint on agricultural growth in Africa, of inaccessibility of markets and poor, costly communications. She refers to 'unintegrated food markets' (giving rise to large differences in the prices for the same products on markets in the same locality) and observes that 'Even where the private sector is allowed to operate freely in marketing and agro-processing as, for instance, in Nigeria, trade by licensed buying agents for cotton and rubber is often said to be far less than competitive' (Lele, 1988: 202).

The pervasiveness of traditional, or informal, financial institutions in African rural economies, which is becoming increasingly well documented, itself attests to the imperfections of formal-sector financial markets mentioned by Lele, for the former have expanded in response to the inadequacies of the latter.[30] The evidence suggests that informal financial institutions in Africa are typically large, broadly based and an important source of saving and credit for the groups using them. Informal institutions, such as local moneylenders, rotating credit co-operatives and community savings and loan associations, are more accessible, innovative and responsive to borrowers' needs, but they do not encourage any but the most short-term investments.[31]

Lele further develops her arguments on the limitations of market mechanisms in Africa in the conclusions of a study of liberalisation and privatisation efforts in agricultural marketing in six African countries:

> The ability of the private sector to function effectively in the area of agricultural marketing depends on the environment in which traders must operate. This environment is defined by many of the elements whose absence in the past served as a rationale for public-sector intervention in the first place.
>
> (Lele and Christiansen, 1989: 23)

These elements include:

- the presence of an entrepreneurial class able to undertake risk;
- competitive markets;
- adequate infrastructure, including transport and communication networks that allow the efficient movement of information, goods and services;
- food security.

The study by Ahmed and Rustagi cited earlier similarly found evidence of rural markets operating less efficiently in Africa than in Asia, with substantially larger price spreads between markets and marketing profit margins three times as large in the African countries studied. These contributed about a quarter of the total difference in the proportion of final price received by the African and Asian farmers (their Table 11.6), further impairing price incentives. Hence, despite highly adverse findings about the inefficiency of state marketing interventions, they urge only gradual state withdrawal from marketing, plus infrastructural investments and other measures to help the development of more efficient private marketing systems (Ahmed and Rustagi, 1987: 115).

To sum up, a combination of explicit or implicit taxes, institutional inefficiencies and market failures have reduced the prices received by African farmers, relative to world or local consumer price levels and by comparison with other parts of the world.[32] Other factors have operated to diminish the relevance of price incentives to farmers, namely poor market information, research, extension and other supporting services; bad or non-existent roads; uncertain input supplies; inadequate credit institutions; unstable economic environments or non-credible policies which reduce the reliability and real value of price incentives and place a premium on risk avoidance.

Weak technological capabilities

In our earlier consideration of Africa's limited ability to take advantage of modern technology, we stressed the importance of technological progress in both industry and agriculture but presented evidence to suggest that progress in this area had lagged badly, by comparison with other developing regions.

Why might this be? An obvious line of explanation is to point out Africa's severe disadvantages in terms of the supply of modern skills. At independence, the countries of Africa suffered from an acute shortage of educated and trained personnel, reflecting the weak development of the educational system until the last years of colonial rule. The number of people with advanced education was often negligible. There were few universities or even technical schools to provide industrial and managerial skills (Fieldhouse, 1986: 35). In consequence of these neglects, the proportion of people in 1960 enrolled in tertiary education relative to the population aged twenty to twenty-four was less than 0.5 per cent in sixteen of the eighteen African countries for which estimates exist, compared with 2 per cent for all low-income countries taken together, 4 per cent for middle-income countries and 17 per cent for industrialised countries (World Bank, 1981: Annex Table 38). The newly independent states were largely populated by illiterate and innumerate people.

Despite the large educational expansion that has occurred since, Africa's relative disadvantage persists, with substantially lower school enrolment rates than in any other developing region. Table 6.6 showed low literacy rates; Table 6.7 suggests even larger disadvantages at higher and more

Table 6.7 Comparative human resource indicators, 1987

	Sub-Saharan Africa	Asia	Latin America
1 Educational enrolment at 2nd level as % of age group	18	56	55
2 Enrolment at 3rd level, science and technology, per 100,000 population	19	411	435
3 Enrolment at 2nd level vocational training per 100,000 population	103	815	1,323

Source: UNCTAD (1993: Table III–3). The figures presented are means of the individual country entries provided in the source table for 1987 or the closest available year.

technical levels of education. For further evidence compare Tables 9.1 and 9.2 of Lall's contribution to this volume. Moreover, while governments can point to rapid educational expansion this has probably been undermined by a decline in quality. Data on teacher–pupil ratios do not support this view, showing no deterioration, but the UN publication, *Africa Recovery*, noted a decline in real government expenditures and commented:

> The declines in educational spending have directly translated into an erosion in the quality of schooling in much of Africa. Severe shortages of textbooks and other school materials became even worse as funds available for their purchase dried up. In many African countries, the whole infrastructure of support services – school inspection and super-vision, in-service teacher education, school health services, and the maintenance of schools' furniture, equipment and physical facilities – has deteriorated.
>
> (UNDP, 1992: 13)

Governments can also point to expenditure levels on agricultural research and development at least comparable with other regions. Mosley (1992: 10, 13) reports that public-sector spending on agricultural research in Africa is above the developing-country average, relative to agricultural output, and that spending on extension services is also well sustained. Governments can also show that in recent years they have responded quite vigorously to the technology gap in the form of newly created agencies dealing with science and technology. Bwisa (1989, Table E) reports UNESCO data showing the number of such bodies to have risen in Africa from sixty-nine in 1973 to 197 in 1986 (latest available).

However, the effectiveness of the institutions and the productivity of expenditure programmes and of newly educated graduates present more deep-seated problems. The weakness is less that of numbers of people and agencies than the framework within which they work. Thus, in Chapter 9 Lall argues that industrialisation in Africa has been crucially held back by shortages of what he calls 'industrial capabilities', referring to the skills, institutions and organisational arrangements that will permit firms to utilise suitable technologies and deploy their resources efficiently. He further suggests that, given the minuscule base of skills and industrial experience in Africa, only countries with large non-African populations with access to the necessary skills have stood a chance of developing an efficient and flexible manufacturing sector. Similarly in the agricultural area, Ruttan and Thirtle (1989: 26) urge the importance of the 'institutionalisation of capacity to supplement indigenous knowledge with science-based knowledge and craft-generated technology with industrial inputs which embody advances in scientific and technological knowledge'. They argue that this has been neglected in Africa and join Lele (1992: 574–5) in complaining that the agricultural research agenda has been unduly driven by external aid donors. Suggestions about poor communications with potential users of research outputs – farmers and industrialists – are particularly common. Thus Mosley states:

> The problem, then, at least in some countries, may be not that extension services do not exist at the requisite level, but rather that these services are unable to bridge the information gap between the farmer and the most productive technology that is available to him or her, either because the information is presented in the wrong way (e.g. without financial analysis) or because it is simply not credible because it is not adapted to local resource conditions, or because no opportunity to escape from the costs of a wrong decision exists for the farmer.
>
> (Mosley, 1992: 14)

Similarly, in a study of industrial science and technology policy in Cameroon which illustrates a number of the institutional weaknesses described above, Forje (1990: 234) complains of the absence of an infrastructure to link the research capabilities of higher education institutes to manufacturing industries. Kydd's (1989) study of the failure of maize research in Malawi draws attention to a further element in the complex of conditions which contribute to countries' technological capabilities: the disincentive effects of inadequate rural infrastructures and economic services. Over the twenty-eight years during which high-yielding hybrid maize varieties have been available, their adoption by farmers has been closely correlated with waves of investment in rural infrastructure, which improved access to financial services, markets and reliable supplies of seeds and fertiliser.

In short, it seems that the organisational and institutional infrastructure has not developed in ways that diminish transaction costs and ease technological progress. Further symptoms of lagging institutional development are incompetent or corrupted police forces and judiciaries, outdated laws and hidebound or venal public administrations, which introduce avoidable uncertainties and transaction costs in the definition and enforcement of property rights. We are thus once again led back to the failings of the state – in this instance, its inability to create an environment supportive of the adoption and adaptation of modern productive technologies.

Unresponsive political systems

Various policy weaknesses have now been identified. These were far from being restricted to Africa; many of the same mistakes were made in Asian and Latin American countries. What perhaps placed Africa in a special category was the slowness with which its governments responded to the clearly adverse consequences of the measures they had adopted. Why were dysfunctional policies kept in place for so long despite deteriorating economic results, even though governments' popularity, even legitimacy, was undermined by the resulting economic decline?[33] Why was it commonly left to the IMF and the World Bank to initiate the eventual policy reforms? And why has progress with these been slow? To answer such questions we need to go outside the frontiers of economics, to examine political, historical and cultural factors.[34]

The effects of political systems

In a passage inserted at the prompting of its African advisers, the World Bank sketched an answer to the question why African governments have apparently been so unresponsive to the shortcomings of policy:

> Underlying the litany of Africa's development problems is a crisis of governance. . . .Because the countervailing power has been lacking, state officials in many countries have served their own interests without fear of being called to account. In self-defence individuals have built up personal networks of influence rather than hold the all-powerful state accountable for its systemic failures. In this way politics becomes personalised, and patronage becomes essential to maintain power. The leadership assumes broad discretionary power and loses its legitimacy. Information is controlled, and voluntary associations are co-opted or disbanded.
>
> (World Bank, 1989: 60–1)

Two competing models of the state in Africa are popular among political scientists. One is the *rational-choice* model, of which the writings of Robert

Bates are often cited as examples.[35] This model can be characterised as having a view of the state in which politicians, bureaucrats and other actors in political processes are presumed to act to promote their own interests, to maximise their own welfare, as distinct from – often in opposition to – the welfare of the wider population. In the absence of accountability and democratic checks and balances, political actors are free to use the resources of the state for the benefit of themselves and their supporters, constrained only by the necessity to maintain sufficient backing to be able to hold on to office.

A second model views the African state in terms of *personal rule* (e.g. Jackson and Rosberg, 1984; Sandbrook, 1985). This sees the position of the ruler and his government as maintained by patron–client relationships, based mainly on familial and ethnic loyalties. Followers are rewarded with preferential access to loans, import licences, contracts and jobs. Institutional rules and constitutional checks and balances are swept aside by the competition for patronage and the struggle to maintain power. Rulers get themselves voted 'president for life'; the dubious virtues of one-party rule become the official ideology; open political competition is banned or carefully delimited; the distinction between the public and private domains becomes blurred.[36] Callaghy (1984) and MacGaffey have provided vivid accounts of the consequences of personal rule in the extreme form it has taken in Zaïre and the consequential decay of the state. MacGaffey states:

> In Zaire those with political position have used the power of their office to seize control of the economy . . . to acquire manufacturing, wholesale and retail businesses and plantations. However, they have neither managed their enterprises in a rational capitalist fashion nor invested their profits in expansion of their businesses and improved production . . .
>
> (MacGaffey, 1988: 175)

> The ruling class is not a true economic bourgeoisie; it is one that loots the economy and collapses effective administration. It is thus unable to exercise the control over production necessary to maintain its dominance and must resort to consolidating its position by participating in the more lucrative activities of the second [parallel] economy.
>
> (MacGaffey, 1988: 172)

Fortunately, only a minority of African countries have been driven to the benighted condition of Zaïre. Here especially we must beware of overgeneralisation and should remember that some African countries have established democratic traditions (Botswana, The Gambia, Senegal, more recently Namibia).

Nonetheless, in the more typical situations of slight accountability and weak democratic traditions, both the rational-choice and personal-rule models are persuasive in illuminating various of the policy weaknesses described earlier. The proliferation of state enterprises and growth of the public sector; choice of direct and discretionary controls over policies which work impersonally through price incentives; a pro-urban, anti-smallholder bias; the politicisation of credit allocation and investment decisions are all explicable within the parameters of either of these models. For present purposes, this helps to explain the unresponsiveness of governments to anti-developmental policies long after their ill-effects have become apparent, because their primary function was to provide personal benefits and/or rewards to supporters in order to maintain rulers in power, rather than to promote development.

Indeed, even democratic forms offer no assurance of responsive governments. Radelet's 1992 study of economic reforms in The Gambia finds that the rational-choice model gives 'a compelling set of answers' to the question why the Gambian government continued with discredited policies for so long:

> [The ruling party] was comfortable with its rural political base, and saw government expansion as a means of solidifying urban support and extracting resources for their own individual economic benefit. The government established several urban-based parastatals, increased public investment over 700 per cent in six years, and doubled the size of the civil service. Urban-based businesses . . . reaped the benefits of 'developing certificates' that gave generous tax breaks and loan guarantees. Urban residents also gained from low-interest government loans; the over-valued exchange rate; protective tariffs; and subsidized rice, utilities and transport fares.
>
> (Radelet, 1992: 1090)

In the end – and this is a story retold in many African countries – emerging economic crisis and the palpable unsustainability of existing policies eventually forced the government to turn to the IMF and the World Bank. Reforms were embraced but late and reluctantly, and in the meantime the welfare of the population had been compromised.

The lines of explanation offered above are also consistent with the stress in Chapter 11 by Seddon and Belton-Jones on the importance of the autonomy of the state in determining its freedom of choice and capacity for rapid response. Given the low level of development of the institutions of civil society in most African countries, it might appear that the state would typically enjoy a high degree of autonomy. However, the story told above is of governments seeking to compensate for a lack of popular legitimacy by using the resources of the state to bribe the support of key groups: the armed forces; the bureaucracy; the urban labour force; the trading and industrial élites; key ethnic groupings. The government is hemmed in by the alienation of the people from it, and it is in no position – except through desperation –

to get tough with key interest groups whose support is contingent on a continuing flow of favours.

The influences of history and social structure

Personal rule, self-serving politicians, weak states and clientelist-based politics are not, of course, confined to Africa but they do seem particularly pervasive there. Again, we must ask, why? To take this further requires examination of the historical experiences and the social values and structures which underlie the political condition of the continent – treacherous territory for an economist. Various questions arise. How did history and social structure influence the economic policy choices that were made after independence? How are they connected with the spread of anti-developmental political systems? Above all, how do they help us to understand why Africa's economies appear less flexible than those of other developing regions?

One feature which is different from, say, most of Asia is low population densities.[37] A number of writers see this characteristic as having far-reaching implications for contemporary political processes. In pre-colonial times, most Africans were either pastoralists or cultivators with few obligations to feudal overlords or landlords. They hence enjoyed an autonomy impossible in the highly regimented agriculture of pre-colonial Asian civilisations (Hyden, 1986: 54), although this did not altogether prevent the development of centralised political systems, e.g. in pre-colonial Nigeria and Uganda. The favourable land–labour ratio and the low carrying capacity of much of Africa encouraged dispersed settlements and voluntary migration in search of food, pasture and trading opportunities (Hopkins, 1986: 1479). These factors and the prevalence of pre-modern cultivation techniques meant low productivity in agriculture and the absence of a surplus with which to support a highly stratified and urbanised society. In most cases the political unit remained the village or clan, with social obligations determined by the ties of kinship.

Such social structures were, of course, modified by colonialism, for example through the alienation of land and the forced commercialisation of agriculture, but they were rarely transformed by it (see Fieldhouse, 1986; Hopkins 1986). A key feature of colonialism – covering all colonial systems – was their insistence that colonies should pay their way and not become a burden on the metropolitan budget. It led in the British case to 'indirect rule', as a cost-effective way of governing an empire with few personnel. It committed the British authorities to support traditional rulers, and the relations of production on which they depended, often enhancing, even creating, ethnic divisions.[38]

In principle, the French colonial philosophy was different, embodying the notion of the 'assimilation' of colonial peoples, under which those who qualified became French citizens entitled to elect Deputies to the French National Assembly. In practice, however, only a tiny proportion of colonial peoples achieved this status, partly because of a financially induced neglect of the educational system (see Fieldhouse, 1986). Many bureaucrats in the French territories still owed their position to the status they enjoyed in traditional society. The principle of the balanced budget was thus in conflict with the modernisation of French and British colonies alike. The position of territories colonised by Portugal was even worse, where tight budgetary restrictions were accompanied by little desire to modernise in any case (Mayer, 1990).

In the view of writers like Hyden, the survival of traditional social structures during the colonial period, and the superficiality of any social modernisation as a result of European rule, make Africa unique in the developing world and impart a special character to the nature of its political organisation. In urban areas immigrants continue to seek support from members of their tribe or village and as a result urban dwellers continue to behave in ways more akin to villagers than to an urban proletariat. Hyden (1986) calls this structure 'the economy of affection' and views the role of ethnicity in African politics as closely tied to this perpetuation of links to the countryside. It results, he argues, in the vertical (ethnic) and not horizontal (class) political groupings which characterise African society, and in structures hostile to formal bureaucratic principles.

Without the power and authority of their imperial overlords and as the cement of anti-colonialism lost strength, post-colonial rulers lacked adequate legitimacy to rule over the ethnically diverse communities that had comprised the colonial state. Despite the grafting-on of democratic forms during decolonisation, the colonialists left a dominant legacy of authoritarianism and group rights, derived from the tradition of indirect rule and the co-optation of traditional authorities (Young, 1986). Artificial colonial borders which lacked geographical or ethnic integrity made matters worse, committing governments to the maintenance of contrived unions, sometimes in the face of considerable opposition. Expenditure on security was consequently an important component of the growing fiscal deficit, sometimes intensified by the impact of the Cold War. Inexperienced political leaders were thus faced with the daunting task of maintaining their authority, and the integrity of their nations, in the face of divided societies and fragile states. In response, they often sought to maintain their positions through a concentration of power reinforced by a system of rewards.

Returning to the question why governments have been so unresponsive in the face of demonstrated policy failures, the argument sketched here is that there was a conjuncture of demographic, social and historical influences that made the African continent particularly fertile ground for the spread of clientelist-based politics. Of course, political systems world-wide contain elements of clientelism; what we are discussing here is a matter of degree.

The contention is that conditions in post-colonial Africa particularly encouraged this way of doing political business. That such systems came into being in fragile nation-states reinforced the incentive to use patronage and a centralised authoritarianism to hold the state together. These factors resulted in the persistence of many of the policy choices which hindsight shows to have been anti-developmental.

IV CONCLUSIONS

While it is dangerous to offer continent-wide generalisations and Africa by no means offers a uniformly adverse situation, we have marshalled evidence here which indicates a generally low degree of economic flexibility: a slow pace of modernising structural change; a rather adverse record with 'structural adjustment'; a poor revealed ability to take advantage of trading opportunities; a similarly laggard response to technological advances; and rather low supply elasticities in agriculture. Moreover, we have shown that these factors interact with each other, so that in combination they have a powerful sclerotic effect.

We have contrasted this evidence of inflexibility with the demonstrated responsiveness of African peoples to economic incentives and have sought to resolve this paradox by examining various constraints which prevent their responsiveness from resulting in adaptable national economies. Following the suggestions of Chapter 1, we looked first at evidence on the quality of information flows, finding that such flows are relatively weak in Africa. Second, we found evidence of seriously deficient incentive systems, resulting largely from adverse policy interventions but aggravated by market failures and other domestic constraints.

Thirdly we highlighted the importance of weak technological capabilities, flowing from Africa's particularly severe shortages of skills and knowledge, the weaknesses of its institutional base and the resulting depressed productivity of such skilled labour as does exist. Finally, since many of the deficiencies just mentioned may be attributed to past policies, we have examined why political systems have proved so unresponsive to the proven inadequacies of previous interventions – a task which led us also to examine the influences of history and social structures.

What conclusions might we now draw from this exploration?

First, that there has been value-added from the focus on flexibility. Admittedly, some evidence and diagnoses, particularly as they relate to the foreign-exchange constraint, supply elasticities and the failings of policy interventions – have merely presented familiar materials in an unfamiliar setting. But some of the other discussion has covered less well-trodden ground – for example, that relating to technology lags and capabilities, and the responsiveness of political systems. In addition, the analysis has gained from being able to comprehend a wide range of materials that would not normally be considered in combination, to show the ways in which they interact and contribute to the overall problem of inflexibility.

On the negative side, the analysis is not rigorous. The concept of flexibility is too imprecise and multi-faceted, and the evidence too incomplete, for this essay to be more than an exploratory first attempt. It would, for example, have been highly desirable to explore the hypothesis that the relative absence of a modern entrepreneurial culture, of business people with access to the know-how necessary for modernisation, has been a further crucial factor holding back the adaptability of African economies. One view on this is that there is no such shortage, only an economic environment which provides poor access to important information and discourages the expansion of private enterprise (see Elkan, 1988; Marsden, 1990) and direct foreign investment, but there is simply not enough evidence to bring to bear on that.

In any case, rigour is not the sole criterion by which research should be judged. There are also questions of relevance and richness, as much of the 'rigour' which afflicts present-day economics constantly reminds us. What this exercise has also shown is the importance of adopting a multi-disciplinary approach, of going beyond the boundaries of economics into the realms of the political scientist, sociologist and historian. This can be seen as a positive, enriching, virtue (although whether my amateurish entry into this unfamiliar territory has been successful is another question). Nevertheless, it can be readily conceded that this chapter would have been stronger had it been possible to assemble a larger amount of reliable evidence in a more systematic way.

A further conclusion that suggests itself is that flexibility matters: that the inflexibility of African economies has had powerfully negative welfare effects. For example, there is a direct and obvious link between the inability of Africa's exporters to take advantage of developing trade opportunities in the way that their counterparts in other developing countries have done and the severity of its foreign-exchange constraint. There are similarly clear connections between the slow pace of technical progress, depressed productivities and lagging per capita incomes.

We are reminded here of North's (1990) suggestion that the growing specialisation, de-personalisation of transactions and complexity of economic structures which are intrinsic to development give rise to disproportionate increases in transaction and enforcement costs. The emergence of institutions which minimise these costs is thus imperative if economic development is not to be frustrated, *but there is no necessary reason for this to occur*. Our arguments concerning the contribution of historical, political and social factors to the inflexibility of Africa's economies can be interpreted as pointing to a failure of the necessary institutional development and hence avoidably high transaction costs which are the hallmark of an inflexible economy.

We began this chapter with the hypothesis that there is a positive relationship between an economy's flexibility and its level of development. To a considerable extent, the African case supports this suggestion. In a variety of ways, Africa's economic inflexibility can be attributed to underdevelopment: poor infrastructure and communications; weak institutions and markets; shortages of skilled and experienced labour, with resulting weak technological capabilities. To a considerable extent, Africa is inflexible because it is poor, as well as being poor because it is inflexible.

However, we should not take too deterministic a view of the influence of underdevelopment. At various points in this chapter, evidence has been marshalled which adversely contrasts the African experience with other developing regions, including countries which were severely underdeveloped two or three decades ago but have since made substantial progress. There has, in addition, been an 'Africa factor'. In finding this we are in agreement with the results of Easterly and Levine's more formal study of Africa's growth performance:

> we find that even after controlling for policies, human capital endowments, terms of trade shocks, and 'catch-up' factors, Africa grows more slowly for reasons that the cross-country model does not explain. Africa is different.
>
> (Easterly and Levine, 1993: 4)

They reject (p. 15) as unscientific and unreliable the introduction of political, cultural and institutional factors to explain 'the mysteriously poor performance of Africa'. However, this seems to come close to saying that only quantifiable economic variables are 'real' evidence, which takes the claims of the economics discipline a bit far. While we admit the pitfalls and loss of rigour, we have sought to persuade that the influences of political systems, history and social structures are relevant to an understanding of the 'Africa factor'.

Finally, the chapter has implications for the efforts of those African governments – and of the IMF, the World Bank and the donor governments which stand behind them – which are attempting to improve economic performance through programmes of structural adjustment. If the analysis above is accepted, it indicates that such programmes are addressing major factors holding back the responsiveness of African economies, e.g. by addressing many of the policy deficiencies identified earlier as blunting incentives and weakening the institutional base.

At the same time, our analysis indicates that a focus on moving away from interventionist policy stances, and on 'getting prices right', is too narrow. It is important to attend to a wider range of factors, bearing upon technological capabilities, institutional development, information flows, the adequacy of the infrastructure and of the provision of other public goods. Indeed, to the extent that adjustment programmes are associated – as they are – with reduced public-sector service provisions and investments, these will make it all the harder to adapt the economies of Africa to present-day realities.

NOTES

I should like to thank Stephen Bailey-Smith for valuable assistance in preparing materials for this paper.

1 See Killick (1991, Table 1) showing that in 1980–8 aid to Africa was equivalent to 33 per cent of investment (ten times as high as the average proportion for other developing countries) and 26 per cent of imports (five times as high).

2 World Bank (1992c: 3). The above discussion has been based on the results summarised on pp. 1–5 and in chapter 1.

3 See Killick (forthcoming) for a review of the evidence on economic performance in sub-Saharan Africa and explanations of this. See also Easterly and Levine (1993) who find that Africa has under-performed relative to other developing countries, in terms of the predictions of standard growth models.

4 See Bond's 1987 survey, which finds no evidence to support the hypothesis of a backward-sloping supply curve for labour in Africa.

5 A large number of empirical studies have found positive, sometimes large, supply elasticities. See the evidence summarised for a number of cash crops in World Bank (1986: Table 4.4), also Bond (1987).

6 There is a growing body of evidence on this. See especially Berthelemy and Morrisson's 1987 study of twelve African economies. Also Bevan et al. (1987) who find this in Tanzania; and Guillaumont and Bojean (1991) showing how price responses in agriculture can be largely nullified by shortages of imported incentive goods.

7 They are tiny when measured by the value of economic activity. I have estimated for African and similar developing countries that the average market for industrial goods is only about one three-hundredth of that of an average-sized industrial economy (Killick, 1993: 91–2). The 1991 dollar value of the GDP of Africa's economic 'giant', Nigeria ($34.1bn), was smaller than that of Ireland ($39bn); and the aggregate GDP of the whole of sub-Saharan Africa ($164.3bn) was about the same as that of Austria ($164bn) (World Bank, 1993a, Table 3).

8 Thus, Matin (1992) undertakes econometric tests on four alternative indicators of openness and obtains the result, robust for all four measures, of a statistically strong association between openness and African economic growth.

9 Calculated from IMF, 1992b: Table A35. The average for 1988–90 was an estimated 25 per cent.

10 See World Bank (1992d) which shows that sub-Saharan Africa had in 1991 a far higher debt to GNP ratio than any other region. The extent to which African countries were unable to maintain scheduled service payments may be gauged from the fact that during 1980–92 there were no less than 535 Paris and London Club rescheduling agreements in a total of thirty-nine African countries (calculated from World Bank, 1992a: Table A1.5, and 1992d: Appendices II and III; and *Annual Reports* and other publications of the IMF).

11 Calculated from IMF, 1992: Table A43. The comparable averages for other developing regions were: Asia 32 per cent, Western Hemisphere 26 per cent.

12 Both Ali et al. (1991) and Svedberg (1991: 26–31) caution that there is no necessary connection between African export diversification and improved export earnings growth or stability. This, it may be surmised, is because the limited

amount of diversification that has occurred has largely been into different 'non-traditional' primary commodities.

13 For valuable detailed country studies see Riddell (1990a) on Zimbabwe; Stevens (1990) on Ethiopia and Kenya; and McQueen (1990) on Mauritius. See also McQueen and Stevens (1989) for further evidence on ACP export diversification to European Community countries under the Lomé IV arrangements.

14 This is an unweighted mean for nine commodity categories estimated by Kox (1990) from UNDP and World Bank data and reproduced in Baban and Greene (1992: Table 11).

15 See Khan and Knight (1988) for strong econometric evidence of the adverse effects of import compression on export performance, based on data from thirty-four developing countries. See also the studies cited in Note 6 above, showing adverse production effects from shortages of imported 'incentive goods'. At a more microeconomic level, Mbelle and Sterner (1991: 343, Table 2) show for two Tanzanian manufacturing industries that, on a range of alternative production function formulations, the elasticity of output is far greater with respect to the availability of imported materials than of labour or capital.

16 Thus, Lele et al. (1989: 5): 'In many parts of Africa over 80 per cent of the value added in smallholder agriculture comes from a production process where the hand-hoe is frequently the only other major input besides labour.'

17 Calculated from data in UN ECA (1991: Tables 1 and 19).

18 See also Lall (1992: 120) where he also suggests that firm-level R&D is very rare in Africa.

19 The statistics record the mean accumulated number of US external patents granted in 1962–87 per million of the 1980 population for a sample of developing countries in each region. Source: UNCTAD (1993: Table III–2).

20 Readers should be cautioned, however, that the results of elasticity estimates are highly sensitive to the period chosen and the model specification so that no great reliance should be placed upon the specific values reported in the table. There are particularly large questions about the long-run elasticity estimates.

21 Jaeger (1991: 21–2) tested for the existence of a trade-off between the production of food and export crops and found no statistically significant evidence of this. Indeed, his results tended to suggest positive associations between the production of these two crop types.

22 Lele et al. (1989: Table 3) undertook three alternative measures of food self-sufficiency for a sample of six African countries and found that the period averages diminished between 1960–9 and 1980–6 in all but one of the countries (Malawi).

23 See Grilli and Yang (1988) and Ardeni and Wright (1990), who, using different methods, both estimate a long-term trend rate of decline of −0.6 per cent p.a. Subsequent articles by Boughton (1991) and Sapsford et al. (1992) also find a long-run trend decline.

24 See United Nations (1992, Table A.22). This, for example, indicates that world food export prices halved in real terms in 1981–91, i.e. when deflated by a price index of manufactures.

25 For substantiation see Killick (forthcoming, Table 5) showing a median currency appreciation of 40 per cent during 1969–71 to 1978–80. The effect of over-valuation was in practice mitigated by the growth of parallel foreign-exchange markets in many countries (although not in the Franc Zone because of currency convertibility), although this in turn gave rise to serious economic distortions. For example, in the early 1980s the parallel rate for foreign exchange in Ghana was twenty to thirty times the official rate and a high proportion of all foreign-

exchange transactions were conducted through the parallel market, but the huge profits that could be made from access to imports at the official rate led to widespread corruption and other forms of rent-seeking. Similar, if less extreme, situations existed in many other African countries.

26 On the implicit taxation of African agriculture see also Beynon (1989) especially Table 1; Krueger, *et al.* (1988) also provide valuable information, although not confined to Africa.

27 This could reach extreme levels. Thus, in Tanzania, where there was limited fiscal taxation of exports, escalating marketing costs (in combination with currency overvaluation) absorbed increasingly large shares of the total local-currency proceeds of commodity exports. Rwegasira (1984) provides the following figures on the percentages of world prices being passed on to Tanzania's farmers:

	1969	1980
cashew nuts	70	35
coffee	81	45
cotton	70	45
tobacco	61	48

28 Statistically the result was highly significant; the response was recorded as simultaneous (or very short-run) but lagged variables were not tried. Diakosavvas cites Elias (1985) as having reached similar conclusions.

29 See Jaeger (1991: 39–43) for some illustrations along these lines. See also Helleiner (1986) for econometric evidence of an inverse relationship between export performance and import instability. See also Guillaumont and Bojean's 1991 study of Madagascar for evidence of stabilisation, *per se*, associated with improvements in agricultural production.

30 For excellent studies of relationships between formal and informal financial systems in Africa see Aryeetey (1992) on Ghana, and Chipeta and Mkandawire (1991) on Malawi.

31 The example of the poorly developed nature of the financial sector illustrates the difficulties of disentangling the failings of the public and private sectors, for the shallowness of the financial sector in most of Africa is partly the result of policies of financial repression, but these policies may, in turn, be partly a response to the non-competitive nature of the formal financial system. Note that Easterly and Levine (1993: 9) find growth in Africa to be strongly linked to the level of financial development.

32 For a directly analogous analysis, see Mosley and Smith (1989: 337–43) for a detailed specification of a wide range of factors which reduce the proportion of the benefits of a currency devaluation being passed on in farm-gate prices. Their conclusion is similar to ours: when these various factors are borne in mind, it is not surprising if the evidence indicates only muted agricultural responses to devaluations.

33 In support of this proposition, El-Farhan (forthcoming, Chapter 6) finds a statistically significant relationship which runs from GDP growth to political stability: the slower the growth the greater the incidence of instability.

34 The following pages borrow heavily from Killick (forthcoming). They are much influenced by the work of my colleagues John Healey and Mark Robinson (1992), from which I have borrowed extensively. They provide an excellent

survey of the literature on the political systems of Africa and their economic consequences.

35 See especially Bates (1981 and 1991). However, see also the special section on his writings on the political economy of development in Africa in the June 1993 issue of *World Development*, pp.1033–81, from which it appears that he can only loosely be located in the rational choice school.

36 Thus, it has been said of Malawi that 'the private sector is alive and well – and owned by President Banda!' Pryor (1990, Chapter 4) offers some supporting evidence.

37 As at 1960 population densities (per km^2) were estimated as follows, although such averages of course conceal huge inter-country differences within each region (United Nations, 1975: Table 2): Africa 13, Asia 80, Latin America 15.

38 In fact, ethnicity in modern Africa is viewed by some as a relatively modern creation, in which the experience of colonisation played an important part. For a survey of approaches to ethnicity in modern Africa see Vail (1986), who also presents case studies.

REFERENCES

Ahmed, Raisuddin and Narendra Rustagi (1987) 'Marketing and price incentives in African and Asian countries: a comparison', in Dieter Elz (ed.) *Agricultural Marketing Strategy and Pricing Policy*, Washington, DC: World Bank.

Akiyama, Takamasa and Donald F. Larson (1989) 'Recent trends and prospects for agricultural commodity exports in sub-Saharan Africa', Working Paper no. 348, Washington, DC: World Bank, December.

Ali, Ridwan, Jeffrey Alwang and Paul B. Sigel (1991) 'Is export diversification the best way to achieve export growth and stability?', Working Paper no. 729, Washington, DC: World Bank, July.

Ardeni, Pier Giorgio and Brian Wright (1990) 'The long-term behavior of commodity prices', Working Paper no. 358, Washington, DC: World Bank, March.

Aryeetey, Ernest (1992) *The relationship between the formal and informal sectors of the financial market in Ghana*, Research Paper no. 10, Nairobi: Africa Economic Research Centre, October.

Askari, Hossein and J.T. Cummings (1976) *Agricultural Supply Responses: A Survey of Econometric Evidence*, New York: Praeger.

Baban, Roy C. and Joshua E. Greene (1992) 'The export performance of sub-Saharan Africa, 1970–90: a survey', Working Paper no. 92/55, Washington, DC: International Monetary Fund, July.

Balassa, Bela (1990) 'Incentive policies and export performance in sub-Saharan Africa', *World Development* 18(3), March: 383–92.

Bates, Robert H. (1981) *Markets and States in Tropical Africa*, Berkeley, CA: University of California Press.

—— (1991) 'Agricultural policy and the study of politics in post-independence Africa', in Douglas Rimmer (ed.) *Africa 30 Years On*, London: Royal African Society and James Currey.

Berthelemy, J.C. and C. Morrisson (1987) 'Manufactured goods supply and cash crops in sub-Saharan Africa', *World Development* 15(10–11): 1353–68.

Bevan, D.L., A. Bigsten, P. Collier and J.W. Gunning (1987) 'Peasant supply response in rationed economies', *World Development* 15(4), April: 431–40.

Beynon, J.G. (1989) 'Pricism v. structuralism in sub-Saharan African agriculture', *Journal of Agricultural Economics* 40(3), September.

Binswanger, Hans (1990) 'The policy response of agriculture', *Proceedings of the*

World Bank Annual Conference on Development Economics, 1989, Washington, DC: World Bank.

Binswanger, H. and P. Pingali (1988) 'Technological priorities for farming in sub-Saharan Africa', *World Bank Research Observer* 3(1), January: 81–98.

Bond, Marion E. (1987) 'An econometric study of primary product exports from developing country regions to the world', *IMF Staff Papers* 34(2), June, Washington, DC: International Monetary Fund.

Boskin, Michael and Lawrence Lau (1990) *Post-War Economic Growth in the Group-of-Five Countries*, Stanford, CA: Center for Economic Policy Research, Stanford University.

Boughton, James M. (1991) 'Commodity and manufactures prices in the long run', IMF Working Paper 91/47, Washington, DC: International Monetary Fund, May.

Bwisa, H.M. (1989) 'Scientific Co-operation for Development in Africa', *African Development Review* 2(1), June: 1–19.

Callaghy, Thomas M. (1984) *The State-Society Struggle: Zaire in Comparative Perspective*, New York: Columbia University Press.

Chander, Ramesh (1990) 'Information systems and basic statistics in sub-Saharan Africa', Discussion Paper 73, Washington, DC: World Bank, February.

Chhibber, Ajay (1989) 'The aggregate supply response: a survey', in Simon Commander (ed.) *Structural Adjustment and Agriculture*, London: James Currey and Overseas Development Institute.

Chipeta, C. and M. Mkandawire (1991) *Informal Financial Markets and Macroeconomic Adjustment in Malawi*, AERC Research Paper no. 4, Nairobi: African Economic Research Consortium.

Cleaver, Kevin (1985) 'The impact of price and exchange rate policies on agriculture in sub-Saharan Africa', Staff Working Paper no. 728, Washington, DC: World Bank.

DeRosa, Dean A. (1990) *Protection and Export Performance in sub-Saharan Africa*, IMF Working Paper no. WP/90/83, September, Washington, DC: International Monetary Fund.

—— (1991) 'Protection in sub-Saharan Africa hinders exports', *Finance and Development* 28(3), September 42–5.

Diakosavvas, Dimitris (1989) 'Government expenditure on agriculture and agricultural performance in developing countries', New Series Discussion Paper no. 3, University of Bradford: Development Project Planning Centre, April.

Diakosavvas, Dimitris and Colin Kirkpatrick (1990) 'Exchange-rate policy and agricultural exports performance in sub-Saharan Africa', *Development Policy Review* 8(1), March: 29–42.

Easterly, William and Ross Levine (1993) 'Is Africa different? Evidence from growth regressions', Washington, DC: World Bank, April, mimeo.

Elbadawi, Ibrahim A. (1992) 'Have World Bank-supported adjustment programs improved economic performance in sub-Saharan Africa?', World Bank Working Paper WPS 1001, Washington, DC: World Bank, October.

Elbadawi, Ibrahim A., Dhaneshwar Ghura and Gilbert Uwujaren (1992) 'Why structural adjustment has not succeeded in sub-Saharan Africa', World Bank Working Paper no. 1000, Washington, DC: World Bank, October.

El-Farhan, Hania (forthcoming) 'Analysis of the growth performance of sub-Saharan African countries, 1960–85', London: School of Oriental and African Studies (PhD thesis).

Elias, J.V. (1985) *Government Expenditures on Agriculture in Latin America*, Research Report no. 23, Washington, DC: International Food Policy Research Institute.

Elkan, Walter (1988) 'Entrepreneurs and entrepreneurship in Africa', *World Bank Research Observer* 3(2), July: 171–88.

Faini, Riccardo and Jaime de Melo (1990) 'Adjustment, investment and the real exchange rate in developing countries', Working Paper WPS no. 473, Washington, DC: World Bank, August.

FAO (1993) *Data Series*, Rome: FAO.

Fieldhouse, D.K. (1986) *Black Africa 1945–1980: Economic Decolonization and Arrested Development*, London: Allen & Unwin.

Forje, John W. (1990) 'Small and poor countries in a world of big science and technology. The management of science and technology for industrial development in Africa: the case of Cameroon', *Science, Technology and Development* 8(3), December: 234–44.

Grilli, E.R. and M.C. Yang (1988) 'Primary commodity prices, manufactured goods prices and the terms of trade of developing countries: what the long run shows', *World Bank Economic Review* 2(1), January: 1–48.

Guillaumont, Patrick and Catherine Bojean (1991) 'Effects on agricultural supply of producer price level and stability with and without goods scarcity: the case of coffee supply in Madagascar', *Journal of International Development* 3(2): 115–34.

Healey, J.M. and M. Robinson (1992) *Democracy, Political Change and Economic Policy: Sub-Saharan Africa in Comparative Perspective*, London: Overseas Development Institute.

Helleiner, G.K. (1986) 'Outward orientation, import instability and African economic growth: an empirical investigation', in Sanjaya Lall and Frances Stewart (eds) *Theory and Reality in Development*, London: Macmillan.

Hopkins, A.G. (1986) 'The World Bank in Africa: historical reflections on the African present', *World Development* 14(12), December: 1473–87.

Hyden, G. (1986) 'African social structure and economic development', in R.J. Berg and J.S. Whitaker (eds) *Strategies for African Development*, Berkeley, CA: University of California Press.

International Monetary Fund (1992a) *Annual Report 1991/92*, Washington, DC: International Monetary Fund.

—— (1992b) *World Economic Outlook*, Washington, DC: International Monetary Fund, May.

Jackson, Robert H. and Carl G. Rosberg (1984) 'Personal rule: theory and practice in Africa', *Comparative Politics* 16(4), July.

Jaeger, William (1991) 'The impact of policy in African agriculture', Working Paper WPS 640, Washington, DC: World Bank, March.

Khan, Mohsin and Malcolm D. Knight (1988) 'Import compression and export performance in developing countries', *Review of Economics and Statistics* May.

Killick, Tony (1991) 'The developmental effectiveness of aid to Africa', in I. Husain and J. Underwood (eds) *African External Finance in the 1990s*, Washington, DC: World Bank. See also World Bank Working Paper no. 646 (1991).

—— (1993) *The Adaptive Economy: Adjustment Policies in Small, Low-Income Countries*, Washington, DC: World Bank, and London: Overseas Development Institute.

—— (forthcoming) 'Explaining Africa's post-independence development experiences', in E. Grilli and D. Salvatore (eds) *Handbook of Comparative Economic Development*, Westport, CT: Greenwood Publishing. Earlier version published as Working Paper no. 60 (1992), London: Overseas Development Institute.

Kindleberger, Charles P. (1962) *Foreign Trade and the National Economy*, New Haven, CT: Yale University Press.

Klitgaard, Robert (1991) *Adjusting to Reality*, San Francisco: ICS Press.

Kox, Henk L.M. (1990) 'Export constraints for sub-Saharan growth: the role of non-fuel primary commodities', Amsterdam: Vrije Universiteit, December, mimeo.

Krueger, Anne O., Maurice Schiff and Alberto Valdés (1988) 'Agricultural incentives in developing countries: measuring the effects of sectoral and economywide policies', *World Bank Economic Review* 2(3), September: 255–72.

Kydd, Jonathan (1989) 'Maize Research in Malawi: Lessons from Failure', *Journal of International Development* 1(1), January, 112–44.

Lall, Sanjaya (1992) 'Structural problems of African industry', in F. Stewart, S. Lall and S. Wangwe (eds) *Alternative Development Strategies in Sub-Saharan Africa*, London and Basingstoke: Macmillan.

Lele, Uma (1988) 'Comparative advantage and structural transformation: a review of Africa's economic development experience', in Gustav Ranis and T. Paul Schultz (eds) *The State of Development Economics: Progress and Perspectives*, Oxford: Basil Blackwell.

—— (ed.) (1992) *Aid to African Agriculture*, Baltimore, MD: Johns Hopkins University Press.

Lele, Uma and Robert E. Christiansen (1989) 'Markets, marketing boards and co-operatives in Africa', MADIA Discussion Paper 11, Washington, DC: World Bank.

Lele, U., R. Christiansen and K. Kadiresan (1989) 'Fertiliser policy in Africa: lessons from development programs and adjustment lending, 1970–87', MADIA Discussion Paper 5, Washington, DC: World Bank.

MacGaffey, Janet (1988) 'Economic disengagement and class formation in Zaire', in Donald Rothchild and Naomi Chazan (eds) *The Precarious Balance: State and Society in Africa*, Boulder, CO: Westview Press.

—— (ed.) (1991) *The Real Economy of Zaire*, London: James Currey.

McQueen, Matthew (1990) 'ACP export diversification: the case of Mauritius', Working Paper no. 41, London: Overseas Development Institute, August.

McQueen, Matthew and Christopher Stevens (1989) 'Trade preferences and Lomé IV: non-traditional ACP exports to the EC', *Development Policy Review* 7(3), September: 239–60.

Marsden, Keith (1990) 'African entrepreneurs: pioneers of development', Discussion Paper no. 9, Washington, DC: International Finance Corporation.

Matin, Kazi M. (1992) 'Openness and economic performance in sub-Saharan Africa', Working Paper WPS 1025, Washington, DC: World Bank, November.

Mayer, Jean (1990) 'Development problems and prospects in Portuguese-speaking Africa', *International Labour Review* 129(4): 459–78.

Mbelle, Ammon and Thomas Sterner (1991) 'Foreign exchange and industrial development: a frontier production function analysis of two Tanzanian industries', *World Development* 19(4), April: 341–8.

Mosley, Paul (1992) 'Obstacles to the spread of the green revolution in Africa: some initial thoughts', IDPM Discussion Paper 32, Manchester: Institute of Development Policy Management, University of Manchester.

Mosley, Paul and Lawrence Smith (1989) 'Structural adjustment and agriculturel performance in sub-Saharan Africa, 1980–87', *Journal of International Development* 1(3), July: 321–55.

Moussa, Antoun and Robert Schware (1992) 'Informatics in Africa: lessons from World Bank experience', *World Development* 20(12), December: 1737–52.

Mukohya, Vwakyanakazi (1991) 'Import and export in the second economy in North Kivu', in J. MacGaffey (ed.) *The Real Economy of Zaire*, London: James Currey.

Newman, John L., Victor Lavy, Raoul Salomon and Philippe De Vreyer (1990)

'Firms' responses to relative price changes in Côte d'Ivoire', Working Paper WPS 550, Washington, DC: World Bank, December.

North, Douglass C. (1990) *Institutions, Institutional Change and Economic Performance*, Cambridge: Cambridge University Press.

Pryor, Frederic L. (1990) *Malawi and Madagascar*, New York: Oxford University Press.

Radelet, Steven (1992) 'Reform without revolt: the political-economy of economic reform in the Gambia', *World Development* 20(8), August: 1087–1100.

Riddell, Roger C. (1990a) 'ACP export diversification: the case of Zimbabwe', Working Paper no. 38, London: Overseas Development Institute, June.

—— (ed.) (1990b) *Manufacturing Africa*, London: James Currey and Overseas Development Institute.

Ruttan, Vernon and Colin Thirtle (1989) 'Induced technological change in African agriculture', *Journal of International Development* 1(1), January: 1–45.

Rwegasira, Delphin G. (1984) 'Exchange rates and the management of the external sector in sub-Saharan Africa', *Journal of Modern African Studies* 22(3), September: 451–68.

Sandbrook, Richard (1985) *The Politics of Africa's Economic Stagnation*, Cambridge: Cambridge University Press.

Sapsford, D., P. Sarkar and H.W. Singer (1992) 'The Prebisch–Singer terms of trade controversy revisited', *Journal of International Development* 4(3), May–June: 315–32.

Scandizzo, Pasquale L. and Colin Bruce (1980) 'Methodologies for measuring agricultural price intervention effects', Staff Working Paper no. 394, Washington, DC: World Bank.

Stevens, Christopher (1990) 'ACP export diversification: Jamaica, Kenya and Ethiopia', Working Paper no. 40, London: Overseas Development Institute.

Svedberg, Peter (1991) 'The export performance of sub-Saharan Africa', in Jonathan Frimpong-Ansah, S.M. Ravi Kanbur and Peter Svedberg (eds) *Trade and Development in Sub-Saharan Africa*, Manchester: Manchester University Press.

UNCTAD (1993) *Analytical Report by Secretariat to UNCTAD VIII Conference*, Geneva: UNCTAD.

UN ECA (1991) *African Socio-economic Indicators 1990/91*, Addis Ababa: UN ECA.

UNDP (1992) *African Recovery*, New York: UNDP.

—— (1993) *Human Development Report 1992*, New York: UNDP.

UNIDO (1993) *Industry and Development Report 1992/93*, Vienna: UNIDO.

United Nations (1975) *UN Statistical Yearbook 1975*, New York: United Nations.

—— (1992) *World Economic Survey 1992*, New York: United Nations.

—— (1993) *World Economic Survey 1993*, New York: United Nations.

Vail, L. (1986) 'Introduction: Ethnicity in Southern African history', in L. Vail (ed.) *The Creation of Tribalism in Southern Africa*, London: James Currey.

Von Braun, Joachim and Leonardo Paulino (1990) 'Food in sub-Saharan Africa: trends and policy challenges for the 1990s', *Food Policy* 15(6), December.

World Bank (1981) *Accelerated Development in Sub-Saharan Africa* ('The Berg Report'), Washington, DC: World Bank.

—— (1986) *World Development Report 1986*, New York: Oxford University Press.

—— (1989) *Sub-Saharan Africa: From Crisis to Sustainable Growth*, Washington, DC: World Bank.

—— (1991) *World Development Report 1991*, New York: Oxford University Press.

—— (1992a) *World Development Report 1992*, New York: Oxford University Press.

—— (1992b) *Global Economic Prospects and the Developing Countries, 1992*, Washington, DC: World Bank.

—— (1992c) *The Third Report on Adjustment Lending: Private and Public Resources for Growth*, Washington, DC: World Bank.

—— (1992d) *World Debt Tables, 1992–93*, vol. I, Washington, DC: World Bank.

—— (1993a) *World Development Report 1993*, New York: Oxford University Press.

—— (1993b) *Global Economic Prospects and the Developing Countries*, Washington, DC: World Bank.

World Development (1993) Special supplement on the writings of Robert Bates on the political economy of development in Africa, 21(6), June.

Yeats, Alexander J. (1990) 'On the accuracy of economic observations: do sub-Saharan trade statistics mean anything?', *World Bank Economic Review* 4(2), May: 135–56.

Young, C. (1986) 'Africa's colonial legacy', in R.J. Berg and J.S. Whitaker (eds) *Strategies for African Development*, Berkeley, CA: University of California Press.

7

EXPLAINING 'FLEXIBLE RIGIDITIES' IN EAST ASIA

Ha-Joon Chang

I INTRODUCTION: FLEXIBLE RIGIDITIES

The rise of East Asia, headed by Japan, and followed by the so-called 'Four Little Dragons' (South Korea, Taiwan, Hong Kong and Singapore), and increasingly by the 'Big Dragon' itself (i.e. China), has been the most important phenomenon of postwar economic history. Not only have these countries raised the living standards of their people at a rate unprecedented in human history. During this period, they have also, through their spectacular successes in many export markets, forced the policy-makers, managers, and workers of the older industrial powers of Western Europe and North America to accept that they may have to change at least some of the ways in which they organise their national systems of production and distribution.[1]

The success of the East Asian economies is even more striking when we consider that they all have very high population densities and relatively poor natural resource endowments, even if we exclude the city states of Hong Kong and Singapore (as we shall continue to do in the rest of this chapter). Despite these constraints, the East Asian economies, by which from now on we shall mean Japan, Korea and Taiwan, showed remarkable ability in transforming their production structures and enlarging their shares in world markets.[2] They were especially successful in those industries like electronics and automobiles which are subject to rapid shifts in technology and in final demand composition, and therefore require rapid adaptation of the organisation of production and corporate strategy. They have also shown surprising ability in adjusting to major external macroeconomic shocks like the two oil crises of the 1970s, the large currency appreciations of the late 1980s (in which, for example, Japan experienced almost a doubling of the value of its currency) and the debt crisis in the case of Korea (the fourth largest debtor in the world at the time of the outbreak of the crisis in 1982).[3] In other words, the East Asian economies have shown remarkable flexibilities during the last few decades.

These flexibilities are frequently interpreted by those economists who can be broadly defined as 'neo-liberal' as a result of 'free market' policies which allowed economic agents to respond quickly to changing price (and hence profitability) signals (for some recent assessments, see Toye, 1991; Chang and Rowthorn, forthcoming, Chapter I; Colclough, 1991 provides an assessment in the developing country context). In the view of these economists, the incapacity of some European economies to engineer an efficient structural change in the face of East Asian competition was the outcome of excessive government regulations and interest-group (especially trade-union) pressures which prevented the movement of resources into activities rendered more profitable by changing relative prices. This is the so-called 'Eurosclerosis' argument (for a representative sample, see Giersch, 1986; also see Olson, 1982, for a discussion on institutional sclerosis in general).

Similarly, the slowdown in the pace of industrialisation from the 1970s on and the inability to adjust to various external shocks of the 1980s shown by many developing countries (especially in Africa and Latin America) were interpreted as the results of a set of 'market-unfriendly' government policies associated with what is frequently (and somewhat misleadingly) called the import-substitution industrialisation (ISI) strategy (the term 'market-friendly' originates in World Bank, 1991; for a critique, see Singh, 1992). Hence the pressure by the World Bank and the IMF on recipient countries for rapid privatisation and liberalisation during the last decade or so. The same sort of policy package, if a more radical version, has been recommended by these international financial institutions and the newly established EBRD to the ex-socialist countries currently undergoing systemic reforms (see, for example, Blanchard *et al.*, 1991; for some critiques, see Bhaduri, 1991; Amsden, 1992; Chang and Nolan, forthcoming).

To put it more simply, the neo-liberal economists, who obviously have great confidence in the ability of the price mechanism to induce quick (and, by implication, 'desirable') adjustment, regard the 'artificial' restrictions created by the government and 'interest groups' as the major, if not the only, sources of economic difficulties in many countries, developed and developing.[4] They regard conditions of free entry and exit as essential for the 'free' exchanges which would allow the movements of resources into more profitable (and, with some qualifications, socially more desirable) activities. In their view, all rules, legislation, or other institutions, other than those which are necessary for market exchange to occur at all (e.g. laws on property rights and contracts) are 'rigidities' preventing such movements. They argue that such rigidities not only reduce the ability of an economy to adjust to external shocks but also reduce its ability to generate long-term growth. Their usual recommendations for domestic deregulation and international opening-up naturally follow from such analysis.[5]

Many neo-liberal economists have supported their arguments by contrasting the 'failures' of the 'sclerotic' economies (of Western Europe, Latin

America, Africa, and South Asia) with the 'success' of the 'flexible' ones in East Asia (Japan in the case of OECD countries and South Korea or Taiwan in the case of developing countries). According to them, the East Asian economies, being much freer (if not absolutely free) from such 'rigidities', are much more responsive to price signals and hence are better at adjusting to external shocks and seizing newly emerging profit opportunities.

In the more simplistic (but not necessarily the older) version of the argument, the East Asian successes are attributed to their states which provided an environment conducive to relatively unrestrained individual wealth maximisation, most importantly through their interaction with world markets.[6] More informed versions accept that there has been rather widespread state intervention in East Asia, but argue that it was at best irrelevant and at worst harmful but somehow neutralised. One version, namely, the virtual free trade argument (Little, 1982; Lal, 1983; World Bank, 1987), contends that the 'harmful' interventions (e.g. import substitution) were cancelled out by countervailing ones (e.g. export promotion). Another version, namely the theory of prescriptive vs proscriptive state intervention (Bhagwati, 1988) asserts that state intervention in these economies, while being quite extensive, still left a lot of room for private initiative, unlike, say, in India. The most recent study from the World Bank (World Bank, 1993), while admitting that some interventionist measures like credit rationing worked to a limited extent, comes up with a largely negative verdict on the effectiveness of state intervention in East Asia, especially on the ground that sectoral industrial policy did not work (for a detailed criticism of this argument, see the Appendix to this chapter). All in all, these 'informed' versions acknowledge that there was a lot of state intervention in East Asia, but contend that these countries succeeded not because of these interventions, with some minor exceptions, but despite them. Thus, these versions preserve the theoretical thrust of the neo-liberal argument that state-created rigidities are harmful to the economy, while accepting that there was quite widespread state intervention in East Asia.

However, many recent studies have revealed that the East Asian economies, especially the three largest, namely, Japan, South Korea and Taiwan, did not succeed on the basis of free market policies, or even 'virtual' free market policies.[7] These studies show that, contrary to what we would expect from the neo-liberal arguments, these countries were full of the kinds of 'rigidities' which the neo-liberal economists usually associate with economic troubles in other countries. What they demonstrate is not simply that state interventions (and the associated 'rigidities') existed in these countries, but also how they played a crucial role in the economic development (and not simply being there as at best irrelevant variables) by *providing the resources and opportunities for enterprises to upgrade their technologies by means of learning* (see also Lall in Chapter 9 in this volume).

Empirically the studies show that the East Asian countries experienced wide-ranging and much more forceful state intervention than is accepted by even the more informed versions of the neo-liberal arguments (for more detail on this point, see Chang, 1993). Strong sectoral industrial policy in these economies (sometimes directly imposed by the government and sometimes administered by government-supported private-sector cartels) meant that firms in many industries had to face tough restrictions on entry and exit, capacity expansion and reduction, pricing and the choice (especially importation) of technology. Their financial markets, especially the banking sector, have been heavily regulated (in Korea and Taiwan, the majority of banks are still owned by the state), with the overall objective of channelling subsidised loans into certain 'strategic' sectors (Amsden and Euh, 1990; Somel, 1992). Capital outflow was tightly controlled, and all incoming foreign direct investment and foreign borrowings had to be cleared with the government. The labour markets in these economies are often argued as being very flexible, but even here there are quite a few government-imposed practices which defy the simple picture of a 'free labour market' depicted by the neo-liberal economists. The East Asian governments frequently use (implicit and explicit) incomes policy, and have enforced certain 'protective' labour legislations which are often associated with labour market sclerosis in other economies (on the Japanese case, see Koike, 1987; on the Korean case, see You and Chang, 1993).[8]

These studies also reveal that 'rigidities' in East Asia are not only created by state intervention. Private-sector agents in these economies, notably in Japan but also in Korea and Taiwan, have exhibited many 'rigidities' in their behaviour, some of which were deliberately created by themselves (sometimes with government encouragement, as is the case with Korean subcontracting networks). Let us take some examples from Japan, which is a leader in this respect. Some (but by no means all) of its consumer goods markets are very difficult to penetrate because of the exceptionally high degree of consumer loyalty (which does, of course, get eroded over time; on this point, see Dore, 1986). Many industries are organised through a robust network of subcontracting, supported by cross-holdings of shares, exchanges of personnel, and preferential lending and/or technical assistance by the 'mother firms'. This networking, which makes changing trading partners almost impossible in the short run, obviously means that the members of the network have to sacrifice profitable trading opportunities outside the network (for a recent study of the Japanese subcontracting network, see Sako, 1993). Industry associations frequently organise cartels during periods of recession or major investment booms, often with the help of the state through special legal and administrative provisions suspending the anti-trust legislation. As a result, industrial restructuring in Japan often involves complex and highly 'politicised' negotiations concerning capacity, market share and choice of technology among the members of the industry (see Dore, 1986; Okimoto, 1989). A sizeable section of the workers in large firms and the so-called 'core workforce' in some small firms, which together means about one-third of the total workforce in the country, can expect lifetime employment. Wages are determined to a large extent by seniority and not by effort or level of qualification, as a freely operating labour market would require. These are the kinds of labour market practices which the proponents of Eurosclerosis would dread to see.[9]

In short, the East Asian economies possess many characteristics which do not fit into the picture of a 'flexible' market economy as depicted by the simpler version of the neo-liberal account of the East Asian experience. Moreover, even the more informed version, which does recognise the existence of state intervention in East Asia, does not provide a satisfactory answer. For one thing, as we pointed out earlier, the range and depth of state intervention in East Asia goes far beyond what these versions admit. More importantly, even the more coherent virtual free trade argument and the prescriptive state argument (not to mention the recent World Bank report [World Bank, 1993], which lacks a coherent overall theoretical framework) suffer from major theoretical problems (for details, see Chang, 1993). The theory of virtual free trade ultimately bases its argument on the traditional theory of comparative advantage, which has very little to say about growth issues (as even one of the leading mainstream trade theorists admit; see Krueger, 1980), which really are at the heart of the whole debate on East Asia. The theory of prescriptive state intervention does not recognise the simple fact that, in a world of scarce resources, prescriptions by the state (especially if they are as wide-ranging as in East Asia) inevitably limit the range of initiatives open to private sector agents.

How, then, have the East Asian economies been able to succeed in the face of so many rigidities, which are supposed to prevent efficient economic adjustments? In other words, how can we explain their 'flexible rigidities', as the title of a major book on Japanese industrial policy by Ronald Dore nicely puts it (Dore, 1986)?

In the following section of this chapter, we provide some theoretical discussion to help us explain this paradox, drawing on the works of Joseph Schumpeter, Herbert Simon, and other more recent works on institutional economics. In the final section, we provide an explanation of the 'flexible rigidities' of the East Asian economies, using the Japanese economy as the 'archetypal' East Asian economy, but with examples from Korea and Taiwan brought in wherever useful.

II SOME THOUGHTS ON FLEXIBILITY

The inevitability of rigidities

All rule-bound behaviour would be 'sub-optimal', if we possessed what Simon (1983) calls Olympian rationality. If agents have boundless abilities to absorb and process information, as is assumed in conventional economic theory, then rule-bound behaviour will inevitably limit their abilities fully to exploit profitable opportunities. Nevertheless, as Simon (1957, 1983) argued earlier and Heiner (1983) and Loasby (1991) elaborated more recently, agents with bounded rationality need some behavioural rules which limit the flexibility of their actions, in order to cope with the complexity of the world.[10] In other words, '[a]n omni-flexible world would be so uncertain [to the agents with bounded rationality] as to make action completely imposs-ible' (Nielsen, 1991: 8). Hayek's discussion of the role of 'tradition' is also based on the idea that the unquestioned acceptance of certain rules is necessary for the development of reasoned behaviour (Hayek, 1988: 11–28). On a less abstract level, Williamson and others have shown that in a world inhabited by agents with bounded rationality, a hierarchical mode of co-ordination, which restricts the flexibility of actions of its members, may be more efficient when investments involve asset specificity (Williamson, 1975 and 1985).

Thus seen, contrary to what the neo-liberal economists say, 'rigidities' are an essential part of our life, rather than 'artificial' fetters which would not exist except for the government or interest groups which are often beyond market discipline and only incompletely disciplined by representative democracy (the 'public choice' argument; see Mueller, 1979). Without certain rigidities, no complex system inhabited by agents with bounded rationality can be run efficiently, or run at all. Therefore, certain degrees of rigidities are a prerequisite for the existence of a complex modern economy. The kind of flexibility assumed to be ideal in the neo-liberal model may not be able to sustain anything more than an economy made up, to borrow Coase's analogy, of lone individuals exchanging nuts and berries on the edge of the forest (Coase, 1992: 718).

The inevitability of rigidity, however, does not mean that all existing rigidities are 'optimal' in the strict sense and therefore that there is no room for improvement. For one thing, our rationality which designs the rules is imperfect and cannot therefore construct an 'optimal' set (or sets) of rules (and hence rigidities) except perhaps at a very local level.[11] If we were so 'rational' as to be able to discover what is the optimal combination of flexibilities and rigidities for the entire economic system, we probably would not have needed any rules in the first place. Of course, some 'evolutionary' forces may ensure that 'better' rules have higher chances of survival, but at least within the timeframe which is relevant for many policy-making situ-ations, such forces are unlikely to come into full operation. Once estab-lished, all rules are difficult to change, and therefore can outlive their functions for a considerable time. One reason for this difficulty is that rules which do not claim to be (and, to an extent, are) beyond manipulation by calculating individuals will be very ineffective as rules. A rule which is too easily changeable is as good as no rule at all; rules therefore have to be difficult to change. Another reason for the difficulty of abolishing obsolete rules is that many of them need to be supported by investments in specific physical and human assets, which create incentives for those who made the investments to defend them against attempts to change the rules for the sake of more global interests.

Thus seen, we need to accept that certain rigidities are necessary for the existence and running of a complex system. Of course, this does not mean that all existing rules are optimal, because we cannot 'meta-optimise' by designing 'optimal' rigidities, and because dysfunctional rigidities will not necessarily be instantly 'selected against'. Rules are, by their very nature, difficult to change, and there may also be vested interests in sustaining certain dysfunctional rules. This means that any point in time there are bound to be lots of outdated and dysfunctional rules in a society.

However, does this mean that there is therefore nothing we can do to improve the world? According to Hayek (1988), the very belief that we can tinker with the existing 'spontaneous order', which is beyond all human comprehension (what he calls 'rational constructivism'), is the main source of trouble with modern societies. However, contrary to what Hayek says, the world is full of 'constructed orders', represented by large modern organisations, and not just 'spontaneous orders' emerging out of evolution; this is why Simon (1991) suggests that the modern economy is better described as the 'organisation economy' rather than the 'market economy'. However imperfect it may be, purposeful attempts to design new institutions and improve existing institutions is a defining characteristic of the human race.[12] The fact that such attempts at improvements are likely to be highly imperfect and sometimes even dysfunctional does not mean that there is no point in trying to improve things.

Short-run vs long-run flexibility

Many modern production technologies involve locking up resources in capital goods which are 'specific' to their current uses. And the same phenomenon of 'specificity' exists in respect of particular human skills, although in this case the problem is less severe because of the higher malleability of human beings (thanks to their ability to learn new things, although within clear limits). The limited resource mobility arising from asset specificity leads to a certain limit to the flexibility of the owner of that asset in responding to changing profit opportunities.[13] For example, the owner of a steel mill cannot quickly convert his or her factory into a computer factory simply because profits are higher in the computer industry; although this did happen to a Japanese steel producer, New Nippon Steel, which shifted part of its resources into the computer industry, it was only by means of purposeful long-range planning.

However, this does not mean that flexibility will necessarily be increased by the use of less 'specific' resources. Whether this is the case will depend on our timeframe. Locking up resources in specific capital goods or investing in specific skills definitely reduces the range of actions open to an agent. On the other hand, over time, investments in specific assets bring higher incomes (otherwise we would not live in a world full of specific assets), and higher incomes in general (if not necessarily) provide more options and therefore more flexibility. Chapter 6 in this book shows how low productivity was one of the major reasons behind the inability of the African continent to respond flexibly to external shocks. Moreover, higher incomes usually come about through a process of experience in production (except in the case of hitting upon mineral or other natural resources), which generates increased 'technological capabilities', which in turn will increase an agent's flexibility even further by allowing him to adopt courses of action which are not open to less 'capable' agents. An example of this is the ability of Japan to deal with an oil-price hike by the introduction of energy-saving production techniques, an option which is not open to, say, a very poor African country. Thus seen, using less specific assets may increase flexibility in the short run, but may reduce it in the long run. This means that there may be a certain trade-off between short-run and long-run flexibility in a modern economy which uses specific assets.

Schumpeter was a champion of this type of argument (Schumpeter, 1987). According to him, innovation, the crucial activity for growth in productivity, requires 'long-range planning' (pp. 102–3), which is possible only in a stable environment provided by what he calls 'monopolistic practices'. Obviously, such practices create rigidities in the firm's short-term response to changes in external conditions. However, according to Schumpeter, this does not mean that we should get rid of such rigidities, because 'in the spurts and vicissitudes of the process of creative destruction . . . perfect and instantaneous flexibility may even produce functionless catastrophes' (p. 105). Part of the reason is that short-run price wars during a recession in industries with large specific assets may result in 'unnecessary' bankruptcies, which are 'wasteful' from the social point of view (for a detailed argument, see Chang, 1994, Chapter 3). More importantly, however, it is because an unstable environment inhibits technical progress which often involves a long-term commitment of resources in specific assets, as Schumpeter himself and the modern scholars of technology and innovation have argued (see the essays in Dosi et al., 1988). Innovative activities also require 'learning' through repeated practice, which requires a stable environment and therefore may have to be supported by 'institutionalised routinised behaviour' (Johnson and Lundvall, 1991: 38).

In other words, in a world where productivity enhancement requires investment in resources with limited mobility, there exists a certain trade-off between short-run and long-run flexibility. A good example is the famous Just in Time (JIT), or 'lean', production system in the Japanese automobile industry, which operates on the basis of a well-connected and co-operative subcontracting network which can deliver inputs of consistent quality precisely on time (see Best, 1990; Womack *et al.*, 1991, for details). This system is said to have increased the flexibility of Japanese producers to cope with rapidly changing demands in the consumer market, but it required building a subcontracting network that can provide a timely delivery of inputs of consistent quality. And building this network meant that the short-run profits from being able to switch from one subcontractor to another according to their prices had to be sacrificed. In the short run, such investment certainly reduced flexibility of action, but in the long run the sacrifice of such short-run flexibility paid off in the form of greatly increased ability to cope with rapidly changing demands in the world market.[14]

We can extend this argument to the national level. Those who have invested in specific assets have an incentive to restrict the movement of other complementary assets which are more mobile, as they will suffer disproportionately from such movement. They will refuse to accept the 'market' outcome and will resort to 'collective action' in order to prevent the cuts in their incomes that follow from restructuring. One obvious way to reduce such resistances is to ban any collective action, as many neo-liberal economists argue. However, this may have an adverse consequence for the long-run flexibility of the economy, as it will discourage investments in specific assets which are often necessary for the enhancement of productivity, which in turn increases the long-run flexibility of the economy. Thus, an attempt to increase the short-run flexibility of the economy may result in a reduction in its long-run flexibility, if it reduces the 'safeguard' for investments in specific assets. This is an extension of the familiar argument in favour of 'socialisation of risk', with a modern twist.

The point, then, is that, when 'commitment' is necessary for productivity growth, too much possibility of 'exit' provided by the lack of 'rigidities' makes commitment too costly and therefore militates against that growth (on the concept of exit, see Hirschman, 1970). And if an expansion of wealth, and the increase in technological capabilities generated in the process of that expansion, increases an agent's (or a country's) ability to deal with changes in the long run (that is, increases the long-run flexibility of its actions), policies designed to increase short-run flexibility may impair long-run flexibility. If this is the case, limiting the short-run flexibility of certain aspects of the national economy may actually have a beneficial effect on its long-run flexibility. In the model of perfect competition which serves as the ideal bench-mark for neo-liberal economists, there is no conflict between long-run and short-run flexibilities only because perfect resource mobility (together with perfect foresight) is assumed. If this assumption does not hold, long-run flexibility may be obtained only at the cost of short-run rigidities, which suggests some serious flaws in neo-liberal policy prescriptions.

Individual vs national flexibility

When we talk about the flexibility of the national economy, we need to bear in mind that the national economy is a complex system made up of many agents (individuals and organisations). Neo-liberal economists assume uncritically that the maximum flexibility of the national economy is achieved by allowing maximum flexibilities for individual agents. However, flexible behaviour by some agents may result in a reduction in the overall flexibility of the national economy to which the agents belong (also see Chapter 2 of this book). A good example of this is the case of capital flight, where a flexible reaction on the part of individuals to a 'national' economic problem can lead to a foreign-exchange crisis and eventually to a collapse in investments, which will reduce the flexibility of the national economy in both the short and the long run.[15]

The point is that individuals, firms, or sectors in a national economy may react in the most flexible way to the changing environment, but with disastrous results for the flexibility of the national economy as a whole. It is no coincidence that the only survivor among the major debtors in the debt crises of the early 1980s was Korea, which exercised notoriously harsh control on the movement of foreign exchange out of the country, as mentioned earlier (see Note 3). If there is a conflict between individual and national flexibilities, it may be desirable from the point of view of the national economy to limit the flexibility of the actions of its constituent parts. But why is there this conflict between individual and systemic (in this case, national) economic flexibilities?

In the real world, different assets in a national economy have different mobilities partly because of their physical characteristics (e.g. specific capital goods have much less mobility than financial assets) but also due to the fact that they are subject to different degrees of restriction on their mobilities across national borders. For example, financial assets have much higher international mobility than, say, unskilled labour (which, being non-specific, is in fact quite mobile in its purely physical characteristic), partly because of politically determined restrictions on international migration. The trouble is that when the more mobile factors are allowed to move freely out of a national economy in search of better profit opportunities, the less mobile factors left behind may not be able to generate as much output as before. This will lead to a reduction in national income, which will reduce the ability of the national economy to respond flexibly to changes in the environment. Of course, this need not happen if the out-migrating factors repatriate their incomes, but there is no guarantee that this will happen.

If this is the case, there may be grounds for restricting the freedom of action of those who own resources which are highly mobile across national borders, especially liquid financial assets (for a similar argument, see Amadeo and Banuri, 1991). This certainly restricts the flexibility of the owners of such assets to respond to changing profit opportunities, but it may increase the flexibility of the national economy. Our earlier discussion on capital flight highlights this issue.

Thus, the differential mobility of different assets in a national economy creates the potential for conflict between national flexibility and the flexibility of its component parts. In a world with more than one nation, if different assets have different abilities to move across national borders, the flexibility of action of those who own the more mobile factors (e.g. financial capital, professionals with foreign language skills) may, under certain circumstances, result in a reduction in the national income and therefore actually reduce the flexibility of the national economy. If this is the case, there may be a reason to restrict the flexibility of action of some agents for the sake of the flexibility of the national economy.

III EXPLAINING FLEXIBLE RIGIDITIES IN EAST ASIA

In the previous section, we argued that a certain degree of rigidity is essential for the existence of all complex systems inhabited by agents with bounded rationality – which, needless to say, will include all real-world economies. We also pointed out that the neo-liberal argument that allowing freedom for individuals to react with maximum flexibility to changes in short-run relative prices is the best economic policy appears to be inadequate, because it may entail conflicts between short-run and long-run flexibilities, on the one hand, and between individual and national flexibilities, on the other hand. How do these points help us explain the 'flexible rigidities' of the East Asian economies?

Increasing the capability of the national economy

One distinguishing feature of the East Asian economies was that they were not satisfied with merely reacting to immediate changes in the economic environment (i.e. attaining short-run flexibility) but deliberately set about improving their resource base and technological capabilities, both of which gave them enhanced ability to deal with changes in the economic environment in the future (i.e. attaining long-run flexibility). To be sure, when faced with external shocks, they showed impressive ability in quickly switching the composition of their final demands by means of devaluation and real wage restraints. But the more important part of the story was that these adjustments were seen not simply as an exercise in getting short-run macroeconomic balances right but as one step within a continuous transformation of their economic structures towards the status of high-technology industries (what is called 'upgrading' by East Asian bureaucrats). In short, we can describe one purpose of state intervention in East Asia as that of increasing the long-run flexibility of the national economy (which will help the economy attain high growth, if nothing else) by increasing its capabilities, if necessary at the cost of suppressing short-run flexibility.

As discussed in the first section of this chapter, this policy orientation involved a wide range of forceful state interventions in almost all areas of the economy, most of which, in short, can be described as attempts to enhance the long-run flexibility of the economy, if necessary by suspending the price-responsiveness of firms in the short run.

One example is provided by the operation of state-supported cartels in Japan (for more details, see Okimoto, 1989; Singh, 1992; and Chang, 1994, Chapter 3). In Japan adjustment in the capacity of industries with large sunk costs was not left to the price mechanism, but was carefully controlled through investment cartels (to reduce excessive entry during a boom) and recession cartels (to prevent price wars and thereby excessive exit during a recession). This was because of the recognition that 'flexible' actions on the part of individual firms in the short run can have potentially harmful effects on the availability of investible resources and the accumulation of technological capabilities by means of production experience (learning-by-doing), which affect the long-run flexibility of the economy.

Another example is the policies to promote 'strategic' infant industries (e.g. steel, shipbuilding, automobile, electronics, etc.) through protection and various direct and indirect subsidies (for details, see Magaziner and Hout, 1980; Amsden, 1989). These policies provided the time and resources for the firms in these industries to accumulate technological capabilities through learning, which proved critical in their later foray into world markets. This inevitably involved limiting the flexibility of enterprises to operate in labour-intensive industries which were currently more lucrative according to short-run price signals, but, by increasing the capabilities of the national economy, it contributed to increasing the long-run flexibility of the economy.

Of course, as the neo-liberal economists will be only too willing to point out, the suspension of the price mechanism does not necessarily lead to the enhancement of the long-run flexibility of the economy, as we have seen in many developing countries. In East Asia, such a result was achieved because the state made it quite explicit that the suspensions of the price mechanism which it had initiated or supported were short-term measures intended to increase the long-run flexibility of the economy. Infant industries which failed to 'grow up' were wound down, import protection was gradually reduced as the protected industries acquired technological capability, and cartels were usually disbanded as soon as their aims were achieved.

In view of this observation, many commentators have rightly pointed out that the lessons other countries can draw from the East Asian experience may be limited, because the success of this policy regime depended critically on a strong state with commitment to long-run productivity growth, a situation which was 'unique' to the East Asian economies (see also Chapter

11 in this volume). Many have also pointed out other conditions which were 'unique' to them – for example, the large inflow of US aid into Korea and Taiwan in the 1950s, the start of their export drives under favourable world demand conditions, and (more controversially) Confucian culture – and which make their experience less than relevant to other countries.

It is undeniable that many (but not all) of these conditions are indeed unique. However, the 'uniqueness' of their experience should not mean that they are irrelevant for other countries (Chang, 1993; Wade, forthcoming). For one thing, the East Asian countries did not have a strong state committed to productivity growth from the beginning. The incompetence of the Kuomintang government before it moved to Taiwan and the incapacity of the Korean state during the 1950s show that construction of such a state is not something which is beyond human capacity. To take another example, Confucianism, especially given its disdain for commercial and industrial activities, is not necessarily conducive to economic development, any more than any other culture (Chang, 1993). More generally, all 'success' stories of industrialisation have their own 'unique' conditions which are difficult to replicate elsewhere – for example, the strong state in Bismarck's Germany, the abundant natural resources and the massive immigration into the USA in the late nineteenth century, the corporatist compromise in post-1930s Scandinavia, the efficient local governments in postwar Northern Italy – but that did not keep the 'follower' countries (including the East Asian ones) from learning from the previous success stories. There is no experience so unique as to prevent others from learning something from it, although what exactly is to be learned and to what degree from a particular experience is bound to be different for each country.

Systemic view of flexibility

Another important point in explaining 'flexible rigidities' in East Asia is the systemic view that the East Asian countries took of flexibility. They were under no illusion that maximum flexibility for individuals automatically led to maximum flexibility for the national economy. East Asian policy-makers acknowledged that certain types of individual flexibility could be harmful for national flexibility, and took measures to limit their extent.

One example of this policy is the restrictions on the outflow of capital (especially important in Korea and Japan in the earlier stages of development). Given the limited international mobility of labour, the potentially damaging effect of capital flight was recognised (see above), and state control therefore reduced the ability of the owners of financial assets to maximise their wealth by moving their assets across national borders. This also made their economies less vulnerable to the possibility of macroeconomic shocks turning into crises through the self-reinforcing process of capital flight. Needless to say, this statement should not be interpreted as meaning either that capital control is sufficient in itself for rapid economic growth (many developing countries provide counter-examples) or that without capital control countries will not grow (a good counter-example is Malaysia). However, it is clear that in East Asia reducing the flexibility of individual actors to use their financial power contributed to national flexibility.

As another example, let us take the case of controls on the importation of technology. Policy-makers in these countries recognised that, in the face of technological interdependence, allowing individual producers to choose their technologies according to the changes in returns on different factors might well lead to an economic structure which reduced the overall ability of the system to react flexibly to changing world market situations. (In fact this was a critical insight behind many early theories of industrialisation like those of Rosenstein-Rodan and Hirschman; see Chapter 2 of this volume). This meant that, despite their eagerness to import foreign technologies, the East Asian policy-makers carefully controlled technology imports in accordance with national development projects.

It was accepted that allowing flexible adjustment of prices to individual producers in industries with large sunk and/or specific assets might some-times lead to an unnecessary destruction of those industries (see Chang, 1994, Chapter 3), thereby reducing the resource base of the national econ-omy and long-term (if not necessarily short-term) flexibility. Consequently, various restraints were imposed on the terms on which private (and public) enterprises could compete with each other, in such a way as to reduce such potential damage.

Of course, it is quite inadequate to suggest that imposing controls on private-sector decisions is enough to secure national flexibility. That this is not the case is too well known to need further discussion. However, there are clearly cases where individual flexibilities clash with national flexibility (as we have discussed above), and the willingness and ability of East Asian states to impose restrictions on individual behaviour in such cases proved beneficial for their national economy's flexibility.

Moreover, we are by no means suggesting that the East Asian economies succeeded because they each operated like a single enterprise in which the interest of the parts is categorically suppressed via a hierarchical decision-making mechanism, as the proponents of the 'Japan Inc.' view would lead us to believe. Although it is quite correct to point out that individual flexibili-ties were often suppressed for the sake of national flexibility, the picture is much more complex.

For one thing, the process involved a complex system of political bargain-ing, which we shall discuss in more detail below. Moreover, we have to square the fact of higher incidences of co-operation among private sector agents in East Asia with the widely acknowledged existence of fierce compe-tition among the same set of firms. Of course, these two observations are not necessarily incompatible. Collusive behaviour among East Asian firms is often confined to precisely defined areas with specific purposes (e.g. rationalisation cartels to keep firms which are upgrading their equipment from being undercut in the short run by those which are exploiting the upgraders' teething problems), and therefore does not suppress competition in general. And if one is willing to accept that, in a world where specific investments and 'learning' are necessary for productivity growth, it will immediately be realised that the possibility of socially beneficial co-operation (or collusion, if you will) is much greater than what is usually suggested by conventional welfare economics (e.g. infrastructure, education, health).

The politics of flexible rigidities

Another important key to explaining the 'flexible rigidities' of the East Asian economies is the explicit and implicit acceptance on the part of their policy-makers and private sector agents of the fundamentally 'political' nature of the market. While these policy-makers would agree with the neo-liberals that producer groups may organise to prevent the reallocation of resources with undesirable social consequences, they did not share the neo-liberal dream of sanitising the resource reallocation process of politics by means of deregulation (which presumably would make it pointless to bring political pressures to bear on the state). They implicitly recognised that, in a world full of immobile assets, deregulation would not necessarily eliminate incentives to resist structural change by means of 'political' action, and therefore accepted that conflicts arising during the process of large-scale structural change are better managed in an explicitly 'political' manner rather than simply left to take care of themselves (on the notion of conflict management, see Amadeo and Banuri, 1991; for its discussion in a 'dynamic' context, see Chang and Rowthorn, forthcoming, Chapter 2, and Chang, forthcoming). Industrial policy in East Asia therefore openly incorporates a 'political' element in its design and implementation.

One good example is the successful scaling-down of certain Japanese industries in the 1970s (for details, see Dore, 1986). When faced with the need to shut down certain labour-intensive and energy-intensive industries, the Japanese state did not allow the 'natural' forces of the market to take over wholesale. Instead, it encouraged the producer groups to strike deals which were unashamedly 'political'. As a result, the final deals on restructuring partly reflected considerations of national economic efficiency in the narrow sense – for example, the acceptable (but not necessarily 'optimal') vintage structure of the capital stock – but also considerations like the power of the status quo (current market shares) and the question of fairness (large firms bearing larger burdens). For example, in the case of the Japanese shipbuilding industry,

[t]he large companies and efficiency-oriented civil servants wanted to

see the big companies cut capacity, and many of the small companies to close down. The small companies wanted the large ones to take all the cuts. Companies which had newly invested in up-to-date berths . . . wanted special exemptions.

(Dore, 1986: 145)

In this particular case, reflecting the concern for 'fairness' which was essential if the deal was not to be vetoed by the smaller producers, exit was ruled out and cuts were graduated to the size of the firm, ranging from 40 per cent for the seven biggest firms to 15 per cent for the twenty-one smallest (Dore, 1986: 145).

Another example is provided by the so-called Industrial Reorganisation Programme of 1980 in Korea, where the state openly intervened to streamline the heavy industries which were in trouble and forced the private sector firms to strike deals on exits, mergers, market-sharing by means of segmentation, and market swapping in several industries (for details, see Chang, 1993).[16] There was no compelling economic reason why the deals had to be struck in the ways they were. In fact, as almost none of the companies involved in the restructuring were making a profit, there was no reason to believe that any of these deals made 'economic' sense. If the only concern was immediate profitability, all these enterprises should have been closed down. However, things could have been worse if these deals had not been struck at all, and striking openly 'political' deals seemed to be the only way to do it, as most of the enterprises involved were members of powerful conglomerates who could veto, or at least delay, the whole restructuring process.

Neo-liberal economists would argue that such 'political' management of the resource reallocation process is undesirable, because it reduces the economy's flexibility. However, when it comes to a large-scale structural change, 'political' management of the process may in fact increase the flexibility of the economy in the long run, by preventing the industries from being stuck in a costly 'war of attrition'. Our case is further corroborated by the Scandinavian experience, where the most 'rigid' labour markets produce 'flexible' adjustments by providing safeguards to the workers for their investment in skills by means of a combination of unemployment benefits, relocation assistance, and retraining (Pekkarinen et al., 1992). In other words, when specific assets are involved and there are therefore incentives for political renegotiation of current market prices (which, as we argued above, is totally justifiable under certain circumstances), resource reallocation may be facilitated by explicitly facing up to such pressures rather than by denying their existence and pretending that the 'market solution' is somehow 'natural'. Although 'excessive' (given the capacity of the state and the balance of power between groups) politicisation of economic policymaking is not desirable, it is equally undesirable that we should pretend that politics has nothing to do with economics (see also Note 4).

IV CONCLUDING REMARKS

In this chapter, we have argued that there are good theoretical reasons to believe that all complex modern economies with specific assets and non-off-the-shelf technology require various institutional 'rigidities' in order to socialise risk in specific investments and provide a stable environment for learning. In such a world, we argued, there is an inherent conflict between short-run and long-run flexibilities, as short-run flexibilities may discourage productivity-enhancing investments, which are likely to increase long-run flexibility by providing a larger resource base and increased technological capabilities. We also argued that, in a world which has more than one national economy and assets with different mobilities, allowing individuals total flexibility may lead to a reduction in the flexibility of the national economy, because it may reduce the resource base and hamper the growth of productivity in the national economy.

The East Asian cases provide ample examples to support our arguments. These economies are full of 'rigidities' of the kinds which the neo-liberal economists usually associate with economic failures, but have shown remarkable flexibilities at the national level. The explanation of these 'flexible rigidities' is found in the ability of their states and private-sector agents to develop institutions which enhance long-run national flexibilities at the cost of short-run individual flexibilities. It was also argued that, by acknowledging the inherently 'political' nature of the resource reallocation process in a world full of specific assets, these economies were able to devise policies which facilitated the restructuring process by incorporating political considerations into their implementation.

To conclude, our discussion shows that the neo-liberal ideal of a regulation-free and collusion-free economy is, even if it can be obtained, not desirable in a world where agents have limited capacity to process information and where productivity growth requires specific investments and learning. If the neo-liberal programme of deregulation and opening-up is ill-suited for the purpose of constructing flexible national economies, we need to start our search for an alternative programme which is both politically more realistic and institutionally richer. This, in turn, will require some serious rethinking about the costs and benefits of competition and co-operation, the relationship between the economic and the political, and the theory of institutional change and the role of the state in it. The experience of East Asia may provide some 'spicy' food for that rethinking.

APPENDIX

'Failures' of East Asian Industrial Policy – a comment on the World Bank's *East Asian Miracle* Study

The World Bank study (1993) (henceforth called the Report) claims that in East Asia, and especially in Korea (which consistently comes out as supporting the Bank's view on every criterion), 'promoting specific industries generally did not work' (p. 354). This is argued on the following grounds. First, the changes in the sectoral composition of industries were 'market conforming'. Secondly, 'activities that were not promoted (for example, textiles) had TFP [total factor productivity] performance as impressive as those that were' (p. 316). Thirdly, there were significant financial costs associated with such a policy (for example, Box 6.3 on Korea). All three points look robust at first sight, but once we probe deeper they reveal a number of factual and methodological problems. Let us take each of these arguments in turn, referring basically to the Korean case (which should be to the Bank's advantage).

In relation to the 'structural' argument, the Report argues that the Korean industrial structure was not very different from what would be expected from a projection based on factor endowments. This is claimed on the grounds that: (i) the Korean textile and clothing industry, which the Report regards as the quintessential labour-intensive sector, is much larger than the international norm (Table 6.15 and pp. 313–14); (ii) there is a negative correlation between the changes in an industry's share in total manufacturing value added (MVA) and its level of wage or value added per worker (p. 315 and pp. 330–4).

A big problem with this argument is that we cannot equate 'high wage' (used in the Report as a proxy for capital intensity) or 'high value added' sectors with 'promoted' industries. There were all sorts of reasons other than a high value added component or high capital intensity to promote an industry, including in particular its foreign-exchange earning capability. The prominent case in point is in fact the textile industry, which the Report regards as one of the 'activities that were not promoted' (p. 316), when it was, in fact, one of the most heavily promoted industries. Primarily thanks to its foreign-exchange earning capacity, it was one of the seven industries provided with a special 'promotional law' (for details, see Chang, 1993). And as the major export industry, it received a large amount of subsidised 'export loans' at interest rates well below the official deposit rates (and substantially negative throughout the 1970s) and also other subsidies and tax rebates which were not available to more 'domestic-market-oriented' industries (for details, see Amsden, 1989). Thus, the fact that Korea has an 'exceptionally large' textile and clothing industry is not proof that industrial policy did not work but in fact suggests that it worked really well, as this was one of the most heavily promoted sectors. Add to this the fact that Korea has an 'exceptionally large' metal products and machinery sector (Table 6.15), which even according to the Report itself was the result of selective industrial policy, and there is very little basis for arguing that 'industrial policy only marginally altered industrial structure' (p. 312). The second component of the industrial structure argument based on the correlation analysis also falls, as there is no simple correspondence between the degree of 'promotion' and the level of an industry's wages or value-added per worker.

More fundamentally, in arguing that the East Asian countries would have developed their current production structure without state intervention, the Report is assuming that this structure would have evolved through market forces. However, this assumption ignores the fact that there are formidable entry barriers for developing countries attempting to move up the ladder of the international division of labour – because of cumulative causations in technical progress (as emphasised even by recent mainstream literature on new growth theory), imperfect domestic and international financial markets (which the Report itself, in Chapter 5, admits to be substantial), and a lack of marketing skills and infrastructure, and so on. Thus, without the full-scale backing of the state, few 'new' industries set up in Korea and other 'industrial policy states' in East Asia would have been able to organise their finances, let alone become competitive in the world market by accumulating technological and marketing capabilities. In the absence of an actual example of market-based progress towards an advanced industrial economy during the last century or so (barring the exceptional case of the colonial city-state, Hong Kong), we have yet to see whether the assumption is true that 'advanced' industries are likely to spring up on their own in developing countries.

Regarding the TFP argument, we should first of all point out that this argument also suffers from the 'mistaken identity problem' discussed above (especially with respect to the textile industry). Secondly, the evidence on sectoral TFP growth is ambiguous even from the studies which the Report actually uses. For example, one of the TFP studies cited, namely, Dollar and Sokoloff (1990) shows (in Table 4) a quite different result from the table in the Report (Table 6.16) concerning relative rankings of different industries in terms of TFP growth. This is obviously because measuring TFP is fraught with problems. As Abramovitz (1989) points out, the result will depend critically on all sorts of underlying assumptions about the shape of production functions, the adjustment made for the improving 'quality' of inputs (especially the supply of a more educated labour force), and assumptions regarding the 'interaction' between technology, physical capital, and human capital. In the case of a country like Korea, which experienced very rapid structural change, the result will also critically depend on the period covered. For example, the Report uses data for 1966–85, but in at least the first half of this period, many 'promoted' industries did not get promoted and, worse still, many of them did not even exist in their modern forms (e.g. iron and steel, shipbuilding, semiconductors). For some industries which started in the late 1970s (e.g. heavy machinery, automobiles), the period covered is almost irrelevant, once we allow for a period of 'maturation' of several years.

A yet more fundamental question is whether TFP growth is the single best indicator of the 'success' or otherwise of an industry. Chang (1993) shows the impressive balance-of-payments contributions made in the late 1980s by those Korean industries 'promoted' through the Heavy and Chemical Industrialisation (HCI) programme in the 1970s. The 'promoted' industries could also generate spillovers which are not captured by sectoral TFP growth figures. The Report uses TFP growth at the 2-digit level on the grounds that 'spillover' exists only within the boundary of 2-digit sectors, stating that a recent study 'on the pattern of spillovers of R&D in industrial economies demonstrates that the major beneficiaries are closely related sectors, often sectors that would be identified with a two-digit classification' (p. 326). However, this study, which is on R&D spillovers in industrial economies, is of only limited relevance for developing economies, where more important forms of spillover may be such things as the formation of a skilled labour force and the increase in generalised engineering capability.

The Report's third line of argument against industrial policy is that it incurs costs in the forms of: (i) direct fiscal/financial costs in the form of subsidies through policy loans and tax exemptions; (ii) costs from 'writing off' the principal of non-performing loans; (iii) the issuance of subsidised funds to 'rationalised' firms and preferential access to Central Bank discounts. This argument also has problems. First, the fact that the HCI programme had certain 'costs' is beside the point. The object of the exercise was to obtain long-run benefits even if some short-run costs were incurred. The important point is: what was the net benefit? Secondly, it has to be pointed out that how big one believes these 'costs' to have been depends on the counterfactual one employs, as even the Report itself admits in its sombre moments. Even if we accept the counterfactuals assumed in Box 6.3, the cost is grossly overestimated, because the non-performing loans were largely accounted for by the construction and shipping industries, which had very little to do with the HCI programme. According to Amsden (forthcoming), the construction industry alone accounted for 60 per cent of the non-performing loans.

NOTES

I want to thank Ronald Dore, Herbert Simon, and Hugh Whittaker for helpful suggestions, and Bob Rowthorn, Hans Singer, Ajit Singh, John Toye, and Robert Wade for discussing some of the ideas presented in the appendix.

1 Between 1950 and 1987, per capita income in Japan grew at 6 per cent p.a., 3 percentage points above the average of the sixteen largest OECD economies

(including Japan), the next best performers being Austria and West Germany, which grew at 3.9 per cent and 3.8 per cent p.a. respectively. During the same period, Taiwan grew at 6.1 per cent p.a., making it the fastest growing economy in the world, while Korea, at 5.5 per cent was in the third place in the world league, after Taiwan and Japan. See Maddison (1989) for details.

2 While there are notable differences in various areas between the three countries – for example, state ownership of banks (absent in Japan), the importance of public enterprises (very important in Taiwan, important in Korea, relatively unimportant in Japan), the role of private sector conglomerates (unimportant in Taiwan), the emphasis on heavy and chemical industries (less important in Taiwan), and so on (see also in Chapter 9 of this volume), there are significant commonalities among them which warrant talk of an 'East Asian model'. Such commonalities include: the commanding heights occupied by the state in the economy; the importance of an activist elite bureaucracy; the dominance of the executive branch of the state over the legislature; the prominence given to industrial policy.

3 Korea's survival of the debt crisis is due to many factors, whose relative importance is a matter of debate. Frequently cited reasons include: a 'better' use of the funds borrowed in the sense that they were not consumed but were largely invested, particularly in foreign-exchange-generating activities; the continued commitment on the part of policy-makers to exporting which gave confidence to the creditors; the tight control on capital outflow, which prevented the capital flight which magnified the impact of the debt crisis in other debtor countries; and other more 'historically contingent' factors, such as the limited exposure to the so-called 'contagion effect' (see Sachs, 1989; Hughes and Singh, 1991).

4 Of course, describing all government regulations and collective actions as 'artificial' and somehow going against the 'natural' order of the market is one important characteristic of most mainstream economics, and not just neo-liberal economics. This belief in the institutional primacy of the market stems from the belief in the market as a self-contained and self-regulating machine (Polanyi, 1957), which is separable from other spheres of life, in particular the political. However, all markets are basically 'political' at least for two reasons. First, the establishment and distribution of property rights and other entitlements is a highly political exercise. Secondly, at least one fundamental set of prices which affect all sectors of the economy, namely, wage rates, are determined by the 'politically' decided restrictions on international migration. Historically, also, states created markets, rather than the other way around, as depicted in the Contractarian myth (Chang, 1994, Chapter 1; also see Coase, 1988). In short, the border between the 'economic' and the 'political' is fuzzy. We were clearly reminded of this in the recent British coal crisis, when the British miners were told to accept 'world market' prices, which turned out to be determined by the 'political' decisions of the German government to subsidise their coal, of the French government to allow the export of their subsidised nuclear electricity, and of the Colombian government to allow child labour in their mines, and so on.

5 One additional ingredient in the neo-liberal agenda is privatisation, which space does allow us to discuss in this chapter. For some criticisms of the neo-liberal arguments in favour of privatisation and some alternative perspectives, see Chang and Singh, 1993; Rowthorn and Chang, 1993.

6 For example, as late as 1988, Balassa was arguing that 'apart from the promotion of shipbuilding and steel', the role of the state in Korea 'has been to create a modern infrastructure, to provide a stable incentive system, and to ensure that government bureaucracy will help rather than hinder exports' (Balassa, 1988: S286).

7 On Japan, see Johnson (1982); Dore (1986, 1987); Okimoto (1989); Sheridan (1993). On Korea, see Jones and Sakong (1980); Amsden (1989); Chang (1993). On Taiwan, see Amsden (1985); Wade (1990).

8 For example, it is interesting to note that one labour law in (the then) West Germany particularly heavily criticised by a leading proponent of Eurosclerosis, namely, the priority of severance pay over other obligations in cases of bankruptcy (Giersch, 1986: 16), is practised in as anti-labour a country as Korea (see You and Chang, 1993).

9 Koike (1987) points out that lifetime employment and the seniority wage system are in fact not unique to Japan, as most white-collar workers in all OECD economies (including Japan) enjoy them. According to him, what is unique in Japan is that a sizeable section of the blue-collar workers also enjoy them.

10 And Heiner argues that the rigidity in behavioural rules should be higher for agents with less intelligence.

11 Loasby (1991) sums up the point in a succinct way: 'We try to make sense of the world by imposing patterns on it, and sticking to them as long as they are tolerably successful in allowing us to feel that we understand what we observe and what we experience (p. 6). . . . People prefer not to have to think; but what they like even less is the feeling that they do not understand, and in such a situation they are driven to seek an explanation. A satisfactory explanation is one that will somehow associate the disturbing phenomenon with what is already familiar, and thus restore a pattern of coherence (p. 7).'

12 The simple but rarely recognised fact that there is a wide-ranging institutional diversity even among the countries which are usually classified as 'capitalist' supports this observation (on the question of institutional diversity of capitalism, see Chang and Kozul-Wright, 1994).

13 With the rise of so-called flexible manufacturing, this characteristic of modern production may have been partly alleviated, as more machines have now become more general, thanks to computer technology (Piore and Sabel, 1984; Best, 1990). But it is unlikely that flexible manufacturing will become the dominant mode of industrialisation in the foreseeable future, especially in developing countries (Schmitz, 1988).

14 Also, from the point of view of the subcontracting firms and the workers, the involvement in JIT imposed the short-run cost of not being able to reap gains by cleverly using 'exit' options, although again in the long run they benefited from the increased flexibility and hence competitive success of their 'mother' firm (in the case of the subcontractors) or their firms (in the case of the workers).

15 Needless to say, this statement should not be interpreted as meaning that imposing capital controls will on its own lead to greater national flexibility.

16 Under this programme, four existing companies in the power-generating equipment industry were merged into Korea Heavy Industries and Construction Co. (KHIC), which was subsequently nationalised on the ground that the state support needed to make it profitable was too big to be given to a single private firm. In the passenger car industry, one of the three existing producers (Kia) was forced to exit and specialise in trucks and buses with a promise that it would be allowed re-entry when demand picked up; this actually occurred. One of the three companies in the naval diesel engine industry (Daewoo) was forced to exit, and the other two were obliged to split the market into two segments and specialise (Hyundai in over-6,000 hp and Ssangyong in under-6,000 hp engines). In heavy electrical machinery industry, where there were eight companies, three (Hyosung, Ssangyong and Kolon) were merged into one (Hyosung) and allowed to produce only highly specialised and expensive products. A subsidiary of

Hyundai was asked to produce only for its sister companies. Four other minor companies were forced to produce only less sophisticated and cheaper products. Each of the four companies in the electronic switching system industry (Samsung, Gold Star, OPC, and Daewoo) was forced to specialise in a different product. The two companies in the copper smelting industry were merged by forcing one to buy the other' s equity, supported by equity participation by the state-owned Korea Development Bank (KDB) and a moratorium on the repayment of bank loans.

REFERENCES

Abramovitz, M. (1989) 'Thinking about growth', in *Thinking about Growth and Other Essays on Economic Growth and Welfare*, Cambridge: Cambridge University Press.

Amadeo, E. and T. Banuri (1991) 'Policy, governance, and the management of conflict', in T. Banuri (ed.) *Economic Liberalisation: No Panacea*, Oxford: Clarendon Press.

Amsden, A. (1985) 'The state and Taiwan's economic development', in P. Evans, D. Rueschemeyer and T. Skocpol (eds) *Bringing the State Back In*, Cambridge: Cambridge University Press.

—— (1989) *Asia's Next Giant*, New York: Oxford University Press.

—— (1992) 'Can Eastern Europe compete by "Getting the prices right"?', Political Economy Working Paper no. 37, New York: New School for Social Research.

—— (forthcoming) 'Why isn't the whole world using the East Asian model to develop?: Review of the World Bank's *East Asian Miracle Report*', *World Development*.

Amsden, A. and Y-D. Euh (1990) 'Republic of Korea's financial reform: what are the lessons?', UNCTAD Discussion Paper no. 30, Geneva: UNCTAD.

Balassa, B. (1988) 'The Lessons of East Asian development: an overview', *Economic Development and Cultural Change* 36(3), supplement: S273–90.

Best, M. (1990) *The New Competition*, Cambridge: Polity Press.

Bhaduri, A. (1991) 'Conventional stabilisation and the East European transition', Vienna: Vienna Institute for Comparative Economic Studies, mimeo.

Bhagwati, J. (1988) *Protectionism*, Cambridge, MA: MIT Press.

Blanchard, O., R. Dornbusch, P. Krugman, R. Layard and L. Summers (1991) *Reform in Eastern Europe*, Cambridge, MA: MIT Press.

Chang, H-J. (1993) 'The Political Economy of Industrial Policy in Korea', *Cambridge Journal of Economics* 17(2): 131–57.

—— (1994) *The Political Economy of Industrial Policy*, London and Basingstoke: Macmillan.

—— (forthcoming) 'State, institutions and structural change', in *Structural Change and Economic Dynamics*.

Chang, H-J. and P. Nolan (eds) (forthcoming) *Reforming the Communist Economies – Against the Mainstream*, London and Basingstoke: Macmillan.

Chang, H-J. and R. Kozul-Wright (1994) 'Organising development: comparing the national systems of entrepreneurship in Sweden and South Korea', *Journal of Development Studies*.

Chang, H-J. and B. Rowthorn (eds) (forthcoming) *Role of the State in Economic Change*, Oxford: Oxford University Press.

Chang, H-J. and A. Singh (1993) 'Public enterprises in developing countries and economic efficiency – a critical examination of analytical, empirical, and policy issues', *UNCTAD Review* no. 4: 45–82.

Coase, R. (1988) 'The firm, the market, and the law', in *The Firm, the Market, and the Law*, Chicago: University of Chicago Press.
—— (1992) 'The institutional structure of production', *American Economic Review* 82(4): 713–19.
Colclough, C. (1991) 'Structuralism versus neo-liberalism: an introduction', in C. Colclough and J. Manor (eds), *States or Markets? Neo-liberalism and the Development of Policy Debate*, Oxford: Clarendon Press.
Dollar, D. and K. Sokoloff (1990) 'Patterns of productivity growth in South Korean manufacturing industries, 1963–79', *Journal of Development Economics* 33(2): 309–27.
Dore, R. (1986) *Flexible Rigidities: Industrial Policy and Structural Adjustment in the Japanese Economy 1970–80*, London: Athlone Press.
—— (1987) *Taking Japan Seriously – A Confucian Perspective on Leading Economic Issues*, London: Athlone Press.
Dosi, G., C. Freeman, R. Nelson, G. Silverberg and L. Soete (eds) (1988) *Technical Change and Economic Theory*, London: Pinter Publishers.
Giersch, H. (1986) *Liberalisation for Faster Economic Growth*, Occasional Paper no. 74, London: Institute of Economic Affairs.
Hayek, F. (1988) *The Fatal Conceit – The Errors of Socialism*, London: Routledge.
Heiner, R. (1983) 'The origin of predictable behavior', *American Economic Review* 73(4): 560–95.
Hirschman, A. (1970) *Exit, Voice, and Loyalty*, Cambridge, MA: Harvard University Press.
Hughes, A. and A. Singh (1991) 'The world economic slowdown and the Asian and Latin American economies: a comparative analysis of economic structure, policy, and performance', in T. Banuri (ed.) *Economic Liberalisation: No Panacea*, Oxford: Clarendon Press.
Johnson, B. and B. Lundvall (1991) 'Flexibility and institutional learning', in B. Jessop, H. Kaastendiek, K. Nielsen and O. Pedersen (eds) *The Politics of Flexibility – Restructuring State and Industry in Britain, Germany, and Scandinavia*, Aldershot: Edward Elgar.
Johnson, C. (1982) *MITI and the Japanese Miracle*, Stanford, CA: Stanford University Press.
Jones, L. and I. Sakong (1980) *Government, Business and Entrepreneurship in Economic Development: The Korean Case*, Cambridge, MA: Harvard University Press.
Koike, K. (1987) 'Human resource development and labour–management relations', in K. Yamamura and Y. Yasuba (eds) *The Political Economy of Japan*, vol. 1, Stanford, CA: Stanford University Press.
Krueger, A. (1980) 'Trade policy as an input to development', *American Economic Review*, 64(3): 288–92.
Lal, D. (1983) *The Poverty of Development Economics*, London: Institute of Economic Affairs.
Little, I. (1982) *Economic Development*, New York: Basic Books.
Loasby, B. (1991) *Equilibrium and Evolution*, Manchester: Manchester University Press.
Maddison, A. (1989) *The World Economy in the 20th Century*, Paris: OECD.
Magaziner, I. and T. Hout (1980) *Japanese Industrial Policy*, London: Policy Studies Institute.
Mueller, D. (1979) *Public Choice*, Cambridge: Cambridge University Press.
Nielsen, K. (1991) 'Towards a Flexible Future – Theories and Politics' in B. Jessop, H. Kaastendiek, K. Nielsen and O. Pedersen (eds) *The Politics of Flexibility –*

Restructuring State and Industry in Britain, Germany, and Scandinavia, Aldershot: Edward Elgar.

Okimoto, D. (1989) *Between MITI and the Market: Japanese Industrial Policy for High Technology*, Stanford, CA: Stanford University Press.

Olson, M. (1982) *The Rise and Decline of Nations*, New Haven, CT: Yale University Press.

Pekkarinen, J., M. Pohjola and B. Rowthorn (eds) (1992) *Social Corporatism*, Oxford: Clarendon Press.

Piore, M. and C. Sabel (1984) *The Second Industrial Divide*, New York: Basic Books.

Polanyi, K. (1957) *The Great Transformation*, Boston, MA: Beacon Press.

Rowthorn, B. and H-J. Chang (1993) 'Public ownership and the theory of the state', in T. Clarke and C. Pitelis (eds) *The Political Economy of Privatisation*, London: Routledge.

Sachs, J. (ed.) (1989) *Developing Country Debt and the World Economy*, Chicago and London: University of Chicago Press.

Sako, M. (1993) *Prices, Quality and Trust*, Cambridge: Cambridge University Press.

Schmitz, H. (1988) 'Flexible specialisation – a new paradigm of small-scale industrialisation?', IDS Discussion Paper no. 261, University of Sussex.

Schumpeter, J. (1987) *Capitalism, Socialism and Democracy*, 6th edition, London: Unwin Paperbacks.

Sheridan, K. (1993) *Governing the Japanese Economy*, Cambridge: Polity Press.

Simon, H. (1957) *Administrative Behaviour*, 3rd edition, New York: Free Press.

—— (1983) *Reason in Human Affairs*, Oxford: Basil Blackwell.

—— (1991) 'Organisations and markets', *Journal of Economic Perspectives*, 5(2): 25–44.

Singh, A. (1992) '"Close" vs. "strategic" integration with the world economy and the "market-friendly approach to development" vs. an "Industrial policy": a critique of the World Development Report 1991 and an alternative policy perspective', Cambridge University, Faculty of Economics and Politics, mimeo.

Somel, C. (1992) 'Finance for growth: Lessons from Japan', UNCTAD Discussion Paper no. 44, Geneva: UNCTAD.

Toye, J. (1991) 'Is there a neo-political economy of development?', in C. Colclough and J. Manor (eds) *States or Markets? Neo-liberalism and the Development of Policy Debate*, Oxford: Clarendon Press.

Wade, R. (1990) *Governing the Market*, Princeton, NJ: Princeton University Press.

—— (forthcoming) 'The role of the state in East Asia', in H-J. Chang and B. Rowthorn (eds) *Role of the State in Economic Change*, Oxford: Oxford University Press.

Williamson, O. (1975) *Markets and Hierarchies; Analysis and Antitrust Implications*, New York: Free Press.

—— (1985) *The Economic Institutions of Capitalism*, New York: Free Press.

Womack, J., D. Jones and D. Roos (1991) *The Machine that Changed the World: The Story of Lean Production*, New York: Harper Perennial.

World Bank (1987) *World Development Report*, New York: Oxford University Press.

—— (1991) *World Development Report*, New York: Oxford University Press.

—— (1993) *The East Asian Miracle – Economic Growth and Public Policy*, New York: Oxford University Press.

You, J. and H-J. Chang (1993) 'The myth of free labour market in Korea', *Contributions to Political Economy* 12: 29–46.

8

A COMPARATIVE STUDY OF FLEXIBILITY IN THE RESPONSE OF NATIONAL ECONOMIES TO THE OIL-PRICE SHOCKS

Peter Smith and Alistair Ulph

I INTRODUCTION

In this chapter we consider what light can be thrown on the question of why some countries are able to respond more flexibly than others to various shocks. This is done by considering the responses to the oil-price shocks of the 1970s and 1980s. We begin with a brief account of the oil-price shocks, followed by an equally brief discussion of what we mean by flexibility, what factors might affect flexibility, and whether it is possible to give some empirical content to the notion of flexibility. In particular (in Part II) we shall attempt to develop an index of the degree of flexibility of different countries.

As we shall discuss in Part II, there are two forms of adjustment to oil-price shocks that countries need to carry out, and two levels at which these adjustments can be studied. The first form of adjustment is the microeconomic response, which focuses on adjustments that take place within the oil market or (more broadly) the energy markets. Faced with an oil-price increase, countries should seek to reduce their demand for oil and expand their domestic supply of oil or oil substitutes. This can take place at the level of individual households and firms, whose responses can be broadly summarised by considering elasticities of supply and demand, and at the level of government policy, which can both affect the speed with which exogenous changes in prices get transmitted to domestic markets and may supplement individual responses to market prices, perhaps because of market failures. Part III will examine the evidence on individual market responses, while Part IV considers government microeconomic policy responses.

The second form of adjustment to oil-price shocks relates to the macroeconomic response, reflecting the fact that if oil is a significant part of a country's trade, then large oil-price shocks will imply large transfers of resources between oil-importing and oil-exporting countries, which individual countries will need to accommodate by adjustments in domestic factor rewards and the allocation of resources between traded and non-traded sectors of the economy. In principle, these adjustments will require responses at both the individual and the government level, but since many of the individual responses relate to issues of labour market flexibility and trade flexibility covered elsewhere in this book, we shall focus only on the government level of responses. Part V deals with the macroeconomic response.

II OIL-PRICE SHOCKS AND FLEXIBILITY: SOME GENERAL CONSIDERATIONS

The nature of the oil-price shocks that occurred in the 1970s and 1980s is now familiar, and can be summarised in Figure 8.1 which shows the real dollar price of oil (chosen because oil prices are denominated in dollars). This shows that after two decades in which the nominal oil price remained almost constant, with the real price drifting downwards, real oil prices began rising from 1970, and climbed sharply in 1973 when the nominal price tripled. A further tripling occurred in 1978–9. Oil prices were successively cut during the period 1980–5 and collapsed sharply in 1985, since when they have fluctuated around a relatively constant level. Various explanations have been advanced to explain this pattern of oil prices (see Cremer and Salehi-Isfahani, 1991; Heal and Chichilnisky, 1991 for useful summaries). However, commentators are agreed that over this period the oil market underwent a profound structural change, from a situation of strong vertical integration through the major oil companies, with the oil price being virtually a transfer price, to a situation where production and consumption decisions are taken independently and linked by arm's-length trade through active spot and futures markets. The oil market is now much more like a conventional market for primary products, so that in addition to the major price changes that constituted the three oil-price shocks (the increases in 1973 and 1978–9 and the collapse in 1985), there is now more short-term volatility in the price. Most of our discussion will focus on the three oil-price shocks, rather than the increased volatility of prices.

To assess the flexibility with which countries adapted to these oil-price shocks, we need first to discuss briefly what we mean by flexibility. If we are to ask questions about whether increased flexibility implies that economies will perform more successfully, we have to be able to define flexibility in a way which is not simply synonymous with success. We shall argue that one can go further than this, in that there need not even be a monotonic relationship between flexibility and success; in other words, there is a notion of an optimal level of flexibility, implying that beyond some point increasing flexibility will be harmful.

At the level of individual agents, the question of flexibility arises when

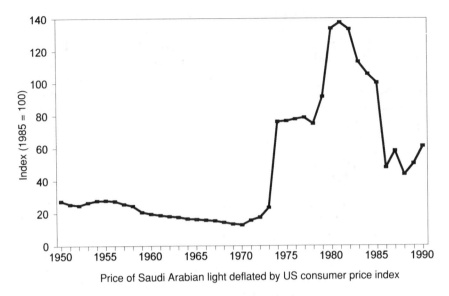

Price of Saudi Arabian light deflated by US consumer price index

Figure 8.1 Real price of oil

agents have to take decisions in one period which have consequences for future periods, but where agents are uncertain about the state of the world in the future. Flexibility relates to the extent to which decisions taken now constrain the ability of agents to respond in the future to the state of the world that actually materialises (see Jones and Ostroy, 1984 and Kreps, 1979 for formal analyses of how to rank decisions in terms of their degree of flexibility). In the context of responses to oil-price shocks, such intertemporal decisions arise naturally because, on the demand side, energy use is closely tied to the use of particular types of capital equipment, while, on the supply side, at least for commercial energy, the energy production and distribution sectors are among the most capital-intensive in the economy, and decisions on energy-using or -producing equipment have to be taken in a context of uncertainty about future fuel prices. It is possible to vary the flexibility of energy demand or supply investments. For example, it is possible to install dual-fired boilers which allow energy users to switch fuel types in response to changes in prices, while electricity supply systems can vary the diversity of types of generating stations they operate. If such flexibility were costless, agents would always choose the maximum degree of flexibility, but in general increasing flexibility increases capital costs, and agents have to trade this off against the expected saving in future operating costs by being able to optimise *ex-post* fuel-use decisions. The optimal level of flexibility will thus be low either if the demand for flexibility is low (for example, if agents expect that there will be little variation in future relative

224

prices of fuel, or that future variations will be very short-lived), or if the cost of providing extra flexibility is very high (which will largely be determined by technology). It follows that the degree of flexibility in energy demand or supply could be expected to vary over time.

Recent developments in economic analysis move this notion of optimal flexibility in a further direction. In practice, the optimal degree of flexibility is likely to be quite low, so that even allowing for the ability to carry out some *ex-post* adjustments in response to future energy-price changes, agents will be left bearing a considerable degree of risk. In such circumstances, there is another dimension to agents' decisions – the timing of major investment and disinvestment decisions. One response to fluctuations in prices such as the oil-price shocks might be to wait to see whether they are going to be sustained or not. More precisely, the literature on irreversible investment and hysteresis effects (see Dixit, 1992 and Pindyck, 1991 for good recent surveys) shows that when, for example, the US dollar began to appreciate in 1980, it would not have been optimal for foreign producers to respond immediately – rather they should wait until it reached some critical level before expanding sales to the USA. Similarly the fall in the dollar from 1985 to 1987 would not trigger an immediate reduction in foreign firms' sales – they would wait till it fell below a critical level before pulling out. Thus what may look like rather inflexible lags in firms' responses is actually part of the optimal response to uncertainty. But in order to distinguish this kind of optimal delayed response from sub-optimal, inflexible, responses, it is important to note that the optimal response implies that lags should vary with the level of prices. For our purposes, optimal responses would imply a faster response to the second oil-price shock than the first.

This general discussion can be made more precise by taking particular applications, and indeed in such contexts it is sometimes possible to provide quantitative measures of optimal flexibility. In the context of energy demand, Ingham, Maw and Ulph (1992) estimated a sophisticated vintage model of production for UK manufacturing which allows the calculation of an index of the degree of flexibility that producers incorporate (by means of investment) in new plant and equipment in terms of their ability to respond to future changes in relative prices of fuels. Figure 8.2 shows this index for 1971–89. In the early 1970s producers did not expect future changes in energy prices and so chose very low flexibility. Following the first oil-price shock, as they became more convinced that future energy prices were becoming increasingly uncertain, they increased the flexibility of their investments. By the 1980s, with the change in the structure of the oil market, producers saw future oil prices as likely to be subject to more short-term volatility and began to reduce the degree of flexibility. On the energy supply side, Ulph (1989) calculated a diversity premium for the UK electricity supply system showing how much more it would be sensible to pay in non-fossil-fuel generating costs in order to diversify the electricity supply

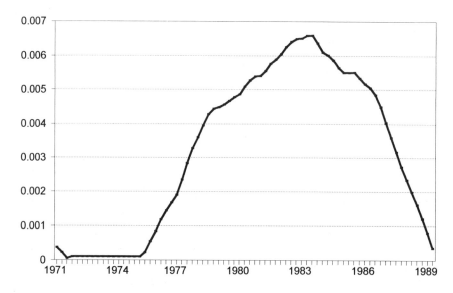

Figure 8.2 Index of flexibility, UK manufacturing

Source: Ingham et al., 1992

system and reduce its dependence on fossil-fuelled generation, subject to uncertain future fossil-fuel prices, principally oil prices. Finally, Wright and Hurn (1993) analyse the time lags in the process of investing in new oil-fields in the North Sea and show that, as the oil price rises, the length of lag falls.

The above discussion concerned flexibility as it relates to individual decision-making. We now turn to flexibility at the level of the whole economy. Economic analysis provides less guidance for defining flexibility at the economy-wide level. Obvious factors of relevance would include the way in which institutional structures (particularly in the labour and financial markets) expose agents to risk, and hence affect their decisions on flexibility of investments, or the extent to which governments might isolate domestic economies from changes in world prices, and thus reduce the incentive for agents to invest in flexibility. Rather than trying to provide a precise definition we shall think of flexibility rather loosely as the speed of adjustment to shocks, and look at what factors might affect this. Here we shall focus on the question of what factors might make an economy more flexible, and provide an empirical test of these factors.

Killick (1993) discusses the attributes of a flexible economy, identifying two key sets of conditions. First, the economy must have efficient information and incentive systems, ensuring that stimuli reach economic decision-makers, and that they are encouraged to respond appropriately. Second, decision-makers must be receptive, and prepared to respond appropriately. We have conducted a test of these ideas, within the limitations of data availability. We argue that, comparing two economies exposed to the same set of external shocks, the more flexible economy would be one which is better able to reduce the impact of these shocks on the domestic economy, as measured by the standard deviation of the growth rate of GDP. We therefore conducted a cross-section analysis of nineteen developing countries, all classified by the UNDP as being at 'low' or 'medium' levels of human development (UNDP, 1993). We proceeded by regressing the standard deviation of the growth rate of GDP over the period 1974–90 in each country against two sets of variables (we started with a larger number of variables and eliminated insignificant variables following the general-to-specific modelling methodology; we report only the final regression).

The first set includes variables which control for different exposure to external shocks. These are: (i) the proportion of the labour force in the industrial sector, to capture the notion that the more diversified an economy, the less vulnerable it is to shocks in any one sector; (ii) the level of GNP per capita, capturing the notion that more developed economies may be exposed to more shocks, with the previous variable controlling for the diversification aspect of this; (iii) the proportion of exports in the category of fuels, minerals and metals, reflecting the greater instability of this sector in terms of volatility of world prices. The second set of variables includes those which determine how flexibly an economy will respond to external shocks; these are: (i) mean years of schooling in 1980, capturing the notion that a more educated workforce is likely to be more flexible, more receptive to change; (ii) the proportion of GDP devoted to investment, reflecting the fact that shocks will require mobility of resources (especially capital) between sectors of the economy, and this will be easier to carry out if there is a high level of investment which can be redirected between sectors; (iii) a dummy variable representing whether a country had a flexible exchange-rate regime or not, a proxy for a broader index of how far governments allow world prices to feed through into domestic prices. This variable was compiled using information in Killick (1993).

Table 8.1 shows the outcome of this regression, in which we interpret a negative sign as indicating a factor which has enabled a country to achieve lower variability in growth rate. The results show that we have a well-determined relationship in which all the variables have their expected signs. We then used the coefficients on the three variables which determine flexibility to construct a general index of flexibility for the different countries in the sample, as reported in Table 8.2. The index is constructed such that higher values indicate more flexibility. Notice that the index may be calculated for a wider range of countries than we were able to include in the estimation process. We shall use this general index of flexibility at later stages in the paper.

Table 8.1 Factors influencing country flexibility

Regressor	Coefficient	t-ratio
Gross domestic investment as % of GDP	−0.11599	−4.3617
Mean years of schooling, 1980	−0.87857	−3.8538
Flexibility of exchange rate (dummy variable)	−0.72706	−1.4986
% of labour force in industry	−0.08975	−2.8266
GNP per capita	0.00583	5.1667
% of merchandise exports which are fuels, minerals and metals	0.02838	3.8953
Intercept	5.9422	10.0460

R-bar squared	=	0.7481
$F(6,12)$	=	9.9107
χ^2 (1) Functional form	=	0.7797
χ^2 (2) Normality	=	0.7758
χ^2 (1) Heteroscedasticity	=	1.4237

Table 8.2 A general index of flexibility

Country	Index
Bangladesh	3.149
Bolivia	5.517
Burundi	2.467
Côte d'Ivoire	2.653
Dominican Republic	6.245
El Salvador	5.106
Guatemala	5.633
Haiti	3.321
Honduras	4.871
India	4.601
Indonesia	7.626
Kenya	4.541
Malawi	3.697
Morocco	4.597
Nepal	3.669
Nigeria	3.345
Pakistan	4.424
Sierra Leone	2.706
Uganda	2.270

III ENERGY DEMAND AND SUPPLY ACROSS COUNTRIES

As we indicated in the introduction, there are two forms of adjustment to oil-price shocks that countries need to carry out: first, there are responses within the oil market, or more generally energy markets, with a rise in oil prices requiring reduction in demand for oil and expansion of domestic supplies; second, there will be further economy-wide repercussions, essentially caused by the transfer of resources from oil-importing to oil-exporting countries and the need to adjust the balance of resources between traded and non-traded sectors, and also to adjust the level of factor incomes. In this and the next section we concentrate on the former set of responses. In this section we analyse the responses made by individual agents, while in Part IV we discuss government responses.

In Part II we discussed what we meant by flexibility in relation to individual decisions and gave some examples of how this concept had been implemented in three contexts related to energy demand and supply in the UK. We cannot carry out such sophisticated studies for developing countries, so we need to find some cruder indices of flexibility. To analyse individual responses to oil-price shocks we shall work with elasticities of demand and supply for oil or, more generally, energy. The absolute values of these elasticities could be taken as measures of flexibility, with larger values indicating greater flexibility. However, the discussion in Part II points to two rather more subtle uses of elasticities to capture flexibility. First, we argued that flexibility had to do with how far decisions taken in one period (in particular, investment in energy-using or energy-producing capital) would constrain future responses to oil-price changes. This might suggest that we could use the long-run elasticity of demand or supply as an indicator of the maximum response individuals can make to oil-price changes; this could vary across countries because of different industrial structures, different preferences, different geographical or cultural features. Perfect flexibility would be a situation where this maximum long-run response could be obtained instantaneously, and so the short-run elasticity would be identical to the long-run elasticity. Thus the relative difference between long-run and short-run elasticities could be an indicator of flexibility.

Second, we argued that while the optimal degree of flexibility might be quite low, so that we could expect quite long lags in the adjustment process and hence marked differences between short-run and long-run elasticities, the work on hysteresis effects would suggest that the length of lags should depend on the level of oil prices. This would suggest that if agents were acting optimally the response to the second oil-price shock should be faster than the first, while response to the third oil-price shock (since it is in the opposite direction) should be slower than the second. We shall try to test whether short-run elasticities varied over the different oil-price shocks. If they did not, that would suggest inflexibility. The next two sub-sections deal with demand and supply responses respectively.

Energy demand

We begin our study of energy demand by looking at a widely used index – the aggregate energy: output ratio for countries, as calculated, for example, by Dunkerley and Gottlieb (1987) for a range of developing and developed countries. The limitations of such an index are well understood, but the key point is that, while average energy intensities are roughly comparable in developing and developed countries, the range is much wider in developing countries. As Dunkerley and Gottlieb note, an important factor in this is the sectoral structure of energy demand and the way this changes as development proceeds, with the household share of energy falling from 50 per cent in low-income countries to 20 per cent in middle- and high-income countries; thus the sectoral shares of energy in countries such as Argentina and Brazil can be seen to be broadly comparable with those of Western Europe. There were also important sectoral changes over time, with all developing countries for which data are available experiencing a fall in the share of energy in the household sector over 1971–81, but a rise in the share in electricity generation, while industry and transport shares remained constant.

Table 8.3 shows calculations of the energy:output ratio for 1990 for a sample of developing countries. These figures reveal that for a number of countries, the energy:GDP ratio is at a level comparable with that of industrial countries. It is also worth noting that the poorer countries with highest values for the ratio, such as Tanzania, Ethiopia and Kenya, are countries which continue to obtain a significant proportion of their energy requirements from traditional, rather than commercial, sources. If we focus only on commercial energy, the ratio naturally shows a very different pattern. However, even here it is clear that there are a number of developing countries which have ratios of commercial energy consumption to GDP which are comparable with those in Japan and the USA – notably Egypt, India, Korea and Singapore. These figures should be borne in mind when interpreting our later results, in which the emphasis is on commercial energy.

As Pachauri (1989) and Siddayo (1987) note, in the early days after the first oil-price shock there was a belief among many policy-makers that, allowing perhaps for changing sectoral effects, there was a strict proportional relationship between energy demand and income, so that the only way energy consumption could be reduced was through reductions in income. There was also a belief that the income elasticity of demand for energy in developing countries was higher than in developed countries. This seemed to be confirmed by an early pooled cross-section time-series study by Zilberfarb and Adams (1981) which suggested that the energy/GDP elasticity was 1.35 for developing countries, compared to a unitary elasticity for developed countries. The usual explanation of this finding was that

Table 8.3 Energy:GDP ratios, 1990

Country	Energy:GDP	Commercial energy:GDP
Costa Rica	6.496	3.928
Cyprus	7.930	7.930
Ecuador	9.365	7.047
Egypt	11.585	11.150
Ethiopia	22.814	1.918
Kenya	17.107	3.177
Korea (Rep.)	11.955	11.848
Philippines	6.491	3.885
Sri Lanka	3.974	1.677
Tanzania	22.820	1.907
Japan	8.497	8.492
USA	14.072	13.900

Note: Energy:GDP ratios constructed as the ratio of Total Energy Requirements (in terajoules) to GDP (in PPP$). Energy in column 2 includes traditional fuels.

developing countries were at a stage, where they were in the process of expanding energy-intensive industrial sectors so that the energy intensity of GDP could be expected to rise. Desai (1986) argued that it was more sensible to capture this effect through other variables reflecting the structural differences between economies, and he carried out a cross-country study similar to that of Zilberfarb and Adams, but including *per capita* capital stock and a dummy for agricultural or industrial countries; when these variables were included, the elasticity of energy demand with respect to income fell below 1.

Economists have argued that there was no such rigid relationship between energy use and GDP and that energy demand would react to higher energy prices. This seems to have been confirmed by the data, for while oil demand in developed countries grew by 7.5 per cent p.a. in the period 1967–73, it fell by 2 per cent p.a. over the period 1973–83. By contrast, in developing countries oil demand, which had risen by 8 per cent p.a. in 1967–73, continued to rise at 4 per cent p.a. from 1973 to 1983. An important question is how large is the price elasticity of demand in different countries? Studies of energy demand in the early 1970s suggested that price elasticities were indeed relatively low, but these studies were rather crudely based, and there has been an explosion of literature developing more sophisticated models of energy demand (see Watkins, 1992 for a good recent survey), which has uncovered rather higher estimates of energy price elasticities. Thus, for example, Pindyck (1979) finds the long-run own-price elasticity of energy demand to be -1.1 for the residential sector and -0.8 for the industrial sector, in a pooled cross-section time-series study of ten OECD countries. Much of this work has been restricted to the analysis of developed countries, and there are formidable difficulties in trying to conduct similar studies for developing countries (see Bhatia, 1987 for a comprehensive review). However, we present a brief review of the evidence produced in some of the studies of energy demand that have been carried out for developing countries.

Seale *et al.* (1991) conducted a large pooled cross-section time-series (fifty-one countries, three years, 1970, 1975, 1980) study of the pattern of consumption for eleven goods, including energy. While the model is the same for all countries, differences in income and consumption levels lead to different elasticities for different countries. The authors show that the (long-run) income elasticity of energy demand ranges from 1.173 in the richest country (USA) to 1.424 for the poorest country (Tanzania), while the own-price elasticity ranges from −0.855 to −1.038 for the same two countries. At a more detailed sectoral level, Siddayo *et al.* (1987) reported own-price energy elasticities for a number of industries in a selected number of Asian economies. The striking features in this study were relatively high elasticities for Thailand and the Philippines, and it is interesting to note that these are countries which followed high pricing policies – essentially moving domestic energy prices to world price levels.

As we said in the introduction to this section, the notion of flexibility is reflected in more than just the level of demand elasticities. Also of relevance are the size of the short-run elasticity relative to the long-run elasticity and the extent to which the lags between short-run and long-run adjustment depends on the level of oil prices, in particular whether the response to the second oil-price shock was faster than the first. We now turn to these other measures.

A number of studies have calculated long-run and short-run elasticities. At the aggregate level, Ibrahim and Hurst (1990) present estimates of long- and short-run income and price elasticities for thirteen developing countries. In fact, they were able to estimate long- and short-run elasticities only for the oil-importing countries, and for some countries they were not able to obtain significant price elasticities, a fact which they attribute to the existence of energy rationing in those countries. Their figures suggest that income elasticities are perhaps not as high as earlier estimates had indicated, although in most cases they are above 1.0, the oil-exporting countries having rather lower income elasticities, which perhaps reflect the greater degree of industrialisation in these countries. Long-run price elasticities are quite low and, with a few exceptions, not significantly different from the short-run elasticities. A further study by Koshal *et al.* (1990) of five Pacific countries found that the short-run elasticities were very similar for all countries, while the long-run elasticities showed no clear pattern between developed and developing countries. The Philippines had a very high income elasticity, but Korea was quite low, comparable to Japan and Canada and significantly below the USA. The price elasticities are very similar for the developed countries, but while the price elasticities for Korea are somewhat lower than for the developed countries, those for the Philippines are again strikingly high, and it is perhaps worth noting that Korea was one of the developing countries which kept its energy prices rather low. Finally, we note that Abdel-Khalek (1988) calculated long- and short-run elasticities of energy demand for Egypt and found them to be -0.15 and -0.52 with respect to own-price, and 0.26 and 0.88 with respect to income, so that there is quite a marked difference between the flexibility of energy demand in the short and long run in Egypt. We argued above that in addition to considering the absolute values of short-run and long-run elasticities, some light could be shed on the question of flexibility by considering two further tests – the ratio of short-run to long-run elasticities (with higher ratios indicating greater flexibility) and differences in response to the different oil shocks (with short-run elasticities being higher after the second than the first shock, but lower after the third than the second). To test this out we carried out our own analysis of demand elasticities for a sample of 11 countries, but the results were disappointing (see Smith and Ulph [1993] for details). For the first test the results were not sensible. For the second the results were slightly more encouraging, with short-run elasticities being higher after the second shock than the first for 7 out of 11 countries, although in many cases the differences were slight. We believe this might be a fruitful area for further research, although the difficulties in estimating energy demand elasticities alluded to earlier may severely limit the reliability of the extra tests that one can carry out on these elasticities.

Energy supply

In principle, the concept of flexibility developed in Part II for energy demand and illustrated above for some cross-country comparisons applies equally to the energy supply side. As we have been unable to find studies of energy supply elasticities for developing countries, we shall confine ourselves to providing some factual background to inform discussion in Part IV on policies towards energy supply. The first obvious supply response for countries faced with a shock to oil prices is to adjust their domestic supplies of oil, if they have any. In 1967 only fourteen non-OPEC developing countries produced oil, and this accounted for less than 8 per cent of non-OPEC, non-communist crude supply; by 1988 these figures had risen to forty countries with a share of 20 per cent. Some of these countries had gone beyond self-sufficiency to become significant exporters (Angola, Syria, Malaysia, Tunisia and Mexico) – see Choucri et al. (1990)).

The second response to a positive oil-price shock is to expand supplies of other fuels, including traditional fuels such as dung, fuelwood, charcoal or bagasse, and new renewable sources such as wind, solar, mini-hydro, or biomass. Table 8.4 shows the percentage of total energy requirements being met from traditional sources in three key years for a sample of ten develop-

Table 8.4 Traditional energy supply

Country	% of energy from traditional sources		
	1980	1985	1990
Costa Rica	41.5	48.6	39.5
Ecuador	27.4	27.0	24.7
Egypt	5.1	4.5	3.7
Ethiopia	93.3	93.5	91.6
Kenya	79.2	86.9	81.4
Korea (Rep.)	6.5	4.1	0.9
Philippines	39.9	45.2	40.2
Sri Lanka	59.3	60.7	57.8
Tanzania	89.8	90.8	91.6
Japan	0.1	0.1	0.1
USA	1.4	1.8	1.2

ing countries, together with data for the USA and Japan. These data seem to suggest that the supply of traditional fuels offers scope for flexibility in adjusting to relative price changes. In the majority of countries, reliance on traditional fuels increased after the second oil-price shock, i.e. between 1980 and 1985. This is even evident in the data for the USA. Furthermore, it can be seen that these sources became less important between 1985 and 1990 (during which time oil prices fell) in all countries except Tanzania. Data are not available on the use of the new renewable sources of energy.

IV MICROECONOMIC POLICIES AND THE OIL-PRICE SHOCKS

In this section we shall analyse the microeconomic response to oil-price shocks at the level of government, by examining their microeconomic policies aimed at influencing either the supply or the demand for energy. Much of the discussion centres on the question of the setting of energy prices. We begin with a brief discussion of the principles involved and an assessment of the impact of policies on energy demand and supply.

Principles of energy pricing

The discussion of flexibility based on analysis of elasticity of demand for energy or of the adequacy of supply responses rests on the key assumption that domestic oil prices reflect the changes in world prices. However, this may not necessarily be the case if governments decide to cushion domestic consumers from the full impact of the shocks. Such interventions may impede the adoption of more flexible technologies, although this is, of course, unlikely to have been the intention of the policy. It was apparent that, following the first oil-price shock, many developing (and some developed) countries responded by keeping domestic energy prices below the new world prices. There were a number of reasons for this:

(i) as already noted, there was a belief that energy price elasticities were very low, if not zero, and that the role of markets in developing countries is very different from those of developed countries;

(ii) even if the own-price elasticity of demand for energy is significantly non-zero, there may be distortions to the market for energy which make energy prices a relatively ineffective instrument compared with other policies;

(iii) as well as distortions in energy markets there are distortions in other markets which warrant deviations from efficiency in energy markets;

(iv) there was a belief that energy is part of the basic needs of households and any attempt to raise energy prices would worsen inequality and poverty;

(v) there was a concern for the inflationary impacts of raising energy prices.

We have seen that point (i) is not tenable and in many developing countries energy elasticities are comparable with those in developed countries. We shall deal with point (ii) in the next sub-section, and with point (v) in Part V. This leaves us with points (iii) and (iv), and we shall briefly discuss the principles of energy pricing to address these points. (We summarise the lengthier discussion of these issues found in Pereira, Ulph and Tims, 1987, Chapter 7.)

If the government was concerned solely with economic efficiency, if there was no need to raise government revenue, and if there were no distortions elsewhere in the economy, we would want to set energy prices at their efficient level. For traded energy goods, such as liquid fuels, this would imply setting domestic prices equal to border prices, and for non-traded energy goods such as natural gas or electricity, setting prices equal to marginal costs of production. If the government has concern for equity as well as efficiency, or if it needs to raise revenue, then it will still be appropriate to set efficient prices within the production sector, but there may now be a need to set consumer prices at a different level from producer prices. There would be two considerations in this. To the extent that household demand for some fuels was relatively price-inelastic, revenue-raising would dictate taxing such fuels; to the extent that some fuels form a larger share of the budgets of poor than of rich households, and there are no other ways of redistributing income to poor households, then this may warrant a subsidy to those fuels.

There are two further considerations. First, within the production sector, it may be that there are already other substantial forms of distortion (e.g. trade protection) which the government is not prepared to remove; standard second-best considerations tell us we would want this to be reflected in energy prices. However, the implications of this are not at all clear. For example, a study by Dixit and Newbery (1985) showed that in Turkey it would have been appropriate to subsidise the use of oil by producers in the non-energy sectors, despite the fact that in these sectors producer prices were above their efficiency levels, because it was desirable to try to reduce the effect of these distortions in the energy-intensive sectors. However, using a very similar model for Iran, Frewer (1984) found that it would be desirable to tax oil. Since the correct policy turns out to be very sensitive to the structure of economies, the nature of their distortions, and parameter values such as elasticities, Newbery (1984) concludes that it might be as well simply to set producer prices at their efficient level.

The second additional factor is that it has been assumed that it is possible to set different prices for different fuels and also for different sectors (household/production). But there may be limitations to this. For metered fuels such as electricity, it may be possible to set different prices for households and producers; but it would be impossible to set different gasoline prices for these groups. Similarly, in principle it may be desirable to set very different prices for diesel, gasoline and kerosene, with diesel prices being set close to their efficiency level as they are mainly an input to production, gasoline being taxed because it is consumed by wealthy households, and kerosene being subsidised because it is consumed by poor households. However, these products are close substitutes and any large differential in price will lead to such responses as the substitution of diesel for gasoline or the adulteration of gasoline with kerosene. For instance, in Zambia it was observed that producers substituted kerosene for fuel oil. These considerations suggest that there may be important limitations on the extent to which it is possible to set low prices for energy products for households, even if equity considerations suggested that it was desirable, and it may be better to find other policies to protect poor households.

One final point should be noted. This discussion has concerned the pricing of energy products. Of course, if efficient energy prices were set in the production sector that would have implications for the product prices of energy-intensive goods. Efficiency considerations say that we want these energy prices to be passed through to product prices, in order to discourage consumption of energy-intensive goods. Again, this may conflict with equity (e.g. food-processing), but this is not an argument for not setting efficient energy prices to producers. At best, it would be an argument for considering subsidising the consumption of such energy-intensive goods.

To illustrate some of these points we consider briefly some of the evidence on energy pricing in some developing countries. First, for petroleum products (gasoline, diesel, fuel oil and kerosene), Lohani and Azimi (1992) provide figures for the average ratio of retail prices to border prices for twenty-seven developing and developed countries for the years 1974, 1977,

1980 and 1983 and show that they range from 0.2 (in Venezuela) to 2.4 (in Germany). Subsidies to oil products are given predominantly by developing country oil exporters (Colombia is the exception), taxes are imposed by oil importers, with the ratio being highest (2 or above) for European developed countries (the exception being Ghana where the ratio is 2.2). They also quote prices for electricity in India (1988–9) which show that the average generation cost (which is below marginal cost) is 0.91 Rs/kwh, while average prices are 0.16 Rs/kwh for agriculture, 0.54 Rs/kwh for domestic use and 0.98 Rs/kwh for industry.

Policies and energy demand

The above discussion is concerned with the structure of energy pricing in developing countries, but even if there are good arguments for deviating from efficient pricing, at least for the household sector, that does not suggest that the level of energy prices should not be adjusted in line with external shocks. As already indicated, the response to the first oil-price shock in many developing countries was not to pass the price increases through to the economy. We now summarise briefly the findings for some other developing countries, beginning with the studies analysed by Pereira, Ulph and Tims (1987).

In Peru energy prices were kept constant in nominal terms from 1971 to 1975, but were then raised, though significant subsidies remained. Egypt kept prices well below the world level throughout the 1970s (they were 15 per cent of f.o.b. prices in 1980), but they were allowed to rise slowly during the 1980s, although still remaining well below world prices. Colombia kept its energy prices constant until 1976 and then began raising them towards world prices which they had almost reached by 1979. Costa Rica and Zambia gradually raised their energy prices to world levels by the end of the 1970s, while maintaining subsidies for fuels such as kerosene.

Pachauri and Srivastava (1988) note that India pursued a policy of administered prices for petroleum, but kept other oil-product prices above international levels, except for diesel and kerosene which were kept lower than international prices until the mid-1980s. As part of a policy to encourage switching from oil to coal, wholesale prices of coal rose only fivefold between 1973 and 1983, while those for fuel oil rose eightfold. Hsueh (1992) noted that, following the first oil-price shock, Taiwan kept energy prices low; thus, while the real costs of crude oil rose by 277 per cent between 1971 and 1978, gasoline and fuel oil prices rose by only 8 per cent and 6 per cent respectively, while diesel oil prices fell by 24 per cent. For other Asian countries, we have already noted that Thailand and the Philippines pursued a policy of world pricing, while other countries, such as Korea and Singapore, adjusted more slowly, perhaps because their economies were under less pressure than Thailand and the Philippines (Siddayao, 1987).

Table 8.5 Ratio of weighted average retail prices to the price of Arab light

Country	1978	1979	1980	1981	1982	1983	1984
Argentina	n.a.	n.a.	n.a.	1.35	0.79	0.92	n.a.
Ecuador	n.a.	1.14	0.75	0.61	0.52	0.55	0.43
Brazil	2.65	2.11	1.85	2.00	1.79	1.62	n.a.
Sudan	n.a.	2.07	1.50	1.04	1.03	1.47	1.52
Thailand	1.77	1.71	1.81	1.68	1.52	1.66	1.63

Source: Krapels (1987).

In respect of the later oil-price shocks, Krapels (1987) calculated the ratio of average retail prices of petroleum products relative to crude oil prices in a number of developing countries for the period 1978–84, as shown in Table 8.5. Only Thailand kept this ratio relatively constant, consistent with its policy of setting world prices. In the other countries there was some erosion of product prices relative to crude oil prices, so the second shock was not being fully passed through. Hsueh (1992) showed that, for Taiwan, in the period 1979–81 real crude oil costs rose by 92 per cent, and the prices of fuel oil, diesel and gasoline rose by 88 per cent, 58 per cent and 43 per cent respectively; when real crude oil costs subsequently fell, real product prices did not fall as quickly. So there is further evidence that developing countries moved more quickly to adjust domestic prices to world prices following the second oil-price shock than they had done after the first shock.

Two questions remain – how successful were policies of raising energy prices in constraining energy consumption, and what other policies did countries use to constrain energy demand? On the first, it is difficult to assess precisely the impact of individual policies. Hsueh (1992) notes that, for Taiwan, in the period 1973–9 following the first oil-price shock, when domestic energy prices were not adjusted in line with world prices, energy efficiency (in terms of energy intensity) improved by 1.0 per cent p.a.; in 1979–83, when domestic energy prices were moved in line with international prices, energy efficiency improved by 3.78 per cent p.a.; while in the period 1983–7, when energy prices fell, though not as fast as international prices, energy efficiency improved by only 0.75 per cent p.a. Of course, this is little more than temporal correlation. As already noted, Lohani and Azimi (1992) have analysed the ratio of domestic retail energy prices to their corresponding border prices for twenty-seven developed and developing countries. They regressed the 1983 energy:GDP ratio for these countries against the value of this ratio for 1983, and found that higher ratios of domestic prices to border prices did significantly reduce the energy intensity of countries. Siddayao (1987) argued that where countries had used prices to influence energy consumption, as in Singapore for petroleum products and electricity, and in the Philippines for motor fuel, reductions in energy use had occurred.

What other policies did countries use to constrain energy demand? Where countries did not use price increases, resort was often made to some form of rationing. In India, in 1973–4 the government set up a system for allocating petroleum products to industrial units, based on the previous year's consumption reduced by a set proportion. This caused the share of petroleum products in total energy use in the industrial sector to fall from 20.8 per cent in 1972–3 to 17.4 per cent in 1975–6 (Pachauri and Srivastava, 1988). Sudan also introduced rationing of fuel imports (as part of a broader policy of import rationing), but this led to shortages occurring which affected production and exports (Pereira *et al.*, 1987). Siddayao noted that, even if formal rationing is not introduced, the use of administered prices can also lead to shortages, and pointed out that these can have important effects in reducing the profitability of production and hence the attractiveness of a country for foreign investment; such difficulties affected the Philippines. Similar distortions to pricing can affect the supply of electricity in terms of both inadequate total capacity and inadequate maintenance, and Siddayao noted that the World Bank had criticised the Philippines for unnecessarily large subsidies to residential urban consumers.

However, it must be noted that, even where countries used pricing policies close to efficient pricing, that was not the only form of energy policy used. Referring back to the discussion of the previous sub-section, there is a view that there are important market failures in energy markets which suggest that governments cannot adopt an entirely *laissez-faire* approach. This applies particularly to the question of energy conservation, where it is frequently argued that setting appropriate energy prices may not be sufficient to guarantee an efficient level of investment in energy saving. These arguments apply to developed and developing countries, and the alleged market failures can be briefly summarised as lack of information about available technologies and capital market imperfections. (Ingham *et al.*, 1992 provide a test for these market failures for UK manufacturing, and conclude that there is little evidence to support them.) Lohani and Azimi (1992) note that the information problem is probably more acute for developing countries, even among energy planners, and, of course, the problem is compounded by distorted energy prices.

The steps that are taken to overcome these market failures, apart from reforming energy prices, are the use of subsidies for energy conservation investments, the provision of information, requirements to conduct energy audits, hire energy managers, etc. Siddayao (1987) provides a table listing which of these policies have been adopted among the East and South Asian countries she studied, but provides little detail of actual policies. Hsueh (1992) provides a detailed account for Taiwan. Briefly, there are various subsidies to investment in energy conservation which amount to a 25–30 per cent reduction in investment costs. However, these have gone largely to the large industrial energy-using producers, and this may have prevented a restructuring of the industrial sector away from energy-intensive goods, such as chemicals, non-metallic minerals and primary metals. There have also been requirements that certain firms appoint an energy manager, and report data on energy utilisation twice yearly; but there have been low compliance rates for these regulations (about one-third). Taiwan has also imposed some tough energy efficiency standards on products such as air conditioning, where standards are at Californian levels but short of the Japanese level. Finally, for small and medium-sized firms an Energy Service Corps was set up in 1983 to provide them with information and technical assistance, and this has proved successful. The Corps has since been made an independent, non-profit-making institution. Lohani and Azimi (1992) report similar, but less successful, policy moves for India. The Bureau of Indian Standards has laid down energy efficiency standards for a wide range of products, but lack of proper testing facilities means that relatively few products have been certificated (three for refrigerators, ten for air conditioning). The Industrial Development Bank of India issues subsidies for conducting energy audits, with a list of seventy-two approved energy consultants. By 1990 only 150 audits had been conducted.

The discussion so far has been about policies in developing countries, the main focus of this chapter, but it is perhaps worth making a few comments about Japan, which is often considered to have been the major success story in terms of policies to reduce energy demand, some of which have already been alluded to. Without disparaging the substantial progress Japan has made in energy conservation, we shall argue that the real difference between Japan and other countries in terms of reducing energy demand has lain in broader areas of economic policy, in particular, policies which are linked to the kind of macroeconomic policy considerations we shall discuss in Part V.

Table 8.6 shows the sectoral composition of the change in oil demand in Japan compared to OECD countries, following the oil-price shocks. It is clear that the major difference between Japan and other OECD countries occurred in the industrial sector. This success is usually attributed to a range of policies, similar to some already discussed (see Dore, 1982 for further discussion). Primary emphasis is put on the role of investment in energy conservation. For example, the *Economic Survey of Japan 1980–1* noted that in 1980 investment in the steel industry was 105.5 per cent higher than in 1979, and of this 17 per cent was investment in energy conservation; Suzuki and Tanaka (1981) discuss this more broadly. This investment was partly the response to market forces (the *Economic Survey of Japan* noted that success in controlling inflation rates in Japan meant that there was a more pronounced increase in relative oil prices) but was also due to incentives for investment in energy conservation (modest reductions in interest and special tax depreciation allowances) and a variety of energy advisory services. All plants consuming more than a certain quantity of energy were required to have energy managers trained and certificated to standards set by the

Table 8.6 Change in oil demand by sectors

| | 1973–9 | | 1979–83 | |
	Japan	OECD	Japan	OECD
Industry	−0.6	+1.5	−17.2	−8.9
Transport	+5.5	+7.4	−3.2	−2.3
Household	+1.4	−2.4	+2.1	−4.9

Source: Economic Planning Agency, 1985.

Table 8.7 Percentage change in energy use in manufacturing, 1973–87

| | | Component factors | | | |
Country	Overall	Output growth	Aggregate intensity	Industry structure	Actual intensity
Japan	−16.7	+51.3	−45.0	−11.5	−36.4
USA	−20.2	+43.2	−44.5	−14.8	−32.4
Germany	−21.3	+14.9	−31.2	− 6.1	−27.2
France	−35.7	+13.4	−35.7	− 7.2	−30.3
UK	−31.8	− 4.1	−29.2	− 0.8	−28.9
Denmark	−15.6	+26.6	−33.9	− 5.2	−27.4
Sweden	−13.1	+19.8	−27.2	− 6.2	−22.5
Norway	− 1.4	+ 8.7	− 9.8	+21.2	−20.2

Source: Howarth *et al.* (1991).

government. An Energy Conservation Centre ran courses for these certifi-
cates, and it also published information booklets and ran regional seminars
to help disseminate information on energy conservation.

But how far were these policies central to Japan's performance in reducing
industrial energy demand? Howarth *et al.* (1991) break down the change in
energy use in the manufacturing sectors of eight OECD countries over the
period 1973–87 into a number of factors, as shown in Table 8.7. The first
column shows that Japan's reduction in energy use was not in fact all that
striking in aggregate terms, but this is largely explained by column 2 which
shows Japan having the highest rate of growth of aggregate manufacturing
output; correcting for this gives the reduction in energy intensity across
countries, which indeed shows Japan (closely followed by the USA) having
the highest reduction in energy intensity, significantly higher than in
Europe. But the next two columns break this down into factors – a change in
industrial structure (between high energy-intensive industries and low
energy-intensive industries) and the actual change in energy intensity within
each industry on average. The final column of Table 8.7 shows far smaller
differences between Japan, the USA and European countries in the
reduction in energy intensity comparing industry by industry. The major

241

difference was in the ability of the industrial structure to respond to changes in the relative costs of production induced by changes in energy prices. This much more reflects the differences in labour or capital markets discussed elsewhere in this book than specific differences in energy policy responses.

It is perhaps worth noting for later discussion in Part V that the outliers in Europe in terms of both overall growth of manufacturing output and the change in industrial structure were Norway and the UK. This reflects the fact that these were oil-exporting countries; for them the implications of higher oil prices were a squeeze on the manufacturing sector as non-traded goods expanded and a relative switch to energy-intensive industries to exploit their comparative advantage. Oil importers, in contrast, needed to expand their traded goods sectors (primarily manufacturing) and switch away from energy-intensive industries.

To complete this section we assess how far the different policy packages chosen by different governments were successful in changing patterns of energy demand. In Figure 8.3 we show the share of oil consumption in total energy demand for two countries – Korea and India – over the 1980s, the only period for which data were available. From the discussion earlier in this sub-section it is clear that Korea followed relatively flexible policies in this period, allowing domestic energy prices to reflect changes in world prices and supplementing this by policies designed to improve energy conservation; India used administered prices backed by rationing, and its policies to boost energy conservation were not particularly well designed. So we take Korea as representative of a flexible policy approach and India as representative of an inflexible policy approach. Figure 8.3 shows that while Korea's oil consumption relative to total energy moved inversely with oil prices, India's rose slowly throughout the period irrespective of oil prices. The change in oil's share of energy consumption in Korea over the two five-year periods before and after 1985 is striking. As we shall see later, this distinction between Korea and India in terms of flexibility of micro-based policies is consistent with the classification of the two countries in terms of their flexibility with respect to macroeconomic policy adjustment, and, in turn, that is consistent with the general index of flexibility of countries as developed in Part II.

To conclude, successful adjustment to the oil-price shocks required governments to reflect movements in world oil prices in domestic prices for fuels. There are plausible arguments about why market forces may be insufficient to reduce energy demand, but they are not arguments for refusing to allow domestic energy prices to adjust to world prices, but rather for supplementing market prices with policies that address the sources of market failures, namely information problems and, perhaps, capital market failures. However, these policies need to be carefully designed and targeted. Adopting these pricing and supplemental policies can lead to substantial changes in the patterns of fuel consumption over short periods.

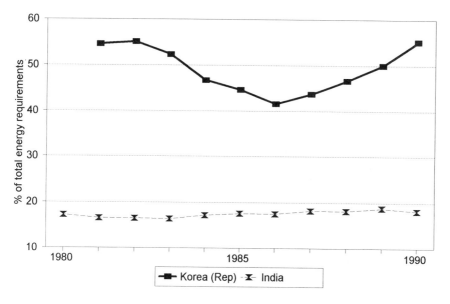

Figure 8.3 Share of liquid fuels

Policies and energy supply

Microeconomic policies are just as important for the energy supply sectors of an economy, and again the policies in some developing countries have not helped to expand domestic energy supplies in an efficient manner. An important aspect of policy is the prices set in domestic energy markets, and we shall give some examples of this. We have already noted that, in Peru, oil prices were held below world prices after the first oil-price shock, and only began to be raised in 1976. During the 1980s prices were again held down, with the result that the state oil company, Petroperu, accumulated losses of $2bn, and in both public and private sectors investment in exploration was cut, leading to a sharp fall in reserves and a large increase in oil imports (Mayorga-Alba, 1992). On the other hand, the same author notes that many African countries operate a cost-plus basis for product pricing, so that small outdated refineries, built to meet security or socio-development needs, are operated with resulting product prices well above those prevailing in world markets.

Choucri *et al.* (1990) used a simulation model of the Egyptian oil industry for the period through to 2000 to examine the impact of changing Egypt's policies on oil pricing (which kept oil product prices for domestic consumers well below world prices – at one-third of world levels in 1985) and on profit sharing between the government and the oil companies (the government share was 80 per cent in 1985), which affects incentives for discovering new

243

reserves. In the base case they assumed that domestic oil prices would increase gradually but still only reach two-thirds of world prices by 2000; under this scenario, the growth of domestic oil consumption would outstrip domestic production, leading to total exports falling from 510 thousand barrels per day in 1988 to 291 tbd in 2000, with government exports falling from 204 tbd in 1988 to only 31 tbd in 2000. By contrast, if domestic prices were set equal to world prices from 1990, this would constrain the growth of domestic consumption by 25 per cent, and allow government exports in 2000 to rise from 31 tbd to 194 tbd. As a further experiment Choucri and his colleagues analysed the effects of cutting the government's profit share from 80 per cent to 75 per cent. While this means a short-term loss of revenues for the government, it causes exploration and hence production to rise throughout the 1990s, resulting in government revenues being higher than in the base case from 1996 onwards. The problem here is not just the high government share, but the fact that the production-sharing arrangement is a rather crude form of resource-rent taxation, and it might be better to impose a properly designed resource-rent tax (see Pereira *et al.*, 1987 for further discussion).

A related point is that another way in which developing countries have sought to extract a reasonable share of resource rents from domestic oil reserves is by setting up national oil companies. This leads to the familiar problems of internal inefficiency. Similar problems also arise in state electricity companies. Mayorga-Alba (1992) quotes some comparative indicators of efficiency of electricity production from a World Bank study of 100 developing countries. Two indicators are used: electricity losses in the generating and transmission system, and customers served per employee; for OECD countries losses average between 6 per cent and 8 per cent, while customers per employee are usually above 200 (Japan was the highest with 450). By contrast, for nine of the developing countries he quoted, losses are between 12 per cent (Zaïre) and 26 per cent (Burundi and Colombia), while customers per employee are below 25 for five African countries, and between 150 and 200 for four Central and Latin American countries; only Korea had a performance close to those of developed countries. Mayorga-Alba believes that an analysis of national oil companies would show similar results.

Finally, we turn to the role of alternative energy supplies in developing countries. A recent survey of experience in developing countries (Desai, 1992) is salutary. As with energy conservation, many of the alternative energy sources were introduced with government subsidies, and these were often quite substantial: ethanol in Brazil 45–53 per cent; ethanol in the Philippines, 49 per cent; gasifiers in the Philippines had a 90 per cent loan, often not repaid; biogas plants in China, 66 per cent; biogas in India, 25–45 per cent for families, 100 per cent for communities; micro-hydro in China, 23 per cent at its lowest point. Despite these subsidies, many of these schemes failed. Biogas plants in China fell from 7.1 million in 1978 to 3.8 million in 1984. This was because many plants were built just to meet targets, and were unusable; of those that were usable many gave insufficient gas for cooking. In India, 25–50 per cent of the biogas plants were not working. In the Philippines of 201 gasifiers installed with foreign assistance in 1981–5, only one was in use in 1990; 165 needed repair; and thirty-four had gone out of use.

Desai also quotes some examples of successful alternative projects, many of which had little government support. He concludes that there are a number of reasons why government policies have proved to have limited success. Subsidies are usually given to producers, and, in an attempt to regulate quality, only a few producers are licensed, so subsidies rarely get passed to consumers. Moreover, the producers recognise that large subsidies are unlikely to be sustainable, and so are discouraged from making long-term investments in quality; subsidies are usually tied to specific technologies, which freezes technology in a field where there is rapid technical progress. Desai believes that better designed policies could be successful – e.g. providing subsidies to intermediaries such as leasing firms. Again there is a need to link this to more rational energy pricing, in particular making energy prices reflect transport costs so that alternative technologies can be developed for niche markets, where it would be very expensive to introduce conventional energy.

V THE MACROECONOMIC IMPACT OF THE OIL-PRICE SHOCKS

To understand the macroeconomic implications of an oil-price shock it will be convenient to consider an oil-importing country faced with a sustained upward shock to oil prices. To fix ideas, let us begin by supposing that the country makes no adjustment whatsoever, and pays for the higher oil bill either by running down foreign reserves or, more plausibly for developing countries, by borrowing. As we shall discuss later, this was a much easier response to the first oil-price shock than to the second, when the level of indebtedness was already high. The country could just try to carry on with this policy and make no adjustments, but clearly such a response is not sustainable, as loans will at some stage need to be repaid, and the country will be forced to make adjustments. Part of the adjustment process involves the microeconomic responses designed to reduce the demand for oil or to increase the supply of domestically produced oil or oil products, in order to reduce the size of the net oil import bill. These were discussed in the previous section.

However, part of the response will also involve economy-wide changes in resource allocation. At the heart of such changes is the need to switch resources into the production of traded goods and out of the production of non-traded goods, in order to help pay for the increased oil bill, and this will require two macro-level changes. First, to ensure that production of traded goods expands there will need to be a reduction in real returns to domestic factors of production, which for most countries will mean wages. This reduction in real wages is necessary both to cut costs of production in order to improve the competitiveness of the traded goods sector, and to cut domestic demand for both traded and non-traded goods. Second, there will need to be a reduction in the prices of non-traded goods relative to traded goods, and this will require a real devaluation.

These macroeconomic adjustments are clearly going to be painful, but as Solow (1980) has argued, the policy problem is not to undo the real effects of the shock, for as long as the real price of oil can be raised by cutting oil output, macroeconomic policy cannot make oil cheaper in real terms. Rather, the role for macro policy is to minimise and perhaps smooth the costs of adjustment. To minimise the costs of adjustment the macroeconomic policies of cutting real wages and the real exchange rate should be implemented, but the effects of cutting real wages on reducing consumption could ideally be smoothed by providing transfer payments, particularly to low-income families, perhaps financed by government borrowing. In practice, such transfers are infeasible for many countries, and so the smoothing of adjustment will take the form of slowing down the reduction in real factor prices and increasing the long-run cost of adjustment to the oil-price shock. Similar comments apply to the real exchange rate. These failures to adjust are likely to show up as increased inflation as the oil-price increases just get passed through the economy in higher prices for goods and factors of production, and increased unemployment as real wage resistance erodes the competitiveness of the traded goods sector. Thus these failures to adjust will simply increase the long-term cost the economy has to incur as a result of the oil-price shocks, and the reduction in real incomes will be that much greater.

We can summarise the above discussion in terms of the implications for GDP in Figure 8.4. The solid line represents the path of output the country would follow in the absence of the oil-price shock. A country which was able to carry out its microeconomic and macroeconomic adjustment instantaneously (perfect flexibility) would have a path like that in A', showing that the oil-price shock essentially represents sustained reduction in the level of output corresponding to the minimum amount of income transferred to the oil-exporting countries by the price rise when all the adjustments have been carried out. Allowing for the fact that in practice even quite flexible countries will face smaller adjustment costs in the long run than the short run, and that countries may therefore wish to carry out some short-term smoothing of the reduction in income, would lead to a path like A', where the immediate and short-term reduction is smaller than A as a result of smoothing, the medium-term reduction in income is larger than A' because of the greater short-term costs of adjustment, and where the long-term path lies slightly below A' because of the need to pay for the costs of smoothing. A path like B would correspond to an inflexible country where

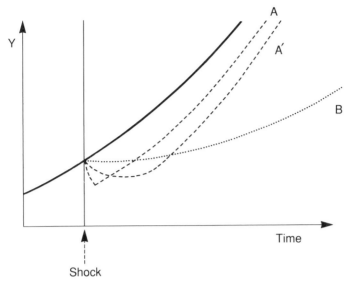

Figure 8.4 Alternative adjustment paths

adjustment is very slow so that the country not only has a larger cost to pay for its oil, but also the cost of paying off its increased debt. Finally, note that oil exporters will experience a positive oil shock; for such countries the process of adjustment will be the opposite of the one described earlier and will correspond to what is referred to as the Dutch-disease problem (see Neary and van Wijnbergen, 1986 for a useful overview).

To assess the macroeconomic experience of developing countries we first summarise briefly the paths of the main macroeconomic variables of interest for the group of non-oil developing countries (NODCs) and contrast this with the experience of the industrialised countries. Table 8.8 presents summary information comparing these two groups of economies. In the period prior to the first oil-price shock, NODCs had been growing somewhat faster than the industrial economies as a group, although not as much faster as convergence would demand. Inflation was higher, but not excessively so. Growth rates in the industrial economies dipped in 1974–8 and again in 1979–85, perhaps beginning to recover after oil prices fell in the mid-1980s. NODCs contrived to maintain the momentum of growth, especially in 1974–8, when they were buoyed up by other booming commodity prices, and by increased borrowing. However, a substantial contrast between the two groups of countries is seen in respect of inflation, where the industrial economies brought inflation under reasonable control while the NODCs saw marked acceleration of price changes. Of course, these broad pictures disguise appreciable differences in the performance of individual regions and economies.

247

However, we are more interested in the differences in macroeconomic performance across developing countries. To assess this we begin by using the distinctions in flexibility of performance in terms of GDP that we drew in Figure 8.4. To make this operational, for 33 countries we constructed simple time-series models of GDP prior to the first oil-price shock in 1973 (in a few cases where we had insufficient data on GDP prior to 1973 we used the second oil-price shock), and used these models to predict what might have happened to GDP from 1973 to 1990 in the absence of the oil-price shocks; we then compared actual paths of GDP over these periods with the predicted paths, and classified each country into one of five categories according to the observed patterns. Table 8.9 defines the five categories, and Figures 8.5–8.7 show the resulting patterns for a representative member of each of the first three groups.

Now obviously the exercise we have carried out can be criticised for being extremely simple, and in particular for ignoring all the other shocks impinging on countries' GDP; for example, the boom in primary commodity prices following the first oil-price shock probably explains the countries falling in Category D. However, what is striking is that despite the simplicity of the exercise we were able to classify all but three of the thirty-three countries according to the simple theoretical discussion underlying Figure 8.4.

Table 8.8 Macroeconomic performance of the non-oil developing countries (NODCs)

Period	Average annual growth rate of real GDP (%)		Average annual inflation rate (%)	
	Industrial economies	NODCs	Industrial economies	NODCs
1960–73	4.7	5.0	3.7	9.6
1974–8	2.6	5.2	9.8	15.9
1979–85	2.3	3.8	7.6	41.4
1986 onwards	2.5	4.1	3.6	71.8

While the classification of the oil-importing countries into the A and B categories in Table 8.9 contains few surprises, we obviously want to explain more fully why some countries responded flexibly and others did not. We begin by returning to the general analysis of flexibility we carried out in Part II. We discussed there the construction of a general index of flexibility of different countries and in column 3 of Table 8.9 we show the calculated value of the index for those countries for which data were available. The results are quite interesting. Those countries which we classified as A have flexibility indices in the range 6.7–10.8, with an average of 8.4; those countries in category B have an index ranging from 1.6 to 9.8 with an average

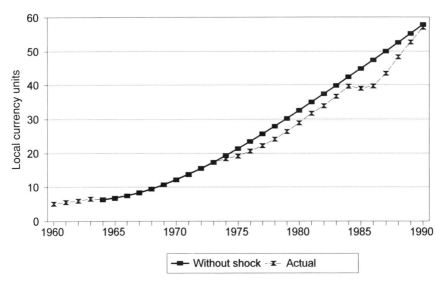

Figure 8.5 Typical category A country: Singapore
Source: IMF.

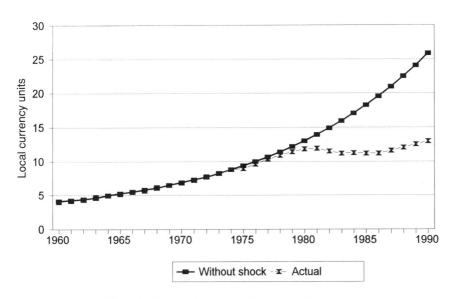

Figure 8.6 Typical category B country: Guatemala
Source: IMF.

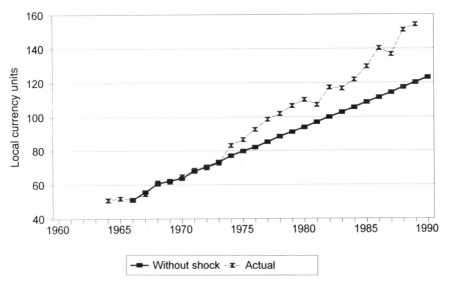

Figure 8.7 Typical category C country: Morocco
Source: IMF.

of 5.4. Thus our general analysis of flexibility is able to discriminate reasonably well between those countries which adjusted flexibly to the oil-price shocks and those which did not.

We need to go beyond the rather general set of factors determining the differences in flexibility of macroeconomic responses discussed in the previous paragraph to look more closely at the actual policy differences implemented by different governments. We shall consider examples from countries in categories A and B to illustrate the differences in policies that contributed to the differences in performance.

On the basis of our index, Korea shines out as the potentially most flexible of the countries in the sample. Had we been writing from the vantage point of the 1970s, this might have been seen as a surprising result. Korea grew very rapidly indeed throughout the 1970s, but with a very strong government influence. A combination of economic incentives and government decree had directed the economy in the direction desired by the authorities, with the help of a receptive private sector prepared to respond to signals from the government (Kwack, 1990a). However, in the wake of the first oil-price shock few attempts were made to make appropriate adjustments; inflation was allowed to rise (Scitovsky, 1990), and the government borrowed heavily in an attempt to maintain the momentum of growth. A programme of conscious restructuring (towards heavy manufacturing industry) behind high tariff protection was vigorously followed during the late 1970s.

Table 8.9 Categorisation of countries by adjustment path

		Index of flexibility
Category A: flexibility in readjusting to the growth path	Cyprus	n.a.
	Indonesia	7.626
	Korea (Rep.)	10.817
	Mauritius	6.730
	Singapore	8.326
	Sri Lanka	8.111
	Philippines	9.077
Category B: inflexibility in response to the oil-price shocks	Argentina	6.315
	Bolivia	5.517
	Brazil	6.178
	Costa Rica	9.011
	Dominican Republic	6.245
	Ecuador	7.675
	El Salvador	5.106
	Ghana	1.740
	Guatemala	5.633
	Honduras	4.871
	Kenya	4.541
	Malawi	3.697
	Mexico	6.561
	Panama	7.039
	Tanzania	4.657
	Zambia	1.624
Category C: oil-price shocks have a positive impact on real output	Egypt	4.888
	Morocco	4.597
	Syrian Arab Republic	4.260
Category D: a positive response to the 1973/74 shock, but negative response in 1979/80	Côte d'Ivoire	2.653
	Paraguay	7.320
	Trinidad and Tobago	7.331
	Venezuela	6.427
Category U: unusual patterns	Chile	7.767
	Ethiopia	2.386
	Thailand	7.367

By the time of the second oil-price shock, Korea seemed to be facing potential chaos: inflation was high, outstanding international debt was soaring (relative to GDP), credibility of the restructuring programme was low (Tan, 1992), President Park was assassinated (in 1979), and the grain harvest of 1980 showed a 20 per cent real fall. Yet, real output growth in 1981 was back to 7.1 per cent. Previous policies towards inflation (i.e. to ignore it) were now reversed, and monetary policy was designed to bring inflation under control. Exchange rates were manipulated to ensure that competitiveness was maintained. The Korean won was devalued against the US dollar by 36 per cent in 1980, and depreciated further over the following five years (Kwack, 1990b). Between 1980 and 1985, the real won exchange-rate depreciation was around 15 per cent. The restructuring policies were discontinued (possibly the 'greatest policy achievement of the period', according to Noland, 1990), or at least redirected. In addition, reforms were introduced to enable market forces to play an increasing role in the allocation of resources (Kwack, 1990b). Thus it was in the 1980s that Korea was seen to adopt policies specifically designed to encourage recovery and enable rapid adjustment. This whole package of measures seems to have had the effect of facilitating a flexible response to the crisis. In particular, it has been argued (Mazumdar, 1993) that it was Korea's willingness to engineer appropriate changes in unit labour costs that was the key to the success that it undoubtedly enjoyed through the 1980s. Indeed, Mazumdar states that the unit cost of labour when measured in US dollars fell by 26.32 per cent p.a. in 1979–81. Real wages fell (by 4.6 per cent in 1980 and by 0.9 per cent in 1981), but the continuing growth of real labour productivity cushioned the effects. Nonetheless, it would be misleading to suggest that labour's co-operation in this was totally voluntary. Reforms in the late 1980s which allowed more freedom to the trade unions unleashed a wave of labour unrest (Noland, 1990).

Perhaps an extreme example from Category B is Tanzania (see Hyden and Karlstrom, 1993). Throughout the 1970s and the first half of the 1980s Tanzania had pursued policies based on the belief that prices played little role in resource allocation, and so nominal prices, in particular exchange rates and interest rates, were kept fixed. The need to adjust following the first oil-price shock was partially offset by a boom in coffee prices and rising flows of aid. However, the second oil-price shock was accompanied by a fall in coffee prices and declining aid flows. The terms of trade declined by 40 per cent between 1978 and 1982; to deal with the balance-of-payments problem without having to adjust prices, imports were licensed, causing import volumes to fall by 50 per cent, leading to bottlenecks in production. The main rationale for not adjusting prices, especially the exchange rate, was the need to protect living standards, but official statistics showed real GDP per head falling at 0.5 per cent per annum over the period 1965–85. Household surveys showed a worse picture, with living standards falling by 50 per cent on average between 1969 and 1984, with urban incomes and living standards falling even faster (65 per cent) since rural families could fall back on subsistence agriculture to support themselves. In the second half of the 1980s there was a change in policies; exchange rates were gradually adjusted, agricultural producer prices were raised, and imports began to be freed; as a result real GDP rose at 4 per cent per annum between 1986 and 1990, and has also risen in *per capita* terms.

VI CONCLUDING REMARKS

In this paper we have tried to assess how countries differed in the flexibility of their responses to the three oil-price shocks of the 1970s and 1980s. We have analysed the response both within the energy markets and more broadly in the economy as a whole, and at the level of individual agents' responses and of government policies.

In Part II we tried to formalise the concept of flexibility, particularly at the individual level, and there are examples of quite sophisticated applications of our notion of flexibility to energy supply and demand in developed countries. However, when we came to apply the concept of flexibility to developing countries, in Part III, we had to use somewhat more ad hoc measures, based on elasticities of demand or supply, and in particular on the relationship between short-run and long-run elasticities and how this might vary depending on the level of oil prices. The empirical findings here were not particularly encouraging, although analysing how the length of response to oil-price shocks varied over the three shocks gave some interesting results, reported in Smith and Ulph (1993).

At the economy-wide level we developed a general index of flexibility, depending on factors such as education, the share of investment in GDP and an index of the nature of governments' exchange-rate policies. For micro-based policies we showed that countries which allowed domestic prices to move in response to changes in world prices, supplemented with well-designed policies to deal with market failures related to energy conservation, could be successful in achieving quite large changes in patterns of energy consumption over quite short periods of time. The countries which adopted the more flexible micro-based policies were those which were classified as being more flexible by our general index of flexibility. However, as the case of Japan showed, an equally important factor in changing energy demand was the nature of broader economic policies which affected the flexibility with which industrial structure could change in response to changes in costs of production.

At the level of macroeconomic policy responses, we argued that key policy variables to stimulate a flexible economy-wide response are the real exchange rate and real wages. We studied patterns of GDP response to the three oil-price shocks and classified countries in terms of their flexibility according to the pattern of GDP response they displayed. This indicator of macroeconomic flexibility was closely correlated with the classification of countries using our general index of flexibility. A more detailed analysis of the macroeconomic policy responses in a few countries confirmed that those countries identified as having a flexible macro-policy response were those which allowed exchange rates and real wages to adjust in response to the oil-price shocks, while countries which were inflexible tried to prevent external factors such as the oil-price shocks from feeding through into real wages or exchange rates. The result was that countries which responded inflexibly faced significantly greater costs of adjustment than those which responded more flexibly.

REFERENCES

Abdel-Khalek, G. (1988) 'Income and price elasticities of energy consumption in Egypt', *Energy Economics* 10(1): 52–9.

Bhatia, R. (1987) 'Energy demand analysis in developing countries: a review', *The Energy Journal* 8: 1–34 (special LDC issue).

Choucri, N., C. Heye and M. Lynch (1990) 'Analysing oil production in developing countries: a case study of Egypt', *The Energy Journal* 11(1): 91–116.

Cremer, J. and D. Salehi-Isfahani (1991) *Models of the Oil Market*, London: Harwood.

Desai, A.V. (1992) 'Alternative energy in the Third World: a reappraisal of subsidies', *World Development* 20(7): 959–66.

Desai, D. (1986) 'Energy–GDP relationship and capital intensity in LDCs', *Energy Economics* 8(2): 113–7.

Dixit, A.K. (1992) 'Investment and hysteresis', *Journal of Economic Perspectives* 6: 107–32.

Dixit, A.K. and D.M.G. Newbery (1985) 'Setting the price of oil in a distorted economy, *Economic Journal (Conference Papers)* 95: 71–82.

Dore, R. (1982) *Energy Conservation in Japanese Industry*, Energy Paper 3, London: Policy Studies Institute.

Dunkerley, J. and M. Gottlieb (1987) 'The structure of energy demand and energy conservation', *The Energy Journal* 8: 35–56 (special LDC issue).

Economic Planning Agency (1981) *Economic Survey of Japan 1980–81*, Tokyo: Japanese Government.

—— (1985) *Economic Survey of Japan 1984–85*, Tokyo: Japanese Government.

Frewer, G. (1984) 'Policies towards oil pricing in developing countries', MSc thesis, Department of Economics, University of Southampton.

Heal, G. and G. Chichilnisky (1991) *Oil and the International Economy*, Oxford: Clarendon Press.

Howarth, R., L. Schaffer, P. Duerr and S. Strom (1991) 'Manufacturing energy use in eight OECD countries', *Energy Economics* 13(2): 135–42.

Hsueh, L.M. (1992) 'An evaluation of Taiwan's energy conservation policy in 1980s', *Energy Policy* 20(5): 444–9.

Hyden, G. and B. Karlstrom (1993) 'Structural adjustment as a policy process: the case of Tanzania', *World Development* 21(9): 1395–1404.

Ibrahim, I.B. and C. Hurst (1990) 'Estimating energy and oil demand functions: a study of thirteen developing countries', *Energy Economics* 12(2): 93–102.

Ingham, A., J. Maw and A.M. Ulph (1992) 'Testing for barriers to energy conservation – an application of a vintage model', *The Energy Journal* 12(4): 41–64.

International Labour Office, *Yearbook of Labour Statistics*, Geneva: ILO, various issues.

International Monetary Fund, *International Financial Statistics*, Washington, DC: IMF, various issues.

Jones, R. and J. Ostroy (1984) 'Flexibility and uncertainty', *Review of Economic Studies* 51: 13–32.

Killick, T. (1993) *The Adaptive Economy: Adjustment Policies in Small, Low-Income Countries*, Washington, DC: World Bank and London: Overseas Development Institute.

Koshal, R.K., K. Luthra and J. Lindley (1990) 'Production and high energy prices', *Energy Economics* 12(3): 197–203.

Krapels, E.N. (1987) 'Implementing efficient petroleum product pricing programs in developing countries', *The Energy Journal* 8(1): 39–52.

Kreps, D. (1979) 'A representation theorem for "Preference for Flexibility"', *Econometrica* 47: 565–78.

Kwack, S.Y. (1990a) 'The economic development of the Republic of Korea, 1965–1981', in L.J. Lau (ed.) *Models of Development: A Comparative Study of Economic Growth in South Korea and Taiwan*, San Francisco: ICS Press.

—— (1990b) 'The economy of South Korea, 1980–1987', in L.J. Lau (ed.) *Models of Development: A Comparative Study of Economic Growth in South Korea and Taiwan*, San Francisco: ICS Press.

Lohani, B.N. and A.M. Azimi (1992) 'Barriers to energy end-use efficiency', *Energy Policy* 20(6), 533.

Mayorga-Alba, F. (1992) 'Revisiting energy policies in Latin America and Africa: a redefinition of public and private sector roles', *Energy Policy* 20(10): 995–1004.

Mazumdar, D. (1993) 'Labor markets and adjustment in open Asian economies: the Republic of Korea and Malaysia', *World Bank Economic Review* 7(3): 349–80.

Neary, P. and S. van Wijnbergen (eds) (1986) *Natural Resources and the Macroeconomy*, Oxford: Basil Blackwell.

Newbery, D.M.G. (1984) 'Equity, efficiency and the pricing of petroleum products in Asia', Paper presented at the Energy Pricing Workshop, Regional Energy Development Programme, Bangkok.

Noland, M. (1990) *Pacific Basin Developing Countries: Prospects for the Future*, Washington, DC: Institute for International Economics.

Pachauri, R.K. (1989) 'Energy and growth: beyond the myths and myopia', *The Energy Journal* 10(1): 1–19,

Pachauri, R.K. and L. Srivastava (1988) 'Integrated energy planning in India: a modelling approach', *The Energy Journal* 9(4): 35–48.

Pereira, A., A.M. Ulph and W. Tims (1987) *Socio-economic and Policy Implications of Energy Price Increases*, Aldershot: Gower.

Pindyck, R. (1979) *The Structure of World Energy Demand*, Cambridge, MA: MIT Press.

—— (1991) 'Irreversibility, uncertainty and investment', *Journal of Economic Literature* 26, 1110–48.

Scitovsky, T. (1990) 'Economic development in Taiwan and South Korea, 1965–1981', in L.J. Lau (ed.) *Models of Development: A Comparative Study of Economic Growth in South Korea and Taiwan*, San Francisco: ICS Press.

Seale, J.L., W.E. Walker and I.M. Kim (1991) 'The demand for energy: cross-country evidence using the Florida Model', *Energy Economics* 13(1): 33–8.

Siddayao, C.M. (1987) 'Policy and energy use: Asia's adjustment to the changing energy picture', *The Energy Journal* 8: 57–84 (special LDC issue).

Siddayao, C.M., M. Khaled, J.G. Ranada and S. Saicheua (1987) 'Estimates of energy and non-energy elasticities in selected Asian manufacturing sectors: policy implications', *Energy Economics* 9(2): 115–25.

Smith, P. and A.M. Ulph (1993) 'The flexibility of national economies in response to the oil-price shocks', University of Southampton Discussion Paper in Economics and Econometrics no. 9322.

Solow, R. (1980) 'What to do (macroeconomically) when OPEC comes', in S. Fischer (ed.) *Rational Expectations and Economic Policy*, Chicago: Chicago University Press.

Suzuki, K. and H. Takenaka (1981) 'The role of investment for energy conservation',

Energy Economics 3(4): 233–63.

Tan, G. (1992) *The Newly Industrializing Countries of Asia*, Singapore: Times Academic Press.

Ulph, A.M. (1989) 'A note on a method of quantification of the benefits of diversity in relation to fluctuations in fossil fuel prices', Document S4165, *Evidence to the Hinkley Point Inquiry*, London: HMSO.

United Nations Development Programme (1993) *Human Development Report 1993*, New York: Oxford University Press for UNDP.

Watkins, G. (1992) 'The economic analysis of energy demand', in D. Hawdon (ed.) *Energy Demand: Evidence and Expectation*, Guildford: Surrey University Press.

Wright, R. and A. Hurn (1993) 'Geology or economics? Testing models of irreversible investment', University of Glasgow Discussion Paper no. 9303.

Zilberfarb, B. and F. Adams (1981) 'The energy–GDP relationship in developing countries', *Energy Economics* 3(4): 244–8.

9

INDUSTRIAL ADAPTATION AND TECHNOLOGICAL CAPABILITIES IN DEVELOPING COUNTRIES

Sanjaya Lall

I INTRODUCTION

A flexible economy is one in which ends and means are readily adjusted to changing constraints and opportunities. This includes flexibility in the institutional base of the socio-economic system, as well as flexibility on the part of the government in adapting policies to changing conditions. It implies an economy in which movement of resources among alternative uses is relatively low friction, low cost and rapid, and leads to changing factor proportions, technologies and composition of output. . . . The *response speed and the costs that must be incurred* to achieve a given adjustment are the key indicators that differentiate flexible from rigid economies. (Emphasis added.)

(Killick, 1993, 47)

Defined thus, flexibility (or adaptability) is in many ways a *sine qua non* of success and growth in the context of the manufacturing sector. There is growing pressure on industries in developing countries to adapt and change. Industrial technologies are evolving rapidly and constantly, probably faster than in other economic activities. Their skill, infrastructure and informational needs are changing in concert. Competition is increasingly on a global scale, and in most developing countries policy is moving to greater openness and outward orientation. All this raises the need for existing industries in the developing world to raise their productivity and competitiveness to world standards, and this, in turn, calls for flexibility in government policies, institutions, factor markets and technological efforts within firms.

Important issues arise, therefore, about the forms that industrial adaptability may take, the national and firm-level factors that influence adaptability, and the role of the government and institutions in promoting adaptability. Despite much debate about the determinants of industrial success in developing countries, which directly or indirectly touches on the flexibility of government, institutional or industrial responses, many of these issues have not been satisfactorily resolved (see Lall, 1990, 1992a, 1993a). This chapter examines the nature and determinants of industrial flexibility in developing countries, contrasting the main approaches to the analysis of technological performance, and taking examples from economies at different levels of industrialisation and displaying very different degrees of flexibility in the face of technological change and international competition.

Flexibility in industry may be analysed at several levels: firm, industry and economy-wide. At the firm level, enterprises in developing countries must be able to do two closely related things. First, since many developing country enterprises tend to operate well below international levels of 'best-practice' technical efficiency (Pack, 1988), they must improve the efficiency with which they use given technologies. This involves moving away from lines that are inherently inefficient, and boosting the productivity and quality of activities that are potentially competitive by investing in improvement in organisational and technological capability. Second, they must upgrade and add to their range of technologies. This requires further investments in technological and organisational capabilities, even where most of the new information and hardware is purchased abroad. The emerging close relationship between technological and organisational innovation, most clearly in evidence in the growth of 'flexible specialisation' (Kaplinsky, 1993; Ferraz et al., 1992), accentuates this need, placing new demands on skills, training, information requirements and interactions with other agents in the economy.

At the industrial level, greater adaptability to technical progress and growing international competition calls for a restructuring of existing activities and for entry into new, generally more complex, activities. Restructuring involves the closure of inefficient firms, the selection or creation of facilities of a size and capability to compete in world markets, and the promotion of inter-firm specialisation and linkages that are conducive to the effective transfer of technology and information. The undertaking of new activities involves the development of new support activities (infrastructure, suppliers, intermediaries) and institutions, and of a complex of inter-industry linkages.

All these processes have implications at the macroeconomic level. Apart from the management of macro policies, the promotion of industrial flexibility calls for an incentive regime conducive to investment in capacity and capabilities. It may also call for interventions in factor and product markets, to help develop the new factors (skills, information, infrastructure, institutions) that technical progress entails.

Part II of this chapter focuses on how the individual firm develops technological competence and copes with changes in the world technological frontiers. Part III moves on to consider the determinants of industrial adaptability: the international environment and the national incentive

258

regimes provide the 'demand' for technological effort to become flexible and competitive, while finance, technical skills, effort and institutional support provide the 'supply side'. Part IV analyses the role of the government in providing the appropriate demand and supply conditions for industrial flexibility, taking the East Asian newly industrialising countries (NICs) as examples of flexible economies and the least industrialised countries of sub-Saharan Africa as examples of inflexible economies. Part V draws the main conclusions.

II NATURE OF INDUSTRIAL COMPETENCE AT THE FIRM LEVEL

There are two broad approaches to the explanation of how firms in developing countries gain technical competence and achieve the adaptability needed to compete in world markets. It is important to understand how these approaches differ, since these differences are important for policy purposes and for the issues addressed by this book.

The standard neoclassical approach

The most common approach to how firms in developing countries grow and adapt is based on textbook models of the neoclassical firm, the anonymous unit that operates in perfectly competitive markets to optimise resource allocation and production. This model, with all its simplifying assumptions, serves as the bedrock of much of the current understanding of technology and industrial development in developing countries.[1] It also provides the rationale for important elements of policy-making on trade and industrial policy, for instance in structural adjustment programmes.

In the world of simple theory, firms everywhere are assumed to operate with full knowledge of all possible technologies. Given the right (market-determined) prices for inputs and outputs, they pick the one that is appropriate to their national factor endowments. All firms in an industry facing the same prices choose the same technologies; otherwise they are allocatively inefficient. The international technology market is assumed to work efficiently, and all firms are taken to have full knowledge of the technologies available so that they can buy the right one 'off the shelf'. All firms can, moreover, immediately use imported technologies with the same degree of efficiency (and at best-practice levels). There is no theoretical reason to expect the persistence of technical inefficiency. If such inefficiency exists, it is, *ex hypothesi*, due to managerial slack or incompetence, and to government interventions that allow inefficient firms to continue in production.

This approach gives rise to simple policy prescriptions. Interventions in efficient product and factor markets are deemed undesirable. Since developed countries are the main source of industrial technology, and search and absorption are costless, it is recommended that developing countries adopt policies as open as possible to all channels of information flow (foreign direct investment, licensing, capital goods imports and so on). Openness in all its forms is seen as desirable, and the possibility that there are imperfections in finding and purchasing technology, and costs and risks in absorbing this is not taken into account. Moreover, the possibility that different modes of technology transfer may have different effects on learning and industrial flexibility is not considered. The rapid growth of export-oriented economies is attributed, at least partly, to their general 'openness' to trade and technology transfer, with technology flowing effortlessly and being aborbed by a process of osmosis.[2]

Where extra costs of introducing new technologies in developing countries are admitted, a simplified view is taken of the learning process. The learning curve is believed to be fairly short and predictable – largely confined to 'running in' a new plant until it reaches rated capacity and the benefits of automatic learning-by-doing are realised. It is generally assumed that such costs are relatively trivial, predictable, and similar across industries. The learning process is, moreover, relatively passive rather than one that involves investment, risk and, in some activities, long maturation periods. Firms know what to do to reach best-practice levels. There is consequently no need to devise measures to stimulate the capability to absorb new technologies, or to distinguish between industries in the financing of learning and start-up costs.

Firms are assumed to acquire and use technologies as individual units, essentially in isolation.[3] There are no linkages between them, and no externalities resulting from individual efforts to generate skills and information. The development of specialisation among firms and industries thus relies on information exchanged in anonymous market transactions. There is no need to create or foster the information networks and institutions that have evolved in advanced industrial economies. Since there are no technological externalities, there is also no need to co-ordinate investment decisions (in physical assets or capability-building) across activities that may themselves have intense linkages. Nor are some sets of activities more significant for industrial development than others because they have more beneficial externalities: no sector has the claim to be more 'strategic' than another.

It is assumed that firms have the foresight to finance 'running in' costs in capital markets. If capital markets are not fully efficient, the market failure has to be addressed at source. In the interim, infant-industry protection (or subsidies) may be granted, only as a second-best measure, at moderate levels and uniformly across activities to minimise the risk of resource misallocation. Since no technologies are more difficult, or involve more externalities, than others, there is no need for policy-makers to be selective in their promotion of particular industries or technologies. There is also no need to devise different policies according to the level of development of the countries in question, since markets are assumed to operate with equal degrees of efficiency.

In this essentially static framework, comparative advantage evolves according to the gradual accumulation of factor endowments, rather than by the deliberate efforts of industrial enterprises. As endowments grow, firms automatically move to the right factor combinations, costlessly absorbing the technologies concerned. It is generally admitted, however, that in developing countries some factor markets may not operate efficiently, in particular in the creation of skills and the diffusion of information. In this case policy interventions are needed to support factor markets, but this support has to be non-selective. The allocation of resources should not be influenced to encourage or support activities that governments consider desirable.[4] In sum, industrial flexibility is only possible in the context of non-interventionist policies and adherence to free markets.

The capability approach

The assumption that technology is costlessly absorbed in efficient factor and product markets is an important, but often misleading, simplification. Empirical work in many different developing countries suggests that most industrial technologies are generally operated at low levels of technical proficiency, and that technical inefficiency is a much larger source of low productivity than allocative inefficiency (see Pack, 1988 for a brief review). The process of selecting, mastering and adapting technology, and later improving upon it, requires the development of new knowledge, skills, organisational forms and interlinkages between enterprises. It is based, in other words, upon the acquisition of new technological capabilities (TCs). The significance and costs of such acquisition are ignored in the textbook models, with important implications for policy analysis.

Technological capabilities in industry may be defined as the information and skills – technical, organisational and institutional – that allow productive enterprises to utilise equipment and information efficiently. Such capabilities are firm-specific, a form of institutional knowledge that is made up of the combined skills and experience of its members (see Nelson and Winter, 1982 and Bell *et al.*, 1984). The development of TCs should not be thought of as the ability to undertake frontier innovation, though innovative capabilities are one form of TC. It comprises a much broader range of effort that every enterprise must itself undertake in order to absorb, adapt and build upon the knowledge that has to be utilised in production. The growth of capabilities may be defined as industrial technology development (ITD); this process is evolutionary, and depends on the conscious and purposive efforts under-taken by every enterprise.[5]

The successful transfer of a new technology to a developing country has to

261

include a major element of capability building: simply providing equipment and operating instructions, patents, designs or blueprints does not ensure that the technology will be properly used (see Nelson, 1987; Nelson and Winter, 1977; Pack and Westphal, 1986). These 'embodied' elements of a technology have to be accompanied by a number of 'tacit' elements that have to be taught and learned. Only when such learning (entailing training, searching for new technical information, and in-house engineering and experimentation)[6] has taken place, and the necessary adaptations made to local operating and market conditions, can the technology be considered to be 'mastered' in a static sense. Only then, that is, can it be used at or near the best-practice level of technical efficiency for which it was designed. The achievement of flexibility in a dynamic setting, with new technologies, changing market demands and the entry of new competitors, is a far more complex and demanding process than in the neoclassical model.

Technological mastery, whether in a static or a dynamic sense, cannot be an automatic or passive process. In other words, in order to successfully absorb and deploy new technical information, prior investments have to be made in human capital and organisational capabilities to 'decode' new technical information, and to incorporate it into manufacturing processes. Technological capability is not, however, simply the sum of the education and training of a firm's employees. It is based on the learning undergone with reference to particular technologies, and depends on the way in which the firm combines all the individual skills to function as an organisation (see Enos, 1992 and Chandler, 1992).[7]

To some extent, of course, any enterprise that tries to use a new technology acquires some TCs as an automatic result of the production process. Such passive learning goes some way to developing the necessary capabilities. In simple industries, say the assembly of imported kits or garment manufacture for the domestic market, this may be enough for efficiency. Such passive learning is, however, generally insufficient to ensure efficiency as more complex technology is considered, or if more demanding markets are tackled. For more complex industries, to reach even static best-practice levels as established in advanced countries involves an enterprise in a longer and more demanding process, sometimes taking years of production, engineering and research.[8]

This learning process means that different firms can experience quite different rates of technological development, and end up with different levels of efficiency in using the same technologies. Adaptability is necessarily firm-specific. There is no predictable learning curve down which all firms travel. Moreover, in most developing countries the learning process itself may have to be learned.[9] The systematic launching of the training, engineering, search and experimentation process that comprises capability development is generally not understood by the typical entrant to modern manufacturing in developing countries. And even if the need for capability development is recognised, enterprises may not know the best way to go about it: information of this sort cannot be assumed to be widely available in developing countries.

Manufacturing enterprises do not develop capabilities in isolation. They operate, in most industries, in a dense network of formal and informal relationships with suppliers, customers, competitors, consultants, and technology, research and educational institutions. These networks take the form of complex, long-lasting contractual and non-contractual relations.[10] These linkages help individual firms to deal with each other, to gain access to expensive ('lumpy') information and facilities, and to create information, skills and standards that all firms need but no individual firm will generate on its own ('public goods').

The need for such linkages differs by industry and enterprise. Some simple activities that rely mainly on primary inputs and use low skill techniques may not need many linkages to be efficient. Others need constant flows of information, skills and other inputs from outside to maintain their efficiency and to make rational decisions to invest in physical and human assets. As the role of complex activities grows with economic development, so does the need on the part of firms to take account of linkages. This process is a necessary part of the increasing specialisation between firms that is essential to industrial development. In the context of technological progress, it is vital to maintaining flexibility.

The learning process for complex technologies is thus long, risky and uncertain. In a new environment, with a new plant or process, different physical conditions, underdeveloped supply networks and inexperienced workers and managers, no such process can be entirely predictable. Investments in TC acquisition are, like other investments, highly sensitive to the incentive environment, the cost of the investment, and the availability of the investible resources: apart from the finance, these are access to skills, technical information and support, and interactions with related firms. Thus, firms in certain environments undertake larger TC investments than in others because of their more stable and favourable macroeconomic policies, more stimulating market environment, greater stocks of the relevant skills, and better technology institutions (see below).

The complexity, costs and risks of TC investments rise with the sophistication of the technology and the pace of technical change. The cost of building up a viable level of TC in, say, automobile manufacturing is far greater than in the making of simple machine tools, which in turn is more than in garments. Within engineering industries, the cost is higher for rapidly moving technologies like electronics than for relatively stable mechanical engineering.

Finally, indigenous capability development depends crucially on the import of technology and skills from advanced industrial countries. For most developing countries, the thrust of TC building is essentially to absorb imported technologies, and there is no necessary conflict between 'making' and 'buying' technology. However, two points have to be noted.

First, as capabilities develop and technologies in use grow more complex, there arises a make–buy choice in technology generation. The same technology can be transferred with many different combinations of foreign and local technological effort. The optimal combination would vary by country and technology, but there is a general case for deepening local capabilities (into basic design and engineering, and into an understanding of the research methodologies involved) as industrialisation progresses.[11] The case rests on the increase in the ability to better adapt imported technologies and to import effectively more sophisticated new technologies, the externalities that a deepening of TCs generates (in terms of spillovers to innovations in other activities), and the possibility of increasing the use of local materials. It is possible to deepen the industrial structure without greatly deepening local technological content (in other words, to set up more complex industries while remaining wholly or largely dependent on imported technologies, equipment and skills). The process is, however, likely to be more costly, and possibly less dynamic, and may result in an industrial structure that is less flexible and responsive to technological challenges.

Second, the mode of technology import can have an effect on local TC development. Internalised modes (like foreign direct investment, where the seller of technology retains ownership and control of the utilisation of the technology) tend to centralise the innovation process in developed economies and transfer the results of research to affiliates. In externalised modes (licensing, equipment purchase, copying, etc.), the recipient may not obtain the technology as rapidly, and it generally has to do much more 'homework' to absorb and build upon it. But it may, if given the right incentives and skills, be able to develop its innovative capabilities far more than if it never had to develop the skills that it imports.

This concludes the description of the process by which firms develop technological capabilities in the real world. It is evident that this description can lead to very different, and more complex and differentiated, policy conclusions on how industrial flexibility may be promoted from the standard neoclassical approach. Just 'getting prices right' may not be sufficient – it may not even be desirable, if it means sole reliance on market forces when market failures are endemic and widespread. Interventions, sometimes selective, may thus be a necessary and desirable element of policies to develop industrial flexibility. The nature of the policies cannot be standard, but should vary by country and industry.

III DETERMINANTS OF INDUSTRIAL COMPETENCE AND FLEXIBILITY

The investments that an individual firm makes in TC acquisition are driven by 'demand' and 'supply' factors. Demand factors are produced by the incentives thrown up for capability development by local and international markets and conditions. Supply factors are the skills, information and physical investment that it can tap to feed into its own capabilities. Random firm-level differences apart, the efficiency of the product and factor markets and supporting institutions that firms face therefore determine their success in developing competence.

'Demand' factors

The set of market and non-market incentives facing the firm determine the 'demand' for technological effort. A number of these do not merit separate discussion here, but are noted in passing. First, the most fundamental incentive for a firm to develop its technological capabilities, regardless of the trade and industrial regime, is the initial need to get into production. Second, the political and macroeconomic environment, and prospects for growth, both domestic or foreign, are clearly strong influences on decisions to invest in TCs. *Ceteris paribus*, a stable, predictable and high growth environment is far more conducive to such investments than any other. Third, the rate of technological progress internationally affects the optimal pace and content of ITD. No modern manufacturing technology is static, and no developing country can afford to ignore world technological trends if it wishes to stay internationally competitive. Organisational innovations are also of vital importance, and mass production is being rapidly replaced by flexible specialisation in many engineering industries as the key to production and innovation efficiency (see Ferraz *et al.*, 1992; Hoffman, 1989; Kaplinsky, 1993).[12]

The incentive factors that need more discussion are those that arise from competition, both domestic and foreign. Competitive markets provide perhaps the most potent stimulus to investments in capability acquisition, and correct market signals guide firms in investing to the right extent, and in the right forms, in ITD. Thus, artificial restraints to competition can hold back ITD investments, or can lead firms to develop the wrong kinds of capabilities.[13] In some circumstances, however, interventions in competition may be justified with reference to market failures: this needs some discussion.

Exposure to international competition is given by the trade regime. It is now universally accepted that classic import-substitution industrialisation strategies have been inefficient. The benefits of outward orientation to industrial development are well established, and need not be analysed in detail here. The empirical evidence on the relative success of outward orientation over import substitution is overwhelming. This paper has no dispute with the superiority of export-orientation strategies: what it does want to look at is the nature of their impact on industrial competitiveness and flexibility.

In neoclassical development theory, the benefits of export orientation arise from the country's conformance to comparative advantage. There is a clear and powerful proof in neoclassical economics of the welfare benefits of free trade (and outward orientation has long been presented as reproducing conditions of free trade) that arise from optimal resource allocation. The superior performance of export-oriented economies is traced by neoclassical development economists like Balassa and Krueger to the realisation of these allocative benefits. In theory, however, these benefits obtain only when the assumptions of perfect competition and efficient markets hold. Once they are relaxed, the conclusions and welfare implications drawn do not necessarily follow. Two points need to be made in this context.

First, the theoretical case for free trade does not establish the links between optimal resource allocation in a static sense and higher rates of growth over time. Under neoclassical assumptions, the theory proves only that free trade optimises static resource allocation. With the usual assumption of diminishing returns to investment, it does not lead to higher rates of growth: neoclassical development economists are not true to neoclassical theory (see the new growth theorists like Lucas, 1988; Young, 1991). A sustained increase in the growth rate can only come from investments in human capital and technology that do not suffer decreasing returns because they can raise the productivity of other factors of production. Analysts of import liberalisation have also noted that the theoretical link between a move to free trade and improved efficiency is tenuous (Rodrik, 1992), and the empirical support for the hypothesis is weak (Havrylyshyn, 1990).

The neoclassical development economists have argued that export orientation does provide dynamic, not only static reallocation, benefits. World-class competition is a powerful catalyst to efforts to cut costs, improve quality, introduce new products and keep up with technical progress. Selling to world markets allows the realisation of scale economies. It restricts the scope for unproductive rent-seeking activity. It also provides constant, and generally free, feedback for product design and process improvements. More broadly, it breeds dynamic managerial attitudes by virtue of openness.

However, while these benefits do exist, many of them are not really dynamic. For example, the realisation of scale economies and the benefits of facing world competition are once-for-all effects. The flow of information provided by exports is not a neoclassical benefit, since in theory all firms have access to the same information costlessly – the benefit must arise because there are market failures in technology flows. Neoclassical development economists straddle the worlds of theory and reality rather awkwardly. In any case, the addition of information externalities from trade does not suffice to explain the dynamic growth of export-oriented (E-O) countries. There are many other countries that have been outward oriented, and have participated for long periods in international trade (as primary exporters), that have exhibited little dynamism. There has to be something in the receptive abilities of developing countries that accounts for the enormous variation in their industrial performance and competitiveness. The international trading environment offers a variety of benefits for those that can access and exploit it; for others it offers little.

The literature on the significant and persistent differences in the competitiveness and flexibility of OECD countries, all highly open and trade-oriented, does in fact focus on these receptive factors rather than on incentive regimes. Differences in productivity and flexibility are explained by factors like education, training, R&D, innovation support and financing, and so on. Since these factors differ far more among developing countries than among developed ones, there is a strong presumption that they play a role in explaining relative industrial performance. This is not to deny the significance of incentives from trade strategy. It is clearly important that incentives should be conducive to capability development, but it is the interaction of incentives with trade strategy that determines industrial success (see also Lall, 1990). What the right set of incentives for TC development consists of is considered now.

Second, once the assumption of efficient markets is relaxed and market failures admitted, it is not clear that free trade is necessarily desirable on welfare grounds. Since the absorption and effective utilisation of industrial technologies are not instantaneous, costless, predictable or automatic processes, and require a variety of information and inputs from product and factor markets they can face a variety of market deficiencies in both sets of markets. These deficiencies may call for corrective government interventions.

The economic case for interventions rests on the nature of the industrial deepening process, and the main difference from the neoclassical approach lies in the assumption made about the time, investment and effort taken to reach world levels of efficiency in complex technologies. Given the intrinsic cost disadvantage that an industrial latecomer in a developing country would face and the externalities, uncertainties and information gaps under which learning is generally conducted, in a free market such an enterprise would find it extremely difficult to bear the costs involved. Moreover, capital markets in developing countries would also not be prepared to finance such a process. Thus, there is no assurance that resource allocation would be optimal under free trade.[14]

There are thus valid infant-industry arguments to protect new industries. As John Stuart Mill, after his forceful and extended critique of arguments for protection, put it in 1848:

The only case in which, on mere principles of political economy, protecting duties can be defensible, is when they are imposed temporarily (especially in a young and rising nation) in the hopes of naturalising a foreign industry, in itself perfectly suitable to the circumstances of the country. The superiority of one country over another in a branch of production often arises only from having begun it sooner. There may be no inherent advantage on one part, or disadvantage in another, but only a present superiority of acquired skill and experience. A country which has this skill and experience yet to acquire, may in other respects be better adapted to the production than those which were earlier in the field; and besides . . . nothing has a greater tendency to promote improvements in any branch of production than its trial under a new set of conditions. But it cannot be expected that individuals should, at their own risk, or rather to their certain loss, introduce a new manufacture, and bear the burden of carrying on until the producers have been educated to the level of those with whom the processes are traditional. A protective duty, continued for a reasonable time, might sometimes be the least inconvenient mode in which the nation can tax itself for the support of such an experiment. But it is essential that the protection should be confined to cases in which there is good ground for assurance that the industry which it fosters will after a time be able to dispense with it; nor should the domestic producers ever be allowed to expect that it will be continued to them beyond the time necessary for a fair trial of what they are capable of accomplishing.

(Mill, 1940: 922)

What better, more cogent, statement can we have, from the staunchest classical supporter of free trade, of the case for protecting the learning period under export orientation?

Two important implications may be drawn from the case for interventions to promote learning. First, it is plausible to argue, and indeed a branch of the 'new growth theory' literature suggests just this (see, for instance, Young, 1991), that there are particular sets of industrial activities that are more conducive to flexibility and productivity increase than others. Technologies that are more skill-, technology- and perhaps capital-intensive tend to pose greater 'learning' challenges to enterprises, and may offer higher long-term rewards in terms of developing the capabilities to carry out further diversification, improvement and innovation. These may thus be more desirable for the promotion of industrial flexibility than simpler technologies, which may offer lesser possibilities for the application of new technological knowledge and also more limited prospects for longer-term learning of innovative capabilities. Industrial flexibility over the long term may then depend on the ability of countries to move from the second set (say, textiles, garments, leather, food processing, or simple metal products) to the first (like machinery, chemicals, electricals and electronics). In terms of policy requirements, the move calls for infant-industry promotion not just of single activities but of entire sets of 'modern' activities.[15]

Second, once the case for protection is accepted, there is no analytical basis for the usual neoclassical case for providing low, uniform rates of effective protection. The duration and extent of protection should not be uniform when different technologies have different learning costs and periods. Complex, skill-intensive technologies necessarily require greater protection than those which have simple processes. The garment industry, for instance, may be able to reach competence in three months, while automobile manufacture may, depending on the level of local content, take ten to fifteen years (Jacobsson, 1993).

The success of outward orientation then has to be examined in the context of whether, and how, their governments succeeded in promoting learning, and overcoming the market failures that confront capability development. It is now widely accepted, and the argument is taken up below, that outward orientation did not mean the absence of selective trade and other interventions for the majority of East Asian NICs.[16] The infant-industry case has now got a bad name because of the many horrors that have been perpetrated in its name: this is not, in itself, an argument against carefully selected interventions to promote infant industries.

The lessons of the East Asian NICs are therefore rather different from those normally implied by the development literature. They grew, not because they replaced imperfect interventions with efficient markets, but because they remedied imperfect markets by well-directed and selective interventions to promote entry into new sets of activities. The benefits of export orientation arose, not from the static benefits to resource allocation, but from the discipline and incentives they provided that enabled infant industries to be carefully selected and to invest in their capabilities.[17] The extent and nature of interventions differed between the NICs, leading to different industrial structures and capabilities; this is taken up in a later section, after the 'supply side' factors have been considered.

Here it would be relevant to note the World Bank's recent (1993) 'miracle' study, which is attracting attention for its analysis of interventions in East Asia. This study describes many of the interventions undertaken and specifically dismisses the neoclassical argument that the NICs were non-interventionist. It also admits, as noted earlier, that there is a possibility of market failure in resource allocation under free markets. However, it concludes that while some interventions in capital markets (allocating credit to efficient firms) may have worked, there is little evidence that 'industrial policy' in terms of protection and targeting had much success. The success of the High Performing Asian Economies (HPAEs) was due to getting macro policies right, investing in education and being export-oriented. This is a biased and misleading analysis.

Since I have completed a lengthy review of this study (Lall, 1994), only the main points need be noted here. The Bank's analysis suffers from several faults, not least among them that it has to defend the institution's approach (in structural adjustment and other policy work) that selective interventions be abolished and governments confined to 'market friendly' interventions in factor markets. There are many ways in which the data and analysis are used (or misused) in the 'miracle' study to achieve this.

The first is that the market failures that the study lists are narrowly defined in neoclassical terms and ignore issues of technological deepening (which was a specific objective of interventions in the larger NICs and Japan). Second, even the market failures mentioned are not empirically explored – how they were tackled is totally ignored. Third, the evaluation of interventions takes no account of the policy aims of the countries, and so is grossly deficient. Many market failures that policy makers were trying to remedy cannot be identified with reference to static neoclassical models that ignore the capability-building process. Fourth, the empirical tests used to evaluate the effects of industrial policy are biased and inadequate, and ignore such basics as differences in industrial structure, export composition or R&D activity resulting from interventions. The fact that the most successful industrialising countries (Japan and Korea) had severely 'distorted' prices (apparently more so than import-substituting countries like India) is mentioned but not evaluated in terms of developing complex industry. It is also deficient in its analysis of supply side factors – the market friendly interventions that it favours – as noted below.

The strongest point of the World Bank study is that it identifies some of the reasons why the East Asian states were able to devise and implement interventionist strategies so successfully, by insulating their bureaucracies from vested interests and developing skills. However, the evident lesson to be drawn from this, to improve the quality of selective intervention in other countries, are ignored because of the basic premise that such interventions are wrong.

'Supply side' factors

These factors may be considered under three broad headings: skills, technical effort and finance. Each of these has its own sets of private markets, and each may suffer from market failures (see Justman and Teubal, 1986). Each has evolved over time institutional intermediaries to remedy such failures. The efficiency of the supply side thus depends on the efficacy of markets in combination with supporting institutions, many of which have been originally set up by governments.

Skills The human capital needed for industrial flexibility comprises the skills imparted by the formal education and training system, as well as those created by on-the-job training and experience. Less advanced or more specialised firms need a smaller range than those in large-scale and technologically complex industries. But even the simplest technology, if it is to be operated at world levels of efficiency, needs a range of worker, supervisory, maintenance, quality-control and adaptive skills. At the lowest end of the technological spectrum, simple literacy and some vocational training, complemented by a few higher-level technical skills, may be sufficient to ensure adequate TCs (even garment assembly for export requires good supervisory, layout and maintenance skills). In more sophisticated technologies, the requirements are more diverse and the range of special skills wider.

While primary and secondary schooling provide the necessary base for building shop-floor capabilities in all activities, more advanced technical training becomes critical as the industrial structure develops. Since many forms of high-level skills are not fungible (a textile engineer cannot, for example, design electrical equipment), the range of specialisation grows with industrial complexity. The education system has to match the skill needs of the industrial structure, not just in the quantity of the people it graduates in different disciplines, but also in the quality of the training and the relevance of the curriculum.

Formal pre-employment education is only one component of the skill creation process. The other is on-the-job training and experience, and also further formal training of employees sponsored by the enterprises. The latter is a rapidly increasing activity among developed country firms. Most enterprises in developing countries, however, invest relatively little in upgrading the skills of their employees.

This may be due to several market failures. First, there may be an information failure: managers may not be fully aware of the skill needs of the technologies they are using. Or they may be rooted in traditional ways of manufacturing and training (such as the apprenticeship system in Africa) that are unsuited to the needs of modern technologies or to the upgrading of existing technologies.[18] Their own level of education may, in certain cases, make them averse to the further training of employees. Second, there may be missing or deficient markets for the provision of skills and training: managers may realise that employee skills are deficient, but may not be able to remedy this. They may not have access to trainers in-house; overseas training may be out of the question; and there may be no local institutions, official or private, that can offer the right level and quality of training. Finally, there may be failures caused by the externalities inherent in training: employers may be unsure of recouping the full benefits of their investments. Trained employees may leave the firm, taking the benefits of training to competitors.

The risk of market failures in skill creation is generally accepted.

Interventions to promote human capital formation are, however, assumed to be purely functional, i.e. they simply strengthen factor markets without attempting to support some activities over others.[19] This assumption is not justified. Many forms of educational investments are non-selective, providing a general base of skills for all activities: particularly for schooling and non-technical higher education. However, by contrast, more specialised forms of tertiary education and vocational training are highly industry-specific, and policies to address these needs have necessarily to be selective. Moreover, the selectivity of educational policies increases with the role that the government plays in determining the direction of industrial growth. If the government has an active industrial strategy, pushing the economy into more complex areas of activity, it has to ensure that the necessary skills are created by the education system: selectivity in one sphere necessarily calls for selectivity in all related, supporting spheres. The conclusion drawn by the World Bank (1993) that education matters is correct – the implication that this is completely neutral between activities is not.

Technical effort   Most of the technological activity that firms undertake to cope with production problems, cost reduction, diversification and so on is an in-house affair. However, the undertaking of such effort may suffer from the types of market failure just mentioned. Many firms in developing countries do not know that they have to undertake deliberate technological effort to resolve those problems. When they wish to undertake the effort, they may not have well-functioning information and technical support services to draw upon. The applied research that industrial firms conduct may need basic research and 'lumpy' testing and other facilities that may not exist in the country. Finally, the returns to investments in technology may be greatly reduced by the danger of losing the knowledge to other firms. Some of these market failures can also lead to underinvestment in technological effort in developed economies, as Arrow's classic article noted many years ago (see Justman and Teubal, 1986).

Government interventions in information and technology markets may be needed to remedy such failures. Let us start with technical information and support. Many forms of technical information are available free to firms: from journals, contacts with capital goods suppliers and buyers of export products, visits to fairs, plants and conferences, interactions with subcontractors and other suppliers, and so on. More complex or closely held information is available commercially from consultants, more advanced firms (on licence), or as part of a package of direct investment. There is little need for policy intervention here, except to guide firms to the right sources of information.

Apart from these, however, there are many information and support services that are not provided by the market in any country, especially by markets in developing countries. There are several technological functions that have 'public goods' features, whose rewards are difficult to appropriate by private firms and so suffer from market failure. These include the encouragement of technological activity in general (overcoming risk aversion and the 'learning to learn' barrier); the development of special research skills; the setting of industrial standards and the promotion of quality awareness: the provision of metrology (industrial measurement and calibration) services; the undertaking of contract research, testing or information search for firms that lack the facilities or skills; other extension services for small enterprises; and the undertaking and co-ordination of basic (pre-commercial) research activities. The provision of these services then has to be undertaken as an infrastructural service, or as a co-operative activity by the enterprises concerned.[20]

The public infrastructure for science and technology may comprise a large range of institutions, from universities and research financing bodies to standards institutes and R&D institutions. The efficacy of this infrastructure has been variable. In many developing countries science and technology (S&T) institutions have been inadequately staffed and poorly equipped and funded. In some a lot of money has been invested, but without a proper linkage between the technological needs of industry and the research or promotion work of the institutions. In the poorest and least developed countries, no industrial research worth the name is conducted, and there is little effective extension work to support small enterprises. In the more advanced countries, the technical extension is somewhat better and some high quality research is carried out, but most of the latter is divorced from industrial technology. There are exceptions, of course, but on the whole the infrastructure has not served the functions for which it was set up.

This is not to say that there is no need for S&T institutions. The promotion of ITD does require infrastructural support, especially as the industrial structure develops and information flows and technical specialisation become more important. Export promotion requires an active standards institute, not merely to inform producers of the required standards and to vet product quality, but to play an active role in helping industry to achieve those standards – a technically demanding task. The observance of standards and the carrying out of research call for precise measurements and calibration, for which a metrology office becomes essential. Contract research is needed by smaller firms, even by larger ones for specific problems, as they try to upgrade their technologies and introduce new products. Access to basic scientific knowledge can help firms to do applied research in some areas. The need for information and technical support grows with the level of TC development, but some needs exist even at the starting levels. The weakness of the support structure is itself a symptom of the low levels of skill and TC development, but the strengthening of the structure can greatly help the technological development process.

Finance   Since the development of TCs is an investment involving time and cost, the availability of finance at the appropriate time, in appropriate amounts and at the appropriate price is an important determinant of ITD. Capital market failures can constitute a barrier to capability development, in general terms by retarding the allocation of resources to, or within, manufacturing activity, and in particular by constricting resources for technology development.

Capital market failures are widespread in developing countries (see Stiglitz, 1989). Some such failures are policy-induced, while others are endemic in the weak economic structures. Policies that lead to the arbitrary allocation of credit, repression of interest rates, suppression of competition among intermediaries, inadequate development of capital markets and segmentation among differing markets for finance, are common causes of resource misallocation in developing countries. Apart from these policy-induced distortions, financial intermediaries may suffer from inadequate information, especially on small borrowers, and may be exceptionally risk-averse because of problems in collecting sufficient information and enforcing contracts. They may be particularly reluctant to finance technological development because of their lack of knowledge of what this involves (they know even less about it than the firms involved), and the risk inherent in all technological activity. Needless to say, capital market failures are likely to be worse for small and medium-sized enterprises than for large ones.

A large part of TC development, especially at the lower levels, is the result not of formal research activity but of problem-solving in the course of production. The financing of this form of TC activity does not require special instruments. The market failures that occur here are part of the broader failures that affect industry in general, and they have to be addressed in context. The rest of TC development is based on more formal technological effort, involving longer-term research and experimentation that may face considerable market risk. This risk persists even if the technology is not new in the international market, but is untried by the developing country firm. The financing of this form of technological activity, which becomes significant as industrialisation proceeds, calls for different mechanisms, such as subsidised R&D, venture capital financing, technology 'incubators' and the like, to overcome market failures.

Conclusions on determinants of TCs

The determinants of industrial flexibility are a complex mixture of demand- and supply-side factors impinging upon the decisions and capabilities of individual firms. These depend partly on the 'initial conditions' in the country – its size, location, resources (physical and human), experience of industrialisation, entrepreneurial culture, and so on – that determine the options open to the industrial sector. They depend also on the policies pursued by the government. Apart from the obvious requirements of sound macroeconomic management and the pursuit of efficiency objectives, policies to remedy missing or faulty markets and improve their functioning, add to the stock of human capital and foster indigenous technological activity, have important effects on industrial flexibility.

Industrial flexibility is thus the result of the interaction of incentives, skills, technological effort and institutional support. One of these factors on its own cannot produce sustained industrial growth or flexibility. Providing 'correct' incentives (free market-determined prices) may lead to static reallocative benefits, but by itself cannot lead to dynamic growth and diversification in developing countries: the ability to cope with technical change and to enter difficult technologies will be held back by learning costs, externalities, uncertainty and lack of information. Yet 'getting prices right' is the main policy prescription of the mainstream neoclassical approach to development economics, supported by the World Bank's 1993 study. At the same time, interventions in the incentive regime carry many risks. The provision of protection or subsidies to infant industries has to be offset by measures to induce them to invest in the necessary learning. And it has to be accompanied by the provision of the skills, information and finance needed from factor markets to allow new technologies to be learnt.

Similarly, the creation of new skills may by itself help industries to become more competitive, but simply adding to skills when incentives are distorted is likely to lead to meagre results. Moreover, simply having skilled employees without investing in technological effort can reduce the pace of industrial development. The same reasoning applies to technical effort and institution-building: the incentive structure has to be conducive to the right kind and intensity of effort and support, and has to be combined appropriately with the other ingredients of industrial competitiveness.

IV GOVERNMENTS AND INDUSTRIAL FLEXIBILITY

So much for theoretical considerations. Let us now look at the experience of governments in promoting industrial flexibility. We examine the experience of two very different groups of countries. The first are arguably the most successful and flexible industrial economies in the developing world, the four East Asian NICs. The second are some of the least developed countries of sub-Saharan Africa, which are evidently performing very poorly and failing to respond to the structural adjustment efforts that are taking hold in the region. It is hoped that, by applying the concepts related to technological learning and market failures discussed above, plausible implications will emerge for flexibility in the developing world as a whole. One interesting aspect of the analysis is that 'flexibility' may not be a uniform, homogeneous quality of industry in different countries: there may be several different kinds of flexibility that economies may aim for.

275

The East Asian NICs

There is a large and growing literature now on the role of government interventions in the industrialisation of the East Asian NICs (see, among others, Amsden, 1989, 1992; Lall and Kell, 1991; Lall *et al.*, 1992; Pack and Westphal, 1986; Wade, 1990; and World Bank, 1993). Apart from the fact that they all combined their export orientation with active support for industrial development, however, the most interesting aspect of their experience is that there is no East Asian 'model' of industrial development. There are separate models for each of the four countries differing in significant respects from each other, and yielding different patterns of industry and technological capabilities. These differences are worth considering here because they have important implications for the kind of industrial flexibility that has emerged. These implications will be drawn out as the cases are discussed below.

It is useful to start with background data on some of the variables that are relevant to TC development. Table 9.1 shows the performance of the four NICs and measures of their education levels, technical effort and reliance on foreign technology in different forms. The data are later compared with those from some of the least industrialised countries from sub-Saharan Africa to illustrate some of the basic needs for industrial development and flexibility.

At one end is Hong Kong, with a *laissez-faire* trade policy that comes closest to the neoclassical paradigm of ideal industrial strategy. The government has not intervened in product markets, either to support particular industries or to protect manufacturing in general. It has not guided investments in other ways, by interfering in the allocation of domestic credit or foreign investments. It has provided a stable administrative and macro-economic regime. Its growth performance has been impressive, if not at the level of the larger NICs.

The Hong Kong government did intervene 'functionally' to provide education and training, subsidised land to manufacturers, export information and support services. The Productivity Centre performed various technological services to help producers to improve their technologies. It even selected the clothing sector to support by setting up a large and well-funded textile and garments design and training centre. However, its interventions were predominantly non-selective, and there was no attempt to 'pick winners'. Moreover, even its functional interventions in education, while impressive by Third World standards, were not as intense as those of the larger NICs.[21] In particular, it lagged in the training of scientists and engineers and in vocational training, and in undertaking research and development locally (though precise data on R&D are not available, all the studies of Hong Kong manufacturing suggest that there is relatively little formal technology development).

Table 9.1 Background data on the East Asian NICs

	Hong Kong	Singapore	Korea	Taiwan
Manufacturing growth				
1965–80	17.0	13.3	18.7	16.4
1980–90[a]	3.0	6.6	12.7	6.9
Manufactured exports (1990)				
US $ billion[b]	27.8	38.4	60.3	62.3
Growth of mechandise exports				
1965–80	9.1	4.7	27.2	18.9
1980–90	6.2	8.6	12.8	10.3[c]
FDI as % of gross domestic investment (1957–87)	7.0	16.8	0.9	3.3
Educational enrolments (1989)				
Primary[d]	105	110	108	99
Secondary	73	69	87	94
Tertiary[e]	13	24	39	31
Tertiary enrolment in science and technology (as % of population)	0.67	0.89	1.39	1.06
Vocational training (per 100,000 population)	800	372	1970	2082
R&D (latest)				
Total (% GNP)	n.a.	0.9	2.3	1.8
Productive enterprises[f] (% GNP)	n.a.	0.3	1.9	1.0
Scientists and engineers in R&D (per million population)	n.a.	960	1283	1426

Notes:
[a] Growth rates for Hong Kong and Taiwan calculated from UNIDO data, in constant 1985 US dollars; rest from World Bank (1992).
[b] *World Development Report* figures.
[c] Calculated from Taiwanese official data, in constant US dollars.
[d] Enrolment figures are with reference to populations in the relevant age group; if enrolments are from other groups, a figure of over 100 per cent is obtained.
[e] Calculated for Hong Kong and Singapore from ESCAP yearbook. Taiwanese data from official statistics.
[f] R&D financed by productive enterprises.

Source: Lall (1992a); Lall and Kell (1991); World Bank (1992); UNDP (1992); Republic of China (Taiwan) (1990, 1992); UNIDO (1992–3); UNESCAP (1991).

Thus the level of intervention was fairly low, and trade was always free. Perhaps this has lessons for other industrialising economies? It does, but not necessarily that *laissez-faire* is everywhere the best way to promote competitive manufacturing. Two important features of the Hong Kong experience have to be noted in this context. First, it started with several unique advantages for industrialisation that other developing countries, even free trade centres, lacked. Its century-and-a-half of entrepot trading experience gave it a range of capabilities and infrastructure for trading and finance. The presence of several British business and finance houses (the 'Hongs') provided a constant supply of foreign skills as well as training for local employees. Most important for manufacturing, its textile, garment and toy industries took off only after the communist take-over, when there was an influx of experienced Chinese entrepreneurs, engineers and technicians from Shanghai. Much of the 'learning' for these industries had already been undergone earlier, and the technologies were sufficiently simple that subsequent training could be given to a workforce with good primary and secondary education. The free trade environment, combined with existing capabilities in trade and finance and a supply of cheap manpower, enabled these advantages to be fully exploited, mainly by Chinese entrepreneurs. There was considerable foreign investment, but in manufacturing the lead stayed firmly in local hands (in sharp contrast to Singapore, discussed later).

Second, the ensuing pattern of industrialisation in Hong Kong reflected the non-selective policies of its government. The colony started and stayed with light labour-intensive manufacturing industry,[22] though within this there was considerable upgrading of quality, a pattern of industrial development driven by the lack of selective interventions to promote more complex industries. Its success was based on the development of operational and marketing capabilities. Despite its dynamism in light industry, however, there was little industrial deepening and diversification. There was little natural progression up the ladder of industrial complexity into more difficult and demanding technologies. As wage and land pressures mounted, the colony had to relocate its manufacturing to other countries, mainly mainland China, and suffered a significant loss of industrial activity at home (over 1986–92 it lost about 35 per cent of its manufacturing employment, and the process is continuing (Havrylyshyn, 1993)).

Hong Kong has been able to continue to grow in services and trade because of its unique location, connections and events in the adjoining mainland. However, its pattern of industrialisation success is clearly not open to other developing countries. Simple recourse to free trade is unlikely to lead to such dynamic growth, even by other small countries, and no other similar free trade centres, of which there are several in the developing world, have achieved much industrial success: they have not been able to undertake even the relatively easy learning required of light industry. More important, even larger economies that can attract labour-intensive foreign investments are unlikely to be able to sustain their industrial deepening by 'natural' progression if they do not undertake interventions to promote the move into more complex activities. Reliance on foreign direct investments can reduce some of the learning requirements, but any development of local technological capabilities is bound to need supporting selective interventions.

The flexibility of the Hong Kong manufacturing sector thus has special characteristics. It consists of moving upmarket in existing light industry and diversifying out of manufacturing altogether, not of taking on the more complex technologies that can enable it to retain a manufacturing base with rising wage costs. By contrast, Switzerland, with only 1 million more people, retains a growing and deep industrial sector (with chemicals, heavy machinery, food processing, and so on) with much higher wages than Hong Kong. The difference lies precisely in the fact that Switzerland, with judicious periods of protection, promotion and disregard of intellectual property laws, has over the past century built up a deep technological base. The industrial flexibility of Hong Kong is in essence to deindustrialise without losing out in growth, a feature that depends crucially on its location and ability to act as a conduit for the mainland.

The relative lack of depth in its industrial structure has, nevertheless, led to considerable disquiet among Hong Kong's policy-makers. As the *Financial Times* survey notes:

> The *laissez faire* prop against which the Hong Kong government has leaned since 1841 has prevented it from adopting the ambitious strategies that have spawned the computer components and telecommunications products of Singapore, South Korea and Taiwan. But as Hong Kong continues to evolve into a financial and services centre, the pressures of some of the highest land and labour costs in Asia appear to have given the government second thoughts about its stance. . . . The government is taking serious measures to encourage the inflow of overseas technologies, so that Hong Kong can retain some kind of industrial base. . . . The government has toned down its *laissez faire* inclinations to permit a new applied research and development scheme. This is a $HK 200m. fund, which will match the investment of any start-up company which fulfils certain criteria, in exchange for an equity stake. This represents the first step towards direct government funding for research and development, and by implication, the creation of a Government industrial policy.
>
> (Havrylyshyn, 1993: 6)

Korea is at the other extreme. Its record of industrial development, in terms of growth, diversification and deepening, is perhaps the most impressive in modern economic history (even more so than Japan's in view of the periods and initial conditions involved). Its government intervened extensively, both functionally and selectively, in all product and factor markets.[23] It offered high, variable and prolonged periods of protection to selected activities, while forcing those that approached competitiveness to export significant parts of their output. It directed domestic investible resources to infant industries, and deliberately fostered the emergence of giant private conglomerates that could internalise various imperfect markets. It invested heavily in education, especially technical education,[24] and forced firms to launch employee training schemes; it also invested in R&D and technology infrastructure institutions, while inducing (through subsidies and other incentives) and cajoling local firms to develop their independent research capabilities (for a case study of the electronics industry see Mody, 1990). All these factor market interventions had highly selective aspects, being integrated into the overall direction of industrial development as driven by trade and industrial policies.

Perhaps the most interesting aspect of Korea's industrial success for present purposes is that it was largely based on indigenous enterprises that imported and assimilated a range of complex technologies, rather than on technology transfer via direct investment. The Korean government was until very recently highly selective towards foreign direct investments, and in some instances induced Japanese firms to sell out to the *chaebol* (large Korean conglomerates) after some years in the country. In technological terms this strategy called for far more domestic skill and technology creation than one that set up the same range of industries but with a heavy reliance on direct foreign investment. Korea's investments in education and R&D, and the fostering of the giant *chaebol*, were a necessary part of its nationalist strategy, driven by the objective of being efficient in world markets. A strategy of nationalism with inward orientation (like India) would have led to far less efficiency, and would consequently have demanded fewer interventions in supporting factor markets. A strategy of outward orientation with reliance on foreign investors, like Singapore, might have led to less deepening, or to lower domestic innovative capabilities.

The fact that Korea has a research and manufacturing base that is able to copy, adapt and build upon state-of-the-art industrial technologies gives it a flexibility that is probably unmatched, especially in advanced manufacturing activities. This flexibility is thus of a completely different order from that of Hong Kong – it conduces to sustained industrial expansion rather than deindustrialisation. It is also different from that of liberalising economies with diverse industrial economies which are heavily dependent on foreign direct investment (FDI) for technology, like Mexico (Mexican enterprises spend some 0.03 per cent of GNP on R&D). Such economies are unable to enter world-class production of new high technology items of the type that Korea is launching, and their most important industrial exports (automobiles in the case of Mexico) are those that have matured behind long periods of import substitution and can now form part of the global sourcing strategies of multinational companies.

The implication of this is that indigenous research capability has many dynamic benefits for the industries that possess the capability. Apart from significantly lowering the cost of technology transfer, it allows independent diversification into more advanced areas than may be permitted by a foreign investor that fully controls the same technology.[25] The underlying market failure with FDI-driven technology transfer is that, in a Korean-type strategy, the local firm is forced to develop more advanced skills and technical knowledge than are needed simply to operate a technology imported in a fully 'packaged' form.[26] The foreign investor who already has access to advanced design, research and development capabilities elsewhere will not find it in its interest to invest in them in a developing host country.

The development of local R&D capabilities can also have several externalities and linkages. It feeds into local capital goods and component production. It enables the accumulated technical knowledge to be applied by other industries or even by competitors. It leads to interaction between industry and the technology infrastructure (universities, research institutions, quality assurance centres, and so on). All this conduces to overall flexibility in the manner displayed by Korea (and also, to a great extent, by Taiwan).

In Singapore, by far the smallest of the NICs, the government has been very interventionist, but the form of interventionism has been very different from that of Korea (see Hobday, 1994). The economy started with a base of trading, ship servicing and petroleum refining. After a brief period of import substitution, it moved into export-oriented industrialisation based overwhelmingly on foreign investment and technology transfer by multinational companies. Unlike Hong Kong, there was a weak tradition of local entrepreneurship, and there was no sudden influx of technical and entrepreneurial know-how from China. There was a decade or so of light industrial activity (garment and semi-conductor assembly), after which the Singapore government acted firmly to upgrade the industrial structure by intervening in the entry of foreign investors to guide them to higher value-added activities, and in education to create specific high-level technical skills.

This latter set of interventions are not reflected fully in the figures in Table 9.1, though the figures for science and technology enrolments at the tertiary level are quite respectable (India, for instance, has 0.21 per cent of its population in these subjects, Mexico 0.7 per cent and Brazil 0.4 per cent; see Lall, 1990). The main thrust of training in Singapore was via the setting-up of institutes jointly with industry to give specialised instruction to employees rather than pre-employment education. This was subsidised by the state, and carefully targeted at the activities to be promoted.

Specific areas of both manufacturing and services (like banking, freighting and aircraft servicing) were selected for promotion, but the policy instruments used did not include trade protection. They comprised a range of incentives, pressure, subsidies and support, that guided the allocation of resources and lowered the cost of entry into difficult activities. Manufacturing activity was highly specialised in particular processes and products, with no attempt to increase local content or the degree of vertical integration. Such specialisation, along with the heavy reliance on foreign investments for technology and skill transfer, greatly reduced the need for indigenous technological investments (as compared, say, with Korea). Thus, while selective interventions led Singapore's industry into sophisticated producer and consumer electronics, precision instruments, optics and so on, the technological depth of the enterprises located there was comparatively low. Some design and development activity did develop over time, again with considerable urging and support from the government (Hobday, 1994), but this is an area that is targeted for the island's future.

The lessons of Singapore, to the extent that an economy of 3 million people can be considered relevant to most of the developing world, are twofold. First, FDI can take a small economy a long way if it is carefully selected and guided, supplied with superlative infrastructure and a disciplined and trained workforce, and given a competitive and stable investment environment. Second, it is not necessary to offer import protection to technologically complex activities if the main sources of operational and other technologies remain foreign, and production is integrated with that in foreign countries (rather than with local suppliers), and concentrated on particular stages of production. This strategy requires both functional and selective interventions by the government; the contrasting experiences of Singapore and Hong Kong with respect to the deepening of industrial activity illustrate this clearly.

For larger countries, however, that wish to develop flexibility *à la* Korea (i.e. to deepen local supply capabilities, develop indigenous enterprise and foster innovative skills), this level of selectivity may not be enough. The significantly higher learning costs involved may only be met by local enterprises receiving higher levels of support (by protection or subsidies), and by the creation of large domestic firms that can partly internalise defective risk, capital and information markets.

Finally, we come to Taiwan. The Taiwanese economy, with about half the size of population of Korea, has been practically as dynamic as the latter. Some thirty years ago Taiwan was considerably more developed than Korea, and was better endowed with human resources. Like Hong Kong, it experienced a large influx of capital, skills and entrepreneurship from mainland China after the revolution. Its development strategy had elements of the Korean-style attempts to select and promote local industries, by protection, credit allocation and selectivity in admitting FDI, in areas of future comparative advantage. However, Taiwan's selectivity was far less detailed than Korea's, and it did not attempt to create giant private conglomerates or to push so heavily into advanced technologies or capital-intensive activities. Its less intense relationship with private industry meant that many of its more ambitious forays into heavy industry had to be led by the public sector, and Taiwan has the largest public sector of the four NICs.

Taiwan's strength has lain in its small and medium-sized enterprises that tapped its large base of human capital and the infant-industry promotion offered by the government to grow and diversify in skill-intensive activities.

The resulting industrial structure is 'lighter' than that of Korea, with greater emphasis on meeting market niches rather than mass production, less in-house R&D, and less emphasis on creating international brand names (see Mody, 1990 on the electronics industry). The inherent disadvantages of small size for technical upgrading have been partly offset by the government's provision of a wide range of technology support services, including R&D, and their inherent flexibility in meeting changing demand conditions have so far enabled Taiwan to maintain nearly as high rates of export growth as Korea.

The flexibility of Taiwanese industry is thus in some respects different from that of Korean industry. A large proportion of small enterprises are specialised in labour-intensive manufacturing which faces the same problems as Hong Kong industry, and may only survive by relocating overseas, perhaps moving upmarket in their domestic operations while winding down manufacturing. Unlike Hong Kong, however, there are many firms with the ability to enter higher value-added activities and to tap a large technology infrastructure. There is also a growing proportion of larger firms that can invest in their own R&D and brand names. This gives the economy some of the flexibility arising from industrial depth, as in Korea. It is a debatable point which of these two economies has the greater flexibility, one dominated by giant *chaebol*, the other with smaller and more nimble, but technologically lighter, enterprises.

This concludes our brief survey of the successful industrialisers. They are all 'flexible' in all common uses of the term. The evidence suggests, nevertheless, that their flexibility has different characteristics – unless these differences are taken into account, there cannot be a correct evaluation of the role and effects of government interventions. Each started with a different set of endowments for industrial growth, and adopted different approaches to improving those endowments and to pushing their enterprises into more productive activities. A variety of models emerged, depending on the strategy chosen to tackle market failures. Each was fairly good in addressing functional failures, especially in physical infrastructure and human capital. They differed in their approaches to capital markets: Korea and Taiwan intervened heavily to direct domestic credit to chosen activities, while Singapore directed FDI inflows to its strategic ends. They also differed in their technology support activities, with Korea and Taiwan investing most heavily in creating an S&T infrastructure.

Their most important differences lay in their trade and industrial policies. Korea intervened most heavily and pervasively, both in trade and in the industrial structure, and also (until the mid-1980s) in deciding what should be produced by whom. It kept foreign firms out of many activities, and intervened in other forms of technology imports to strengthen the hand of local firms. Hong Kong intervened the least, and dynamic local entrepreneurs were able to use the colony's locational and inherited advantages to grow in activities where learning processes were brief and the technical effort needed for efficiency relatively small. The others lay in between.

The nature of the industrial sectors that emerged reflected these different strategies – ignoring this basic fact is perhaps the main weakness of the World Bank's (1993) 'miracle' study. While each country was flexible in terms of coping with world competition, each dealt in a different range and level of industrial technologies. Hong Kong has the least technological depth, and its response has been to move upmarket in light consumer goods and to shift production elsewhere: its flexibility has been in deindustrialising and moving into services (many related to the offshore operations of its industries). At the other end, Korea has developed a very diverse industrial sector with considerable technological depth and R&D capability. Its flexibility has lain in tackling highly complex and risky technologies (with high pay-offs where successful), spawning its own large multinational enterprises, creating a brand image internationally and confronting directly the industrial leaders of the developed world.

Singapore's flexibility derives from its ability to furnish the wherewithal and incentives for developed country firms to upgrade its industries in narrow segments of manufacturing; this may lead it into high technology or out of manufacturing altogether. Finally, Taiwan has been extremely flexible in terms of diversifying the export range of its domestic enterprises, by a mixture of selective and functional interventions. Whether this is as solid a base for longer-term upgrading as in the case of Korea is open to question.

The least industrialised countries

It may be instructive to look briefly at the problems faced by the countries that have obviously not 'made it' in industry. Most of them are in sub-Saharan Africa (SSA), where a combination of external shocks, poor economic management and a tiny base of industrial capabilities has forced a process of massive deindustrialisation (see Lall, 1992b). By any kind of comparison with the NICs, these industrial sectors are clearly not flexible. They find it difficult to compete in world markets except at the rudimentary level of some processing of local natural resources. They tend to operate most technologies at low levels of technical efficiency, and make few significant adaptations or improvements to the technologies that they start with. They have displayed almost no dynamism, even in the well-established industries, in developing new products or processes, cultivating new industrial markets for exports or keeping up with the pace of technological change. There is little development of local supply linkages or domestic diffusion of technologies. By any reasonable standard, therefore, the bulk of SSA industry fails the minimal test of flexibility.

Most explanations for this state of affairs assign a central role to misdirected government intervention. The 'Washington consensus' is that import-substitution strategies, coupled with the push to Africanise ownership of industry under parastatals, led to gross misallocation of resources. The solution is then to 'get prices right', privatise industry, open it to international competition and let efficient activities emerge in areas of natural comparative advantage. This is the essence of the structural adjustment programmes (SAPs) being adopted in a growing number of SSA countries, and the main lesson drawn by the 'miracle' study for other countries. The issue at stake is whether or not the assumptions on which adjustment strategies are founded are valid in SSA. Are SAPs going to inject the flexibility into industry, in a context of revitalised growth, that past inward-oriented, state-led, highly interventionist strategies have patently failed to do?

The earlier discussion suggests that SAPs are based on a simplified view of the development process in which market failures are ignored or minimised. Clearly the extent to which import substitution was carried in most SSA countries was excessive, and too much weight was placed on a public sector that lacked the capabilities to manage industry, and, in addition, was prone to corruption and political interference. But this is not the entire explanation for the abysmal performance of SSA industry. There are many other instances where import substitution yielded far better results, and in the case of the larger East Asian NICs protection was a necessary part of mastering complex technologies.

The reason for the SSA performance lay partly in the common error of import-substitution strategies, i.e. prolonged and non-selective interventions, with no offsetting incentives to invest in developing TCs. It lay also, and in my view more importantly, in the minuscule base of skills and industrial experience that most SSA countries started with in their industrial process (Lall, 1992b). Given the capability requirements of even relatively simple modern technologies, there was no way that an efficient and flexible manufacturing sector could develop (the only partial exceptions were countries with large non-African populations that possessed, or had access to, the skills needed). With enough protection and the subsidies provided by a booming primary export sector, an inefficient sector could, however, survive and grow. When primary exports ran out of steam, and the debt and other macroeconomic problems took hold, the cost of the lack of capabilities and flexibility was a sustained process of deindustrialisation.

Table 9.2 shows some relevant figures on capabilities and skill formation in some leading SSA economies. The contrast between the human resource endowment of SSA and the East Asian NICs hardly needs to be emphasised. In fact, some of the figures given in the table exaggerate the situation in favour of SSA, since they do not take into account the quality of education, completion rates, relevance of the curricula for industry, and so on: in all of these SSA tends to lag. Moreover, R&D figures for Africa appear to be overestimates,[27] and very little of the R&D actually performed is directed to

Table 9.2 Background data on TCs in selected SSA countries

	Tanzania	Kenya	Ghana	Côte d'Ivoire	Nigeria
Education enrolment[a]					
Primary	63	94	75	78[b]	70
Secondary	4	23	39	20	19
Tertiary	0	2	2	3[c]	3
Tertiary enrolments in S&T[d] (% of population)	0.008	0.06	0.05	0.06	0.02
Vocational training (% of population)	0.01	0.04	0.12	0.19	0.09
R&D (% GNP)					
Total R&D	n.a.	0.8	0.2	0.3	0.3
R&D financed by productive enterprises	–	0	0	0	0
Scientists and engineers (in R&D) (per million population)	n.a.	26	12[e]	72	26

Notes
[a] Enrolment data are for 1989 unless stated.
[b] 1985.
[c] 1985.
[d] Around mid-1980s.
[e] Based on fieldwork reported in Lall *et al.* (1994).
Source: Lall (1992b), Lall *et al.* (1994) World Bank (1992).

industry. In a recently completed piece of research on Ghana, which has by regional standards a fairly good technology infrastructure, it was found that only about forty-five graduate engineers or scientists were employed in the whole of public R&D relevant to industry, and that R&D relevant to industry comprised only about 0.02 per cent of GNP (Lall *et al.*, 1994). Industry itself conducted nothing that would be regarded as formal R&D elsewhere, and the level of TCs was so low that many smaller enterprises were not even aware of their skill and technology gaps. There were, in other words, such large information and skill market failures that industrial enterprises had little opportunity to develop their technological capabilities.

In this setting, the impact of SAPs, with their primary reliance on incentive reforms and getting rid of all interventions, is bound to have been disappointing. The pace of reform, where undertaken, has generally been relatively rapid compared with many countries in Asia (though not with some Latin American countries). Depending on the bargaining power of the government concerned, the period in which industry is exposed to severe international competition varies from five years (in Zimbabwe) to about three (in Ghana). Import liberalisation has tended to be uniform across activities, and differences in learning (or relearning) periods have not been given consideration in the design of the phasing of the reforms. More importantly, the need for supporting investments in technical information, training, extension services and the like, has been ignored. In true neoclassical spirit, it has been taken as given that resources will move automatically from less to more efficient uses, and that the relevant factor markets will respond as required.

The real world is very different, and an application of the capability approach would have shown that such assumptions are invalid. Where there are low levels of TCs to start with, as in SSA, and supporting markets and institutions are practically non-existent, sudden exposure to imports is bound to devastate industries exposed to world competition and force economies back to their static, resource-based comparative advantage. Only those activities that have a strong local resource base, are protected by high transport costs or specialise in highly localised (low-income) markets, are likely to be able to survive. These are generally not the base for sustained industrial growth. To create industrial flexibility and evoke a dynamic response from new manufacturing activities needs more than 'getting prices right'; they call for interventions in the incentive regime and in factor markets.

This reasoning is strongly supported by a recently completed project on Ghanaian technology and enterprise development (Lall *et al.*, 1994). These findings are of special interest because Ghana has experienced the longest and most consistent process of structural adjustment in SSA, and for some time has been held up as the model of reform in that region (though Ghana's flagging performance is now turning the spotlight on Tanzania). Let us consider some relevant findings.

The first stage of the adjustment in Ghana started with the Economic Recovery Programme in 1983. This liberalised imports of inputs and equipment, but without offering direct competition to local producers. Since Ghanaian industry was at that stage operating at below 40 per cent of its capacity, the immediate impact was to boost production. The annual real growth rate of manufacturing value-added was 12.9 per cent in 1984, 24.3 per cent in 1985, 11 per cent in 1986, and 10 per cent in 1987. However, this pace of expansion could not be maintained. An easily usable capacity was brought into production (a significant proportion had been run down to such an extent that it could not be used as it stood), the further growth of manufacturing activity called for refurbishing and modernising run-down facilities, the addition of new capacity, and, most important, increases in the efficiency of operations.

Increased efficiency became imperative after 1986 as a series of two SAPs was launched. The trade regime became more open and tariff and non-tariff barriers were reduced to directly competing imports. By 1989, parts of Ghanaian industry were facing severe import competition, with effective rates of protection at a fairly uniform rate of around 20–25 per cent (due to be lowered further in 1990–91). This level of protection might have been sufficient in some countries to allow industry to restructure and grow. In Ghana, given its weak base of TCs and the absence of support for TC development in the design of the SAPs, the rate of growth of manufacturing value-added fell to 5.1 per cent in 1988, 3.1 per cent in 1989 and 2.5 per cent in 1990. There have been few signs of a revival thereafter.

It may be argued that some of this was inevitable: inefficient activities have to die before efficient ones emerge. Certainly there were some intrinsic-ally inefficient units that could not become competitive in a reasonable period or at reasonable cost. However, compared with many SSA countries, Ghana had relatively few 'white elephants' left by the time the SAPs were launched. Much of the industrial sector was already in relatively simple manufacturing. The few large capital-intensive operations left were either fairly efficient enclave operations (like the export-oriented aluminium smelt-ing plant), or else under state control and sheltered from direct import competition (like the oil refinery). It might therefore have been expected that liberalisation would not impose too much hardship, and that a new breed of competitive, even export-oriented, manufacturing activities would emerge in response to the new incentive framework.

However, an examination of the pattern of survival and growth in Ghanaian manufacturing shows three things. First, the adverse impact of liberalisation was strongest in the more modern, large-scale part of the industrial sector. The survivors and new entrants are basically in activities that do not face direct competition (very small-scale, making low-income or localised products, those protected by high transport costs or those based on some processing of local raw materials).[28] Even low-technology 'entry-level' manufacturing activities, like garments and footwear, where Ghana might be expected to have a competitive edge, have been unable to survive the import threat.

At the same time, there is little sign of the emergence of new manufactur-ing activities that are competitive and flexible. New entrants are largely in simple, low-quality metal products and consumer goods that are not exposed to import competition. Foreign investments in manufacturing, running at very low levels of about $5–7 million per annum, are concen-trated in activities with natural protection; hardly any are export-oriented.

Second, as far as manufactured exports are concerned, SAP theory suggests that Ghana's underlying competitive advantages in cheap labour, timber and agricultural products would lead to a dynamic growth of manu-factured exports using these inputs. The data show that while manufactured exports have grown since 1986, the absolute values are extremely small, coming to a total of $14.7 million in 1991.[29] The growth has come mainly from wood and aluminium products, both long established export sectors.[30] There is relatively little sign of a broad-based response on the part of

Ghanaian enterprises based more on local manufacturing activity.[31] There is a striking lack of the capabilities and managerial skills needed to upgrade manufacturing to world levels, and of the institutions needed to help enterprises develop these TCs. There has been some positive response to the improved incentive regime, but the real constraints lie in the lack of capabilities rather than in the incentive regime.

Third, it is particularly relevant to note that cheap labour has not so far emerged as a source of comparative advantage to Ghanaian industry, though the conventional wisdom suggests that this is the main source of comparative advantage in manufacturing for newly industrialising countries. What this ignores is that even the ability to compete internationally in low-technology labour-intensive industries requires a level of labour productivity and managerial and technical skills that is currently lacking in Ghana (compared, say, with the new NICs of South-East Asia).

The relatively well-run enterprises in Ghana were those with foreign management or highly educated local entrepreneurs who had the ability or the foreign work experience to search for relevant technologies, invest in worker training and seek out the technical information they needed to raise productivity. The typical local firm, on the other hand, lacked the ability even to perceive and define its technological problems. The government did nothing to remedy this gap, and the absence of institutions to help firms to upgrade was a crippling constraint.

To generalise on the implications for government policy for countries at this stage of industrial development:[32]

- On the incentive front, the pace of exposure to international competition has to be related to a realistic assessment of the learning or relearning needs of activities that are potentially viable. At the same time, it has to be ensured that the competitive spur to capability investments is not lost; simply reverting to the old system of protection would be disastrous. An appropriate combination of time-bound protection, strong pressures to enter export markets, and free internal entry and exit has to be devised.
- Incentive reforms have to be supported by measures to remedy factor market failures. Enterprises must have access to the finance, information, training, education, testing and other facilities that they cannot provide in-house yet need in order to upgrade competitiveness.
- In particular, the human capital base has to be greatly improved, especially at the middle technical and managerial levels.
- Small improvements in routine production skills can have enormous impact in raising productivity. These inputs may be provided in some cases by foreign investors, but in the bulk of industry they have to be provided by local technical support, diagnostic and consultancy services.
- Many entrepreneurs have to be 'taught to learn': they need to be informed and persuaded that traditional ways of training, production and manage-

ment cannot cope with modern technologies. This may require initial subsidisation of investments in TC development.

- The technology infrastructure has to be greatly improved and made responsive to industrial needs. Current institutions are poorly staffed, motivated and managed. Their own technological capabilities have to be boosted before they can make a significant contribution to industrial flexibility. This applies to basic institutions like the Standards Board as well as to the existing research, extension and information centres.
- Small enterprises are poorly informed about the sources, characteristics, costs and rewards of new technologies. An information service on technology acquisition would be a great help.
- Marketing skills and information, especially in export markets, constitute a big gap in all developing countries, but especially in low-income countries that have been cut off from trade. This gap has to be remedied by appropriate institutional support.
- Finally, government administrations themselves often lack the incentives, skills and knowledge to mount these policies and support services. Since industrial development cannot proceed without such support, it is imperative that administrative capabilities and information be improved.

There remains a large, crucial and difficult role for the government in developing industrial competitiveness in least developed countries. The main question is whether these governments have the capabilities, or can develop them in the relevant period, to fill this demanding role (see Killick, 1993: Chapter 7). The past behaviour and failures of the state in Africa do not offer a great deal of hope. It is beyond the scope of this chapter to analyse the political economy of policy formulation and implementation. However, it is evident that proposing a complex and demanding role for interventions to support industry, based on the experience of East Asia, may be completely irrelevant in cases where the government lacks the desire, discipline and skills to carry out such interventions. However, that experience also offers clues on how government capabilities may be improved and insulated from pressures (World Bank, 1993). If corruption and venality at the highest levels of government could be avoided in SSA, there may be some lessons from Asia on intervention.

Economic theory does not provide clear guidelines concerning the appropriate role of government in any specific set of circumstances (see Shapiro and Taylor, 1990; Streeten, 1991). It would probably be generally accepted that, in the absence of some supporting interventions, especially in skill and institutional development, there would be no economic progress at all. To achieve industrial progress needs more interventions but there is a range of options on what the government can or should do. Is the answer to limit fallible governments to the minimal feasible set of interventions, none of them selective? Is it to permit some selective interventions, but to limit the extent of selectivity (for instance, the degree of selectivity exercised by Korea was greater and more detailed than in other NICs)? If some selectivity is allowed, is the answer to improve the incentive and control systems within governments, and to improve the information and skills available to them? Can the dangers of selectivity be limited by strict adherence to an outward-oriented trade regime, and by setting out clearly the 'rules of the game' (the limited period of protection offered, the performance requirements in terms of exports, investments in training and technological activity)?

The correct policy is probably some combination of the above, with the balance varying by country and, for each country, over time. My own belief is that a very limited degree of selective interventions should be allowed even in SSA, and that external agencies should gear themselves to backing such interventions rather than arguing that there is no theoretical or empirical support for them. African countries should not, at this stage, attempt to 'do a Korea'. Nevertheless, they should not leave industry entirely to imperfectly functioning or missing markets; their interventions should be limited, not very selective, carefully crafted and subject to constant scrutiny.

V CONCLUDING REMARKS

Industrial flexibility is the outcome of a complex interaction of incentives, skills, technical effort and institutional support. All these determinants can be provided by markets. Until markets develop to a high degree, however, developing country industry has to operate with large gaps and imperfections that can distort and stifle the development process. These market deficiencies call for well-directed and well-implemented interventions. The case for only 'market friendly' interventions is not established, either in theory or in practice.

This is not to argue for undiscriminating interventions. The developing world is littered with gross distortions created by interventions. At the same time, there has not been enough intervention of the right type: many developing countries lack international competitiveness and the ability to cope with changing technologies because their policies have not induced the necessary technological capabilities. Those that have managed to develop flexible and competitive industrial sectors are the ones whose governments were able to mount effective interventions to overcome crucial market failures. Their example is relevant to all other countries, even those at very low levels of industrial competence.

There is, however, no unique model of industrial policy. There are many forms of flexibility that economies can develop, each with its own requirements of government intervention. There are also many modes and levels of intervention. Each set of policies has to be defined within its particular economic, social, political and institutional context. This is not a neat solution, but the business of policy-making is not neat. Perhaps the best we can do is to recognise messiness and acknowledge gaps in the theory, rather than to ignore them in the interests of general solutions.

NOTES

I am grateful to Ganeshan Wignaraja for collecting the data used here.

1 This approach is succintly analysed in Nelson and Winter (1977) and Nelson (1981).
2 As noted later, there is some justification in this, but it fails to do justice to the sharply different forms of 'openness' that different countries have adopted, with corresponding effects on the nature and structure of industrial development.
3 There is a quite separate industrial organisation literature on market structure and innovation and the micro-level determinants of research activity in developed countries (for a good recent review, see Cohen and Levin, 1989). This analysis does not, however, generally appear in the industrial policy discussion relevant here.
4 The World Bank's *World Development Report 1991* and its 1993 study are good examples of this view.
5 See recent work on technological capabilities in developing countries by Bell and Pavitt (1993), Dahlman *et al.* (1987), Enos (1992), Katz (1984, 1987), Lall (1987, 1990, 1992a, 1993a), Pack and Westphal (1986), Pack (1992).
6 For a detailed analysis of the constituent elements of the 'learning curve' see Adler and Clark (1991). Mody (1989) has a useful analysis of the need for engineering manpower in the absorption of complex technologies.
7 On the significance of organisational factors in absorbing and innovating technologies in the engineering industry, see Hoffman (1989).
8 For an analysis of the long learning process in the Korean engineering industry see Jacobsson (1993).
9 Stiglitz (1987) has an analysis of 'learning to learn'.
10 On the significance of networks for TC development see Hakansson (1987).
11 Formal R&D efforts are needed both for absorbing and adapting complex foreign technologies and for creating new technologies. On the absorptive functions of R&D see Cohen and Levinthal (1989).
12 As far as this paper is concerned, however, the policy considerations for promoting flexibility raised are very similar to those raised by technology in the more conventional sense, and the conclusions reached continue to apply.
13 Empirical work on capability building suggests, for instance, that highly inward-oriented regimes tend to induce firms to develop skills to use local materials and to 'stretch' the use of equipment rather than to raise quality, lower material use or lower costs. Similarly, restraints on entry and exit conduce to technological sloth and poor manufacturing practice.
14 Some of the market failures in resource allocation arising from externalities, economies of scale, deficient capital markets and learning are acknowledged by the World Bank (1993) study, but their empirical implications are not examined (Lall, 1994).
15 The same case is made with reference to technological externalities, between activities linked in the vertical production process, by Pack and Westphal (1986).
16 On the need for new typologies of trade strategies that can take these complexities into account, see Liang (1992).
17 See Moreira (1993) for an illuminating discussion and a comparison of Korea and Brazil, with the former able to manage the process far better than the latter.

18 This is found in the study of Ghanaian enterprises by Lall *et al.* (1994).
19 This is the reasoning underlying the 'market friendly' terminology adopted by the World Bank in its *World Development Report 1991*, and the 'miracle' study (World Bank, 1993).
20 For a good historical review of institutional support for technological activity in the industrialised countries, see Mowery and Rosenberg (1989).
21 This remains true even if overseas enrolments are taken into account.
22 This essential contrast between Hong Kong and other NIEs is completely ignored in the World Bank (1993) study.
23 The details are now well known, and are given in publications such as Amsden (1989, 1992), Pack and Westphal (1986), Lall *et al.* (1992), Westphal (1990).
24 Interestingly, industrialists participated in setting the curriculum for technical training.
25 The capabilities may be mainly for absorption rather than for frontier innovation, but, as noted, even the absorption, adaptation and improvement of advanced technologies needs substantial local R&D effort.
26 This class of market failures is ignored by the restrictive framework adopted by the World Bank's 'miracle' study. Yet these were clearly recognised as failures by the Korean (and Japanese) governments and addressed in their policies.
27 It appears from my fieldwork in Ghana, for instance, that a lot of testing and extension activity is counted as R&D when this would not be the case in other countries.
28 Apart from the enclave operation of aluminium processing or protected activities like government-owned petroleum refining, these include some food processing, furniture, cement, simple metal products, and uniforms for the army or schools.
29 Note that the definition of 'manufactured exports' here is somewhat different from that used by the Ghana Export Promotion Council. In particular, re-exports and products like common salt and handicrafts are excluded from the sums shown here.
30 The values of the main non-traditional manufactured exports in 1991 were: aluminum $5.5 m., wood products $6.2 m. (of which furniture accounted for $3.6 m. and other wood products for $2.6 m.), canned foods $0.3 m., tobacco $0.4 m., soaps $0.6 m., machetes and iron rods $0.8 m., and others $1.3 m.
31 In wood products, for instance, some 95 per cent of furniture exports come from one foreign affiliate, while scores of local manufacturers operate with such low efficiency and poor quality that they cannot enter world markets. Most of their exports continued to be of builders' products, the lowest category of wood manufacturing.
32 Some of these, especially related to trade policies, are discussed in Lall *et al.* (1994).

REFERENCES

Adler, P.S. and K.B. Clark (1991) 'Behind the learning curve: a sketch of the learning process', *Management Science* 37(3): 267–81.
Amsden, A.H. (1989) *Asia's New Giant: South Korea and Late Industrialization*, New York: Oxford University Press.
—— (1992) 'A theory of government intervention in late industrialization', in L. Putterman and D. Ruschmeyer (eds) *The State and the Market in Development*, Boulder, CO: Lynne Rienner Publishers.
Bell, M. and K. Pavitt (1993) 'Accumulating technological capability in developing

countries', *Proceedings of the World Bank Annual Conference on Development Economics 1992*, Washington, DC: World Bank.

Bell, M., B. Ross-Larson and L.E. Westphal (1984) 'Assessing the performance of infant industries', *Journal of Development Economics* 16(1): 101–28.

Chandler, A.D. (1992) 'Organizational capabilities and the economic history of the industrial enterprise', *Journal of Economic Perspectives* 6(3): 79–100.

Cohen, W.M. and R.C. Levin (1989) 'Empirical studies of innovation and market structure', in R. Schmalensee and R.D. Willig (eds) *Handbook of Industrial Organization*, vol. II, Amsterdam: North-Holland.

Cohen, W.M. and D.A. Levinthal (1989) 'Innovation and learning: the two faces of R&D', *Economic Journal* 99(4): 569–96.

Dahlman, C.J., B. Ross-Larson and L.E. Westphal (1987) 'Managing technological development: lessons from newly industrialising countries', *World Development* 15(6): 759–75.

Enos, J. (1992) *The Creation of Technological Capabilities in Developing Countries*, London: Pinter.

Ferraz, J.C., H. Rush and I. Miles (1992) *Development, Technology and Flexibility: Brazil Faces the Industrial Divide*, London: Routledge.

Financial Times (1993) 'Survey of Hong Kong', *Financial Times*, 6 May: 6.

Government of the Republic of China (1990) *Statistical Yearbook*, Taipei: Government of the Republic of China.

—— (1992) *Statistical Yearbook*, Taipei: Government of the Republic of China.

Hakansson, H. (ed.) (1987) *Industrial Technology Development: A Network Approach*, London: Croom Helm.

Havrylyshyn, O. (1990) 'Trade and productivity gains in developing countries: a survey of the literature', *World Bank Reserch Observer* 5(1): 1–24.

Hobday, M.G. (1994) 'Technological learning in Singapore: a test case of leapfrogging', *Journal of Development Studies*.

Hoffman, K. (1989) 'Technological advance and organizational innovation in the engineering industry', World Bank, Industry Series Paper no. 4, Washington, DC: World Bank, Industry and Energy Department.

Jacobsson, S. (1993) 'The length of the learning period: evidence from the Korean engineering industry', *World Development* 21(3): 407–20.

Justman, M. and M. Teubal (1986) 'Innovation policy in an open economy: a normative framework for strategic and policy issues', *Research Policy* 15(1): 121–38.

Kaplinsky, R. (1993) 'Is flexible specialisation relevant for LDCs?', Paper prepared for the OECD Development Centre, University of Sussex: Institute of Development Studies.

Katz, J. (1984) 'Domestic technological innovation and dynamic comparative advantage: further reflections on a comparative case study program', *Journal of Development Economics* 16(1): 13–38.

Katz, J.M. (ed.) (1987) *Technology Generation in Latin American Manufacturing Industries*, London: Macmillan.

Killick, T. (1993) *The Adaptive Economy: Adjustment Policies in Small, Low-Income Countries*, Washington, DC: The World Bank, EDI Development Studies.

Lall, S. (1987) *Learning to Industrialize*, London: Macmillan.

—— (1990) *Building Industrial Competitiveness in Developing Countries*, Paris: OECD Development Centre.

—— (1992a) 'Technological capabilities and industrialization', *World Development* 20(2): 165–86.

—— (1992b) 'Structural problems of African industry', in F. Stewart, S. Lall and

S. Wangwe (eds) *Alternative Development Strategies in Sub-Saharan Africa*, London: Macmillan.

—— (1993a) 'Understanding technology development', *Development and Change* 24(4): 719–53.

—— (1993b) 'Trade policies for development: a policy prescription for Africa', *Development Policy Review* 11(1): 47–65.

—— (1994) '"The East Asian Miracle" study: does the bell toll for industrial strategy?', *World Development* 22(4): 645–654.

Lall, S. and G. Kell (1991) 'Industrial development in developing countries and the role of government interventions', *Banca Nazionale del Lavoro Quarterly Review*, 178: 271–92.

Lall, S., G.B. Navaretti, S. Teitel and G. Wignaraja (1994) *Technology and Enterprise Development in Ghana*, London: Macmillan.

Lall, S., S. Banerji and F. Najmabadi (1992) *World Bank Support for Industrialization in Korea, India and Indonesia*, Washington, DC: World Bank Operations Evaluation Department.

Liang, N. (1992) 'Beyond import substitution and export promotion: a new typology of trade strategies', *Journal of Development Strategies* 28(3): 447–72.

Lucas, R.E. (1988) 'On the mechanics of economic development', *Journal of Monetary Economics* 22(1): 3–42.

Mill, J.S. (1940) *Principles of Political Economy* (1st edition 1848) with an introduction by W.J. Ashley, London: Longmans, Green & Company.

Mody, A. (1989) 'Firm strategies for costly engineering learning', *Management Science* 33(4): 496–512.

—— (1990) 'Institutions and dynamic comparative advantage: the electronics industry in South Korea and Taiwan', *Cambridge Journal of Economics* 14(3): 291–314.

Moreira, M.M. (1993) 'Industrialization, trade and market failures: the role of government intervention in Brazil and the Republic of Korea', London: University College, PhD thesis.

Mowery, D.C. and Rosenberg, N. (1989) *Technology and the Pursuit of Economic Growth*, Cambridge: Cambridge University Press.

Nelson, R.R. (1981) 'Research on productivity growth and productivity differences: dead ends or new departures?', *Journal of Economic Literature* 19(3): 1029–64.

—— (1987) 'Innovation and economic development: theoretical retrospect and prospect', in J. Katz (ed.) *Technology Generation in Latin American Manufacturing Industries*, London: Macmillan.

Nelson, R.R. and S.J. Winter (1977) 'In search of useful theory of innovation', *Research Policy* 6(1): 36–76.

—— (1982) *An Evolutionary Theory of Economic Change*, Cambridge, MA: Harvard University Press.

Pack, H. (1988) 'Industrialization and trade', in H.B. Chenery and T.N. Srinivasan (eds) *Handbook of Development Economics*, vol. I, Amsterdam: North-Holland.

—— (1992) 'Learning and productivity change in developing countries', in G.K. Helleiner (ed.) *Trade Policy, Industrialization and Development*, Oxford: Clarendon Press.

Pack, H. and L.E. Westphal (1986) 'Industrial strategy and technological change: theory versus reality', *Journal of Development Economics* 22(1): 87–128.

Rodrik, D. (1992) 'Closing the productivity gap: does trade liberalization really help?', in G.K. Helleiner (ed.) *Trade Policy, Industrialization and Development*, Oxford: Clarendon Press.

Shapiro, H. and L. Taylor (1990) 'The state and industrial strategy', *World Development* 18(6): 861–78.

Stiglitz, J.E. (1987) 'Learning to learn, localized learning and technological progress', in P. Dasgupta and P. Stoneman (eds) *Economic Policy and Technological Development*, Cambridge: Cambridge University Press.

—— (1989) 'Markets, market failures and development', *American Economic Review Papers and Proceedings* 79(2): 197–202.

Streeten, P. (1991) 'Review of T. Killick, *A Reaction too Far: Economic Theory and the Role of the State in Developing Countries*, London: ODI, 1989', *Economic Development and Cultural Change* 39(2): 421–9.

UNDP (1992) *Human Development Report 1992*, New York: UNDP.

UNESCAP (1991) *Statistical Yearbook for Asia and the Pacific 1991*, Bangkok: UNESCAP.

UNIDO (1993) *Industry and Development Global Report 1992–93*, Vienna: UNIDO.

Wade, R. (1990) *Governing the Market: Economic Theory and the Role of Government in East Asian Industrialization*, Princeton, NJ: Princeton University Press.

Westphal, L.E. (1990) 'Industrial policy in an export propelled economy: lessons from South Korea's experience', *Journal of Economic Perspectives* 4(3): 41–59.

World Bank (1991) *Development Report 1991*, New York: Oxford University Press.

—— (1992) *World Development Report 1992*, New York: Oxford University Press.

—— (1993) *The East Asian Miracle: Economic Growth and Public Policy*, New York: Oxford University Press.

Young, A. (1991) 'Learning by doing and the dynamic effects of international trade', *Quarterly Journal of Economics* CVI(2): 369–405.

10

FLEXIBILITY IN FINANCE

Maxwell J. Fry

I INTRODUCTION

All financial systems in market economies, whether they are developed or developing, perform two basic functions: (a) administering the country's payments mechanism and (b) intermediating between savers and investors. Both functions are crucial to the financial system's role in promoting flexibility in an economy.

The introduction of money into a society increases flexibility; barter has the well-known drawback of requiring a double coincidence of wants. Historically, money first made its appearance because of uncertainty and the desire to be able to respond flexibly to uncertain events in the future. In this context, liquidity is virtually synonymous with flexibility.

In its role as intermediary between savers and investors, the financial system also promotes flexibility. Without a financial system, investors would be confined to self-financed investments. These would necessarily comprise a small subset of the investment opportunities available when resources can be pooled through a financial system. The additional choice of technique and scale that a financial system permits promotes flexibility. If there is no choice, there can be no flexibility.

A financial system's ability to respond flexibly to changes on the real side of an economy is impaired by: (i) discriminatory taxation through an inflation tax or other forms of financial restriction; (ii) rigid or sticky interest rates that obstruct appropriate responses to inflation; (iii) directed credit policies through which domestic credit is allocated by government decision; (iv) the pursuit of non-commercial objectives by government-owned financial institutions; (v) false credit demands or distress borrowing from insolvent enterprises and non-performing assets which undermine the financial institutions' own solvency; (vi) uncompetitive and oligopolistic market conditions. The first four conditions are imposed by government, while the last two are often caused by one or more of the first four.

Part II of this chapter analyses the way in which inflation reduces flexibility and growth in the medium and long runs. Parts III and IV demonstrate how financial restriction and directed credit policies reduce flexibility, in part by maintaining institutional interest rates below their competitive free-market clearing levels. Part V presents some evidence indicating that flexibility is reduced by a predominantly government-owned financial system that also holds down interest rates. In contrast, Part VI shows how distress borrowing reduces the financial system's flexibility through pathologically high real interest rates. Parts VII and VIII explain how oligopolistic banking systems and non-performing assets reduce flexibility and growth. Finally, Part IX resolves the paradoxical cases of Korea and Taiwan; both economies exhibit high degrees of flexibility and growth but unresponsive financial systems.

II INFLATION AND DEFICIT FINANCE

Financial systems in developing countries, typically dominated by commercial banks, tend to be heavily taxed in a discriminatory fashion. Inflation has long been analysed as a tax and hence as a source of government revenue or seigniorage (Bailey, 1956; Friedman, 1971). The tax collector is the central bank, the tax base is reserve or high-powered money and the tax rate is the inflation rate. Holders of currency pay the tax through the erosion in the purchasing power of their currency. Banks also pay the tax by holding reserves, invariably in the form of required reserves.

A simple example illustrates the effect of a reserve requirement. Suppose that the required reserve ratio is 0.2 and in a zero-inflation environment the loan rate of interest l is 5 per cent. For $100 in deposits, a bank holds $20 in reserves and lends $80. Hence, the bank earns $4 on its loan portfolio. In a competitive zero-cost banking system, the bank would pay a deposit rate of interest d of 4 per cent, $4 spread over $100 in deposits. The wedge between deposit and loan rates is created entirely by the non-interest-earning required reserves. In fact, the relationship between deposit and loan rates in this simplest case can be expressed as

$$d = l \cdot (1 - rrr)$$

where rrr is the required reserve ratio.

If the central bank now generates inflation of 10 per cent and the loan rate of interest rises to 15 per cent, equation (1) indicates that the deposit rate would be 12 per cent, implying a reduction in the inflation-adjusted or real deposit rate $d - \pi$, where π is the inflation rate, from 4 to 2 per cent.[1] In this example, therefore, the banks pass on the inflation tax to depositors. As Martin Bailey (1956: 104) points out, the inflation tax on deposits is $rrr \cdot \pi$. In this example, currency holders face an inflation tax of 10 per cent, while depositors lose two percentage points: 0.2(10). With 100 per cent inflation, the real deposit rate of interest falls from 4 per cent to -16 per cent, i.e., by twenty percentage points.

In general, financial systems in developing countries face high required reserve ratios. Although raising reserve requirements can be used to reduce the money supply and so curb inflation, inflation rates and required reserve ratios are positively correlated both across developing countries and over time within them. The reason for this is that higher reserve requirements increase the tax base on which the inflation tax is levied. For any given inflation rate, therefore, a higher reserve requirement yields higher revenue. A government that makes substantial use of the inflation tax is likely to raise reserve requirements to increase its revenue rather than to reduce inflation. Nevertheless, for any given revenue requirement, inflation will generally be lower the higher is the reserve requirement.

To provide some orders of magnitude, I examine a sample of twenty-six developing countries: Algeria, Argentina, Brazil, Chile, Côte d'Ivoire, Egypt, Ghana, Greece, India, Indonesia, Korea, Malaysia, Mexico, Morocco, Nigeria, Pakistan, Peru, Philippines, Portugal, Sri Lanka, Tanzania, Thailand, Turkey, Venezuela, the former Yugoslavia and Zaïre.[2] These countries comprise developing countries with populations over 10 million for which reasonably good data exist on deposit rates of interest (Gelb, 1989; Hanson and Neal, 1987).

Here I define the tax rate on reserve money as the current inflation rate as measured by the consumer price index; the tax rate on bank reserves is adjusted for any interest paid. The tax base is the geometric average of the beginning-of-year and end-of-year values of currency in circulation plus bank reserves. The two differences between the inflation tax on currency and the inflation tax on bank reserves are: (a) reserves held almost exclusively as deposits in the central bank involve infinitesimal maintenance costs and (b) some interest may be paid on such deposits. In the sample of developing countries examined here, the range of interest paid on required reserves runs from zero to 7.3 per cent after monetary correction (indexation) in the case of Brazil's 20 per cent reserve requirement against saving deposits. In Brazil's case, the tax on these required reserves must be zero or negative at all rates of inflation. Clearly, where indexation is not applied and where nominal interest rates (if any) are sticky, the tax rate on required reserves rises with inflation.

Table 10.1 expresses an approximate measure of the inflation tax or seigniorage revenue as a percentage of GNP and of the government's current revenue. Where possible, data are provided for 1984. Table 10.1 indicates that the inflation tax yielded revenue for the government equal to 2.8 per cent of GNP on average in twenty-six developing countries in 1984; this represented over 17 per cent of the government's current revenue. As a percentage of GNP, seigniorage provides a relatively small source of tax revenue in most of the sample countries. However, where it does produce an above-average amount, it contributes a proportionally larger amount of government revenue. On average, a one percentage point increase in the

Table 10.1 Inflation tax revenue in 26 developing countries, 1984

Country	Percentage of GNP	Percentage of government current revenue
Algeria	1.59	n.a.
Argentina	7.43	46.49
Brazil[a]	2.45	9.09
Chile	0.85	2.66
Côte d'Ivoire	0.44	1.45
Egypt	7.50	16.69
Ghana[a]	0.74	6.17
Greece	3.13	8.72
India	0.98	7.57
Indonesia	0.65	6.17
Korea[c]	0.11	1.39
Malaysia[c]	0.12	0.50
Mexico	7.18	41.88
Morocco	1.67	6.79
Nigeria[c]	0.94	5.05
Pakistan[b]	0.48	2.58
Peru[a]	8.67	58.05
Philippines	2.38	22.09
Portugal	5.25	14.58
Sri Lanka[b]	0.79	3.43
Tanzania[a]	3.14	18.55
Thailand[c]	0.21	1.27
Turkey[c]	2.55	13.92
Venezuela	1.50	5.68
Yugoslavia	9.77	132.79
Zaïre[b]	3.03	16.08

Notes: [a]1985. [b]1986. [c]1987.

Source: IMF, *International Financial Statistics* and World Bank (1990).

inflation tax in relation to GNP corresponds to an increase in the inflation tax in relation to government current revenue of eight percentage points.

Use of the inflation tax reduces the resources available to the financial system in two ways. First, higher reserve requirements (the tax base) reduce funds available to the banking system for lending. Second, to the extent that the inflation tax is passed on to depositors, the real volume of deposits declines. In the simplest balance sheet of the banking system, the banks hold loans L and reserves R as their assets and deposits D as their liabilities:

Assets	Liabilities
Reserves R	Deposits D
Loans L	

The balance-sheet identity implies $R + L = D$. *Ceteris paribus*, an increase in R requires a reduction in L.

This balance sheet identity is still preserved if one divides both assets and liabilities by nominal GNP Y:

Assets	Liabilities
Reserves R/Y	Deposits D/Y
Loans L/Y	

The ratio D/Y falls as inflation accelerates as a result of the higher tax imposed on depositors. So too, therefore, must the ratio $(R + L)/Y$. If the ratio R/L rises during this process, then L/Y falls by a larger percentage than D/Y. Since L/Y is the ratio of bank loans to the nominal value of output, business firms find themselves facing a credit squeeze. Banks find it increasingly difficult to meet normal credit requests from existing clients, let alone take on new borrowers or increase loans to existing borrowers for new fixed investment. This is not a situation in which the financial system can respond flexibly to changing conditions in the real sector of the economy. Indeed, under these conditions some firms may be unable to stay in business because they are unable to obtain the necessary loans to cover the costs of their working capital. The aggregate level of output in real terms would then fall.

In extreme cases of hyperinflation the domestic currency loses its attributes not only of a store of value but also of a means of payments.[3] Under such conditions, financial systems are impeded in performing both of their basic functions. Society turns to substitute means of payments (foreign currencies or barter trade), thereby by-passing the domestic financial system. This substitution is one manifestation of the law of demand. As the opportunity cost of holding money rises, the quantity demanded falls.

In this case, therefore, the deterioration of money reduces the extents to which the banking system administers the country's payments mechanism and intermediates between savers and investors; performances in both functions are related. Since money gives its holders flexibility to buy whatever is being offered for sale, a switch from money to barter reduces flexibility. To the extent that savers and investors are driven to self-financed investments as a result of the rising opportunity cost of holding money, flexibility in investment choice is also reduced.

III FINANCIAL RESTRICTION AND LOW REAL INTEREST RATES

The objective of monetary control conflicts with any fiscal objective requiring an increase in reserve money greater than the amount consistent with monetary stability. There are, however, a variety of measures that raise this threshold, thus enabling more government revenue to be raised without jeopardising monetary stability. These measures are termed financial restriction and are generally administered by the central bank. Although financial restriction reduces the inflationary impact of deficit finance, it impairs the financial system's ability to respond flexibly to changing circumstances in the real sector of the economy as much as, if not more than, the inflation tax does.

Financial restriction encourages financial institutions and financial instruments from which government can expropriate significant seigniorage, and discourages others. For example, money and the banking system are favoured and protected because reserve requirements and obligatory holdings of government bonds can be imposed to tap this source of saving at zero- or low-interest cost to the public sector. Private bond and equity markets are suppressed through transaction taxes, stamp duties, special tax rates on income from capital and an unconducive legal framework, because seigniorage cannot be extracted so easily from private bonds and equities.

Interest-rate ceilings are imposed to stifle competition to public-sector fund-raising from the private sector. Measures such as the imposition of foreign-exchange controls, interest-rate ceilings, high reserve requirements and the suppression or non-development of private capital markets can all increase the flow of domestic resources to the public sector without higher tax, inflation or interest rates (Fry, 1973; Nichols, 1974). Such restrictive measures impair the financial system's performance and hence reduce its ability to respond flexibly to changing demands from the real sector of the economy.

Interest-rate ceilings distort the economy in three ways. First, low interest rates produce a bias in favour of current consumption and against future consumption. Therefore, they may reduce saving below the socially optimum level. Second, potential lenders may engage in relatively low-yielding, traditional investment instead of lending by depositing money in a bank. Third, bank borrowers able to obtain all the funds they want at low loan rates will choose relatively capital-intensive projects. Those rationed out completely by this process will not face the range of choices and thus will not be able to respond so flexibly to changing economic conditions as they would if they had had access to a financial system.

In countries where there are virtually no markets for direct financial claims, the tax derived from financial restriction can be estimated using domestic credit as the tax base and the difference between the parity-adjusted world interest rate and the average domestic rate on the components of domestic credit as the tax rate. An approximate estimate is generally possible in countries which impose interest-rate ceilings on all institutional interest rates. In Turkey, for example, lending interest rates were held at least twenty percentage points below world rates in 1979. With domestic credit averaging TL715 bn, the financial restriction tax was

Table 10.2 Revenue from financial restriction in 22 developing countries

Country	Period	Percentage of GDP	Implicit tax rate	Percentage of total central government revenue
Algeria	1974–87	4.30	10.6	11.42
Brazil	1983–7	0.48	13.4	1.57
Colombia	1980–4	0.24	22.4	2.11
Costa Rica	1972–84	2.33	25.1	12.76
Greece	1974–85	2.53	16.0	7.76
India	1980–5	2.86	11.0	22.38
Indonesia	1976–86	0.00	0.0	0.00
Jamaica	1980–2[a]	1.38	7.4	4.74
Jordan	1978–87	0.60	7.2	2.40
Korea	1975–87	0.25	6.0	1.36
Malaysia	1974–81	0.12	0.5	0.31
Mexico	1984–7	5.77	45.8	39.65
Morocco	1977–85	2.31	16.1	8.89
Pakistan	1982–3	3.23	25.3	20.50
Panama	1977–87	0.69	4.4	2.49
Papua New Guinea	1981–7	0.40	5.6	1.90
Philippines	1975–86	0.45	11.9	3.88
Portugal	1978–86	2.22	15.8	6.93
Sri Lanka	1981–3	3.40	14.5	19.24
Thailand	1976–86	0.38	4.3	2.57
Tunisia	1978–87	1.49	13.4	4.79
Turkey	1980–7	2.20	55.8	10.89
Zaïre	1974–86[b]	0.46	54.5	2.48
Zimbabwe	1981–6	5.52	19.5	19.13
Average		1.82	17.7	8.76

Notes: [a]1981 omitted. [b]1981–3 omitted.

Source: Giovannini and de Melo, 1993: 959.

TL143 bn or 6.5 per cent of GNP. Clearly, this was also the value of the interest-rate subsidy to borrowers, including the government.

Alberto Giovannini and Martha de Melo (1993) calculate the tax revenue from financial restriction in the form of holdings of government bonds at yields below the world market rate. For the sixteen countries in Table 10.2 for which seigniorage tax revenues are presented in Table 10.1, the average tax revenue from financial restriction is 1.9 per cent of GDP. This can be compared with the average tax revenue from seigniorage for these sixteen countries of 2 per cent of GNP.[4] In broad terms, therefore, it appears that financial restriction is as important a source of government revenue in developing countries as is the inflation tax. Similarly, financial restriction's negative impact on flexibility probably equals that of inflation.

IV DIRECTED CREDIT POLICIES AND SUBSIDISED INTEREST RATES

Directed credit policies, which are common components of financial restriction, also reduce flexibility in finance. The techniques employed to reduce the costs of financing government deficits discussed in the previous section can be, and are, used to encourage private investment in what the government regards as priority activities. Interest rates on loans for such approved investment are subsidised. The costs of the subsidies are met by depositors who receive lower deposit rates of interest, by unsubsidised borrowers who pay higher free-market loan rates and by taxpayers as a result of lower central bank profits.

Directed credit policies necessitate financial restriction, since financial channels would otherwise develop expressly for rerouting subsidised credit to uses with the highest private returns. Financial restriction is generally imposed in an attempt to prevent recipients of subsidised credit from round-tripping or relending the funds at market rates. For directed credit policies to work at all, financial markets must be kept segmented and restricted. Where financial restriction does segment credit markets, it ensures that subsidised credit distorts factor prices and encourages inefficient investment. Deliberate market segmentation deliberately reduces flexibility.

There are six major categories of directed credit policy instruments: subsidised loan rates for priority sectors, differential rediscount rates, direct budgetary subsidies, credit floors, credit ceilings and proliferation of specialised financial institutions. The most common directed credit technique in a sample of eleven Asian developing countries is subsidised loan rates for priority sectors.[5] The government sets relatively low loan rates of interest for priority sectors. The main problem, of course, is how to persuade the commercial banks to lend to such sectors at these low rates.

One way of solving the problem is to use differential rediscount rates. Financial institutions are compensated partially, fully or even overcompensated for lending at subsidised rates of interest to priority borrowers when they rediscount priority loans at the central bank on concessional terms. Hence, most priority credit may actually be provided by the central bank. This method can and often does jeopardise control over the cash base, as has happened in Korea. It is the only technique that can be used without direct interest or credit allocation controls.

An extensive directed credit policy implemented through the rediscount mechanism is likely to be accompanied by high required reserve ratios designed to reduce the commercial banks' own funds available for discretionary, non-priority lending. In such a case, the central bank's assets will probably constitute a relatively large proportion of the total assets of the financial sector as a whole. All the eleven sample Asian developing countries still use the preferential rediscount technique, although its scope has been reduced in Indonesia, Korea, Taiwan and Thailand.

The third method of implementing directed credit policies is direct budgetary subsidy. In Indonesia, Pakistan, the Philippines and Sri Lanka, negative differentials between priority loan and deposit rates of interest were financed by explicit budget appropriations in 1980. Due to oil revenue in Indonesia, this technique has been used to a greater extent there than it has in Pakistan, the Philippines or Sri Lanka. In the latter three countries, budget subsidies were confined to a small proportion of priority loans – small, interest-free loans to farmers in Pakistan and loans to the government in Sri Lanka. In 1989, Pakistan's interest-free loans to farmers were abandoned in favour of low-interest loans. By 1990, only the Philippines used direct budget subsidies.

Credit floors constitute the fourth method used to implement directed credit policies in eight of the eleven sample Asian developing countries. The monetary authorities set minimum proportions of total credit or total deposits that must be lent by the banks to specific priority borrowers. In India, 40 per cent of bank loans are allocated to priority sectors. In 1989, policy-directed loans constituted 38 per cent of deposit money bank (DMB) lending in Korea (Park, 1990: 45A). The national banks in Indonesia are obliged to make 20 per cent of their loans to small- and medium-sized industries. The Nepalese commercial banks must use at least 8 per cent of their total deposit liabilities for lending to priority sectors. In the Philippines, 15 per cent of banks' loan portfolios must be devoted to the rural sector. Credit allocation is conducted informally in Sri Lanka through moral suasion. 'Medium' (i.e. medium-sized) business banks in Taiwan are required to devote 70 per cent of their loans to small- and medium-sized enterprises.

The fifth method of implementing directed credit policies is to set credit ceilings either on non-priority lending or on the aggregate volume of loans. Overall credit ceilings are usually promulgated in conjunction with exemptions for priority loans or credit floors for priority sectors. Credit ceilings were used in eight of the sample Asian developing countries in 1980. However, global credit ceilings have become unfashionable; they are now set only in Korea, Pakistan, the Philippines and Sri Lanka. The incentive for a commercial bank to extend subsidised credit springs in the main from the ceiling imposed on normal lending. A subsidised loan may be a more profitable asset than excess cash reserves. However, delinquency and default have plagued priority lending operations, particularly in Bangladesh, India, Indonesia, Korea and Nepal. Even though bank interest rates were deregulated in 1988, Korean DMBs are still subject to quantitative ceilings on lending and loan rates have been kept artificially low and stable (Park, 1990: 43). In Sri Lanka, global credit ceilings were imposed in May 1989 (Aries Group, 1990).

The final method of implementing directed credit policies is heavy reliance on specialised financial institutions. This technique is used in six of the sample Asian developing countries. Funds are extracted from non-specialised depository institutions through high reserve requirements to be channelled to priority sectors on concessional terms by government-owned specialised financial institutions. Proliferation of such institutions has been taken furthest in India, Korea and the Philippines. Financial layering and market segmentation appear to have been the main effects. In these countries, higher required reserve ratios have reduced the total supply of loanable funds in real terms.

A major inherent problem with virtually all specialised financial institutions in developing countries springs from the fact that they are established to lend to borrowers that existing financial institutions – the commercial banks – have avoided. By and large, commercial banks choose not to lend when the perceived risks are too high. Hence, specialised financial institutions are set up deliberately to lend to high-risk borrowers. However, they are not compensated for assuming higher risks with higher loan rates. Invariably, therefore, the specialised financial institution established to support a problem sector of the economy itself becomes a problem institution. Furthermore, priority sectors delineated for special financial assistance rarely embrace innovative entrepreneurs who spearhead economic development. Indeed, one priority group in India consists of sick firms. Some day India may get its own Sick Bank.

Despite the prevalence of directed credit policies in developing countries, in no instance is an innovative sector or a sector not yet in existence singled out as a priority sector. Inevitably, therefore, directed credit policies reduce the economy's flexibility. Financial resources are directed by bureaucratic decision based on some form of development plan. Since allocations are generally determined on an annual basis, flexibility is reduced at least to the extent that new priorities must wait for the next round of allocations. Often, however, new priorities will not be recognised or considered until a new five-year development plan is being designed.

Directed credit policies or programmes increase the financial system's fragility while reducing its flexibility. There is no evidence that they improve the economic efficiency of resource allocation. Portfolio constraints reduce the funds available for discretionary bank lending both directly and indirectly by reducing the attractiveness of deposits.[6] They also increase the fragility of the financial system by forcing financial institutions to increase their risk exposure with no compensating return. Directed credit programmes are partly responsible for the substantial volume of non-performing assets on the books of many financial institutions in developing countries.

Among the Asian developing countries, Bangladesh, India and Nepal have pursued directed credit policies most vigorously. They have also recorded the lowest rates of economic growth, and flexibility is not one of their strong points. These poorer Asian developing countries have been particularly reluctant to abandon directed credit policies, despite the increasing evidence that such policies have hindered rather than promoted development efforts. Part of the difficulty in abandoning these policies lies in the vested interests that they have created. Vested interests invariably prefer the status quo and therefore oppose flexibility which would promote change.

V GOVERNMENT OWNERSHIP OF FINANCIAL INSTITUTIONS

The case for bank nationalisation goes back to the writings of Karl Marx and Friedrich Engels, both of whom advocated the centralisation of credit in the hands of the state through a single national bank with an exclusive monopoly (Hilferding, 1910; Podolski, 1973). Lenin, impressed by the powerful political and economic influence of the European banks in the eighteenth and nineteenth centuries, understood the crucial role of the financial system and was also a keen proponent of bank nationalisation and monopolisation:

> Even before he took power, Lenin envisaged the banking system as becoming the backbone of the socialist state's administrative apparatus. Nationalisation of private banking and establishment of a government monopoly of all foreign exchange transactions were among the first economic measures taken by the Bolshevik government in 1917.
>
> (Garvy, 1968: 19)

None of these political thinkers foresaw the technical difficulties involved in the process of nationalisation and amalgamation.

Lenin duly nationalised all Russian banks in 1918 as the fastest and most effective way of ending capitalism and assuming control over the entire Russian economy. The unforeseen difficulties then encountered were such that by 1921 'the monetary system of the economy had ceased to exist' (Podolski, 1973: 20). It was not until 1931 that the Soviet banking system was operating satisfactorily and could be used effectively as a mechanism for economic planning through the concept of control by the ruble, 'a microeconomic control calculated to check or influence behaviour of individual enterprises' (Podolski, 1973: 12).

The early Yugoslavian experience illustrates the difficulties of running an efficient centralised and nationalised banking system (Goldsmith, 1975; World Bank, 1975). Dimitri Dimitrijevic and George Macesich (1973: 51) conclude that 'the principal deficiencies in the financial institutions came from their administrative character and strong government influence'. These two indictments recur frequently in the literature on nationalised bank performance in developing countries. In the Yugoslavian reforms of 1965 and 1966 banks were given far more autonomy and responsibility for domestic resource mobilisation and allocation (Dimitri and Macesich, 1973: 52). After the reforms, new banks in the former Yugoslavia were established at the instigation of socialist enterprises, which themselves subscribed the initial capital. In this case, as in other Eastern European countries in transition, a full circle has been completed from nationalisation of banks in order to separate them from industrial conglomerates to which they were subservient back to the principle that banks must respond flexibly to the needs of business and hence must be creatures of the industrial class.

Nationalised commercial banks and development finance institutions (DFIs) are pervasive throughout the developing world. Felipe Morris (1985: viii–ix, 19) identifies the following particular problems of the predominantly government-owned financial system in India: (a) proliferation of financial institutions; (b) low resource mobilisation by DFIs; (c) low profitability of commercial banks because of overstaffing, high delinquency rates, risky priority sector lending and low capitalisation ratios; (d) reduced flexibility of banks to undertake discretionary lending; (e) increased administrative requirements for loan processing; (f) reduced scope for financial institutions to allocate credit on the basis of economic criteria; (g) reduced autonomy of top management in the larger financial institutions; (h) poor quality of field staff; and (i) weak management and supervision. India's financial institutions were nationalised in part to prevent industrial concentration and to provide credit to small- and medium-sized enterprises. However, J.S. Uppal (1986: 144) finds that India's nationalised financial institutions discriminated in favour of large enterprises even after the government established a special commission to deter such behaviour. Local observers have also concluded that India's bank nationalisation did not achieve its objectives.

In Argentina, public sector financial institutions in the form of the provincial banks which hold one quarter of total commercial bank assets have caused a number of problems: (a) the provincial governments owning these banks have used them extensively to finance their own deficits; (b) non-performing assets in the portfolios of the provincial banks constitute a much higher percentage of net worth than they do in private commercial banks' portfolios; (c) the central bank rediscount facility is largely pre-empted by the provincial banks; (d) distress borrowing by some provincial banks has contributed to the exorbitantly high real interest rates; (e) as fear of bank failures increased in the 1980s, deposits were transferred from private to provincial banks; and (f) the provincial banks are not automatically subject to central bank directives. Even when they are, as in the case of reserve requirements, these banks have simply failed to comply.[7] In general, Argentinian provincial banks have jeopardised the soundness and flexibility of the private commercial banks through unfair competition (World Bank, 1986).

In Brazil, state financial institutions play a major role, while private financial institutions are becoming increasingly absorbed by business conglomerates. There, public-sector financial institutions provide 50 per cent of all loans to the private sector, many of them under directed credit programmes. Despite the reasonable internal efficiency of federally owned financial institutions, financial markets are segmented, financial institutions are layered and resources are misallocated as a result of these policies (World Bank, 1984). Provincial banks in Brazil are used during election campaigns to finance popular public works. After an election, these banks are invariably in even worse condition than they were before the election.

Almost all developing countries possess specialised financial institutions in the form of DFIs or development banks. Typically, these specialised financial institutions have been established as government-owned institutions to attract foreign resources, to mobilise domestic savings (in part by developing capital markets) and to allocate investible funds efficiently. The record of the past thirty years suggests that DFIs have attracted foreign resources, have failed completely to mobilise domestic resources, and have a mixed (and deteriorating) record in allocating funds to productive investment projects. In general, DFI efforts at promoting the development of capital markets have been disappointing (Gordon, 1983: 16–24).

Very few DFIs have become self-supporting, autonomous financial institutions capable of mobilising resources entirely on commercial terms. This is partly because DFIs have often been required to make loans at low rates of interest, frequently negative in real terms, and partly because they have financed projects evaluated as economically viable but which are not financially viable. About one-third of the DFIs in developing countries are now in serious financial difficulties, due in the main to large percentages of nonperforming loans. The problem of arrears increased substantially with the worldwide recession and deteriorating terms of trade for developing countries in the early 1980s. By the end of 1983, almost half the DFIs in developing countries had more than 25 per cent of their loans affected by arrears. One-quarter of these DFIs suffered arrearages of over 50 per cent (World Bank, 1985: 11). The World Bank concludes, however, that 'current problems of DFIs relate in part to their basic approach to finance, the limitations of their management and frequently their inability to follow sound business practices'. One particular problem identified is the financing of risky investments solely with debt (World Bank, 1985: ii).

According to David Gordon (1983: 19–20), government-owned DFIs have had a poorer record than privately owned DFIs in terms of domestic resource mobilisation and allocation. Political factors influence lending to a greater extent in government-owned than in private DFIs. The World Bank states:

> The DFIs were in the 1970s increasingly viewed and acted as tools of development policy, channelling resources to publicly promoted or owned enterprises and to priority sectors which commercial lenders

were unwilling to finance. The managements of DFIs that were heavily dependent on government resources and operated in highly regulated financial markets were unable to make lending decisions based on independent assessments of business risks and profits. In addition, the intermediaries' spreads often did not reflect the true costs and risks involved in long-term lending to higher risk projects.

(World Bank, 1985: ii)

Public-sector financial institutions can impair flexibility in finance in two ways. First, weak internal management, often the result of political interference or the lack of expertise and incentives, leads to bureaucratic rather than innovative responses to changing conditions. Second, the policy milieu in which public-sector financial institutions are expected to operate can hinder flexible responses to new demands from the real sector of the economy.

As a general premise, government ownership *per se* produces no special issues of concern, as evinced by widespread government ownership of financial institutions in France, Italy and Taiwan. It is certainly the case, however, that Taiwanese banks are strongly criticised for their bureaucratic procedures and lack of initiative. That the publicly owned Taiwanese financial sector has done little damage to the Taiwanese economy lies in the fact that macroeconomic policies, together with the roles expected of the public-sector financial institutions, have been conducive to rapid economic growth.

The worst combination is bad management facing bad macroeconomic policies. Specifically, when public-sector financial institutions are obliged to pursue selective or directed credit policies that have social or political objectives, inflexibility is compounded. Weak management, combined with policy directives to lend on non-economic criteria, is a recipe for insolvency, the ultimate manifestation of inflexibility.

VI DISTRESS BORROWING AND HIGH REAL INTEREST RATES

In part, the critical problem of loan delinquency encountered in virtually all directed credit programmes is due to the fact that the subsidised loan rates, which are typically negative in real terms, discourage prompt loan repayment. High delinquency and default rates that plague financial systems in developing countries reduce flexibility because they reduce credit available for new investment. However, although financial restriction, directed credit policies and government ownership of financial institutions often reduce flexibility because interest rates are too low, flexibility is also reduced by interest rates that are too high.

High real interest rates in developing countries have been triggered by exogenous shocks of various kinds – financial opening, recession and changes in real exchange rates, terms of trade, internal terms of trade, real interest rates, nominal interest rates and other relative prices. Newly liberalised financial sectors subject to inadequate prudential supervision and regulation then magnify the initial shocks by accommodating distress borrowing. In this way banks in these countries compound the problem of insolvency in the real sectors of the economy. Because distress borrowers push real rates of interest to levels at which virtually no economic activity can be profitable, solvent businesses can find themselves in liquidity crises which force them to borrow at rates which they know are unmanageable. Hence, distress borrowing propagates more insolvency.

Manuel Hinds offers the following explanation of this snowball effect:

> Faced with immediate bankruptcy, both bankers and their debtors give priority to their survival over other, longer-term objectives, including profitability. Debtors borrow at interest rates higher than the long-term profitability of their real assets, even if they have no clear idea of how they are going to repay their debts. Bankers refinance bad debtors because failing to do so would force them to increase their write-offs. Furthermore, bankers lend almost exclusively to bad debtors because, to remain liquid, they raise deposit interest rates to levels that the more solvent borrowers are not willing to pay.
>
> (Hinds, 1988: 27–8)

In Indonesia, for example, the predominant form of bank lending, often referred to as evergreen lending, transforms short-term loans into long-term loans by capitalising interest payments. Banks roll over short-term loans, increasing the loan size by the amount of interest due. As David Cole and Betty Slade point out:

> The fact that the customer can borrow additional funds to meet current interest payments has significant ramifications for both the customer and the bank:
>
> 1 The customer does not have to generate any surplus from the cash flow of his business in order to make such payments as long as the line of credit grows.
> 2 The bank may not check, and often does not know, whether the customer is capable of meeting interest payments out of his past or current earnings.
> 3 Most loans under the line of credit will *appear to be sound or performing*. The bank only becomes aware that the loan may be in difficulty when the customer reaches the upper limit of his line of credit, and then is unable to meet interest payments when due because the bank, for some reason unrelated to the particular loan, refuses to increase the line of credit.[8]
> 4 If a borrower cannot meet his interest payments, then the bank faces

a hard choice. If it does not increase the line of credit, and tries instead to get the customer to meet his interest payments from other sources, the bank faces the possibility of having to recognize and provision for a non-performing loan.[9]

5 If the bank's current earnings and capital position are weak, it may prefer to increase the line of credit, thereby realizing interest 'income' and avoiding the need to provision for a non-performing loan.

(Cole and Slade, 1993: 4–5)

Higher interest rates increase rather than decrease the quantity of evergreen loans demanded, since higher interest rates necessitate additional borrowing for their payment. Under these conditions, even solvent borrowers may be relatively immune to interest-rate changes. The transition from business and bank solvency to insolvency takes place under inexorably rising real interest rates. Evergreen lending reduces the banks' flexibility to respond to new credit demands from the real sector of the economy because over time an increasing proportion of the banks' resources become absorbed in the original evergreen loans.

Frank Veneroso (1986: 17) points out that the exceptionally high real interest rates observed recently after financial liberalisation in the Southern Cone countries and in Turkey constitute a new phenomenon. He concludes that in all cases they were caused by distress borrowing in conjunction with deposit insurance. The lack of adequate regulation over banking practices encouraged undue risk-taking on the part of the banks. When non-performing assets rose, the banks raised deposit rates to attract more funds to pay interest on existing deposits. In the Argentinian case, Roque Fernandez (1985: 886) points out that 'each financial institution closed by the Central Bank was offering the highest interest rates in the market' at the time of its closure.

Extraordinarily high real loan rates are observed when a substantial proportion of a country's banks have zero net worth or bank managements believe that shareholders as well as depositors are implicitly insured by the government. The exceptionally high real interest rates produce an epidemic effect: the false credit demand by distress borrowers puts upward pressure on interest rates, which in turn drags down other firms (Corbo and de Melo, 1985). The supply is made available because of deposit insurance. Demand rises because of firms' expectations that the government will bail out non-financial as well as financial enterprises. When net worth is zero, firms have every incentive to gamble on a government bail-out in the future.

Financial distress results in reduced investment and worse resource allocation through the distressed financial sector. When non-performing loans rise, banks have less resources for new lending. Furthermore, banks often extend more loans to large firms unable to repay their old loans, in an attempt to conceal their own losses. In this way, loan demand rises, real interest rates increase and investment declines. Attempts to lower interest rates by government decree in Argentina, Bolivia and the former Yugoslavia made matters worse by accelerating inflation and capital flight. The ensuing disintermediation and lower demand for domestic financial assets compounded the banks' difficulties (World Bank 1989: 74–5).

Ronald McKinnon (1991b) emphasises the adverse selection problem that arises with deposit insurance when inflation is high and unstable. In this context, adverse selection occurs because banks are unable to discriminate between high- and low-risk borrowers. If banks raise lending rates thus deterring some low-risk borrowers, the increased percentage of high-risk borrowers could reduce the banks' average return from lending despite the higher loan rate. The reason for this is that the increased default rate more than offsets the increased lending rate. Hence, banks may maximise profits by holding lending rates below their market-clearing equilibrium rates and rationing loans. In this way, they ensure that there is a higher proportion of low-risk borrowers in the pool of potential borrowers.

McKinnon points out that when macroeconomic instability causes positive correlation between returns on alternative bank-financed projects, banks may no longer seek to reduce adverse selection through credit rationing (McKinnon, 1991b: 84–91). If deposit insurance protects depositors, banks may choose riskier lending strategies when macroeconomic instability produces strongly correlated outcomes. This is because favourable outcomes produce large bank profits, while unfavourable outcomes resulting in massive bank losses are borne mainly by the deposit insurance agency. Hence, instead of lowering the loan rate to reduce adverse selection when instability increases, banks may have an incentive to raise it. When banks operate under such conditions of macroeconomic instability and deposit insurance protects depositors, effective prudential regulation and supervision are imperative. A second-best solution may be to impose a ceiling on loan rates of interest.

There has been increasing recognition that prudential regulation and supervision are key prerequisites for financial stability. In their absence, financial systems are prone to financial crises, as witnessed by Chile which experienced high real interest rates in the 1980s:

> these incredibly high interest rates on peso loans represented, in large part, the breakdown of proper financial supervision over the Chilean banking system. Neither officials in the commercial banks themselves nor government regulatory authorities adequately monitored the creditworthiness of a broad spectrum of industrial borrowers.
>
> (McKinnon 1991a: 383)

The great flexibility of the 1970s in the absence of prudential supervision and regulation led to sclerosis, collapse and renationalisation of the Chilean financial system in the 1980s.

VII MARKET STRUCTURE, COMPETITION AND FLEXIBILITY

One of the disappointments with financial liberalisation in a number of developing countries has been the subsequent lack of change in the behaviour of the financial sector. If financial systems do not respond flexibly to a major change in their environments, such as the abolition of interest rate controls, they can hardly be expected to respond flexibly to any changes on the real side of their economies. In Indonesia, for example, David Cole and Betty Slade (1990: 21) report that after interest-rate controls on state banks were abolished in 1983, these banks simply continued to behave as before '. . . still operating in the bureaucratic control mode'. The monetary authorities in Malaysia and Thailand have also been frustrated by the sticky response of bank lending rates to changes in market interest rates. Turkey provides one of several examples where bank associations have taken over the interest-rate setting function when the monetary authorities relinquished it. In India, the Indian Banks' Association fixed an interest rate ceiling of 10 per cent on the inter-bank call money market rate until May 1989.

The basic problem in all these cases has been lack of competition.

Uncompetitive financial markets have been one of the side-effects of government selective credit policies. Deposit-rate ceilings tend to encourage and condone bank cartels. Overt banking cartels for the purpose of setting interest rates have existed in, among other countries, Hong Kong and the Philippines. In Thailand, the oligopolistic structure of the banking system has led to extreme downward deposit-rate inflexibility because the banks have been anxious not to lose market shares by reducing their rates. Cartels, such as the Turkish bankers' association, tend to raise operating resource costs, so reducing the efficiency and flexibility of financial intermediation:

> Many observers have remarked that the gap between rates on loans and rates on deposits is excessive in Turkey compared to other countries. High costs would appear to absorb a large part of this gap. Why are costs high? One simple answer is that costs are high because the gap is wide. As both loan and deposit rates are fixed, perfect competition does not exist. Non-price competition in the form of massive advertising expenditure, impressive building, etc., takes place. Furthermore, there is no incentive to be efficient. To exhibit large profits is asking the authorities to step in and reduce the gap. This is the kind of market situation in which tacit collusion to maintain high costs and to keep profits within certain limits would flourish.
>
> (Fry, 1972: 127)

In general, specialisation within developing country financial sectors has occurred not because of the efficiency inherent in division of labour, but rather as a result of decrees and prohibitions. Far from reducing intermediation costs, specialisation produced in this manner has generally raised them. In most developing countries, specialised financial institutions have been established with exclusive franchises for particular financial activities or particular sectors of the economy. On the one hand, this has destroyed any actual or potential competition. On the other hand, it has not achieved the goals of adequate and efficient distribution of credit or of flexible responses to changing conditions in the real sector. All too often, the specialised bank has expropriated scarce resources to finance large and inefficient investments. Other small investment projects have been starved of funds.

One response by the authorities to an uncompetitive and oligopolistic banking system has been to permit and encourage competition from unregulated financial institutions such as finance companies. Examples of this method of stimulating competition can be found in Malaysia, the Philippines, Sri Lanka, Taiwan, Thailand and Turkey. In all cases, however, these two-tier financial systems have led to financial crisis, fraud and scandal. While unregulated finance companies may provide competition to a lethargic banking system and can inject flexibility into a moribund financial sector, they do not offer a viable alternative to low-risk deposits. In practice, it has proved politically impossible to avoid providing some protection to depositors in failed finance companies.

Other steps taken in several developing countries to stimulate competition include lowering entry barriers, privatising government-owned financial institutions and abolishing interest-rate controls. Bank ownership by conglomerate business groups has also been blamed for lack of competition and inefficient credit allocation.[10] Another contrasting view comes from advocates of universal banks who argue that competition can be stimulated by despecialising DFIs and commercial banks. The Philippines provides an example of such an experiment. Although a major financial liberalisation programme was carried out in the early 1980s, most observers feel: *Plus ça change, plus c'est la même chose.* The inertia was due largely to increasing concentration within the financial system. For example, the interest-rate ceilings that were abolished under the interest-rate reform were quickly replaced by a cartel agreement linked to the Manila Reference Rate, which was supposed to be, but was not, determined competitively in the free market. Removal of many balance-sheet restrictions produced increased concentration in the Philippine financial system rather than the intended increased competition.

Perhaps the only proven way of successfully stimulating competition in an oligopolistic financial system is for the government to compete by issuing treasury bills and bonds with attractive yields. An experiment along these lines in Turkey succeeded in raising real deposit rates of interest by twenty percentage points in 1981. The rate of economic growth accelerated sharply in that year. Typically, however, government securities in developing countries are held only by financial institutions as part of their required liquidity ratios and by business firms obliged to hold them in order to bid for government contracts. Yields on government securities are so low that voluntary holdings are non-existent. The appropriate interest-rate structure, however, applies equally to the government and the private sector. Indeed, if the government is unwilling to compete in this way, attempts to improve flexibility in finance are doomed.

VIII NON-PERFORMING ASSETS AND FLEXIBILITY

Non-performing assets constitute a major cause of the high costs of credit intermediation in developing countries. Banks, and in particular government banks, in many developing countries hold substantial proportions of non-performing assets. The issue of non-performing assets is particularly acute for DFIs (Gordon, 1983; World Bank, 1985). Here, the World Bank (1985: ii) suggests that much of the problem springs from the increasing use of DFIs as tools of development policy. Arvind Virmani (1985: 2) points out that the forced lending requirement used as part of directed credit policies is a recipe for high arrears, the responsibility for which must be assumed by the government.

Default costs are extraordinarily difficult to measure, since accounting practices regarding non-performing loans vary from country to country. Typically, however, the true default costs are understated. In Bangladesh, for example, financial institutions are required for tax purposes to report interest accrued, whether or not it has actually been received. All DFIs in Bangladesh are insolvent, yet they have taxes assessed on illusory profits every year. In a number of countries, tax regulations specify a maximum percentage of earnings that can be set aside for loss provisions. The magnitude of default losses of DFIs in developing countries appears to be extremely serious. The World Bank (1985: 11) finds that, in general, DFIs make inadequate provision for loan losses. For its sample of DFIs, the average return on assets would have been negative had realistic provisions been made for default costs. One-third of the DFIs sampled by the Bank (World Bank, 1985: 12) were unlikely to survive without radical restructuring.

Delinquency rates are high in developing countries for a variety of reasons. Cultural factors undoubtedly play an important role. The concept of loan repayment is unfamiliar in some countries. When the government is involved in credit programmes, recipients often fail to distinguish loans from grants. In part, this may be because government officials behave, perhaps to encourage recipients of such loans to extend gratuities, in ways that suggest the government is providing assistance. Subsidised credit, of course, does contain a grant component. Since the grant fraction of a subsidised loan is never made explicit, a borrower can become confused into thinking that all of it is a grant. Low subsidised interest rates, negative in real terms, themselves provide a strong incentive to postpone loan repayments.

Morris (1985: 20) finds that the primary cause of high arrears in India is the rapid expansion of lending in response to government pressures to achieve mandated credit-disbursement targets. He lists the following causes of high arrears in India: (a) failure to tie lending to productive investments; (b) neglect of marketing and linking credit recovery to the sale of the product; (c) defective loan policies – delayed loan disbursement, too much or too little credit and unrealistic repayment schedules; (d) misapplication of loans; (e) ineffective supervision; (f) apathy and indifference on the part of bank management with respect to recovering loans; and (g) lack of responsibility and discipline on the part of borrowers.

Yung Chul Park and Dong Won Kim (1990: 31–4) document the trend in non-performing loans in Korea. In the early 1980s, non-performing assets represented 11 per cent of total loans, equal to 2.6 times total net worth (Park and Kim, 1990: 36). Troubled firms were in declining industries like textiles and plywood, others were in heavy and chemical manufacturing, and others in shipping and overseas construction. The government had been responsible for encouraging heavy and chemical industries with tax and credit subsidies. The banks failed to conduct proper risk analyses. Firms plunged into new industries and activities without experience, assuming that the government would take care of them.

The Korean government decided to support the troubled firms and persuaded the banks to carry the bad loans on their books as long as they could. Banks had to pump more credit into troubled firms and this squeezed the credit for healthy firms. The government then had to implement industrial restructuring by providing subsidies to firms to take over troubled firms. It also rescheduled the bad loans, involving reduction of interest and the supply of fresh credit. The Bank of Korea compensated banks for some of their losses (Park and Kim, 1990: 35–6).

The crucial problem of arrears lies in the fact that, if financial institutions are to remain solvent, higher default costs must reduce net returns to savers or raise gross costs to successful investors. They create a wedge, just as administrative costs do, between loan and deposit rates of interest. Arrears also reduce banks' flexibility in that credit cannot be redirected towards alternative activities if it is not repaid. Excessive arrears and default rates indicate inefficiency of one kind or another. The financial institution has either financed unproductive investments or failed to press for loan repayment. In either case, financial intermediation is impaired.

IX THE ANOMALOUS CASES OF KOREA AND TAIWAN

Despite high growth rates, the financial systems in Korea and Taiwan hardly exhibit flexible responses to changing economic conditions in the real sectors of the economies. Indeed, McKinnon describes the Korean financial system as follows:

> Because of its determination to support the development of heavy industry and Korean contractors undertaking major construction projects in the Middle East and elsewhere, the Korean government coerced the banks into making risky long-term loans, many of which became nonperforming. In the 1980s the Bank of Korea still provided subsidized credit lines (official discounting at below-market interest rates) to various commercial banks to enable them to avoid bankruptcy by keeping these old (1970s) loans on their books. This bad loan syndrome continues to hinder the full liberalization of the Korean financial system despite the successful monetary stabilization.
>
> (McKinnon, 1991a: 389)

Sang-Woo Nam (1989: 140) reports evidence on the effects of Korea's directed credit. Over the periods 1971–8 and 1979–85, the output/capital ratio for heavy and chemical industries supported through directed credit policies only in the 1970s was 23 per cent. Other industries (excluding tobacco) posted an output/capital ratio of 28 per cent in the period 1971–8 and 21 per cent over the period 1979–85. Hence, the heavy and chemical industries improved their relative efficiency in the 1980s. Nam concludes: 'cheap capital in the 1970s led to excessive and inefficient investment in heavy and chemical industries'.

The government-owned Taiwanese banking system is strongly criticised for bureaucratic procedures and lack of initiative. Tein-Chen Chou (1991: 31–2) assesses the allocative efficiency of banks in Taiwan by considering bank behaviour. The government banks, which have dominated Taiwan's financial system, have faced a variety of portfolio constraints, including stringent collateral requirements. Until recently, loan officers responsible for bad loans were prosecuted for criminal offences. Hence, bank behaviour was bureaucratic in the extreme. Chou's regression analysis of the determinants of bank loan/external funds ratio to particular sectors of the economy indicates that only the sector's fixed assets/total assets and fixed assets/external funds ratios have positive effects, while sales/assets, profit/sales ratios and the industry's growth rate have negative effects. Chou concludes that banks allocate credit on the basis of safety factors not performance and, hence, that bank loan allocation in Taiwan is inefficient.

Chou's findings are consistent with data reported by Tyler Biggs (1988: 9–14) indicating a strong bias in Taiwanese bank lending in favour of large firms. Biggs then reports evidence that medium-sized firms had returns to capital 9 percentage points higher than large firms in the 1970s. Chou's findings are also consistent with evidence reported by Jia-Dong Shea and Ya-Hwei Yang (1990: 17) that easier access to bank credit for state-owned firms in Taiwan led to more capital-intensive technologies with lower rates of return. They conclude that there was inefficient overallocation of credit to state-owned and large firms.

That directed credit policies in Korea and inflexible bureaucratic bankers in Taiwan have not prevented economic growth may result from their unique curb markets. Korea and Taiwan possess curb markets of a size and scope probably not found in any other developing economies. In Taiwan, curb markets provided 48 per cent of loans to private businesses in 1964. Although this ratio fell to 27 per cent in 1973, it was back at 48 per cent in 1986 (Lee and Tsai, 1988: 51, Table 9). The curb market is also of considerable importance for business finance in Korea (Cole and Park, 1983). Elsewhere, curb markets or informal credit arrangements appear to be used more to meet household rather than business credit demands.

Biggs (1991: 182) argues that the Taiwanese Government supported the curb market through the Negotiable Instruments Law enacted in the 1950s. This law made it a criminal offence to fail to honour a postdated cheque. Hence, curb-market loans could be secured against cheques dated three, six or twelve months in the future since the law also prohibited banks for cashing cheques before their due date. The loan would constitute the discounted value of the cheque. Initially, the postdated cheque might have been issued to a supplier or subcontractor. With endorsement, the holder of a postdated cheque could then discount it in the curb market. A cheque might circulate several times and hence acquire several endorsements before its due date.

> The penalty [for writing a bad cheque] was tough: Failure to redeem a postdated check could result in as many as two years in prison. And the law was vigorously enforced. . . .The law specifically made all endorsers equally responsible for redeeming checks with the issuer. Government agencies policed the system, keeping records on bad check cases and referring malefactors to the courts for prosecution.
>
> (Biggs 1991: 182 and 185)

A similar law supports the use of postdated cheques as promissory notes in Korea. Biggs assessed the effect of this curb market as follows:

> Emergence of a large and thriving curb market has been enormously important to Taiwan's industrial development for at least four reasons. First, the curb market complemented the formal credit market by providing information-intensive, efficient credit facilities, what Scitovsky has called the 'small loans' function of the curb market. Second, the curb market helped to mobilize domestic savings by offering high returns (although riskier) on investable funds. Third, the presence of an active curb market increased the 'fungibility' of financial resources by offering an alternative market-determined interest rate on investment funds: the 'safety valve' function of the curb market.

319

Fourth, many curb market transactions facilitated business dealings ('contracting modes') between heterogeneous firms.

(Biggs, 1991: 189–90)

Another crucial role of the curb market is to reduce the moral hazard problem of deposit insurance and bank bail-outs. The riskier lending business goes to the curb market, which is completely unprotected but does not jeopardise the payments system. Not only does free access to the curb market ensure that the opportunity cost of capital to all firms, both large and small, in Korea and Taiwan approximates the competitive free-market interest rate, but the absence of deposit insurance ensures that real interest rates do not rise to unsustainable levels. Curb markets in Korea and Taiwan appear to respond particularly flexibly to the rapidly changing product mix in their small-scale manufacturing sectors.

X CONCLUDING REMARKS

In this chapter, I argue that both low and high institutional interest rates impede a country's financial system from responding flexibly to changing circumstances in the real sector of the economy. Impaired flexibility subsequently reduces the rate of economic growth. This point is supported by a data set prepared for the World Bank's *World Development Report 1991*. Using these data on real interest rates for a sample of five Pacific Basin developing countries (Indonesia, Korea, Malaysia, Philippines and Thailand) and eleven other developing countries (Argentina, Brazil, Chile, Egypt, India, Mexico, Nigeria, Pakistan, Sri Lanka, Turkey and Venezuela), I detect the following relationship between the rate of economic growth YG, the investment ratio IY, the real rate of interest RD and the rate of growth in exports at constant prices XG using three-stage iterative least squares (297 observations, t statistics in parentheses):

$$YG = 0.164 \hat{IY} - 0.237(\hat{IY} \cdot RD^2) + 0.070 \hat{XG} \qquad (2)$$
$$\quad\;\; (11.541) \quad\;\; (-5.123) \qquad\qquad (12.628)$$
$$R^2 = 0.217$$

The overall effect of a rising real interest rate on growth is illustrated in Figure 10.1.[11] The line C_n denotes two standard deviations below the mean of all negative interest rates in the control group, P_n denotes two standard deviations below the mean of all negative interest rates in the Pacific Basin economies, P_p denotes two standard deviations above the mean of all zero or positive interest rates in the five Pacific Basin economies, while C_p denotes two standard deviations above the mean of all zero or positive interest rates in the remaining eleven countries. Evidently, real interest rates deviated from levels that maximised growth far more in the control group countries than

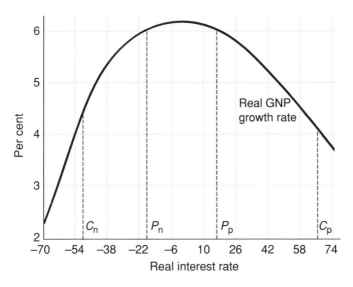

Figure 10.1 Effect of real interest rate on economic growth rate

they did in the Pacific Basin economies. In this chapter, I have argued that pathological financial conditions, such as extremely high or low real interest rates, retard economic growth by reducing flexibility in finance.

NOTES

1 This is exact for continuously compounded interest and inflation rates, but requires the subtraction of $100 \cdot (d/100) \cdot (\pi/100)$ in addition to π for simple rates.

2 Greece and Portugal are no longer classified as developing countries by the UN agencies.

3 James Tobin (1992: 772) states: 'A society's money is necessarily a store of value. Otherwise it could not be an acceptable means of payment.'

4 The observation periods and denominators differ, so the figures are not strictly comparable.

5 This country sample consists of Bangladesh, India, Indonesia, Korea, Malaysia, Nepal, Pakistan, Philippines, Sri Lanka, Taiwan and Thailand. Over the past decade, the scope of priority-sector lending has been reduced substantially in several of these countries.

6 Savers always have the option of using unproductive tangible assets as inflation hedges.

7 State-owned banks often possess a degree of political autonomy, as in Ghana, Kenya and Uganda, which allows them to ignore central bank directives with impunity.

8 For example, the bank may become subject to tighter regulation by Bank Indonesia or must allocate more of its portfolio to certain types of loans.

9 Alternatively, the bank can increase the line of credit to cover interest payments and avoid the problems of technically non-performing loans. Undoubtedly the importance of the customer to the bank will have a bearing on this decision as well as the availability of funds from other banks and abroad. Also, if the bank has ample liquidity, it may be more willing to raise the credit ceiling rather than try to force some actual payment of interest from the customer's own funds.

10 However, this view is challenged by Ben Bernanke and Mark Gertler (1990), who illustrate their analysis with the Japanese practice.

11 This figure is produced using the mean values of all the explanatory variables with the exception of the real deposit rate of interest. The mean value of the real deposit rate is zero with a standard deviation of 23 per cent. Its minimum value is −83 per cent and its maximum value 221 per cent.

REFERENCES

Aries Group (1990) *A Study of Securities Market Institutions: Sri Lanka*, Manila: Asian Development Bank, January.

Bailey, Martin J. (1956) 'The welfare cost of inflationary finance', *Journal of Political Economy* 64(2): April 93–110.

Bernanke, Ben S. and Mark Gertler (1990) 'Financial fragility and economic performance', *Quarterly Journal of Economics* 55(1), February: 87–114.

Biggs, Tyler S. (1988) 'Financing the emergence of small and medium enterprise in Taiwan: financial mobilization and the flow of domestic credit to the private sector', Washington, DC: US Agency for International Development, Employment and Enterprise Development Division, Employment and Enterprise Policy Analysis Discussion Paper no. 15, August.

— (1991) 'Heterogeneous firms and efficient financial intermediation in Taiwan', in Michael Roemer and Christine Jones (eds) *Markets in Developing Countries: Parallel, Fragmented, and Black*, San Francisco: International Center for Economic Growth.

Chou, Tein-Chen (1991) 'Government, financial systems and economic development in Taiwan', Taipei: National Chung-Hsing University, Institute of Economics, October.

Cole, David C. and Yung Chul Park (1983) *Financial Development of Korea 1945–1978*, Cambridge, MA: Harvard University Press for Harvard University, Council on East Asian Studies.

Cole, David C. and Betty F. Slade (1990) 'Indonesian financial development: a different sequencing?', Cambridge, MA: Harvard Law School Program on International Financial Systems, June.

— (1993) 'How bank lending practices influence resource allocation and monetary policy in Indonesia', Cambridge, MA: Harvard Institute for International Development, Development Discussion Paper no. 444, April.

Corbo, Vittorio and Jaime de Melo (1985) 'Scrambling for survival: how firms adjusted to the recent reforms in Argentina, Chile, and Uruguay', World Bank Staff Working Paper no. 764, Washington, DC: World Bank, November.

Dimitrijevic, Dimitri and George Macesich (1973) *Money and Finance in Contemporary Yugoslavia*, New York: Praeger.

Fernandez, Roque B. (1985) 'The expectations management approach to stabilization in Argentina during 1976–82', *World Development* 13(8), August: 871–92.

Friedman, Milton (1971) 'Government revenue from inflation', *Journal of Political Economy* 79(4), July–August: 846–56.

Fry, Maxwell J. (1972) *Finance and Development Planning in Turkey*, Leiden: Brill.

—— (1973) 'Manipulating demand for money', in Michael Parkin (ed.) *Essays in Modern Economics*, London: Longman.

Garvy, George (1968) *Money, Banking, and Credit in Eastern Europe*, New York: Federal Reserve Bank of New York.

Gelb, Alan H. (1989) 'Financial policies, growth, and efficiency', PPR Working Paper WPS no. 202, Washington, DC: World Bank, June.

Giovannini, Alberto and Martha de Melo (1993) 'Government revenue from financial repression', *American Economic Review* 83(4), September: 953–63.

Goldsmith, Raymond W. (1975) 'The financial structure of Yugoslavia', *Banca Nazionale del Lavoro Quarterly Review*, 112, March: 61–108.

Gordon, David L. (1983) 'Development finance companies, state and privately owned: a review', World Bank Staff Working Paper no. 578, Washington, DC: World Bank, July.

Hanson, James A. and Craig R. Neal (1986) *The Demand for Liquid Financial Assets: Evidence from 36 Developing Countries*, Washington, DC: World Bank.

Hilferding, Rudolf (1910) *Das Finanzkapital: Eine Studie über die jüngste Entwicklung des Kapitalismus*, Vienna: Wiener Volksbuchhandlung. [(*Finance Capital: A Study of the Latest Phase of Capitalist Development*), edited with an introduction by Tom Bottomore from translations by Morris Watnick and Sam Gordon, London: Routledge & Kegan Paul, 1981.]

Hinds, Manuel (1988) 'Economic effects of financial crises', PPR Working Paper WPS 104, Washington, DC: World Bank, Europe, Middle East and North Africa Department, October.

International Monetary Fund, *International Financial Statistics*, Washington, DC: International Monetary Fund, various issues.

Lee, Yung-san and Tzong-rong Tsai (1988) 'Development of financial system and monetary policies in Taiwan', Paper presented at the Conference on the Economic Development Experiences of Taiwan, 8–10 June, Taipei: Academia Sinica, Institute of Economics.

McKinnon, Ronald I. (1991a) 'Monetary stabilization in LDCs', in Lawrence B. Krause and Kim Kihwan (eds) *Liberalization in the Process of Economic Development*, Berkeley and Los Angeles: University of California Press.

—— (1991b) *The Order of Economic Liberalization: Financial Control in the Transition to a Market Economy*, Baltimore, MD: Johns Hopkins University Press.

Morris, Felipe (1985) 'India's financial system: an overview of its principal structural features', World Bank Staff Working Paper no. 739, Washington, DC: World Bank.

Nam, Sang-Woo (1989) 'Liberalization of the Korean financial and capital markets', in Korea Development Institute (ed.), *Korea's Macroeconomic and Financial Policies*, Seoul: Korea Development Institute.

Nichols, Donald A. (1974) 'Some principles of inflationary finance', *Journal of Political Economy* 82(2), March–April: 423–30.

Park, Yung Chul (1990) 'Growth, liberalization, and internationalization of Korea's financial sector, 1970–89', Paper presented at the Conference on Financial Development in Japan, Korea and Taiwan, 27–8 August, Taipei: Academia Sinica, Institute of Economics.

Park, Yung Chul and Dong Won Kim (1990) 'The behavior and efficiency of commercial banks in Korea', Paper presented at the Conference on Financial Development in Japan, Korea and Taiwan, 27–8 August, Taipei: Academia Sinica, Institute of Economics.

Podolski, T.M. (1973) *Socialist Banking and Monetary Control: The Experience of Poland*, Cambridge: Cambridge University Press.

Shea, Jia-Dong and Ya-Hwei Yang (1990) 'Financial system and the allocation of investment funds', Occasional Paper no. 9001, December, Taiwan: Chung-Hua Institution for Economic Research.

Tobin, James (1992) 'Money', in Peter Newman, Murray Milgate and John Eatwell (eds) *The New Palgrave Dictionary of Money and Finance*, London: Macmillan and New York: Stockton Press, vol. 2: 770–8.

Uppal, J.S. (1986) 'Public financial institutions and economic concentration in India', *Journal of Development Economics* 20(1), January–February: 135–44.

Veneroso, Frank (1986) *New Patterns of Financial Instability*, Washington, DC: World Bank, February.

Virmani, Arvind (1985) 'Government policy and the development of financial markets: the case of Korea', World Bank Staff Working Paper no. 747, Washington, DC: World Bank, August.

World Bank (1975) *Yugoslavia: Development with Decentralization*, Baltimore, MD: Johns Hopkins University Press for the World Bank.

—— (1984) 'Brazil: financial systems review', Washington, DC: World Bank, July.

—— (1985) 'Financial intermediation policy paper', Washington, DC: World Bank, Industry Department, July.

—— (1986) *Argentina's Banking Sector: The Need for Reform*, Report 6418–AR, Washington, DC: World Bank, September.

—— (1989) *World Development Report 1989*, New York: Oxford University Press for the World Bank.

—— (1990) *World Tables 1989–90*, Washington, DC: World Bank.

—— (1991) *World Development Report 1991*, New York: Oxford University Press for the World Bank.

11

THE POLITICAL DETERMINANTS OF ECONOMIC FLEXIBILITY, WITH SPECIAL REFERENCE TO THE EAST ASIAN NICS

David Seddon and Tim Belton-Jones

There is something wrong with the way we make our decisions . . . there is too much short-termism, too much reacting to events, not enough shaping of events. We give the impression of being in office but not in power. . . . Unless this approach is changed, the government will not survive and will not deserve to survive.

(Norman Lamont, resignation speech
to the House of Commons, 9 June 1993)

I ECONOMIC FLEXIBILITY AND POLICY ADAPTABILITY

Chapter 1 of this book argues that 'the flexibility of national economies is a distinctive concept worthy of separate study which is not adequately treated within the existing literature on market efficiency or long-run development'. We start from the same premise, but examine the determinants of flexibility from a political perspective. While for economists, economic flexibility will be considered as an independent variable in the explanation of economic success, for the political scientist the question is rather what political factors determine the flexibility of a national economy and its overall success in terms of development; economic flexibility becomes a dependent variable to be explained.

We suggest that economic flexibility depends crucially on policy adaptability. This we define as the capacity to change the policy framework within which the economy operates, whether in detail or in overall direction, rapidly, efficiently and effectively, and without undue social or political friction. Policy adaptability is a function both of the character and ethos of the government and the bureaucracy (often referred to interchangeably, but misleadingly, as 'the state') and of their degree of insulation from the immediate pressures of the political arena. Insulation is not the same as isolation. Insulation is possible only if the relationship between the policy-making process and the wider political economy permits the effective regulation of both 'the state' and 'civil society' within certain broadly acceptable parameters. Effective insulation from the immediate pressures of special interests enables policy-makers to respond swiftly and effectively to new circumstances; but the capacity to identify and implement appropriate policies to promote effective medium- and longer-term development requires the maintenance of strategic relations with the wider civil society. When 'the state' is under pressure, when the government or regime is threatened and the bureaucracy harassed or corrupted, there will be reaction (and even over-reaction, leading to policy incoherence) rather than adapt-ability, responsiveness and flexibility. Overall, political stability and continuity, associated with a mode of regulation which ensures the effective insulation of policy-makers from short-term pressures while at the same time rendering them responsive to the medium- and long-term needs of the economy and civil society, constitute the necessary (but not sufficient) conditions for policy adaptability.

In order to examine and develop these hypotheses – or assertions – we consider here the case of the East Asian economies, in particular that of South Korea. There can be no denying the spectacular economic growth and apparent success of the East Asian economies over the past three decades, despite scepticism on the part of some commentators regarding the sustaina-bility of this success through the 1990s (Bello and Rosenfeld, 1991; Bello, 1992). As Jenkins succinctly puts it, 'if successful capitalist development is taking place anywhere in the Third World it is here' (Jenkins, 1992: 5).

The East Asian economies and states vary in important respects, but flexibility, responsiveness, adaptability, and a capacity to 'create compara-tive advantage' with the help of strategic policy-making are all invoked by analysts of very different theoretical persuasions to help explain their success (see Chapter 7). But if all emphasise the importance of policy adaptability and economic flexibility in determining the capacity of the East Asian economies to respond to, and even to anticipate, significant changes in the economic environment to their own advantage, there is considerable dis-agreement about the role of politics and the state in this regard.

In the mid-1980s, Stephan Haggard reviewed the experience of the NICs – and commentaries on this experience – and attempted to develop a system-atic explanation for the relative success of the East Asian NICs. He pointed out that, for many,

> The East Asian 'Gang of Four' . . . are seen to vindicate the liberal prescription for market-oriented policies and close participation in the world economy. Their success has elevated export-led growth into a

new development orthodoxy. Brazil and Mexico, on the other hand, are perceived as exemplifying the costs of inward-looking, import-substituting industrialization. . . . Once growth miracles in their own right, both are now favourite test cases of policy incoherence, economic distortion, inequality and dependence.

(Haggard, 1986: 344)

Certainly, Balassa (1981) emphasised the crucial importance of export-oriented industrialisation in the successful development of the East Asian NICs during the 1970s; for him, Korea and Taiwan broadly vindicated liberal policy prescriptions and provided examples of a general strategy for successful economic development. Moving between positive analysis and advocacy, he argued generally for 'getting the prices right' through market-oriented policy shifts to integrate developing countries into the world economy. These policy shifts were to include domestic pricing and financial reforms, but above all import liberalisation and a realistic exchange rate.

In the same year as Balassa's study was published, Little argued, with respect to the Asian Gang of Four, that 'their success is almost entirely due to good policies and the ability of the people – scarcely at all to favourable circumstances or a good start' (Little, 1981: 25). A decade earlier, Brown had argued that 'the almost irresistible conclusion from Korean development experience is that with proper economic policies and a continuation of reasonable international aid levels, most developing countries could sustain growth rates as high as 10 per cent' (Brown, 1973: 265).

Government policies, while evidently important, appear to be considered simply a matter of choice, and without historical, social or political preconditions. Economic flexibility appears to be intrinsically associated with 'the market', and despite the constant reference to the significance of good policies, the role of the state is regarded essentially as that of providing a package of incentives to encourage efficient allocation of resources and signal to firms their comparative advantage. It is taken as axiomatic that 'a well-functioning market system is conducive to economic flexibility; by comparison central planning creates rigidities' (Chapter 1).

Balassa, for example, is cited by Harris as stating:

experience indicates that countries which have not planned have had a much better economic performance than those that have relied on planning methods. Countries that have (not) planned include Taiwan, Korea, Israel, as well as Brazil; India has planned. Whereas the first group reached rapid rates of economic growth, relying largely on private initiative, in India, investment, production and import controls applied in the process of planning have constrained not only the growth of the private sector but also the growth of the entire national economy.

(Harris, 1986: 131)

In the view of an increasing number of economists, however, the assumption that flexibility is a prerogative of market economies is invalid. Many now emphasise the crucial role of the state in creating the preconditions for flexibility in many of the most successful economies. For Harris, the 'key' to the success of the East Asian NICs has been their capacity to respond rapidly and effectively to changing world circumstances – to the changing nexus of opportunities and constraints afforded by the global political economy – and to adapt. Nevertheless, he also emphasises that, in the case of at least three of the Gang of Four,

> there was no simple reflection of 'market forces' either. Not only did the state direct the process, participating closely, it also – in the case of South Korea and Taiwan – imposed what might be seen as a predatory agrarian policy not unlike those in the Eastern Bloc.
>
> (Harris, 1986: 69)

State intervention, from this perspective, is not an impediment to economic 'flexibility' but a precondition for it.

Others adopt a more cautious position. The World Bank, for example, has come to recognise that, while Hong Kong followed a relatively free-market approach, the other East Asian cases involved greater state intervention (World Bank, 1991: 39). It continues, however, to regard intervention, even in these cases, as problematic ('some economists argue that intervention worked because markets were still freer than in other economies. Some go so far as to argue that intervention set the East Asian economies back, that they would have done even better without it'), and suggests that, in any case, 'intervention in the market in these East Asian economies was, in an overall sense, more moderate than in most other developing economies' (World Bank, 1991: 39). This, as we shall see, is debatable, to say the least.

II POLICY ADAPTABILITY:
REACTING, RESPONDING OR SHAPING?

Since Haggard undertook his review,

> there has been a spate of articles . . . comparing the economic perform-ance of the East Asian and Latin American NICs (Ranis, 1985; Ranis and Orrock, 1985; Sachs, 1985; Evans, 1987; Gereffi and Wyman, 1989). The comparisons made are invariably unflattering to the Latin America countries.
>
> (Jenkins, 1991: 197)

Others, concerned with the even more striking contrast between the per-formance of the East Asian economies and that of sub-Saharan Africa, have considered whether 'superior adaptability helps to explain the economic successes of the NICs of East and Southeast Asia, . . . while . . . the absence of this quality has contributed importantly to the lagging performances of the economies of Eastern Europe and sub-Saharan Africa?' (Killick, 1994).

A review of the recent literature on the NICs in general and the East Asian economies in particular reveals a striking unanimity, despite often considerable differences in emphasis and interpretation, that flexibility and adaptability contributed significantly to the success of the East Asian NICs. Harris, for example, in comparing 'the Gang of Four' with 'the Latin Americans' suggests that no particular model of economic development provided the 'key' to economic success – 'the experience does not vindicate export-promotion policies any more than it repudiates import-substitution industrialization. In practice, an *opportunistic combination* of both approaches was employed' (Harris, 1986: 69). In his view, what all of the Gang of Four had in common was their capacity to respond in a flexible and opportunistic fashion to external demand, combining export orientation and import substitution as and when required. If 'willingness and ability to change policies when these are not giving the desired results' (Jenkins, 1992) is an effective definition of adaptability, then all of the East Asian NICs demonstrated such adaptability.

This suggests an important – perhaps crucial – distinction between 'planning' (as in central planning) and 'policy adaptability'. With respect to South Korea, Harris suggests that:

> although the heart of Korean development was as state capitalist as any East European economy and as Keynesian as any West European social democracy, it was distinguished from both by the flexibility of approach and speed of change. Exports required an opportunism normally excluded from state planning. One commentator described the government style as 'not so much a deliberate one of careful planning and debate, but more one of diving in, getting started, observing results, adjusting policy, and repeating the process until the appropriate mix is found'.
>
> (Harris, 1986: 42)

He then contrasts the East Asian NICs and their flexible, opportunistic approach to economic policies with the Latin American countries, arguing that while the governments of Brazil and Mexico 'recognised that the world was a different place and realised that interdependence had become the condition of survival . . . others [in Latin America] did not see the change . . . – the old conditioned reflexes were skew of the new world order' (Harris, 1986: 92).

Others, of very different theoretical persuasions, adopt a broadly similar approach, even if they link flexibility explicitly with a shift towards an enhanced role for the market. Fischer, for example, writing on the 'crisis' of the Latin American countries during the 1980s, explicitly suggests that 'in contrast to the dynamic Asian economies (DAEs), Latin American countries lacked the flexibility and thrust of policy reforms to respond more rapidly or, indeed, adequately to trends in economic globalisation and interdependence' (Fischer, 1991: 20). And Barsony writing in the same publication, has argued, for the DAEs as a whole, that, in the 1980s 'policy reforms based on market principles further increased the flexibility of the DAEs and contributed to the full exploitation of the extremely favourable external environment' (Barsony, 1991: 15). The World Bank consistently, throughout the 1980s, emphasised the importance of flexibility as an element of economic success (and 'rigidities' as crucial in explaining failure). Adoption of the correct policies (generally aimed at encouraging and promoting market responsiveness) enhances internal flexibility and reduces rigidities, while these in turn affect the success of an economy. At the same time, the capacity to respond rapidly and effectively to changes in external conditions is also regarded as a positive feature.

Suarez-Villa and Han observe, with reference to South Korea's development of high technology, that:

> essentially, what has occurred in Korea's case is that several 'take-offs' have propelled electronics to the most important position among this nation's industries. Each of these take-offs has been characterized by significant changes and new learning curves in productive organization, technology and work processes. What is remarkable is the rapid succession of these take-offs, demonstrating Korea's ability to absorb and adapt foreign technology and to change its productive structure to accommodate the needs of each new wave of industrial activities.
>
> (Suarez-Villa and Han, 1990: 275)

However, what is striking about the general thrust of the specialist literature of the 1980s and 1990s regarding 'the role of the state' in East Asia is that, while the capacity to adapt policies and effect rapid changes in orientation (policy adaptability) is much emphasised, this capacity is seen less in terms of responsiveness to changing conditions than in terms of the capacity of the state to provide support for new initiatives and to create new opportunities through a flexible strategy designed to strengthen the economy for the future (what might be termed strategic and selective intervention). In fact, a good deal of the discussion emphasises the extent to which government policies in the East Asian NICs went explicitly against the directions indicated by comparative advantage and were concerned to create comparative advantage on the basis of a medium- to long-term strategy or plan to change the structure and direction of the economy. This has been seen by some in terms of 'state guidance' and implies a degree of forward planning. As Hall points out, this is, increasingly, a characteristic of many of the more successful advanced capitalist states, like Germany and Japan. He suggests that:

the international market has required the advanced states of capitalist society to progressively rationalise their societies so that they can compete. This has necessitated such states becoming 'stronger' in infrastructural terms, as has been seen clearly in the manner in which the Japanese state plans and markets the products of its industry.

(Hall, 1991: 128)

As regards the East Asian economies, Lee and Yamazawa, for example, argue that in both Japan and South Korea:

changes in the pattern of trade and industrial structure have been guided not by the actual but by the potential comparative advantage in both countries. General trading companies have played this guiding role in Japan with the assistance of the government's industrial policy. In the case of Korea, the government has been more active in guiding the development of new industries.

(Lee and Yamazawa, 1990: 187)

They suggest that, in the case of South Korea:

foreign technology was introduced in the 1960s mainly through imports of machinery and equipment, since the standardized technology easily embodied in machinery and equipment was required. In the early 1970s, technology transfer through direct foreign investment and licensing became important as Korea started building its heavy and chemical industries . . . government intervened in technology, restrictive marketing clauses, the possible impact on the development of new industries, and royalty payment arrangements.

(Lee and Yamazawa, 1990: 187)

Several other authors also emphasise the active role of 'the government' or 'planners' in creating comparative advantage, rather than simply adapting policies in the light of current identified comparative advantage – in effect, making long-term commitments rather than simply responding to the present. Chang in Chapter 7 of this volume also takes up this theme. Similarly, Wade argues that 'the governments of Taiwan, Korea and Japan have not so much picked winners as made them' (Wade, 1990: 334). And Auty suggests that

although the South Korean planners pursued the outward-oriented trade policy favoured by agencies like the World Bank, they also intervened strongly to *create* comparative advantage. Their policy has been accurately defined as dual industrial development . . . in which import substitution industrialization proceeds alongside export promotion. The Korean government intervened to create competitive advantage in HCI (heavy and chemical industry) via tariff protection, infrastructure provision and, most important, cheap finance. (Emphasis added.)

(Auty, 1990: 18)

Amsden (1989) also argues that the Korean government emphasised the need for credit and commodity markets to be distorted away from international price levels and internal uniformity, in order that successive industries could be entered and thus provide a foundation for further diversification. She also points to the continuing commitment to growth during periods of macro-economic instability.

These generalisations can be put into context if we consider, briefly, the evolution of government economic policies in Korea, for example, during the 'miracle' years. Economic policies adopted during this period reflect a complex strategy on the part of the government. At the beginning of the 1960s, the currency, the won, was devalued by half to encourage exports, interest rates were allowed to rise to encourage domestic savings, restrictions on external trade were eased to allow exporters virtual freedom to import provided they exported, and tax incentives to export were increased. The results were extremely positive and encouraged a continuing focus on exports as the key to economic growth. But the government also continued to protect the domestic economy, although on a changing basis (a ban on the importation of cement, metals, chemicals and fertilisers later gave way to a ban on transport equipment and machinery). With success, the government's ambitions grew. Harris argues that 'while the backbone of the export performance of South Korea might be attributable to a genuine comparative advantage, the second generation of growth industries seemed more likely to be the products of government gambles' (Harris, 1986: 41).

Just as the neoclassical economists were hailing the appearance of a Korean strategy which appeared at first sight to vindicate their notions of the free market economy, the government introduced the 1973 Heavy Industry and Chemicals Plan, designed to force the disproportionate growth of capital-intensive industries regardless both of relative prices and of notions of comparative advantage. Between 1973 and 1983, Korea increased its shipbuilding output by 15,000 per cent to take 23 per cent of the world market. Steel output from the state company Posco started at 1 million tons in 1973 and by 1984 had reached about 12 million tons. Automobile manufacturing was another area in which the state made a major commitment to promoting growth, and in 1974, when 9,100 cars were produced, targets were set for an output of half a million by 1980 and one million by 1985. Despite the increase in world oil prices in 1973–4 and deepening world recession, the government persisted in its strategy, increasing its overseas borrowing to ease the domestic shortage of resources. Investment as a share of gross domestic product increased between 1976 and 1979 from 25 to 35 per cent, with four-fifths of it going to the heavy industry and chemical sectors.

All of these commitments would have been impossible without 'a privileged framework of operations provided by the government' (Harris, 1986: 41). Generally, what was true for shipbuilding was true for other areas of industrial development

> it was government that made the difference, financing company expansion in the face of declining demand and low capacity use, forcing mergers and a cartel to reduce domestic competition, and obliging companies to adopt a particular pattern of specialisation. In sum, it appeared that government, not the operation of a free world market, had created a 'comparative advantage'.
>
> (Harris, 1986: 40)

This emphasis on creating comparative advantage ('stealing a march on the competition') gives a very different twist to the idea of flexibility, underlining the importance of anticipation and of strategic and selective intervention to ensure changing 'ahead of the game' rather than simply reacting or responding to changes in circumstances. If pursued systematically, such an overall strategy, combining 'flexibility and foresight', could be seen as enabling states not only to promote economic flexibility and create comparative advantage – changing 'ahead of the game' – but also to begin to have a significant effect on 'the game' itself and its overall direction, and thus to exert a degree of control or hegemony in the global political economy, thereby becoming shapers of international commerce.

The emphasis on policy adaptability as involving a combination of responsiveness and strategic intervention inevitably 'brings the state back in', as we have seen above. However, it is one thing to emphasise the importance of state intervention, of strategic and selective planning or 'guidance' as well as the capacity to shift policy when required (policy adaptability). It is quite another to explain the nature of 'the state' and the conditions which enable it to act in such a fashion; and yet another to explain why some dirigiste states are successful both in encouraging policy adaptability and in promoting economic development, while others are not.

The World Bank has increasingly recognised that flexibility is not confined to 'free-market economies' with minimalist states, and that political factors may significantly affect the capacity to adjust policies rapidly and effectively. Thus, in the mid-1980s, the Bank suggested that:

> the diverse experience of developing countries emphasises certain basic lessons for policy. One can be summarised as the need for flexibility . . . [the capacity] to be able to respond flexibly to changes in the external environment. Countries as varied as India, Indonesia, Korea and Turkey have adapted their economic policies to changed circum-

stances. . . . When for political or other reasons countries cannot adjust their policies quickly, they should be conservative in resorting to foreign borrowing.

(World Bank, 1985: 7)

It would be hard to argue that the four countries cited are prime examples of free-market economies, but all have moved rapidly and relatively effectively at different points over the last decade or so towards new, more 'outward-oriented' policies.

But the 'political factors' referred to are not discussed: neither the 'political or other reasons' which may prevent rapid adjustment, nor the political preconditions for 'flexibility' and rapid, effective change are examined. The relevance of 'the political' is recognised, but not analysed. Furthermore, the language of the Bank – as, indeed, that of most other commentators and analysts of whatever theoretical persuasion – tends to obscure the need to consider the role of the state, or indeed political factors generally, in any detail, for it is 'economies' that are interventionist, and 'countries' that follow policies. There is a real need explicitly to 'bring the state back in' to the analysis, and to consider in some detail the political determinants of economic flexibility.

As Fine (1992) remarks, in his analysis of the South Korean case, the recognition of the crucial role played by the state in East Asian development over the past three decades is very important, but finally insufficient. Simple recognition of the importance of the state leaves unresolved the relationship between the state and the social groups or interests that it represents and advantages, and those that it does not represent and marginalises. These issues have occasionally been acknowledged, but have rarely been addressed. Luedde-Neurath recognises an unresolved issue in the case of South Korea:

neither have we tackled the critical question of *why* the state in Korea was able to intervene so decisively in economic development without causing chaos or provoking large scale defiance among the business interests keen, for example, to circumvent import controls, artificially prolonging their 'infancy', or avoid export obligations. (Emphasis added.)

(Luedde-Neurath, 1986: 5)

White and Wade (1985: 9) acknowledge this in their edited collection on 'developmental states in East Asia': 'what none of the papers on Taiwan and South Korea say much about is the basis of state power, the way it is organised, or the micro-principles with which officials make allocation decisions. These are exceedingly important questions'. However, they console themselves with the achievement of the collection – which is essentially to show why the 'neoclassical' interpretation of the success of the East Asian NICs is misleading.

III THE BASIS OF EFFECTIVE STATE INTERVENTION

In 1986, Haggard remarked that 'there have been few cross regional studies of the NICs . . . nor has there been much effort to analyse the domestic political bases of these alternative paths to industrialization' (1986: 344). This remains largely true even today, although a few attempts have been made, literally in the last few years, notably by Jenkins (1991, 1992), in particular as regards the comparison between the East Asian NICs and the Latin American countries, and by Killick (1992 and Chapter 6 of this volume) in studies of the relatively unsuccessful development experience of sub-Saharan Africa in the 1970s and 1980s, in the light of successful development elsewhere (particularly in East Asia).

But since the mid-1980s there has been an increasing interest generally in the role of the state in economic development, particularly in East Asia. Most of the recent literature on the East Asian NICs broadly rejects the main thrust of the neoclassical approach and explanation of the kind provided by Balassa, on both theoretical and empirical grounds. It emphasises, by contrast, the strategic importance of state intervention in, and state direction of, the economy in the case of the East Asian NICs. The view that the secret of the East Asian NICs' success involved 'getting the prices right' and a minimal role for the state has been widely challenged, particularly in the cases of Singapore, South Korea and Taiwan (by Amsden, 1985; Harris, 1986; Pack and Westphal, 1986; White, 1988, and others).

The majority of economists recognise that economies are not purely self-regulating but actually require the state at least to provide an appropriate framework. Many would go further to argue that the role of 'the state' in determining – through government policies and bureaucratic mechanisms – the shape and direction of economic change cannot be ignored if we are to understand the economic performance of different countries and regions. Those economists and (fewer) political scientists concerned to explain the economic success of the East Asian NICs have tended, increasingly, to come to the same conclusion.

Amsden has argued, with respect to South Korea, that 'when industrialisation began to accelerate, it did so in response to government initiatives and not the forces of the free market . . . these processes can be thought of as general propositions applicable to similar countries' (Amsden, 1989: 27). She also argues that 'it may be said that growth has been faster in Korea not because markets have been allowed to operate more freely, but because the subsidization process has been qualitatively superior . . . in direct exchange for subsidies, the state exacts certain performance standards from firms' (Amsden, 1989: 145, 146). Barsony – who is generally enthusiastic about the 'outward-oriented' development of the East Asian economies in the 1980s – recognises that:

financial policy in Korea and Taiwan, although recently becoming more market-oriented, has generally been characterised by heavy official intervention, particularly through a strict control over interest rates and over the allocation of credits with limited discretion for financial institutions. Moreover, the financial system has been largely closed to international competition.

(Barsony, 1991: 17)

The World Bank too has recognised the significance of 'state' intervention in its more recent analyses, agreeing that, while Hong Kong followed a relatively free-market approach, 'the other economies were relatively more interventionist', and noting that 'Japan and Korea followed policies of protection for inftant industries and of credit subsidies' (World Bank, 1991: 39). Others, such as Wade (1988, 1990), concerned to establish a synthesis between market-led and government-led approaches, recognise the crucial importance of 'governing the market' in East Asian development.

But if the role of the state is broadly agreed to be of major importance, there is less agreement as to precisely what that role is. Furthermore, surprisingly little attention has been paid to the social and political determinants of the state's role or the character of state intervention. In general, however, during the 1980s, and not only with reference to the East Asian NICs, it has been widely argued that 'it has become increasingly evident that resumed and sustainable growth also requires increased state capabilities – not so much a less powerful state as one that plays different roles and does so more effectively' (Nelson, 1989: 10). In the comparison between the economic performance of the East Asian economies and those of Latin America, Jenkins argues that 'it is the effectiveness of state intervention which is the crucial difference' (Jenkins, 1991: 199). Mouzelis also sees that the key issue as effective versus ineffective state intervention and the key question as what precisely explains the prevalence in East Asia of 'a strongly authoritarian state apparatus committed to economic planning and to a highly selective, flexible, and efficacious regulation of the overall economy' (Mouzelis, 1993: 192).

There has long been interest in the relationship between democracy, dictatorship and development, and a general assumption that successful capitalist development and 'democratic forms' were closely linked. Certainly, classical political economy identified a tendency for the two to go together and many today, including neoclassical Marxists like Warren (1981), continue to see development and democracy as closely interrelated. In the 1960s and 1970s the evolution of political regimes in Latin America and in Southern Europe tended broadly to confirm this analysis. More recently, however, particularly in the 1980s, there has been a growing interest in whether authoritarian regimes or democracies are more or less conducive to effective adjustment and continuing economic development.

Killick in Chapter 1 of this book argues that 'a government which is insecure, corrupted, repressive is unlikely to give much priority to economic flexibility, or to have the legitimacy necesssary to carry through policies needed to adjust the economy to changing circumstances', and deploys this general thesis in an explanation of the failure of countries in sub-Saharan Africa to respond swiftly and effectively to the changed conditions of the 1980s (see also Chapter 6). But what of governments that are relatively secure and repressive – such as the government of Pinochet in Chile or the military regime of Turkey after the 1980s coup? Some, like Hall, argue that 'bluntly, forced and fast imitative industrialization requires the centraliz-ation of power – that is, it rules out of court the combination of low despotism/high infrastructure that characterized the rise of the West' (Hall, 1991: 129), although he recognises that the centralisation of power does not guarantee effective development.

The argument, characteristic of much of the radical Left during the 1970s and 1980s – that only strong, authoritarian regimes would be capable of orchestrating the appropriate policies for limited capitalist development in times of global crisis (e.g. Frank, 1981) – pointed towards both the Latin American states and the East Asian NICs (as well as to others, in the Middle East for example). The term 'bureaucratic authoritarianism', used to characterise the regimes that emerged in Latin America during the 1970s (O'Donnell, 1978, 1979) was applied to explain the relationship between industrialisation and authoritarianism in the East Asian NICs, particularly in South Korea during the 1980s (Cummings, 1984; Im, 1987). Towards the end of the 1980s, from a more orthodox position both politically and theoretically, Nelson argued that all of the governments pursuing far-reaching adjustment and economic reform programmes during the late 1970s and early 1980s were characterised by regimes with highly centralised authority:

(in) Chile, Turkey (between 1980 and 1983), and Ghana, military rule ensured control. While Philippine president Corazon Aquino had come to power on a wave of popular support, she ruled by executive decree during her first eighteen months in office. In Sri Lanka and Jamaica, both long-established parliamentary democracies, prime ministers Julius Jayawardene and Edward Seaga both were powerful leaders who thoroughly dominated their cabinets, parties and legisla-tures. (Both also tightened their control after several years in office by maneuvers widely viewed as erosions of democratic tradition.) In all six cases, moreover, organised opposition groups were routed and in disarray for the first years of the new government; in the military cases they were also suppressed.

(Nelson, 1989: 12)

Interestingly, she does not refer to the East Asian NICs in this context. Others, however, like Johnson (1987: 164), have observed that the cases of

Japan and Taiwan, as well as South Korea, illustrate how economic perform-ance is dependent on political arrangements, to argue for 'the essential rationality of the soft authoritarian-capitalism nexus in terms of comparative development strategies', and radicals like Frank (1981) have insisted that capitalist development in 'peripheral' states (including those of East Asia) is only possible under repressive and authoritarian regimes.

As Nelson points out:

> conventional wisdom has long held that authoritarian governments are more likely than democracies to adopt and enforce unpopular econ-omic stabilization and adjustment measures. They are assumed to be better placed to make long-run plans, less influenced by popular pressures and better able to both forestall protest through anticipated repression and suppress protest if it does occur. In the longer run moreover, democracies are perceived to be more likely to develop powerful entrenched interest groups that block flexible adaptation to changing technology or international trends.
>
> (Nelson, 1989: 15–16)

This line of argument has, however, been challenged by studies which argue either that no clear relationship can be identified (e.g. Haggard, 1986; Remmer, 1986; Healey and Robinson, 1992) or that democracies actually provide a more appropriate framework. Nelson also points out, in support of this view, that 'authoritarian systems, especially long-established ones, are hardly immune to problems of inflexible vested interests' (Nelson, 1989: 16), while Killick draws attention specifically to the poor development record of many African states, arguing that this may have been, in part at least, a consequence of the prevalence of authoritarian 'patrimonial' states and military regimes in Africa during the last twenty years (Chapter 6).

Nelson suggests that at least some democracies, especially many of the long-established Western democracies, 'have developed sophisticated chan-nels and procedures to accommodate all major interests while permitting adaptation to changing economic circumstances' (Nelson, 1989: 16). As far as the most successful of the East Asian economies is concerned, Weinstein points out that:

> the Japanese political system has been characterised formally by a parliamentary cabinet form of government and competitive political parties since 1889 . . . and [that] the 1947 constitution also broadened and more firmly guaranteed the civil liberties of Japanese citizens, making Japan among the most free and open nations in the world today.
>
> (Weinstein, 1987: 602)

And the World Bank has emphasised the importance, in the case of Japan, of consensus and avoidance of conflict in relations between government agencies, producers and producers' associations (World Bank, 1991). Even those who would point to the dominance of the conservative government in Japan throughout the postwar period and refer, as does Johnson (1987), to 'soft authoritarianism', concede the formally democratic political regime.

This suggests that a government bound by broadly democratic structures to respond to a variety of special interest groups and accommodate them in some way may, nevertheless, be able to achieve policy adaptability and promote economic flexibility. Nelson also stresses that, even in the cases of regimes with highly centralised authority:

> in each, in the years noted . . . a new government took office, elected with overwhelming majorities in Sri Lanka, Jamaica, and the Philippines; and taking power in military coups but with considerable or sweeping public support in Chile, Turkey and Ghana. In all of these countries, there was clearly widespread support – indeed demand – for major changes, although there were deep divisions in every case regarding the nature of the needed reforms. . . . Commitment to change was a shared feature.
>
> (Nelson, 1989: 12)

As Killick notes,

> change is not impossible even when the state is behoven to interest groups. . . . When combined with strong leadership, public acceptance of the need for change can render politically feasible shifts that would formerly have been judged suicidal.
>
> (Killick, 1992: 17)

The sharp distinction between democracy and dictatorship clearly does not, in practice, hold up under empirical analysis; most regimes combine authoritarian and democratic features in varying ways and to varying degrees at any one point in time. Furthermore, even in the recent postwar historical past, many countries have experienced a shift from one to the other, and in some cases several shifts, both 'backwards' and 'forwards'. While some might argue that there is a general tendency for specific countries to exemplify one or the other and for there to be a general evolution from more authoritarian forms of state to more open democratic forms as economic development takes place, the empirical evidence cannot sustain this argument.

Mouzelis, for example, considers, even in what he terms the parliamentary semi-periphery (which includes for his purposes the Latin American states and those of south-eastern Europe), where it could be argued that a transition took place – in the 1960s to the 1970s – from dictatorship to democracy, that this apparent transition was illusory and that:

> both before and after the military interventions . . . [these states were characterised by] . . . an over-inflated, highly corrupt and inefficient

state apparatus . . . controlled by forces (military, civilian, or a mixture of both) whose concerns for political survival and consolidation more often than not undermine attempts at political and economic modernisation.

(Mouzelis, 1993: 189)

Furthermore, in the rapidly changing world of the 1980s and 1990s, even the advanced capitalist economies have been experiencing the trauma of 'adjustment' and attempting to respond effectively to new possibilities and constraints developing in the global political economy. This is explicitly considered by writers like Jessop. He observes of 'the Western democracies' that, while all are endeavouring to secure greater flexibility ('through changes in technology, production, industrial relations, labour markets, taxation regimes, social security systems, the educational system, and other key sites for economic and societal restructuring' – Jessop, 1988: 10), states are adopting different strategies, all of which imply a high degree of state regulation, if not intervention. His analysis is, we believe, of interest to us in our consideration of the East Asian NICs.

Jessop identifies three major approaches to increasing economic flexibility: the neo-liberal, the neo-corporate and the neo-statist, each of which implies very different economic, social and political 'arrangements'. The neo-liberal variant implies strong state action to promote a market-guided transformation (the restructuring of markets, regulation of monopolies, etc.):

(f)or the public sector it involves a mixture of privatization, liberalization and adopting commercial criteria in the residual state sector; for the private sector it involves deregulation and a new legal and political framework to provide passive support for market solutions.

(Jessop, 1988: 10)

The neo-corporatist variant implies state intervention to orchestrate and support the *ex ante* concertation of the economic decisions and activities of private economic agents. As Jessop explains:

neo-corporatist arrangements must reflect the expansion of relevant interests in policy communities as well as the increasing heterogeneity of the labour force and labour markets. In particular, neo-corporatist concertation could extend beyond the organizations of capital and labour to include other policy communities representing different functional systems (e.g. science, health, education, policing); and policy implementation could be made more flexible through the extension of 'regulated self-regulation' and private interest government.

(Jessop, 1988: 10–11)

Of particular interest, given the general agreement regarding the importance of state intervention in guiding and directing the economic process in the East Asian NICs to promote flexibility and create comparative advantage, is the third of the three variants. Neo-statism involves:

> a state-guided approach to economic reorganization through inter-vention from outside and above market mechanisms. There is little or no consultation with organized economic interests and intervention is based on the state's powers of imperium (imperative coordination) and/or dominium (its own economic resources and/or activities as one actor among others). It involves a mixture of decommodification, state-sponsored flexibility, and state activities concerned to secure the dynamic efficiency of an industrial core. In particular this is associated with an active structural policy in which the state sets strategic targets for flexible accumulation. It pursues an active labour market policy to re-skill the labour force and ensure a flexi-skill rather than flexi-price labour market; it intervenes directly and openly to restructure declin-ing industries and to promote sunrise sectors; and it engages in societal guidance strategies to promote specific objectives through concerted action within varied policy communities which embrace public, mixed and private interests. These activities aim to move the economy up the technical hierarchy by maintaining a coherent and competitive indus-trial core and pursuing a strategy of flexible specialization in specific high-technology sectors. The state must become flexible because of the openness of post-Fordist economies and the rapid changes involved in flexible accumulation.
>
> (Jessop, 1988: 12)

IV STATE AUTONOMY AND POLICY ADAPTABILITY

The above description of the 'neo-statist' strategy, with its emphasis on 'little or no consultation with organised economic interests' – although used in Jessop's analysis to consider the differences between Britain and Germany during the 1980s – is of particular interest, given the recent discussion among East Asian specialists of the importance of what is referred to as 'the autonomy of the state' – often regarded as a crucial prerequisite for effective state intervention in, and regulation of, the East Asian economies. In this discussion, a distinction is usually made between those situations where 'the state' is able to design and implement policies with a relatively high degree of insulation from special interest groups in society (e.g. in East Asia) and those situations where 'the state' is, in effect, hostage to special interests or else is obliged to balance conflicting interests and therefore is unable to act decisively or to orchestrate effective responses to new circumstances (e.g. in Latin America).

As Killick suggests, in Chapter 1, the notion of 'political will' or 'political commitment' (so often invoked as a key determinant of the implementation and success of developing country adjustment programmes) is too superficial to take us far. He suggests that 'it is necessary to dig beneath this surface to discover the forces acting upon the government and, in particular, the degree of autonomy which the government enjoys from class and other special interest group influences when determining its policies'. Others have also identified 'the autonomy of the state' as an important determinant of capacity to implement adjustment programmes. Callaghy has even argued that:

> the success or failure of adjustment efforts to a large degree depends on a government's ability to insulate itself from – and buffer against and adjust to – threatening political, societal and international pressures . . . this requires the policy leeway, resources, statecraft skill, technocratic and bureaucratic capabilities, and coercion, necessary to make and break strategic compromises with key actors based on careful monitoring of the adjustment process in all stages.
>
> (Callaghy, 1989: 120)

Haggard's comparative analysis of the East Asian and Latin American NICs addresses both the general question: what domestic political factors account for the different development trajectories of the two groups, and the more particular: to what extent were 'state élites' relatively autonomous, or insulated from the demands of particular social groups, and therefore able to devise and implement policies with limited 'interference'. He argues (1986: 34) that the specific policy reforms undertaken by the East Asian NICs were 'facilitated by favorable, and probably unique international and domestic conditions' (including, in his opinion, differences in the social organisation of the rural sector, the timing of the political mobilisation of labour, and the interests and strength of domestic entrepreneurs) which 'help to explain the divergence between the Latin American and East Asian development path'. But he also suggests that

> state autonomy is *crucial* in accounting for turning points, such as the shift to export-led growth, when incentives are restructured and a new growth coalition is forged. Without autonomy or 'insulation' from the demands of particular social groups, the pursuit of policies such as land reform, lowering of real wages, raising of interest rates, devaluation, or lifting of subsidies or protection would be impossible. (Emphasis added.)
>
> (Haggard, 1986: 34)

And Alam writing about 'lessons from Korea, Taiwan and Japan', also suggests that:

342

probably the most decisive part in the transition to export orientation in Taiwan and Korea was played by a set of factors that greatly increased their governments' power to detemine policies independently of various reference groups . . . the complete elimination of the power of landed interests, the suppression or co-option of the labor movement, and the elimination of foreign (mostly Japanese) capital that preceded the entry of Taiwan and Korea into import substitution, permitted these governments a much greater latitude in the determination of their economic policies. Moreover this power was exercised resolutely in support of policies that prevented the trade unions from gaining strength and forced private capital into cooperation with government policies.

(Alam, 1989: 20)

Wade also argues for the crucial importance of 'the autonomy of the state' when he lists six elements to explain the success of Japan, Korea and Taiwan: centralisation of the decision-making structure employing the best managers; insulation of the decision-makers from all but the strongest pressure groups; a powerful executive not beholden to the legislature (which tends to reflect popular consumption interests at the expense of investment); the absence of a powerful labour movement (because 'trickle down' from economic growth itself generates improvements in living standards); the absence of conflicts between the owners of natural resources and manufacturers; and the decision-makers' perception that legitimacy is grounded in economic success (Wade, 1988: 158–60).

Recently, Jenkins has concluded that the main factor explaining the superior performance of the East Asian NICs (as compared with Latin America) is greater policy adaptability, determined by the nature of the state and its relationship to civil society:

the key to superior industrial performance of the East Asian NICs does not lie in the general superiority of export-oriented industrialization strategies over import substitution, or of market-oriented policies over state intervention, as some writers suggest. It is rather the ability of the state to direct the accumulation process in the direction which is required by capitalist development at particular points in time which is crucial. This in turn has to be located in the existence of a developmental state with a high degree of relative autonomy from local classes or class fractions.

(Jenkins, 1991: 224)

He argues:

it is tempting to draw parallels between the bureaucratic authoritarian regimes in Latin America and the bureaucratic authoritarian industrializing regimes of East Asia. However, in terms of state autonomy, such

343

comparisons are misleading. Although formally there may appear to be similarities between the triple alliance of state, foreign and local capital in the two types of regime, in Latin America the interests of private capital predominate, whereas in East Asia the state is clearly dominant.

(Jenkins, 1991: 203)

He emphasises that in East Asia the state has pursued policies that have been flexible, highly selective, coherent and directed towards promoting rather than regulating private enterprise; in all these respects the East Asian NICs differed from those of Latin America. It would seem that

> effective state intervention to bring about economic transformation requires that the state is able both to formulate and to implement coherent economic strategies. A prerequisite for formulating a consistent strategy is a degree of autonomy of the state from the dominant class or class fractions, which enables the state to pursue goals that do not reflect the interests of these groups and may even go against their short-term interests. Effective intervention also requires an internal structuring of the state apparatus in terms of an efficient and cohesive bureaucratic machinery and effective policy instruments which gives the state the capacity to implement its economic strategy. Autonomy from both dominant and subordinate classes is also a factor determining the capacity of the state to implement policy.
>
> (Jenkins, 1991, 200–1)

As Fine rightly observes, 'taking the state as the chief agent avoids the issue of classes as agent, other than as obstructive of the state's freedom of action, despite what might be argued to be the state's fundamental dependence upon classes in the (re)formulation, implementation and impact of its policies' (Fine, 1992: 27). But Fine himself, while usefully providing a review and critique of the literature which emphasises the crucial role of the state in East Asian development, and the importance of the 'relative autonomy of the state', does not himself take us much further. The dynamic relationship between 'state' and 'class' (or, more broadly, social interest groups) in the East Asian cases requires further consideration, if we are to understand the basis for the relative autonomy of the state, considered by many to be a crucial prerequisite for effective policy adaptability.

V CLASS INTERESTS AND THE RELATIVE AUTONOMY OF THE STATE

Many have argued that the relative autonomy of the state (the government and the bureaucracy) in the East Asian cases is explained by the relative weakness of all the social classes of civil society, and the lack of a dominant class. All too often, however, the analysis ignores the important process of social transformation experienced over the past decades and its relevance for changes in the relative autonomy of the state.

In Korea, the Japanese initiated the undermining of the traditional ruling class. Then, after the end of the Second World War, the US administration implemented a land reform: Japanese holdings were expropriated, and the new Korean administration under President Synghman Rhee was pressed to purchase all the large landed estates on specially favourable terms, thereby eliminating the landowning class. As Jenkins observes:

> the land reform effectively destroyed the local landlord class which had been weakened in South Korea by its collaboration with the Japanese. . . . Thus a potential obstacle to capitalist development was removed as a political force.
>
> (Jenkins, 1992: 17)

The dispossessed landowners turned first to trade and then to manufacturing. Hamilton argues (1986: 31) that in 1976, nearly 50 per cent of entrepreneurs' fathers had been large to medium landowners. But he also suggests that the social transformation was itself a product of state intervention:

> the recent history of Korea, and of Singapore and Taiwan, identifies the central role of the state in the formation of a class of industrial capitalists and the dominance of industrial accumulation.
>
> (Hamilton, 1986: 117)

He emphasises that 'the Korean state cannot be thought of as the instrument of big business – it has maintained a large degree of autonomy from the power of capital'. In this analysis, both the destruction of the landed classes and the relative weakness of the emerging capitalist class are explained in terms of state dominance. But, as Fine remarks:

> while Hamilton pays closer attention to the evolution and role of class structure, and hence agency, than many other writers, the net result is to enhance the position of the state as primary agent – since it acts to create the class structure and, unsurprisingly in this light, appears able to act independently of it.
>
> (Fine, 1992: 23)

More recently others have adopted a broadly similar approach. Jenkins, for example, when considering why and how the East Asian NICs were able relatively easily to switch industrial strategies, as compared with the Latin American experience, suggests that 'although empirical evidence is scanty, it seems likely that the weakness of the industrial bourgoisie and the consequent high level of autonomy of the state in South Korea and Taiwan were major factors' (Jenkins, 1991: 216). And if it seems 'likely' that the government and the bureaucracy enjoyed a 'high level of autonomy' as regards direct pressures from specific class representatives, there is no doubt that they were insulated from significant pressures from the political arena. After 1972 (the imposition of the Yushin regime), parliament and other representative institutions were further marginalised from the sphere of policy formulation. Under Park, the president was the key figure, and his personal advisers the most influential men in the country. He dealt personally with the heads of various government agencies (e.g. Bank of Korea) and business leaders, as well as the various ministers. The strength of the president's directive role was revealed in the heavy and chemical industry drive that took place, despite the reluctance and scepticism of the *chaebol* (Bello and Rosenfeld, 1991).

In Korea, during the 1960s and 1970s, the state dominated the entire process of economic growth and structural transformation. Between a quarter and a fifth of GNP comprised government spending, and public savings were between a fifth and a third of the whole. The government nationalised the five leading commercial banks in the early 1960s and, with the Bank of Korea and direct public-sector activities, the state controlled two-thirds of national investment. According to Leroy Jones, this was 'the single most important economic factor explaining the distinctly subordinate position of the private sector' (Jones and Sakong, 1980: 296). Datta Chaudhuri remarks that 'no state, outside the socialist bloc, ever came anywhere near this measure of control over the economy's investible resources' (Datta Chaudhuri, 1981: 56). Jenkins underlines the importance of state control over the financial system in both Taiwan and South Korea:

> in common with Japan, they have relied heavily on financial and monetary means to control the private sector. In South Korea, the state had a majority holding in all the major banks until the early 1980s, and the government controlled, directly or indirectly, more than two-thirds of the investible resources in the economy. Similarly in Taiwan, the government dominates the financial sector by owning all but three of the major banks.
>
> (Jenkins 1991: 206)

This is 'dominium' indeed.

Many, however, identify a process of transformation during recent years in which the relative autonomy of the state may have been progressively reduced as the capitalist class has grown stronger. Interestingly, these arguments recall those frequently deployed to explain the state's relative autonomy under 'state capitalism' in many developing countries in Africa, the Middle East and elsewhere, its role in creating a private bourgeoisie and its declining autonomy as the emergent bourgeoisie grows stronger.

Jenkins observes:

> the degree of relative autonomy of the state is neither invariant within regions nor over time. The degree of state autonomy appears to have

been higher in Taiwan than in South Korea, and the growing importance of the chaebols in South Korea and the predominance of small-
scale industry in Taiwan have served to intensify this difference. . . .
Developments in South Korea in the 1980s suggest that the very
success of the state in promoting industrialisation is reducing its
relative autonomy.

(Jenkins, 1991: 224)

A broadly similar thesis is advanced by Steinberg, who suggests that in
Korea, while the 'corporations were more clearly in the government's iron
glove than in the economy's invisible hand' and could be 'originally viewed
as a mere instrument of government policy, the business sector is taking on a
social and political role' (Steinberg, 1988: 28). For Harris, by the mid-1980s
the relative autonomy of the state was already compromised and 'the
chaebol, the fifty giant private companies, were coming of age, although the
Chairman of Daewoo could still complain that "the government tells you its
your duty and you have to do it, even if there's no profit"' (Harris, 1986:
42). And Jenkins argues:

similarly, in Taiwan the small scale of many manufacturing enterprises
has limited their influence politically, although this too is changing as
government policy shifts towards encouraging mergers, and business
representatives are prominent in the Economic Revitalization Committee, established in 1985 to suggest reforms in economic policy.

(Jenkins, 1991: 209)

While many explain the relative autonomy of the state in terms of the
weakness of all classes, and in particular the capitalist class, others argue that
the state is able to appear relatively autonomous and to change policy
rapidly and effectively precisely because of the close links between big
business and the state. Amsden, for example, identifies big capital as clearly
the dominant class in Korea, and sees the state as, on balance, acting on
behalf of large-scale capital as a whole without being permanently captured
by any one sectional interest within that class. As Fine reports her argument:

from this class has been built up a close relationship with the state in
which highly concentrated levels of ownership have resulted both
within individual sectors and across the economy as a whole – as the
conglomerate or *chaebol*, the equivalent of the Japanese zaibatsu,
gained cumulative experience in diversification and an ability to break
into new industries rapidly and cost-effectively.

(Fine, 1992: 17)

Amsden emphasises the high concentration of control in Korean industry;
the combined share in GNP of the top ten *chaebol* increased from 15 per
cent in 1974 to 67 per cent ten years later (Amsden, 1989: 116). From this

perspective, it is significant that concentration is high in Japan and Taiwan also, albeit to a lesser extent; in the early 1980s, the average share of the three largest firms across manufacturing was 56 per cent in Japan and 49 per cent in Taiwan.

Amsden also considers the general relationship of the state to both capital and labour, and insists – as indeed do some other commentators – on the importance for South Korean (and Taiwanese) economic development of the control of the working classes, in part through encouraging low but steadily growing wages and improving living conditions, albeit with a long working week and limited welfare benefits, but in part through direct repression. Indeed, in the view of many commentators, a crucial difference between the authoritarian states of Latin America and those of East Asia lay in the different strategies for the control of labour and its representative institutions. Whereas in Latin America labour ascendancy gave way to harsh repression in the 1970s, organised labour was systematically excluded from political influence by the regimes of East Asia until very recently (Deyo *et al.*, 1987). Deyo emphasises the pre-emptive nature of the authoritarian controls in East Asian states, where the working class emerged under the auspices of relatively developed authoritarian states adept at containing dissidence by coercive and co-optive means.

> the political autonomy of technocratic planners, which has permitted the state to ignore political claims on development policy, has been rooted in the weakness and dependency of domestic social classes, in elite unity, and in external support for authoritarian regimes (in East Asia). Internal unity and autonomy fostered exclusionary regimes at a very early point in industrialization, which preempted organizational efforts during the subsequent emergence of an industrial proletariat and [ensured] that emergent trade unions were closely allied with ruling groups. The early political inclusion of Latin American industrial workers, by contrast, encouraged the development of strong labour movements that later were able to shelter a privileged segment of the labour force from repression.
>
> (Deyo, 1987: 199)

Even within East Asia, the differences in this regard were significant:

> in Singapore, the PAP (People's Action Party)-controlled neighbourhood associations and committees absorbed much of this potential [for organised dissent] from the very start. In South Korea, community controls go little beyond police containment, thus encouraging political activism to seek unofficial and uncontrolled outlets.
>
> (Deyo, 1987: 212)

It should not be forgotten that Rhee's government was brought down in 1960 and Park's was nearly toppled in 1965. Political stability in the East

Asian NICs has been relatively great – an important prerequisite for policy adaptability – but it has not always been complete.

Many radical critics of the 'bureaucratic authoritarian' type of regime in East Asia have drawn attention to the systematic repression of labour and its representative institutions (trade unions) during the 1970s and into the 1980s and have explained the relative autonomy of the state very much in terms of its 'autonomy from demands of labour' and ordinary working people, in the interests of capital accumulation. Others have drawn attention to the more subtle ways in which the labour movement was controlled and co-opted and its resistance often anticipated and thus pre-empted. Others again, including some on the left (e.g. Warren, 1981), draw attention to the significant gains in working conditions and living standards obtained by labour during the last twenty years in the East Asian NICs. Whatever the explanation, the relative quiescence of labour movements in the East Asian NICs during the period of rapid industrial growth in the 1960s and 1970s is remarkable when contrasted with the Latin American countries. The low levels of organisation and militancy in all of the East Asian countries partly reflect the degree of repression of labour and state control over trade unions, but also the structure of employment and the visible improvements in living standards.

This raises the possibility that, in addition to the repressive nature of the state during the period, its relative success in achieving rapid growth and both economic and social development contributed at least to a general acquiescence in the overall strategy for development and the state's relative autonomy, which would enable claims of acting in 'the national interest' to be regarded as broadly legitimate. Alam, for example, argues that, in the cases of Korea and Taiwan, 'the presence of a national purpose, strengthened by the developmental commitment of the national leadership, also left its mark on the ability of the state to force sacrifices on particular groups as well as on society as a whole' (Alam, 1989: 20). And while there must always be doubt about the validity of such a heavily ideological notion as 'the national purpose' or 'the national interest' as a description of the political reality, there is support for emphasis on such a notion elsewhere.

Nelson argues, for example, that a consideration of 'those governments pursuing particularly far-reaching programs of economic re-orientation in the 1980s (plus a few cases from the 1970s)' shared 'a reform syndrome': 'leaders firmly committed to major change, widespread public acceptance or demand for such a change, new governments with strong centralized authority, and a disabled opposition' (Nelson, 1989: 12). Leaving aside the possible contradiction between the idea of 'widespread public acceptance or demand for such a change' and the political reality of 'a disabled opposition', the major features of what are taken to be exemplars of 'the reform syndrome' are leaders strongly committed to change, a strong centralised state and 'widespread public acceptance or demand' for reform or change. Where the state is able to command genuine broad-based support for its general strategy for change it will, it is assumed, be able to act relatively auton-omously with regard to specific tactics (policies). And the government will be able to 'adjust' (shift policies in a new direction, or significantly accelerate tendencies already set in motion) and thereby adapt to new circumstances or conditions.

Certainly, as regards South Korea, Yan Kong insists that the overall development strategy has depended on stimulating the enthusiasm and commitment of crucial sections of society to ensure their compliance, and not simply on control. He also suggests that the state must overcome socio-political constraints to achieve 'some broad consensus' regarding the need for economic development and its strategy for achieving this goal. He notes, however, that it is also crucial that the regime should deliver economic and other pay-offs to those social strata whose support, or at least tacit consent, is vital to the continuation of the industrialisation effort. When it has failed to provide these, he argues, there have been significant increases in social dissent and unrest.

> the insulation of the regime's economic decision-making process must not be allowed to lapse into regime isolation from those whose task it is to translate policy into action. Failure to provide these incentives tends to result in lethargy, social discontent and political instability.
>
> (Yan Kong, 1992: 25)

This distinction between insulation from short term pressures from the political arena and isolation from most sections of civil society is an ex-tremely important one; it is the former that provides support for policy adaptablity, it is the latter that generates the features of the 'patrimonial state' widely considered to be inimical to both economic and political development (see Chapter 6).

Most importantly, he suggests,

> the regime must be able to adapt to the accelerating aspirations of its supporters. . . . Such aspirations might include rising expectations for social development . . . and political development. . . . In short, in order to succeed, a developmental regime has to establish links with at least the key sections of civil society.
>
> (Yan Kong, 1992: 25)

Other authors have drawn attention to the changing character of political regimes in East Asia in the last few years, in part precisely in response to rising expectations and demands, themselves generated by the process of economic and social development. Koo, for example, has suggested:

> one important consequence of industrial development in the East Asian NICs . . . is the emergence of large middle classes. The rise of the middle classess has thus become a significant element in the

evolution of the new industrial order in the East Asian countries. Concentrated in large urban centres, they shape the dominant pattern of consumption and life styles; they make political demands; and they spawn new political debates and tactics. The political stance of the middle classes has become a critical element in the recent transitions from authoritarian rule in South Korea and Taiwan.

(Koo, 1991: 485)

VI THE STATE AND CIVIL SOCIETY

Many commentators have emphasised the degree of autonomy enjoyed by the bureaucracy (Johnson, 1985: 77–81) in both Taiwan and South Korea, and the relative insulation from direct political pressures on economic policy-making (Haggard, 1986: 261). Sida stresses that, even if Hong Kong was characterised by something approaching 'a free market economy', it was also characterised over the decades by a central executive authority and bureaucracy 'which enjoyed the freedoms of a relatively immune top-down policy making procedure' (Sida, 1993: 15). And Singapore is renowned for the capacity of the state to ensure a significant degree of autonomy and independence from external political pressures for the bureaucracy and the decision-making process.

Certainly, in all the East Asian NICs, the supremacy of the executive (the government) over the legislature (the national assembly or parliament) has been decisive. In some cases, the executive has been completely separate from the legislature, in others the effective insulation of government has been ensured by the dominance of one particular political party in the national assembly. Korea (where President Park effectively ruled the country during his period of office) exemplifies the first, Japan (where the conservative Liberal Democrats enjoyed uninterrupted control of the government after 1948) the second.

But if relative autonomy from immediate political pressures is regarded as crucial, there are also strong indications that a high degree of compatibility or congruence between state policies and the wider development needs of civil society are of considerable importance also. For some, close links with 'the workings of the market' are also required:

in order for the capitalist state to engage in economic transformation . . . the workings of (the bureaucratic) machinery must link up with the workings of the market. . . . The more that social relations . . . approach contractual market exchange and bureaucratic organization, the greater is the likelihood of effective state intervention, since market exchange and bureaucratic organization are major institutional forms that encourage instrumental behaviour and protect it by institutional differentiation and insulation.

(Rueschemeyer and Evans, 1985: 51, 71)

This argument involves not only the important suggestion that a Weberian impersonal bureaucracy and the equally impersonal market complement each other in a modern political economy to create the institutional framework for 'rational' decision-making for development, but also the idea that linkages between 'the state' and the civil society (here 'the market') are crucial to ensure that both function in a complementary fashion (providing the elements of a 'positive feedback' system) and keep each other in line. Here, regulation works both ways and relative autonomy does not imply autarky.

Others, like Yan Kong, from a somewhat different perspective, argue that the proponents of 'the relative autonomy of the state' thesis have in fact tended to overstate the independence of the state from the pressures of civil society.

> While the existence of powerful coercive institutions meant that the support of civil society may not have been necessary for the survival of unpopular regimes, it is hard to imagine that the achievement of a high performance economy could have been realized without the ability to solicit such support from at least some key social strata. If so, by what means were these linkages with civil society forged and how did they develop over time? Moreover, how were state power and national developmental objectives maintained in the context of the relaxation of formal economic and political controls, during the post-1983 period for example?
>
> (Yan Kong, 1992: 19)

For Yan Kong, the emphasis on the 'relative autonomy of the state' requires further consideration in the light of a more detailed analysis of, among other things, the role of the bureaucracy in particular and the linkages between government, bureaucracy, the political arena and civil society. He argues, specifically, that those who emphasise the central role of 'the state' or 'the bureaucracy' fail to analyse in any detail the complex structures that constitute these entities or their relationships with the different elements of civil society. They also, he suggests, overemphasise the power of 'the state' and 'the bureaucracy' over civil society.

> After all, Park's regime in South Korea was dependent not only on control and repression but also on balancing the developmental goals of the regime with the interests of a range of social groups (entrepreneurs, middle class, skilled workers, peasants).
>
> (Yan Kong, 1992: 21)

This echoes the views of Haggard and Moon – who argue that Korea is best understood in terms of a model 'in which the state is conceived as having relative autonomy in its ability to define developmental goals and the power to build social coalitions to support them' (Haggard and Moon, 1983: 140) –

and of Alam, who suggests that 'the presence of a national purpose, strengthened by the developmental commitment of the national leadership, also left its mark on the ability of the state to force sacrifices on particular groups as well as on society as a whole' (Alam, 1989: 20).

In Japan, whose economic success is undoubted and where the policy adaptability is well documented, the conventional wisdom is that economic policy is determined by a tripartite alliance of the conservative Liberal Democratic Party, the bureaucracy and big business. Many Japanese writers in particular have attributed great importance to big business (the *zaikai*), and there is little doubt that its influence is considerable and its interests regularly expressed to the government and the bureaucracy. Big business is the major source of LDP funds, and is constantly involved in lobbying, and business executives have numerous links – school, family and social – with politicians and bureaucrats. Big business is organised into four major lobbying groups – the Federation of Economic Organisation (Keidanren), the Committee for Economic Development (Keizai Doyukai), the Federation of Employers' Organisations (Nikkeiren), and the Japan Chamber of Commerce (Nissho). The Keidanren is the best funded and most influential of these, according to Weinstein (1987), with a membership limited to about 800 of Japan's largest corporations, big banks and trading groups.

There seems little doubt, in the case of Japan at least, that, even if government and the bureaucracy are relatively well insulated from the pressures of the political arena – if only because 'politics' in Japan has become very largely distinct from debates over economic strategy and policies and is essentially clientelist in character – they work closely with big business and take its interests into consideration. The regime could perhaps best be characterised as 'neo-corporatist' – certainly not 'neo-statist'. Even so, it is important to recognise the degree to which the bureaucracy is protected from the political arena. Today, while frequent Cabinet reshuffles weaken ministerial authority, they do not lead to instability in Japanese policy-making. The major policy-making ministries and agencies – finance, foreign affairs, international trade and industry, and economic planning – are headed by administrative vice-ministers who are career civil servants. These vice-ministers meet regularly and frequently with the directors of the Cabinet secretariat and the director of the Cabinet's Bureau of Legislation, constituting what is known as 'the little cabinet'. Because they usually hold office longer than their ministers and are extremely well informed and tactful, the administrative vice-ministers exert a powerful influence in shaping Cabinet policy (Weinstein, 1987: 603).

For Yan Kong, Korea's economic success was the result of a combination of factors, the first of which was certainly the autonomy of the Korean state rooted in coercion:

without the military government in 1961, the likelihood of the developmental issue reaching the top of the political agenda would have been doubtful – a government responsive to short-term political pressures would not have been able to guarantee the predominance of national economic priorities over short term sectional interests.

(Yan Kong, 1992: 72)

Second, however,

the regime ensured that its commitment to national economic development was closely interlinked to the interests of key social groups. These mutually reinforcing interests ensured some degree of responsiveness of the dominant (but not all powerful) state institutions to civil society.

(Yan Kong, 1992: 72)

As regards specific social class interests, Yan Kong argues that the regime's principal agency of economic development – the capitalist class – found that it actually paid to comply with government and bureaucratic priorities, while failure to do so meant incurring serious sanctions. The regime was able to rein in the consumption interests of the middle classes and keep them firmly subordinated to national economic priorities such as investment and the conservation of foreign exchange. And, finally, while the poorer sections of society (including workers and peasants) benefited least from the development process and the Park regime was not popular (especially after 1972 when it became explicitly authoritarian), the state was able to prevent open dissent and encourage hard work. This argument suggests that, although they benefited unequally, all sections of society benefited to some extent and were thus in a sense prepared to allow policy-makers the relative autonomy that they required for ensuring policy adaptability.

From a rather different theoretical perspective, but still with regard to Korea, Harris also draws attention to the complexity of the relations between government and the bureaucracy, on the one hand, and the wider economy and society on the other, although his emphasis is very much on 'the means of control and influence' utilised by the former. Having stressed the importance of the dominium of the state (its direct ownership and control of large sectors of the national economy) he suggests that, 'on top of this, by means of political patronage, discriminatory tax, credit and pricing policies, medals and awards, orders, bribery, bullying, and monthly conferences between ministers and businessmen, the wishes of the state (sic) shaped the whole development process' (Harris, 1986: 41–2).

This discussion suggests that the 'relative autonomy of the state' and insulation from the immediate pressures of the political arena do not necessarily mean a relatively low level of interaction with different sections of civil society, or even with specific pressure and interest groups. What they imply is a situation in which the government and bureaucracy maintain effective control of the commanding heights of decision-making and the policy-making process and are able to manage the various competing special interests in such a way that policy adaptability is maximised. The emphasis is less on 'relative autonomy' and more on the forms of control and influence that enable 'the state' – the government and the bureaucracy – to intervene effectively. There is also a suggestion that the most powerful sectional interests in civil society, in effect permit the state to act in the way it does, and exert a significant influence on its overall strategy and even tactics, keeping it within certain agreed parameters. The virtual elimination of powerful landed interests in postwar East Asian society ensures the absence of 'competing élites' and this increases the coherence of the dominant interests in civil society and an unchallenged commitment to industrial capitalist development.

VII THE DEVELOPMENTALIST BUREAUCRACY

Jenkins argues that 'effective state intervention to promote industrial development involves the construction of an adequate bureaucracy which is able to implement government policy' (Jenkins, 1991: 204), while others have declared that 'effective bureaucratic machinery is the key to the state's capacity to intervene'. According to some this 'requires a minimum of coherence and coordination within and among different state organisations, and that in turn presupposes a minimum of autonomy from forces in civil society' (Rueschemeyer and Evans, 1985: 55).

We have already considered the issue of autonomy. In respect of coherence and co-ordination, the state bureaucracies of the East Asian NICs are quite distinctive among developing countries. The World Bank identifies three factors as possible keys to Japan's success: the bureaucrats, the size of interventions and institutions. As regards the first of these, it is observed that

> some see the Japanese miracle as the result of bureaucrats in the Ministry of International Trade and Industry (MITI) guiding firms' production and investment decisions. Since the 1930s at least, Japanese bureaucrats have influenced manufacturers' decisions. They have eased their access to capital and to foreign technology. They have granted subsidies, trade barriers, and tax breaks. They have formulated plans to allocate production. And they have sanctioned cartels. As industrial consultants who can persuade their clients to follow their advice, MITI's officials have a close relationship with manufacturers.
>
> (World Bank, 1991: 40)

In South Korea and Taiwan, as in Japan, economic decision-making has been highly centralised and the role of bureaucratic institutions very important. In South Korea, the Economic Planning Board (EPB) was made responsible for planning and budgeting after the Park coup in 1961. It was also put in charge of price controls, foreign aid, loans and investment and the transfer of technology, as well of organising the collection of national statistics (Luedde-Neurath, 1988: 95). Apart from the EPB, the most important ministries were the Ministry of Finance and the Ministry of Commerce and Industry. The former controlled tax assessment and collection, foreign and domestic financial institutions and overall foreign-exchange control. It also controlled tariff collection through the office of customs administration. The Ministry of Commerce and Industry was in charge of export promotion, controlled industry development, investment applications, project and firm designation, licensing and industry associations. The two ministries were primarily agencies of implementation, with the EPB the 'overlord planning ministry' – a 'super-agency' that, according to Bello and Rosenfeld (1991), became the main instrument of Park's export-first strategy, with a directive capacity that matched or outstripped Japan's MITI. Support from the president is said to have helped insulate the EPB from interest group pressures (e.g. the *chaebol*).

There were producers' associations (as in Japan), but these acted essentially as channels for consultation between industry and government in particular, and as agents through which the government agencies could influence industry, both in general and in particular, although clearly the interaction was, potentially at least, two-way. These associations have been referred to as 'government watchdogs', however, and likened to the 'Self Control Associations' of wartime Japan (Mitchell, 1984). They would compile detailed plans on an annual basis outlining the proposed activities of members, specifying import requirements, production levels, export levels, capacity growth, etc. The information would then be relayed to the various government ministries as a basis for planning. But they also provided the means whereby government was able to modify these plans, suggesting that their function as industrial lobbies was distinctly subservient to their role as government agents.

On occasion, special commissions were established to bypass this entire governmental system. This was the case with the Special Committee for National Security Measures, charged in 1973 with reorganising the heavy and chemical industries. The Board of Audit and Inspection reported directly to the President and operated as a watchdog over the ministries and government agencies as well as over major companies. The system of controls recalls that of the Soviet Union and Eastern Europe as much as any other capitalist state, with the possible exception of the other East Asian NICs.

In Taiwan, the Council on International Economic Co-operation and Development (CIECD), a semi-autonomous body outside the regular ministries, was established in 1963 to formulate and co-ordinate development plans and negotiations for external financial and technical assistance. In 1973 it was reorganised as the Economic Planning Council, which was subsequently merged with the Financial and Economic Committee in 1977 to form a new super-ministry, the Economic Planning and Development Council.

Whatever the differences in the precise balance of power and influence between government, the bureaucracy and big business, it is undoubtedly the case that the development of effective state bureaucratic capacity in the East Asian countries has involved 'a delicate, long-term process of institution building' and that the opinion of some that 'such institutional constructions are likely to require decades if not generations, to become established' (Rueschemeyer and Evans, 1985: 49, 51) appears broadly justified. The evidence suggests that in the East Asian NICs such a bureaucratic capacity exists, and has existed for some time. Unlike the majority of African countries, for example, the development of state bureaucracies in the East Asian NICs (as indeed in Japan and China) has been a long-term process.

One foundation for the construction of an effective bureaucracy is a strong education system, with both a broad base and capacity to provide advanced training. 'Exceptional investment in people' is seen by the World Bank as one of the key elements in Japan's economic success. After the Meiji restoration, the Japanese Government was explicitly concerned to improve not only the level of technology but also the capacity of the population to use it. Education was a priority: by 1872 a universal and compulsory system of elementary education had been introduced and the foundations for secondary education laid. Primary school attendance rates rose from under 30 per cent in 1873 to more than 90 per cent by 1907. The number of secondary schools expanded tenfold between 1885 and 1915. Adult literacy, which was 10 per cent in 1850, had reached 20 per cent by 1880 and 70 per cent by 1910. During the last part of the nineteenth century, Japan consistently expended a greater share of its real GDP on education than any European or other Asian state.

As the most recent arrival to 'developed capitalist status' – and arguably the only one so far – the case of Japan must be of considerable significance in this regard and Dore argues that the feature which distinguishes Japan more than anything else from the other 'advanced capitalist states' is 'the stable integrated nature of its bureaucratic establishment' (Dore, 1986: 20). Historical analysis reveals the longevity of 'the bureaucratic establishment'. In the other East Asian NICs also there is a long bureaucratic tradition, as well as a long-standing commitment to education. In 1990, adult literacy was 96 per cent in Korea, 92 per cent in Taiwan, 90 per cent in Hong Kong and 88 per cent in Singapore. Education has been strongly oriented towards practical training and, particularly at the higher level, to the needs of the industrial economy (cf. Amsden, 1989: Table 9.2; Wade, 1990: 65). The colony of Hong Kong has enjoyed remarkable political stability and bureaucratic continuity for more than a century. Significantly, the Japanese occupation of Taiwan and South Korea further strengthened the indigenous state apparatus in both these countries. Cummings (1984) suggests that the colonial bureaucracies inherited from the Japanese provided them with effective state organisations in the post-colonial period, and most commentators appear to agree that this was of great importance. Mouzelis argues, for example, that a major legacy of the Japanese occupation was 'a strongly authoritarian state apparatus committed to economic planning and to a highly selective, flexible, and efficacious regulation of the overall economy' (Mouzelis, 1993: 192).

In Japan, the higher civil service is a carefully selected, highly trained élite, with powerful influence across the entire range of government and politics. Of a total of some 250,000 civil servants, between 15,000 and 20,000 reach the higher echelons, but only about 1,000 attain the most prestigious and powerful first grade. Access to higher levels is obtained through academic excellence demonstrated in examinations. Top-level bureaucrats are required by law to retire in their early or mid fifties. Many then enter politics. The links between politics and the top bureaucrats are thus close; of the fourteen prime ministers since 1947, seven have been former bureaucrats, most of them having served first in the Ministry of Foreign Affairs or the Ministry of Finance.

Such a close-knit relationship between higher-level bureaucrats and politicians is not, of course, unusual in other developed and developing states, but the commitment to a developmentalist ethos, which prioritises technical, scientific and economic development, is, even in the advanced captitalist states, not always as great as in the East Asian NICs or in Japan. As Amsden argues for South Korea, 'whilst it is recognised that the state-capital relation is neither simple nor free of corruption, it is perceived to have been dominated by developmental goals rather than self-enrichment at the expense of accumulation' (cited in Fine, 1992: 17).

One of the important questions, raised by many commentators, is how one may explain the 'developmentalist ethos' of the bureaucracies of the East Asian NICs. As Fine wonders:

> if it [the state] is free of sectional interests, then it is not clear why it should adopt goals other than those of its own personnel, however these may be determined, and they may not necessarily be coincident with policies to promote growth, unless this is seen as a necessary condition for its own political and military survival. On the other hand, if the state is subject to competing interests, why have these been resolved in favour of a successful growth strategy?
>
> (Fine, 1992: 21)

On the first point, it has been argued, with respect to sub-Saharan Africa, that the very considerable autonomy of the state in that region has encouraged or at least permitted the design and implementation of policies which have failed to promote economic growth; Killick (1992), among others, explains the relative failure of the African economies in the 1980s in terms of the particular characteristics of 'the patrimonial state', which facilitates corruption and presides over stagnation. The World Bank has also emphasised the role of 'the all-powerful state' in Africa's general economic failure during the 1980s:

> underlying the litany of Africa's development problems is a crisis of governance. . . . Because the countervailing power has been lacking, state officials in many countries have served their own interests without fear of being called into account. In self-defence, individuals have built up personal networks of influence rather than hold the all-powerful state accountable for its systematic failures. In this way, politics becomes personalised, and patronage becomes essential to maintain power.
>
> (World Bank, 1989, cited in Killick 1992)

And Mouzelis suggests, in his analysis of Latin American and south eastern European states, that

> if one looks at late-developing countries with even weaker civil societies than those examined here (at African polities, for instance), the obstructive, anti-developmental character of the state is even more pronounced. This frequently takes the form of a straightforward and systematic plundering of national resources, by a kleptocratic state that is controlled by politico-military elites whose overriding concern is the transfer of indigenous national resources into deposits in privately-held bank accounts.
>
> (Mouzelis, 1993: 191)

If the state and 'the technocratic planners', who in Deyo's version appear to command in the East Asian economies, are virtually autonomous, what ensures their commitment to 'development'? As Wade puts it, with reference to Taiwan:

> if development strategy in Taiwan has been defined by state officials, if state officials have stressed market forces so as to create the kind of production structure which they think Taiwan should have, then the question of the basis, organisation and operation of state authority becomes exceedingly important. Given that not a few states are little more than instruments of plunder on behalf of small groups of officials, politicians and the military, why has the state in Taiwan deployed its power benignly rather than malignly? How has the use of public power been disciplined?
>
> (Wade, 1985)

Amsden's (1985) response to this question is heavily dependent on the importance of 'patriotism', and the pressure of the student movement. Jones and Sakong (1980) simply take the regime's commitment to growth and development as an article of faith. Wade does not really answer the question.

It is often suggested that recruitment patterns and the expectations of bureaucrats are of major importance in explaining their 'ethos'. It is generally argued that literacy and education are crucial here in the moulding of a technically capable and well educated, relatively autonomous, bureaucracy. Patterns of recruitment into the bureaucracy, and the kind of education and training required for entrance, may be as important as the criteria for promotion within the system, although both may be crucial in promoting the appropriate 'developmental ethos'. A detailed consideration of the situation in the East Asian states, with reference to the educational and social background of recruits, in particular those reaching the highest positions, would almost certainly be revealing.

A further area for detailed investigation would be the capacity of the bureaucracy with regard to information retrieval, distribution and analysis, for it is plausibly argued in Chapter 1 that 'flexibility is bound to be limited in the face of ignorance about changes in circumstances to which the economy – and policies – must adapt'. Chapter 1 also suggests that 'traditional values' may stand in the way of, or weaken the incentives for, public servants adopting the role orientation necessary for the efficient conduct of their duties. Against this, however, the World Bank (1991: 40) suggests that 'traditional Japanese views on right and appropriate behaviour have affected the resolution of conflicts – and the relations between workers and managers, between large firms and contractors, and between government agencies, producers and producers' associations'. Here 'traditional values' are invoked to explain how differences of interest between, for example, policy-makers and large firms are managed on an essentially consensual rather than a conflictual basis in order to provide a sound basis for the effective management of capitalist development.

Many of these factors may be important in contributing to the establishment and maintenance of a 'developmentalist ethos' among bureaucrats and policy-makers. Nevertheless the major thrust of this paper has been to suggest that, while it appears to be the relative autonomy of the state and its effective regulation of economy and society which has enabled the East Asian governments and bureaucracies to exercise policy adaptability without being unduly constrained by short-term political considerations, it is, nevertheless, the maintenance of strategic relations with important sectional and class interests in the wider civil society, and a degree of responsiveness to those interests, that prevents relative autonomy from becoming isolation and autarky, and ensures a continuing commitment to economic development. The process of social transformation, which is itself both a determinant and a product of state-society relations, will, however, continue to throw up challenges to test the capacity of the East Asian states to maintain their previously high level of policy adaptability and economic flexibility.

REFERENCES

Alam, M. (1989) *Governments and Markets in Economic Development Strategies: Lessons from Korea, Taiwan and Japan*, New York Praeger.

Amsden, A. (1985) 'The state and Taiwan's economic development', in P. Evans, D. Rueschemeyer and T. Skocpol (eds) *Bringing the State Back In*, Cambridge: Cambridge University Press.

— (1989) *Asia's Next Giant: South Korea and Late Industrialization*, Oxford: Oxford University Press.

Auty, R.M. (1990) 'Creating comparative advantage in HCI: Korea, Brazil and Mexico', paper for RPO 675–41, IENIN, Washington, DC: World Bank.

Balassa, B. (1981) *The Newly Industrializing Countries in the World Economy*, New York: Pergamon.

Barsony, A. (1991) 'Cooperation with the dynamic Asian economies', *The OECD Observer* no. 168, February–March: 14–19.

Bello, W. (1992) 'Export-led development in East Asia: a flawed model', *Trocaire Development Review*: 11–27.

Bello, W. and S. Rosenfeld (1991) *Dragons in Distress: Asia's Miracle Economies in Crisis*, London: Penguin.

Brown, G.T. (1973) *Korean Pricing Policies and Economic Development in the 1960s*, Baltimore: Johns Hopkins University Press.

Callaghy, T.M. (1989) 'Towards state capability and embedded liberalism in the Third World: lessons for adjustment', in J.M. Nelson (ed.) *Fragile Coalitions: the Politics of Economic Adjustment*, Oxford (UK) and New Brunswick (USA): Transaction Books.

Cummings, B. (1984) 'The origins and development of the Northeast Asian political economy: industrial sectors, product cycles and political consequences', *International Organization* 38(1): 1–40.

Datta Chaudhuri, M.K. (1981) 'Industrialization and foreign trade: the development the Philippines', in E. Lee (ed.) *Export-led Industrialization and Development*, Bangkok: ILO.

Deyo, F. (ed.) (1987) *The Political Economy of the New Asian Industrialism*, Ithaca, NY: Cornell University Press.

Deyo, F., S. Haggard and C. Moon (1987) 'Labor in the political-economy of East Asian industrialization', *Bulletin of Concerned Asian Scholars* 19(2): 42–53.

Dore, R. (1986) *Flexible Rigidities: industrial, political and structural adjustment in the Japanese economy, 1970–80*, London: Athlone Press.

Evans, P. (1987) 'Class, state and dependence in East Asia: lessons for Latin Americanists', in F. Deyo (ed.) *The Political Economy of the New Asian Industrialism*, Ithaca, NY: Cornell University Press.

Fine, B. (1992) 'Linkage, agency and the state: the case of South Korea', SOAS Working Paper no. 2. School of Oriental and African Studies, University of London, London.

Fischer, B. (1991) 'Growth policies for Latin America', *The OECD Observer* no. 168, February–March: 20–4.

Frank, A.G. (1981) *Crisis in the World Economy*, London: Heinemann.

Gereffi, G. and D. Wyman (1989) 'Determinants of development strategies in Latin America and East Asia', *Pacific Focus* 2(1): 5–33.

Haggard, S. (1986) 'The newly industrializing countries in the international system', *World Politics* 32(2): 343–70.

Haggard, S. and C. Moon (1983) 'The South Korean State in the international economy: liberal, independent or mercantile?', in J.G. Ruggie (ed.) *The Antimonies of Interdependence*, New York: Columbia University Press.

Hall, J.A. (1991) 'Politics and the market: reflections on the rise and current condition of capitalist society', in M. Banks and M. Shaw (eds) *State and Society in International Relations*, Hemel Hempstead: Harvester Wheatsheaf.

Hamilton, C. (1986) *Capitalist Industrialization in Korea*, Boulder, CO: Westview Press.

Harris, N. (1986) *The End of the Third World*, London: I.B. Taurisz.

Healey, J.M. and M. Robinson (1992) *Democracy, Governance and Economic Policy: Sub-Saharan Africa in Comparative Perspective*, London: Overseas Development Institute.

Im, Hyug Baeg (1987) 'The rise of bureaucratic authoritarianism in South Korea', *World Politics* 39(2): 231–57.

Jenkins, R. (1991) 'The political economy of industrialization: a comparison of Latin America and East Asian newly industrializing countries', *Development and Change* 22: 197–231.

—— (1992) 'Capitalist development in the NICs', School of Development Studies, UEA, Norwich, unpublished paper.

Jessop, B. (1988) 'Conservative regimes and the transition to post-Fordism: the cases of Britain and West Germany', Essex Papers in Politics and Government no. 47, Department of Government, University of Essex, Colchester.

Johnson, C. (1985) 'Political institutions and economic performance: the government–business relationship in Japan, South Korea and Taiwan', in R. Scalapino, S. Sato and J. Wandandi (eds) *Asian Economic Development – Present and Future*, Berkeley: Institute of East Asian Studies, University of California.

—— (1987) 'Political institutions and economic performance: the government–business relationship in Japan, South Korea and Taiwan', in F. Deyo (ed.) *The Political Economy of the New Asian Industrialism*, Ithaca, NY: Cornell University Press.

Jones, L. and I. Sakong (1980) *Government, Business and Entrepreneurship in Economic Development: The Korean Case. Studies in the Modernisation of the Republic of Korea, 1945–75*, Council on East Asian Studies, Cambridge, MA: Harvard University Press.

Killick, T. (1992) *Explaining Africa's Post-Independence Development Experiences*, ODI Working Paper no. 60, London: Overseas Development Institute.

—— (1994) 'The flexibility of national economies: a neglected attribute in economic development', in J.D. MacArthur and J. Weiss (eds) *Agriculture, Projects and Development*, Aldershot: Avebury.

Koo, H. (1991) 'Middle classes, democratization and class formation: the case of South Korea', *Theory and Society* 20: 485–509.

Lee, C. and I. Yamazawa (eds) (1990) *The Economic Development of Japan and Korea*, New York: Praeger.

Little, I.M.D. (1981) 'The experience and causes of rapid labour-intensive development in Korea, Taiwan province, Hong Kong and Singapore, and the possibilities of emulation', in E. Lee (ed.) *Export-led Industrialization and Development*, Bangkok: ILO.

Luedde-Neurath, R. (1986) *Import Controls and Export-Oriented Development: a reassessment of the South Korean case*, Boulder, CO: Westview Press.

—— (1988) 'State intervention and export-oriented development in South Korea', in G. White and R. Wade (eds) *Developmental States in East Asia*, London: Macmillan.

Mitchell, T. (1984) 'Administrative traditions and economic decision-making in South Korea', *IDS Bulletin* 15(2): 32–7.

Mouzelis, N. (1993) 'The state in late development: historical and comparative perspectives', London School of Economics and Political Science, London, unpublished paper.

Nelson, J.M. (ed.) (1989) *Fragile Coalitions: The Politics of Economic Adjustment*, Washington, DC: *Overseas Development Council, US–Third World Policy Perspectives* no. 12, Oxford (UK) and New Brunswick (USA): Transaction Books.

O'Donnell, G. (1978) 'State and alliances in Argentina, 1956–76', *Journal of Development Studies* 15(1): 3–33.

—— (1979) 'Tensions in the bureaucratic-authoritatian state and the question of democracy', in D. Collier (ed.) *The New Authoritarianism in Latin America*.

Pack, H. and L. Westphal (1986) 'Industrial strategy and technological change: theory versus reality', *Journal of Development Economics* 22: 87–128.

Ranis, G. (1985) 'Employment, income distribution and growth in the East Asian context: a comparative analysis', in V. Corbo, A. Krueger and F. Ossa (eds) *Export-Oriented Development Strategies*, Boulder, CO: Westview Press.

Ranis, G. and L. Orrock (1985) 'Latin American and East Asian NICs: development strategies compared', in E. Duran (ed.) *Latin America and the World Recession*, Cambridge: Cambridge University Press.

Remmer, K. (1986) 'The politics of economic stabilization: IMF standby programs in Latin America, 1954–1984', *Comparative Politics* 19(1), October: 1–24.

Rueschemeyer, D. and P. Evans (1985) 'The state and economic transformation: towards an analysis of the conditions underlying effective transformation', in P. Evans, D. Rueschemeyer and T. Skocpol (eds) *Bringing the State Back In*, Cambridge: Cambridge University Press.

Sachs, J. (1985) 'External debt and macroeconomic performance in Latin America and East Asia', *Brookings Papers* 2: 523–73.

Sida, E.M. (1993) 'Hong Kong to 1997', draft PhD thesis, University of East Anglia.

Steinberg, D. (1988) 'Socio-political factors and Korea's future economic policies', *World Development* 16(1): 19–34.

Suarez-Villa, L. and P. Han (1990) 'The rise of Korea's electronics industry: technological change, growth and territorial distribution', *Economic Geography* 66(3): 273–92.

Wade, R. (1985) 'State intervention in outward-looking development: neoclassical theory and Taiwanese practice', in G. White and R. Wade (eds) *Developmental States in East Asia*, Brighton, Sussex: IDS Research Report.

—— (1988) 'State intervention in outward-looking development: neoclassical theory and Taiwanese practice', in G. White and R. Wade (eds) *Developmental States in East Asia*, London: Macmillan.

—— (1990) *Governing the Market: Economic Theory and the Role of Government in East Asian Industrialization*, Princeton: Princeton University Press.

Warren, B. (1981) *Imperialism: pioneer of capitalism*, London: Verso, New Left Books.

Weinstein, M.E. (1987) 'Japan', in G. Delury (ed.) *World Encyclopaedia of Political Systems and Parties*, New York: Facts on File Publications.

White, G. (1988) 'Introduction', in G. White and R. Wade (eds) *Developmental States in East Asia*, London: Macmillan.

White, G. and R. Wade (eds) (1985) 'Developmental states in East Asia', Brighton: IDS.

—— (1988) *Developmental States in East Asia*, London: Macmillan.

World Bank (1985) *World Development Report 1985*, New York: Oxford University Press.

—— (1989) *Sub-Saharan Africa: From Crisis to Sustainable Growth*, Washington, DC: World Bank.

—— (1991) *World Development Report 1991*, New York: Oxford University Press.

Yan Kong, T. (1992) 'The state in development: crisis and readjustment. South Korea, 1976–86', unpublished DPhil thesis, University of Oxford.

12

CONCLUSIONS: ECONOMIC FLEXIBILITY, PROGRESS AND POLICIES

Tony Killick

The ball put into play in Chapter 1 is now back in my court. The main questions to be addressed in this final chapter are whether the focus on flexibility has proved fruitful and whether the hypotheses presented in Chapter 1 receive support from the other contributors. In addition, I want in Part II to take up the issue raised in various of the contributions of the nature of the relationship between flexibility and long-run economic development, and in Part III to consider whether and how flexibility can be actively promoted through the instruments of economic and social policy.

I THE FRAMEWORK RE-EXAMINED

Flexibility in a hierarchy of objectives

Chapter 1 presented a *prima facie* case for regarding the adaptability of national economies as important to their long-term prosperity. We can therefore start by asking whether that position receives support from the other contributors to this volume.

The strongest affirmation that this is so comes from the chapters dealing with regional economic performance. A direct link is made between the remarkable economic progress of the economies of East Asia over the last two or three decades and their economic responsiveness. Chang in Chapter 7 agrees with the general opinion on this, writing of these economies as having shown remarkable flexibility, particularly in their management of the large macroeconomic shocks which affected them. A similarly direct link is made in Chapter 6, where evidence is marshalled showing the relative inflexibility of the economies of sub-Saharan Africa and ways in which this contributed to Africa's calamitous economic decline of recent decades. Neuber's study of Eastern Europe in Chapter 5 similarly makes the link between economic deterioration in those countries during the 1980s and the large systemic rigidities imposed by central planning, resulting in small supply elasticities, little innovation, highly imperfect informational and incentive systems, and much structural and institutional inertia.

In fact, it may not be going too far to claim that a large part of the enormous contrasts in the recent economic histories of these three important regions is explicable in terms of their differing degrees of flexibility, for reasons suggested in Chapter 1 and adding support to Hayek's contention that 'the economic problem of society is mainly one of rapid adaptation to changes . . .'

Various of our contributors concur in regarding economic adaptability as of much importance for long-term economic performance. In Chapter 10 Fry argues the importance of the financial sector in terms of its abilities to enhance the overall flexibility of the economy. Smith and Ulph in Chapter 8 similarly draw attention to the important economic consequences of countries' comparative responses to the oil shocks. The historical importance of adaptability as a determinant of economic performance is an underlying theme of Jones in Chapter 4. However, perhaps more significant is the extent to which contributors qualify the idea that flexibility is desirable, for reasons that receive little attention in Chapter 1.

First, the point is made in Chapters 4 and 7 that if we could imagine complete economic flexibility, with no restraints whatever on labour and other factor movements, the outcome would be marked by enormous uncertainties, not to say chaos. Indeed, that there is a trade-off between flexibility and confidence in the future is an organising principle of Chapter 5 (see Figure 5.1) and is also brought out strongly in Chapter 2. Since a sense of security is very important to most people, the desirability of diminishing this in the name of enhancing flexibility should by no means be taken for granted. Jones in Chapter 4 is eloquent on the human costs of adjustment: 'Economies are adaptable only in a lumbering way.' Adaptation involves losses of income, reduced living standards, greater unemployment, the frustration of personal potentialities, even increased morbidity and mortality.

A more technical point about costs also surfaces in several of the preceding chapters. This concerns the tension between flexibility on the part of policy-makers and the credibility of their decisions – what in Chapter 1 is called 'the delicate balance to be struck between flexibility and continuity in government policies'. This point is taken further in Chapters 2 and 11, with the latter seeing policy adaptability as requiring a capacity to combine responsiveness with continuity of purpose.

The modern theory of economic policy places much weight on the attribute of 'pre-commitment', referring to a government's ability to persuade the public that its policy signals can be depended upon as a basis for investment and other decisions about the future by making credible commitments which restrict its future freedom to change these signals. As Basu observes in Chapter 3, having a choice can weaken an agent's ability to pre-commit. What is needed, he suggests, is the capacity for 'strategic inflexibility' – the power to appear inflexible when that is called for. There is a direct link here with the lively debate that occurred in the 1980s about the conduct of monetary policy: whether monetary authorities should implement a fixed rule, such as a constant rate of growth of money supply (as advocated by Milton Friedman), or retain discretion to vary this over time. The jury is still out on that controversy.

Chang's theme of 'flexible rigidities' in East Asia in Chapter 7 is also concerned with the interplay of continuity and flexibility in policy. He sees a frequent trade-off between short-run and long-run flexibility and argues that in this region policy interventions created short-run rigidities in order to achieve greater long-term flexibility, thus creating a stable policy environment in the short term to encourage the long-term planning and investments in specific assets necessary for the creation of flexible economic structures. However, this is a tricky balance to achieve, as we are reminded by the quotation from Oliver Williamson in Chapter 5 concerning Eastern Europe: 'the stability value of socialism turned out to be an immobility burden in the end'. Perhaps it is the peculiar East Asian genius that has enabled that region to maintain this balance so successfully.

Along similar lines, Smith and Ulph also point out in Chapter 8 that rapid-fire response is not necessarily optimal. There can often be merit in deferring action when there are major uncertainties: delay may permit a better-informed response later. What these various considerations remind us, then, is that we should avoid any temptation to elevate flexibility as a goal to pursue above all others and at all times. Because it has costs, its desirability should not be taken as axiomatic; and it needs to be traded off against other desiderata. Its value is an instrumental one, promoting long-term economic progress, but it is only one of the qualities that have such value.

The determinants of national economic flexibility

The introductory chapter presented hypotheses concerning the factors which determine the flexibility of economies. To what extent are they validated by the ensuing chapters? It could not be claimed that they subject the hypotheses to any systematic testing. Nevertheless, they generally tend to confirm the initial suggestions – but add nuances of their own.

It was suggested in Chapter 1 that, in searching for the sources of flexibility, it would be fruitful to focus on the constraints acting upon individuals, dampening their responses to economic stimuli. The chapters on Africa and Eastern Europe implicitly endorse this, each arguing that the marked inflexibility of the economies of these regions has been despite the responsiveness of their peoples.

The responsiveness of Africans as consumers and producers has been demonstrated by their resourcefulness in the face of the economic hardships that so many have experienced (see Chapter 6). To provide but one of many available examples, in Zaïre the economy has been systematically pillaged by a kleptocratic regime, but its citizens have responded by creating a parallel economy which is estimated to be twice as large as the officially recorded one. The profits of this second economy are used to finance the provision of public goods which the state fails to provide: health facilities, schools, road maintenance, etc.

We may also cite the vigour of smuggling in much of Africa, in response not merely to the usual trade barriers but to distortions in exchange rates and in administered producer prices. There may be a well-established smuggling of cash crops from country A to country B – say of cocoa from Ghana to Côte d'Ivoire – but this will quickly be reversed (as it has been in these countries) if movements in relative prices make it profitable to switch.

People in Africa have responded no less vigorously to other opportunities for capturing the rents created by import restrictions, price controls and other market restrictions – contributing to the widespread corruption so widely complained of. In fact, the response has been so vigorous that in several African countries the state is in crisis, with only a tenuous hold on economic life, and forced by its scale and superior efficiency to tolerate a parallel economy which decimates the tax base.

Neuber tells a similar story for Eastern Europe during the period of central planning (Chapter 5). There was the same emergence of a large parallel economy, and of semi-legal activities responding to opportunities for rents gained from scarcity premia in ways which were highly responsive to supply and demand. Managers of state enterprises learned to escape some of the confines of the plan by informal barter deals, or the use of procurement scouts to find scarce inputs. They established 'networks of intimate co-operation' and elaborate systems of payments 'on the side'. They entered into informal shop-floor pacts with their labour forces quite outside the plan framework.

The Eastern European case is one where most of the constraints on individuals were state-made: the whole paraphernalia of controls and price distortions resulting from central planning. However, Chapter 1 suggests that tradition and social norms also constrain. That proposition receives only qualified endorsement. There is support for the view that tradition can exert a powerful influence. Chapter 4 links England's loss of economic adaptability over the last century to the malign influence of its class structure and the obstacles this places in the way of promotion on the basis of individual merit. The same chapter, however, draws attention to an example where tradition has made a positive contribution to flexibility, referring to the ability of governments in Japan to mobilise a consensus in favour of change: 'There can be little doubt that particular cultural and institutional circumstances have eased Japan's responsiveness'. A similar judgement is implicit in Chapters 7 and 11 concerning East Asia as a whole. Seddon and Belton-Jones show how the societal basis of politics in the region has harnessed a large degree of state autonomy from special interest groups to the pursuit of economic development.

A further insight to emerge is that, while the flexibility of the national economy requires that its citizens be – and be allowed to be – responsive to information and incentives, individual responsiveness can take forms that conflict with the flexibility of the economy as a whole. In Chapter 4 Jones cites the Netherlands of the seventeenth century, whose merchants actually invested in the pirates preying on Dutch shipping, and whose provinces were too jealous of their own autonomy to permit effective measures against a cattle plague that would manifestly have been in their collective interest. Chang in Chapter 7 gives the example of capital flight, where the responsiveness of individuals to economic difficulties at home may starve the domestic economy of the investments it needs in order to overcome those difficulties. Sometimes, he suggests, it is desirable for the state to constrain individual responsiveness in the national interest, citing with approval Korea's 'notoriously harsh' exchange controls.

Implicit in several chapters is agreement with the proposition that the nature of a country's polity – and the interventions that emanate from it – exerts a decisive influence on national economic flexibility, for reasons eloquently summarised by North:

> The polity and the economy are inextricably interlinked in any understanding of the performance of an economy. . . . Not only do polities specify and enforce property rights that shape the basic incentive structure of an economy, in the modern world the share of GNP going through government and the ubiquitous and ever-changing regulations imposed by it are the most important keys to economic performance.
>
> (North, 1990: 112)

Each of our regional studies bears this out and Chapter 11 takes the 'relative autonomy of the state' as the central influence on the state's responsiveness and (tacitly) the resulting flexibility of the economy. It approvingly quotes Wade's identification of the factors which explain the success of Japan, Korea and Taiwan: centralisation of the decision-making structure employing the best managers; insulation of decision-makers from all but the strongest pressure groups; a powerful executive not beholden to the legislature; the absence of a powerful labour movement; the absence of conflicts between the owners of natural resources and manufacturers; and decision-makers' perception that legitimacy is grounded in economic success.

However, Chapter 11 is careful to distinguish between insulation and isolation of policy-makers, pointing out that in the East Asian countries there has been a highly intensive degree of interaction between agencies of the state and the private sector, and that this was essential to the effectiveness of policies. A World Bank study of *The East Asian Miracle* (1993: 187) agrees, making the important point that this intense interaction between planners and industrialists had the effect of enhancing the amount of market-related information that was fed into planners' decisions. In other words, autonomy is not enough: it has to be harnessed to access to information and utilised in pursuit of well-informed policies.

But why is it that policy processes have taken this pro-flexibility form in that part of the world, while other countries present a radically different, and usually less impressive, scene? More specifically, if the policy-makers of East Asia were freed from many of the customary restraints, why did they not use this freedom to promote their own interests (as the public choice school predicts and as has happened elsewhere)? The answer presumably has to do with the social roots of political forms. Writers have invoked patriotism, education and expert recruitment policies in the civil service as elements in the answer. Chapter 11 stresses the importance of strategic relations with important sectional and class interests, and a degree of responsiveness to these, as encouraging continuing commitment to economic development. But we are still far from understanding this issue and why outcomes should differ so dramatically across countries.

So a definitive statement of the determinants of economies' flexibility – if only we were in a position to write one – would give greater, but less negative, attention to the influences of tradition and social structure. And it would place even greater weight on the influence of political systems than is done in the opening chapter.

A reading of the preceding chapters also underlines the importance of economies' openness as an influence on adaptability, an issue taken further in Part III below. Similarly with information. The importance of this factor features in Chapter 6's explanations of the inflexibility of Africa's econo-mies, assembling evidence showing that the collection and dissemination of information are particularly poor there and arguing that this has necessarily constrained the ability of economic agents, at all levels, to respond to changing situations, of which they are but poorly informed.

At the beginning of the project I had posed to Jones the question why Britain and certain other European countries had proved more adept than others at utilising new industrial technologies in their eighteenth and nine-teenth century industrial revolutions. His response in Chapter 4 is that the similarities were more important than the differences:

> it may be better to start by turning back from these issues of
> the relative industrial performance of Britain and her neighbours.
> The differential performance of national and regional units was a
> lesser matter than the stimulus which the entire European system
> gave to individual units . . . we should pay more attention to the

commonalities of Europe's competitive economic system than to the particularities.

But how was this stimulus imparted? Through information flows:

> Policy choices in any one part of Europe might be positive, negative or neutral in the eyes of another part but they would seldom remain unknown for long. There was in effect a single market for information, sluggish only by modern standards.

In fact, Jones' chapter is persuasive in arguing that 'path dependence' should be added to any account of the principal determinants of economic flexibility, i.e. the proposition that 'the path whereby the present has been reached influences the nature of the present'. The accounts offered in other contributions concur with this proposition. Syrquin in Chapter 2 cites an important study of regional government in Italy by Putnam *et al.* (1993) as illustrating the deep historical roots of contemporary contrasts between the regions. Neuber in Chapter 5 draws attention to the path-dependent nature of institutional and behavioural norms in Eastern Europe. Chapter 6 finds it necessary to dig below economic explanations to trace present sources of weakness in Africa back to the nature of pre-colonial society and the failures of colonialism to modernise this. Chapter 11 observes that the development of effective state bureaucratic capacities in East Asia involved institutions which took decades to build.

Outside this volume, others have come to similar conclusions about the importance of historical influences on the responsiveness of policy processes. Compare Ranis and Mahmoud on the results of a survey of cross-country differences in development experiences:

> In summary, our findings suggest that the determinants of the long-run pattern of policy evolution are intimately linked to systems' initial conditions. These conditions, given partly by nature and partly by the legacy of history, affect not only their initial level of income and welfare, but also their policy responsiveness and flexibility over time, i.e. the extent to which policy is likely to be accommodative or obstructive of some basic time-phased evolutionary change.
>
> (Ranis and Mahmoud, 1992: 223)

Contemporary Eastern Europe provides a cockpit in which such ideas are now being put to the test, in endeavouring to create polities, institutions, entire economic systems nearly *de novo*, almost in defiance of history. If path dependence imposes the fetters on present possibilities of change averred in Chapter 4, several of the East European experiments may be doomed to fail. However, Neuber in Chapter 5, while stressing the importance of institutions and acknowledging the heavy hand of the past, rejects as simply impractical the gradualism implicit in the historians' view, asserting the sufficiency of introducing private property rights and a market system:

> The reliance on price liberalisation and property rights reform as sufficient conditions must hence be regarded as the strategy most likely to succeed. Gradualism, due to its inherent credibility deficiency, is unlikely to induce the desired changes in behaviour needed to transform the economic system.

Of course, the unique historical and political conjunction in Eastern Europe could provide 'the exception that proves the rule' but, writing this in early 1994, the political sustainability of the radical approach in some of the ex-communist states appeared to be trembling in the balance.

Lastly on the determinants of flexibility, we should note a demographic factor, to be developed in Part II: a youthful population is good for flexibility.

If flexibility is a useful concept, why is it neglected?

Prior to embarking on this project I undertook a search for publications within economics which bore directly upon the flexibility of economies. Remarkably little was found, which explains the tentative or speculative nature of some of the foregoing, although Syrquin in Chapter 2 provides an informative brief survey of the points of contact between the existing literature and our flexibility theme. The past relative neglect should give us pause, for economics has proved remarkably responsive to the emergence of new problems and insights, and its literature covers an awesomely wide range. Given the apparent importance of the adaptability of national economies, it seems surprising that this topic should have slipped through the gaps. Why might this be?

Basu in Chapter 3 suggests a major part of the answer: that the study of flexibility is not easily reconciled with the concerns of the dominant neoclassical paradigm, since perfect flexibility is taken for granted in formal neoclassical models. Of course, perfect flexibility, like perfect anything else, is merely a device of convenience for theoretical modelling. Neoclassicists recognise that inflexibilities occur in the real world, but tend to attribute these to the malign effects of state interventions or institutional deficiencies, or to dispute their importance. Little has put it well:

> a neoclassical vision of the world is one of flexibility. In their own or their families' interests, people adapt readily to changing opportunities and prices, even if they do not like doing so and even if they may take their time. Businesses pursue objectives roughly consistent with the assumption that they maximise risk- and time-discounted profits. . . . There is usually a wide variety of ways of making things such that

production methods can be expected to shift when input prices change. Demand schedules are consequently curves, neither kinked nor vertical . . . most markets usually tend to achieve an equilibrium without wild price fluctuations. In short, the price mechanism can be expected to work rather well.

(Little, 1982: 25)

Justman and Teubal amplify this, taking a more economy-wide view:

The feasibility and continuity of structural change are assumed in the neoclassical view because technology is identified with freely available information such that the notion of technological capabilities is irrelevant, and because it assumes constant-returns-to-scale production functions. . . . The neoclassical view does not distinguish between the allocation of resources for existing industries and for industries that are only beginning to emerge. Structural change therefore is considered an automatic process that is successfully mediated by market forces.

(Justman and Teubal, 1991: 1169)

Of course, if markets are viewed as working well and adjustment as automatic and relatively costless, then indeed flexibility is an uninteresting subject.

The neoclassical view similarly disputes the relevance of two further topics which receive much attention in this volume: institutions and path dependence. As described in Chapter 1, the adequacy or otherwise of institutions determines the extent of avoidable transactions costs. However, if such costs are assumed away within the parameters of a model, or are regarded as of little practical significance, then those holding these views are tacitly assuming institutions to be perfect, or anyway efficient. In this case, institutional development must be seen as no less automatic and painless than market-clearing. On this view institutions are also uninteresting for economic analysis (see Chapters 3 and 5 for discussions of the theory of institutions). So is history, for similar reasons explored in Chapter 4.

So also is disequilibrium. As Fisher has argued,[1] within the neoclassical paradigm 'Economic theory is pre-eminently a matter of equilibrium analysis. In particular, the centrepiece of the subject – general equilibrium theory – deals with the existence and efficiency properties of competitive equilibrium.' As he goes on to argue, mainstream economics has much less to say about what happens out of equilibrium and about how economic agents behave in such situations.

An enquiry into the flexibility of economies is, however, almost by definition an enquiry into disequilibrium behaviour – about how peoples and their governments respond to shocks and to longer-term changes in economic conditions and useful knowledge. We are enquiring into processes of change, not into the properties of comparative equilibria.

For example, we see the ways in which nations respond to, and take advantage of, advances in useful knowledge as a key determinant of their overall ability to adapt to change (Chapter 9), whereas mainstream economics has rather little to say on this subject. Thus, in his survey of technology and economic development Fransman (1986: 3–4 and *passim*) argues that technical change is poorly understood in economics and that attention is now moving from the neoclassical question of choice of factor proportions from a given set of techniques to less static questions about how technologies change over time. (See also Nelson and Winter, 1982: 29 and *passim*, and Stewart and James, 1982: 1.)

The issues raised in earlier chapters, particularly 6 and 7, about economies' abilities to recognise and take advantage of new international trading opportunities imply a similar desire to move away from a resource-based comparative advantage theory which seems too static and remote from the concerns of traders and policy-makers. Here again, we are concerned with dynamics and processes, and to delve beneath given stocks of resources and factor proportions to investigate why otherwise comparable economies achieve such widely varying export records.

There are strong resonances between this volume's concern with flexibility and the well-known literature on structural change, which runs from Kuznets through Chenery to Syrquin and others, and is taken up by Syrquin in Chapter 2. For one way of describing a flexible economy is to say that it will readily and at low cost adapt its structure to accommodate changing circumstances, while an inflexible economy will exhibit structural ossification and large adjustment costs. In the structuralist view, by contrast with the neoclassical position:

> structural changes are causes of growth rather than outcomes of a process of capital accumulation and rising per capita incomes. Moreover, the growth process may be punctuated by periods of discrete shifts in resource allocation ('creative destruction') and growth acceleration rather than being smooth throughout. Structural changes need not be automatic, they require a skill-specific infrastructure of new capabilities which, when established, generate new comparative advantages. Market failures may be pervasive . . .
>
> (Justman and Teubal, 1991: 1167)

Indeed, as their reference to creative destruction signals, the intellectual origin of our present interests owes more to Schumpeter than it does to neoclassicism.

Little takes a similar view of the structuralist position:

> The structuralist sees the world as inflexible. Change is inhibited by obstacles, bottlenecks, and constraints. People find it hard to move or adapt, and resources tend to be stuck. In economic terms, the supply of

most things is inelastic. Such general inflexibility was thought to apply particularly to LDCs. . . . As a result of poverty, demands, too, were inflexible. . . . Demands also were inelastic, especially for food, for imports into developing countries, and for their exports.

(Little, 1982: 20)

Obviously, then, the subject-matter of this book is in the structuralist tradition, but with an important difference. As Little goes on to point out, the viewpoint summarised in the last two quotations is associated with a distrust of market mechanisms, for if demand and supply are inelastic large price changes – with all their associated costs – are needed to bring about small changes in quantity. And if necessary structural changes are not automatic and are costly they need to be engineered in a cost-effective manner. Traditional structuralism is, therefore, associated with a *dirigiste* approach to the fostering of long-term economic development, whereas no such view is collectively taken in this volume. Indeed, the general proposition in Chapter 1 that a well-functioning market system is conducive to economic flexibility emerges largely unscathed, with differences of opinion focusing largely on how well markets actually do function, and how good the state is at rectifying the weaknesses. While all contributors appear to share the position that inflexibility is a real problem, and are hence implicitly critical of its neglect within the neoclassical paradigm, they are certainly not all anti-market and pro-intervention. In fact, a wide range of attitudes is displayed, with the pro-market stance perhaps most strongly represented in Chapters 5 and 10, and a structuralist, pro-interventionist position most strongly represented in Chapters 7, 9 and 11. Other contributions take up no strong position in this matter.

To return to the question why the subject of national economic flexibility has been neglected, a second explanation should be entered, namely the imprecision of the concept and the impossibility of rendering it into measurable units. From Chapters 3 and 4 we might be tempted to think of the flexibility of an economy as a Ghostly Elephant: elephantine because easier to recognise than define and ghostly because barely perceived until challenged. It must be admitted that we have made only limited progress in the matter of definition and that this continuing elusiveness is a major obstacle to taking the subject forward. However, it would be wrong to infer that the topic should revert to a condition of benign neglect. As Basu points out in Chapter 3, usage often precedes definition. Various concepts familiar in mainstream economics have long established their usefulness despite fuzziness and unmeasurability. Basu gives the example of 'luxury goods'. 'Expectations' and 'the social welfare function' also come to mind.

It may be that it is a mistake to search for a general definition. It is likely to be more fruitful to seek partial definitions of flexibility which are useful in the contexts in which they are deployed. For example, we have seen in

Chapter 1's discussion of labour market flexibility that, even though that too is imprecise and not directly measurable, quantifiable proxies have been developed and a useful empirical literature has emerged. Similarly, Smith and Ulph in Chapter 8 develop a model which enables them to capture the notion of flexibility quite precisely, in the context of firms' technology choices. One potentially useful approach to giving the notion of flexibility more operational content might be to concentrate on the identification and measurement of the avoidable transactions, or adjustment, costs which we have identified with inflexibility.

Smith and Ulph also go further than other contributors in providing numerical indicators of economy-wide flexibility from which they derive a composite index (see their Tables 8.1 and 8.2). Indicators include the investment ratio, years of schooling, exchange-rate flexibility, the size of the industrial sector and dependence on commodity exports. They then compare these results with their assessments of country responses to the oil shocks (Table 8.9), concluding that the general index was able to discriminate reasonably well between those countries which adjusted flexibly to the shocks and those which did not.

However, inclusion in an index of flexibility of such variables as the investment ratio and education does pose the question, fundamental to this entire enterprise, of whether it is useful to try to separate out the determinants of economies' flexibility from the sources of their long-term development. The danger of circularity rears its head again. The answer is perhaps best provided by re-visiting boxes 7 and 8 of Figure 1.2 in Chapter 1. In light of the above discussion, we should add to these lists the influences of history and of the age structure of the population. While the suggested determinants can be criticised as vague, and there are important overlaps with standard models of development, they do direct our attention to a substantially different set of influences, especially in the importance given to factors that take us well beyond economics. The adaptability of an economy, it seems, is an input into economic development with fairly (but not entirely) distinctive explanatory variables of its own.

II FLEXIBILITY AND LONG-RUN DEVELOPMENT

The flexibility–development connection

Mention was made a moment ago of the traditional structuralist view that underdeveloped economies are also likely to be inflexible. Reconsideration of the determinants set out in Chapter 1, taken further above, supports this view and we should recall Syrquin's suggestion in Chapter 2 of a roughly ∩-shaped, or inverted-U, relationship. Such a model is illustrated in Figure 12.1.[2] This indicates that at any given level of development both flexibility-raising and flexibility-reducing forces will be at work. The net effect of these

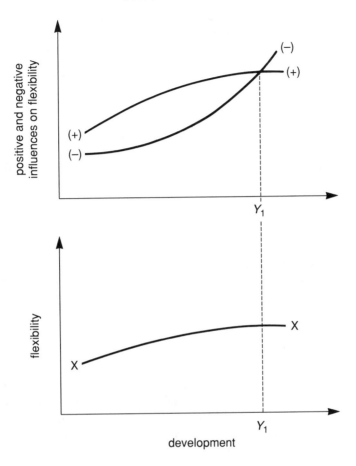

Figure 12.1 The flexibility–development connection

is likely to leave the least developed economies with rigid economies, but for there to be net accretions to flexibility up to some level of development, Y_1, beyond which it diminishes again (although with fluctuations around the trend).

What might be the basis for such a model? Consider first the reasons why flexibility may be enhanced by development. To start with, the data base and information flows can be expected to be poor at the early stages of development. Indeed, for Klitgaard poor information flows are a defining characteristic of developing countries:

one reason why market institutions work poorly in developing countries is that information about prices, quantities and quality is not readily available. One reason why government bureaucracies work poorly is that information about outputs and outcomes, about laudable achievements and illicit activities, is scarce.

(Klitgaard, 1991: 15)

This situation can be expected to improve as the economy develops because it will be feasible to devote larger resources to the collection and dissemination of information, channels of communication will become better developed and a larger part of economic activity will take place within organised, or formal, sectors of the economy that are more amenable to data-gathering.

Further, the hold of any traditional values and modes that impede adaptability is likely to be gradually weakened as development proceeds, education levels improve and modernising attitudes become more the norm. The economy will also become more industrialised. This consideration can be linked with Syrquin's suggestion in Chapter 2 that reliance on primary product exports, characteristic of underdeveloped economies, will add to their initial inflexibility. Industry has greater potential for the rapid response of output to changing price relativities, and for the mobility of resources, because factors of production will be less specific than in the primary sectors.

There are also likely to be agglomeration economies arising from the growing size of the industrial sector, which influence the country's technological capacity. Thus Freeman argues that:

> it is the national system of innovation which is decisive, not the particular range of products. Universities, research institutions, technological infrastructure, industrial training systems, information systems, design centres and other scientific and technical institutions provide the essential foundation which alone make possible the adaptation to structural change in the economy associated with changes in techno-economic paradigm.

(Freeman, 1989: 97)

For these and related reasons, we would expect indigenous technological capacities to increase with development, a transformation further accelerated by the externalities arising from the accumulation of experience and knowledge, adding depth to technological capacities (see Chapter 7).

Partly because the domestic market will be enlarged by development, competition among domestic producers will grow, increasing the pressures upon them to be responsive. Markets will be better integrated and dualism reduced, for dualism is largely a feature of early-stage developing economies. Markets will be more complete. In other respects too we would expect the market mechanism to work better and for factors to be more mobile.

The larger size of developed economies can be an advantage in other ways. Being less reliant on external trade, they will not be so vulnerable to shocks transmitted from the rest of the world. And their more diversified structures of demand and production will facilitate the movement of resources, and perhaps demand, between products.[3] At the same time, the advantage of a simple economic structure – that transactions costs tend to be low – may not be realised because weak institutional development leaves such costs higher than necessary.

For these reasons, we hypothesise that the less developed an economy the less flexible it will be – a view consistent with the conclusions of Chapter 6 on Africa. There is thus something of a vicious circle at work: inflexibility retards development but underdevelopment retards flexibility. Indeed, in some cases this may understate the case. A substantial proportion of the least-developed economies of Africa and elsewhere not only experience the rigidities just mentioned but have suffered serious economic and social deteriorations: declining incomes and living standards, decaying infra-structures, a worsening quality of health and education services, a shrinking tax base leading to inflationary pressures and adding to already acute balance-of-payments problems. In at least some of these cases, there has been a simultaneous decay in the capabilities of the state, with economic life being increasingly conducted through unregulated parallel markets, exten-sive corruption, a serious erosion of senior personnel and morale in the public services, and widespread alienation of the people from the actions of their governments.

Where such conditions prevail, the difficulties of successful adaptation are greatly increased. However, we would not be justified in going so far as to describe this as a low-level trap. The association of inflexibility with under-development is not likely to be so strong as to dominate outcomes. We shall shortly introduce some qualifications to the hypothesis of a ∩-shaped relationship and, in any case, there are things that the governments of even the poorest, most run-down, countries can do to increase the adaptability of their economies, figuratively shifting the X–X schedule in Figure 12.1. That is what the structural adjustment programmes of the World Bank seek to do. What is suggested, however, is that, other things being equal, progress along the X–X schedule will tend to be slower in the early stages and to gather pace as the economy modernises. The least developed face an uphill task and require more 'adjustment' time than more advanced economies.

What now of the upper turning point of an economy's development, when flexibility begins to diminish? The argument here is one particularly associated with Mancur Olson's book, *The Rise and Decline of Nations* (1982, especially Chapter 3). This postulates that, as an economy matures, society will become more articulated into special-interest organisations and that these will grow in relative influence. Many will be 'distributional' coalitions, such as trade unions and producer cartels, primarily concerned to protect their memberships and to enhance their share of national income rather than with the expansion of aggregate income or with the national interest. Hence, Olson sees distributional coalitions as reducing factor mobilities and slowing down a society's capacity to adopt new technologies and reallocate resources in response to changing conditions (pp. 61–5).

Giersch (1986) argues a related case, to the effect that the economies of Western Europe are becoming increasingly rigid.[4] Like Olson, he relates this to the increased strength of special-interest groups, especially of industrialists and organised labour, introducing major labour market rigidities (e.g. through large enforceable severance-pay obligations) and undermining governments' abilities to achieve change through consensus. He writes of 'Eurosclerosis', linking his argument to governments' post-World War II commitments to full employment and arguing that the pursuit of Keynesian demand-management policies in pursuit of this turned into 'promises to protect'. He sees a resulting growth in protectionism acting as a brake on structural change and on the adoption of technological advances.

We should also recall from Chapter 1 the suggestion that transactions costs tend to rise as economies become more complex – unless cost-reducing institutions develop fast enough to offset this tendency. The arguments about distributional coalitions and Eurosclerosis could be reinterpreted along these lines, as part of a broader hypothesis that there is some tendency for transactions costs to outstrip institutional innovation at the more advanced levels of economic development.

Demographic dimensions can be added to these arguments. The more mature industrialised economies are characterised by populations which are growing only slowly, if at all, and are therefore ageing.[5] An ageing population may reduce flexibility in a number of ways. First, it necessitates a shift in the provision of public services away from education (which can be thought of as an investment in human capital and technological capabilities) in favour of welfare provisions for the elderly (which do nothing to enhance future productivities). Moreover, when, as in the modern world, there is a rapid pace of technological progress, an ageing labour force is liable to be less adept at absorbing these changes than a youthful one. Older workers are apt to be more resistant to retraining and, in any case, the profitability of investments in retraining diminishes sharply with the age of the trainees. Similarly, an ageing labour force can be expected to exhibit less mobility than a younger one, and this will reduce an economy's ability to let old industries go and enter successfully into new ones, or will increase the 'adjustment costs' of doing so.[6]

An economy's maturity may also work to reduce adaptability through its effect on the age structure of the stock of physical capital and the technologies embodied in it. A mature economy will be relatively capital-intensive. The volume of new investment in any one period will be small relative to the existing capital stock, and that stock can therefore be changed only rather slowly. It is for such reasons that it is reckoned to have been an advantage for the German and Japanese economies that much of their capital stock was destroyed during World War II, giving them subsequently a more modern capital base than most of their European and North American competitors. (See also Chapter 8 for a variant on this argument.)

Caveats

To the case for a ∩-shaped development–flexibility relationship some caveats must now be entered. Some of the reasons why rigidities may increase with maturity are symmetrical, working to the advantage of the 'immature'. Thus, developing countries have rapidly expanding populations and youthful age structures, which, if we invert the earlier arguments, should give them positive advantages. Similarly, with the capital stock. Holding other conditions equal, an economy at an early stage of development is likely to be adding to its capital stock at a proportionally faster rate than a more mature economy. It should thus be better able to alter the disposition of the capital stock across activities and to incorporate technological advances into its productive system. Note also that in Chapter 4 Jones disputes the ∩-curve hypothesis by reference to economies' resilience in the face of shocks, such as crop failures, with the decay of traditional customs and institutions which had buffered vulnerable populations from the worst effects of such shocks uncompensated by the emergence of any equivalent 'modern' safety nets.

It should also be said that most of the arguments in this section are speculative, with little hard evidence in either direction. Both the shape and the stability of the ∩-curve are hence in question. Furthermore, some of the arguments appear rather transient. For example, Giersch's arguments about Eurosclerosis, although made only a few years ago, already seem dated in some of their important details, for the Conservative Revolution of recent years has diminished the power of trade unions and appears to have increased the flexibility of Europe's labour and capital markets.

It is not, in any case, suggested that the degree of flexibility is an invariable function of the stage of development. Government actions, such as the creation of the European Community, that enhance exposure to international competition are among those that can raise flexibility. So can other types of policy intervention. In short, the X–X curve can be induced to shift upwards. Indeed, it may be that the development–flexibility relationship cannot be reduced to simple geometry at all. What is clear, however, is that there are a number of channels through which these variables influence each other. There is much scope for fruitful empirical research here. My own money would go on a ∩-curve being validated.

III WHAT ROLE FOR THE STATE?

Policy as a decisive factor

It may not be going too far to say that common to virtually all the contributions to this volume is a view that policies – and the way they are executed – have a decisive influence on the flexibility of a national economy, for good or ill. Some contributors emphasise the malign effects of past interventions. Others emphasise positive contributions. Both viewpoints may be right in the particular contexts of which they were written. All agree that the actions of the state have major ramifications for the adaptability of economic systems.

This perhaps comes out most strongly in the regional studies. In the case of Eastern Europe, the inflexibilities induced by central planning, well described by Neuber in Chapter 5, are scarcely a matter of controversy any more. My analysis of the inflexibility of African economies in Chapter 6 similarly emphasises the negative consequences of many interventions and finds it essential to enquire into the nature of African political systems in order to try to understand the persistence of dysfunctional policies. The contrast between the recent histories of these two regions and that of East Asian countries could scarcely be starker, not least as it relates to the effects of state interventions, with Chang in Chapter 7 emphasising the flexibility-enhancing nature of many of the chosen interventions.

Quite apart from the specific consequences of particular measures, these regional studies bring out the importance of the overall policy environment. There are externalities here, positive or negative, with the overall effect being larger than the sum of the parts. Syrquin in Chapter 2 emphasises this and points out the high degree of uniformity within countries in trends in total factor productivity across sectors as evidence for the powerful influence of the overall economic environment. Lall joins him, stressing in Chapter 9 the strong influence of the political and macroeconomic environment on decisions concerning investments in the creation of the technological capabilities which are so crucial to the adaptability of the manufacturing sector. Finally, Chapter 6's analysis of the inflexibility of African economies can be read as pointing to the powerfully negative consequences of an unfavourable macroeconomic environment.

While governments need to maintain a steady pro-adaptation policy environment, they need also to be responsive to evidence on the effectiveness of past policies and on changing circumstances – what Seddon and Belton-Jones in Chapter 11 call 'policy adaptability'. It is evident from our regional studies that there were large contrasts in the policy adaptability of governments in Africa and East Asia. It is worth repeating the conclusions of the World Bank study of *The East Asian Miracle* (1993: 86) already quoted in Chapter 1, commending 'the pragmatic flexibility with which governments tried policy instruments in pursuit of economic objectives. Instruments that worked were retained. Instruments that failed or impeded other policy objectives were abandoned.' Governments' capacity for such responsiveness presumes, of course, that there are monitoring mechanisms for feedback from the wider economy which is keyed into policy decision processes.

The case for active state promotion of flexibility

We turn now to consider how best the state can promote the adaptability of the economy. Our basic position that a well-functioning market system is conducive to economic flexibility conditions what is likely to be the optimal role for the state: *to promote market efficiency and to respond to the remaining weaknesses of the price system (market failures)*. In the promotion of flexibility, to what types of intervention does this guideline point us?

First, we have already observed the possibility of conflicts between individual responsiveness and the flexibility of the national economy. Since it is the state's task *par excellence* to safeguard the general welfare over particular interests, it should stand ready to intervene when such conflicts become apparent (although how that would translate in practice would have to be defined by the specificities of the case in question). Relatedly and as argued in Chapter 11, it is for the political leadership to seek to mobilise a social consensus on the desirability of change, and on how its costs and benefits should be distributed within society. Observers frequently point to the consensual nature of policies in the East Asian economies as enhancing the effectiveness of adjustment policies and hence overall flexibility. The World Bank study just cited suggests there were further advantages from the consensus-building Consultation Councils set up in the region, particularly in Japan and South Korea:

> From an economic standpoint, deliberative councils facilitate information transmission. They enable the bureaucracy to gather information about world markets, technology trends, and the impact of regulations, domestically and abroad, synthesize the information into an action plan, and communicate the plan back to the private sector. Self-interested behaviour is more or less constrained by the repeated nature of the collaboration. This in part helps to establish credibility – private sector participants believe cheating and reneging are less likely.
>
> (World Bank, 1993: 187)

Various of our contributors, particularly of Chapters 4 and 5, draw attention to the potentially large costs of flexibility. That this is so is scarcely in question. Indeed, an increasing part of the literature on the 'structural adjustment' programmes of the World Bank is concerned with this. The structural changes that are intrinsic in processes of economic adaptation inevitably give rise to bankruptcies and job losses. The necessary changes in relative prices and the exigencies of macroeconomic management are also bound to impact on the distribution of income and may well jeopardise the welfare of poverty groups.

If this be accepted, it is hard to resist the corollary that it is the job of the state to minimise these costs – e.g. through transitional provisions, 'safety nets', worker re-training schemes – and to ensure that the way the burdens are shared is regarded as fair. If the state will not do it, the market provides no mechanisms that will fill this vacuum, and it is a task too large to be left wholly to civil society.

There are other types of market failure which can retard national economic flexibility and which, therefore, constitute *prima facie* reasons for state action, unless the costs of intervention seem likely to exceed the benefits. Information has received a good deal of attention in this study as a prime determinant of economic responsiveness, but there are well-known reasons, mainly relating to the difficulties of restricting access, why market mechanisms are liable to underproduce information and to disseminate it poorly. Indeed, unfettered markets may well generate misinformation, e.g. through untruthful advertising.

The potential value of active state intervention in this area could contribute considerably to flexibility (see Chapter 9). Thus Mody (1990: 311) notes that the proven ability of the electronics industry of Taiwan to respond was enhanced by a variety of public-sector productivity, research, standardisation and marketing agencies which served to gather and disseminate information to the industry. Rhee and Belot (1990: 52) draw attention to similarly important informational contributions by public agencies in a study of 'success stories' drawn from countries outside East Asia.

There is quite wide acceptance that this is an important task for the state. Similarly there is little controversy about the public-interest case for state provision of the education and training which have also emerged as crucial determinants of economic flexibility. As Lall comments in Chapter 9, the risk of market failures in skill creation is generally accepted. However, he goes on to argue the economic case for a considerably wider range of interventions. This he does in terms of time, investment and effort, arguing that there are many positive externalities in the development of industrial capabilities, which, moreover, is itself risky and expensive. Enterprises find it 'extremely difficult to bear the costs involved, and capital markets in developing countries are usually not prepared to risk such a process'. Chang argues along somewhat similar lines in Chapter 7, in favour of socialising some of the risks involved in investments in specific assets and non-standard technologies.

Even in the absence of externalities and market failures, there would still be a case for state actions to promote the 'well-functioning' market system which we see as favourable to flexibility. But what kinds of actions?

Some, undoubtedly, should be acts of withdrawal: divestment, deregulation, disengagement. That was most obviously the case with the centrally-planned economies of Eastern Europe at the end of the 1980s. Neuber in Chapter 5 shows how the rigidities induced by the central planning of the communist era have impeded the transition to a decentralised economic system.

Fry's essay on flexibility in finance in Chapter 10 is, in effect, a sustained argument that the interventions characteristic of developing countries have not only prevented financial systems from playing their important role of raising the overall responsiveness of the economic system but have so reduced the competitiveness of these markets that they do not respond well to policies of financial liberalisation. Even in East Asia, he argues, the effects of state interventions in the formal financial system were adverse, saved only by the vigour and responsiveness of the (largely unregulated) curb market. His solution is essentially the *laissez-faire*, ring-holding one of creating an institutional framework for effective prudential regulation and supervision. Although not everyone sees government policies in financial markets in quite such exclusively negative terms,[7] the literature on financial repression has amply established how policies to hold down interest rates and influence the allocation of credit have had adverse consequences for the ability of financial institutions to respond efficiently to economic needs. In other areas too – labour markets, price controls, agricultural marketing, etc – there is often much scope for deregulation or divestment which would enhance the elasticity of the economic system.

It was hypothesised in Chapter 1 that policies which fostered openness to international competition would be beneficial for national economic flexibility, on the grounds that international commerce is a potent medium for both the transfer of information and the transmission of incentives to adapt. This proposition receives quite strong support from other contributors. In Chapter 9 Lall describes the benefits of outward orientation for industrial development as being well-established and the empirical evidence in favour of this over import substitution as being 'overwhelming'. Jones writes in Chapter 4 of protectionism as 'the classic instance and reinforcement of unadaptability'. My chapter on African inflexibility draws attention to the unfavourable consequences for structural adaptation of the particularly high barriers erected against import competition with domestic manufacturing. While the specifics of how best to increase openness and phase out protectionism have to be determined case by case, and harm can be done by premature liberalisation, the benefits for flexibility of exposure to international competition, investment and know-how seem clearly established (although see below on defensive versus promotional protectionism).

Overall, then, we see a case for a combination of pro-active interventions and strategic withdrawals, in promotion of the well-functioning market system which is the chief vehicle for national economic flexibility: safeguarding the national interest, minimising adjustment costs, responding to market failures and getting rid of regulations and other policy instruments which hamper the efficient working of markets.

The nature of the state as an economic agent

In presenting this somewhat conventional conclusion, however, are we not guilty of naïvety? Can we, for example, take for granted that the nature of the state is such that it will promote the general welfare over specific interests, and that it will not minimise costs (or shift gains) in favour of already advantaged groups, to the detriment of the more vulnerable? Modern political-economy theory warns us not to make such assumptions, and so does the analysis in Chapter 6 of the nature of African political systems.

Much of this boils down to the 'state autonomy' which is the *leitmotif* of Seddon and Belton-Jones in Chapter 11: the relative insulation of policy-makers from the lobbying of special interest groups seeking favours. With this we might link Basu's advocacy in Chapter 3 of the superiority of 'partitioned' over 'overlapping' democratic rights, i.e. of decision structures where not so many interested parties are able to have a say on any given issue as to cancel each other out and result in the *immobilisme* with which he characterises the Indian case.

One of the features which distinguishes East Asia is that, by and large, policy-makers enjoyed relative autonomy, while remaining in touch with the felt longer-term needs of the private sector and general public. This leaves the question of why in some societies the state is so beholden to particular interests, to Olson's 'distributional coalitions', while in others policy-makers enjoy an autonomy which allows them to respond readily and pragmatically to new information and emerging problems – and why, possessing such freedom of manoeuvre, they do not abuse it to enhance their own interests, or in pursuit of harmful policies. Chapter 11 answers this by reference to a consensus on policy goals in East Asian countries, which leaves policy-makers relatively free from short-term lobbying, while still constraining them by longer-term social forces:

> it is . . . *the maintenance of strategic relations with important sectional and class interests in the wider civil society, and a degree of responsive-ness to those interests* that prevents relative autonomy from becoming isolation and autarky and ensures a continuing commitment to economic development.

Whether other nations could replicate such conditions and achieve equally beneficial results remains doubtful, however.

In taking a view of the desirable character of state interventionism, the most divisive issues concern industrial policy and the lessons that might be learned from the approaches of the newly industrialising economies of East

Asia. How should key decisions about industrial investments be taken: exclusively by private entrepreneurs acting on current market prices or together with government planners seeking to 'pick winners' in anticipation of future market developments? Should governments have an industrial policy?

The industrial policies of East Asian governments are discussed in Chapters 7, 9 and 11, all of whose authors are broadly supportive of the approaches adopted (although Lall in Chapter 9 makes it clear that there were major differences in specific policies employed within the region). A sceptical view is presented by the World Bank study (1993), whose authors argue that East Asian industrial policies were largely ineffective and that promoting specific industries generally did not work. This controversy is briefly visited in Chapters 7 and 9 – see especially the appendix to Chapter 7.

One of the issues here is the extent to which protection can be recommended as a positive instrument of industrial development, for all the East Asian governments (except Hong Kong) offered protection to local industry. The mere contemplation of such an approach appears to contradict our earlier presentation of protectionism as 'the classic instance of unadaptability' and of the benefits for national economic flexibility of openness to foreign competition. However, we might make a distinction here between defensive protection, aimed at preventing or slowing down the decline of industries which have lost their international competitiveness (an obvious example of protection as an obstacle to adjustment), and offensive (or infant-industry) protection designed to anticipate or create future comparative advantages and to help industries become internationally competitive.[8] There is no argument about the desirability of eliminating defensive protectionism (except as a temporary means of alleviating adjustment costs), but what of offensive protectionism?

In Chapter 9 Lall asserts the validity of 'carefully selected interventions to promote infant industries', suggesting that East Asian industry grew not because governments 'replaced imperfect interventions with efficient markets, but because they remedied imperfect markets by well directed and selective interventions to promote entry into new sets of activities'. In Chapter 7 Chang similarly views the infant-industry protection practised in the region as having been crucial for firms' abilities to raise their technological capabilities sufficiently to become competitive on world markets.

However, he is careful to point out an important feature of East Asian approaches to infant-industry protection. Good results were achieved:

> because it was made explicit by the state that the suspensions of the price mechanism which it had initiated or supported were short-term measures intended to increase the long-term flexibility of the economy. Infant industries which failed to 'grow up' were wound down,

import protections were slowly reduced . . . and cartels were usually disbanded as soon as their aims were achieved.

He is therefore cautious about the lessons that other countries might draw from East Asia. The policies depended critically on the existence of a 'strong state,' the qualities of which are explored further by Seddon and Belton-Jones in Chapter 11. The evidence suggests that such qualities are rarely found elsewhere. Confronted with the probability of bankruptcies and job losses, governments are notoriously 'soft' in winding down the protectionism long enjoyed by 'infants with big teeth' (to quote Ghana's Minister of Finance). Lall is similarly cautious:

> proposing a complex and demanding role for interventions to support industry, based on the experiences of East Asia, may not be relevant where governments lack the desire, discipline and skills to carry out such interventions.

In the end, then, these apparently technical questions of industrial policy boil down to political-economy judgements about the nature and motivations of governments. That this should be so is fully in line with the policy stance arising from so-called 'new trade theory' – there is a theoretical case for intervening but governments are not to be trusted to confine their interventions to economically justifiable cases. (For a useful overview of this stance see Krugman, 1987, especially p. 143.) However, we need not be wholly negative about the replicability of the East Asian model. At least some elements of what constitutes 'strong' government in the sense just used can be nurtured, if with difficulty, in particular the creation of a trained, competent, properly paid and well-motivated public service. Similarly with mechanisms of consultation and consensus-building. However, attempts to reproduce in other parts of the world the socio-cultural climate that permits the relative autonomy of the state in East Asia are less likely to be fruitful.

Flexibility and 'structural adjustment'

At this point let us recall the origins of the present project. Having devoted a good deal of attention in recent years to studies of the policies of the International Monetary Fund and the World Bank (collectively, the IFIs) and the design of the adjustment programmes which spread so rapidly in the 1980s among indebted developing countries, I was increasingly struck by the unevenness with which different economies responded to broadly similar programmes, and increasingly dissatisfied with explanations of these differing capacities to adjust. It was a desire to understand this better which led me to this study of flexibility.

In the light of the discussion so far, how might we understand the term structural adjustment? Since we have shown that the policy environment has a potent influence on an economy's flexibility, we might think of adjustment as induced or planned adaptation, with adjustment policies as the instruments deployed to achieve the desired adaptations and to enhance the economy's flexibility. Structural adjustment should logically be regarded as measures targeted at specifically structural variables, in particular the productive system and the physical and institutional infrastructure.

In the early 1980s, when structural adjustment first became common in the language of development, both IFIs placed priority on means of strengthening borrowing countries' balances of payments. The second oil shock had had a particularly severe impact on oil-importing countries, the debt crisis broke in late 1982, and even prior to that shortages of foreign exchange were seen as the most common constraint on development. As required by its Articles, the IMF continues to give precedence to the goal of restoring balance-of-payments viability, but it has joined the World Bank in extending the policy stipulations attached to its credits (its 'conditionality') beyond its traditional concentration on demand and exchange-rate management into supply-side and other structural measures.

The World Bank has offered the following description of its usage of 'structural adjustment' (which is also in line with IMF usage):

> *Adjustment.* Policies to achieve changes in internal and external balances, changes in the structure of incentives and institutions, or both.
>
> *Structural adjustment.* Reforms of policies and institutions – microeconomic (such as taxes), macroeconomic (such as fiscal imbalance), and institutional (public sector inefficiencies). These changes improve resource allocation, increase economic efficiency, expand growth potential, and increase resilience to future shocks.
>
> (World Bank, 1988: 11)

There are clearly areas of overlap between this conceptualisation and our own view. They have in common that adjustment is a response to changes in the economic environment; that this involves policy changes, i.e. is a planned process; that it is not a short-term task; and that it involves attention to an economy's basic structure. However, there are also important differences.

Our own approach, outlined in Chapter 1, has stressed a wider range of influences to which economies must adapt. In addition to shocks which impinge upon the availability of foreign exchange, we have also introduced trends such as the accelerating pace of technological progress, the decelerating growth of the mature industrial economies, and long-term shifts in the patterns of demand and international trade. We have also brought in a wider range of factors which influence adjustment, most notably political and social influences. And, as seen in Chapter 4, we have taken a longer-term perspective.

In other words, we can think of the structural adjustment programmes of the IFIs as an important subset of our own understanding of the process: more confined in time and coverage, but nevertheless addressed to some of the most pressing of economic adaptation problems. Given the similarities of approach, what lessons might be derived from this volume for the design of IFI adjustment programmes?

There are first a number of points emerging which are strongly congruent with the approaches of the IFIs. At the broadest level, we agree with the IFIs that national economic flexibility is a quality which is capable of conscious promotion and that the policy environment makes a crucial difference to the responsiveness of an economy. We can also agree about the potentially heavy costs of deferred adjustment. If governments decline to act, or seek to avert change, the economy will not cease to respond to outside pressures but it will be able to do so only by imposing heavy avoidable costs on its members (see Chapter 8).

Take the case of a balance-of-payments crisis. A shortage of foreign exchange imposes adjustment and the only choice is whether that adjustment will be planned or involuntary. If the government persists, say, with an overvalued exchange rate or other policies which discriminate against exporters, import supplies will dry up as international creditworthiness is eroded, reserves become exhausted and the availability of foreign exchange to pay for imports shrinks. The economy will be forced to live with whatever reduced volume of imports can be financed, and adjustment will take the form of reduced output, incomes, employment and consumption standards.

Turning to the characteristic policy content of the IFIs' programmes, there is much here that is fully congruent with the thrust of this chapter: the importance of active, well-designed macroeconomic management; of measures to improve the workings of markets, including policies of deregulation, divestment and trade liberalisation, when pragmatic calculations (as distinct from ideological predilections) indicate that such actions are likely to bring net improvements; and of improving incentives for structural adaptation, of which the exchange rate is a price signal of exceptional importance.

It is also easy to concur with the support given by the IFIs for fiscal reforms. In Chapter 3 Basu points to one of the many ways in which taxes can impede responsiveness. And Neuber in Chapter 5 draws attention to how the 'soft budget constraint', which notoriously confronted public enterprise managers under East European central planning, dulled enterprise adaptability, discouraging innovation and reducing their sensitivity to price and policy signals. IFI attempts to strengthen institutional, policy-making and administrative capabilities are also commendable in intent if not always in effect (see below).

In these ways and others, IFI adjustment programmes typically seek to move the institutional and policy environment in directions which enhance economy-wide flexibility, shifting Figure 12.1's X–X curve upwards. Inevitably, however, there are also doubts to express.

First, there is a danger that in some respects the programmes may be counter-productive. One is the continuing prospect that the sometimes heavy hand of IFI conditionality will undermine the development of indigenous policy-making capacity. Relatedly, conditionality can give the impression that programmes are being imposed upon a reluctant government even when that is not the case. Such public perceptions may undermine the legitimacy of a programme and hence the likelihood that it will be implemented and sustained. Even where that does not occur, extensive IFI determination of programme content will weaken what the Bank calls the government's sense of 'ownership' of the programme, which may well be the most important determinant of its success.[9] Although the IFIs are aware of the danger, the modalities of programme negotiation do little to foster government identification with it.

Such circumstances are liable to throw up programmes which governments do not regard as their own and of which, therefore, they will implement only the inescapable minimum. Consequently, some governments have become adept at finding ways that do not formally contravene the agreed policy conditions but which effectively restore the *status quo ante*. One of the difficulties is that, by insisting on major policy changes, the IFIs *ipso facto* become important players on the domestic political stage but without the ability to assemble a coalition of interests sufficient to sustain the reforms, particularly if the economic situation improves and felt pressures diminish.

There is also a rather widely perceived danger that there is an ideological, or doctrinal, element in IFI programme design which gets in the way of a properly pragmatic selection of strategy and policies. While there have often been good grounds for wanting to diminish the extent of state participation in the economy, both agencies have sometimes been seen as adopting too exclusively negative a view of past state interventions in economic life. One way in which this bias has expressed itself is in the reluctance of the Bank to go beyond a drive for reduced protectionism to support active industrial policies of the type explored earlier. This is taken up explicitly in Chapter 9, where Lall offers a range of specific policy recommendations.

Yet another manifestation of doctrinal bias is the IFIs' reluctance to admit the validity of a plurality of approaches to enhancing economic flexibility. While the oft-repeated charge that they prescribe the same policies wherever they go is not borne out by the evidence, there is undoubtedly a uniformity of general approach across programmes and an implicit insistence that there is only one way. This surely is a myth that will not survive any examination of the wide variety of initial conditions in adjusting countries. The East Asian case similarly raises doubts about the appropriateness of a standardised approach, whether or not the policies adopted in those countries are replicable elsewhere. With remarkable success, the East Asian countries worked out for themselves an approach which appeared best suited to their own traditions and circumstances. That is what other countries need to do as well.

Lastly, the relative narrowness of IFI programmes, identified above, also carries dangers. It is worth repeating the conclusion of Chapter 6 (and implicit in most other chapters) – that a focus on moving away from interventionist policy stances, and on 'getting prices right', is far too narrow. It is important to attend to a wider range of factors, bearing upon technological capabilities, institutional development, information flows, the adequacy of the infrastructure and the provision of other public goods. Indeed, to the extent that IFI programmes are associated – as they are – with reductions in public sector services and investments, they will make it harder for economies to adapt to present-day realities. This volume should aid the task of re-design.

NOTES

In this chapter I draw extensively on the preceding contributions. My thanks are due to the authors for providing such a rich storehouse for me to plunder and for their generosity in commenting on an earlier draft. The Chapter, however, is a personal interpretation, for which I alone am responsible.

1 The quotation is from his entry in Eatwell et al., vol. I: 26, but see also Fisher, 1983, for a fuller statement of this position.
2 I should like to acknowledge the helpful suggestions of Moshe Syrquin in improving this presentation.
3 Thus the United Nations World Economic Survey, 1985 (p.15) commented that the larger and more diversified economies with large production capacities were better able to adjust to external shocks, taking advantage of under-utilised manufacturing capacity and an ability to switch from home to foreign markets in order to expand their exports.
4 Note, however, that his argument does not really fit into the hypothesis of a ∩-shaped relationship, for he compares Europe not so much with countries at an earlier stage of development as with the USA and Japan.
5 For a good survey of these issues see Richter, 1992, from whom I have borrowed freely.
6 These arguments can be related to those of one of the few economists to have written about the flexibility of economies. Cornwall, 1977, sees such flexibility as a major influence on long-run growth, although he defines this, curiously, as the rate of growth of factor supplies (p. 39). He argues (pp.181–2) that expanding capital stocks and labour forces are means of overcoming market imperfections and rigidities because they facilitate the reallocation of resources into new lines of production, and allow firms to take advantage of new technologies and the possibilities of increasing returns to scale.
7 Even the World Bank East Asian Miracle study (1993, Chapter 6) has positive things to say about the policies of directed credit pursued in various of the region's countries.

8 Moshe Syrquin draws my attention to a similar distinction, between 'promotional' and 'restrictive' use of trade policy made in Pack and Westphal, 1986, in a paper highly germane to the topic currently under discussion.
9 Thus Mills (1989) reporting on a series of World Bank seminars on adjustment in Africa states (pp. 9–10) that most participants – chiefly government officials – saw African governments as having only a superficial input into the design of structural adjustment programmes, for reasons only partly related to the limited capacities of recipient governments.

REFERENCES

Cornwall, John (1977) *Modern Capitalism: Its Growth and Transformation*, London: Martin Robertson.

Eatwell, John, Murray Milgate and Peter Newman (eds) (1987) *The New Palgrave Dictionary of Economics*, London: Macmillan.

Fisher, Franklin M. (1983) *Disequilibrium Foundations of Equilibrium Economics*, Cambridge: Cambridge University Press.

Fransman, Martin (1986) *Technology and Economic Development*, Brighton: Wheatsheaf Books.

Freeman, C. (1989) 'New technology and catching up', *European Journal of Development Research* 1(1), June: 85–99.

Giersch, Herbert (1986) 'Liberalisation for faster economic growth', Occasional Paper no. 74, London: Institute of Economic Affairs.

Justman, Moshe and Morris Teubal (1991) 'A structuralist perspective on the role of technology in economic growth and development', *World Development* 19(9), September: 1167–84.

Klitgaard, Robert (1991) *Adjusting to Reality*, San Francisco: ICS Press.

Krugman, Paul R. (1987) 'Is free trade passé?', *Journal of Economic Perspectives*, 1(2), Fall: 131–44.

Little, Ian M. (1982) *Economic Development: Theory, Policy and International Relations*, New York: Basic Books.

Mills, Cadman A. (1989) 'Structural adjustment in Sub-Saharan Africa', Washington, DC: World Bank, EDI Policy Seminar Report no. 18.

Mody, Ashoka (1990) 'Institutions and dynamic comparative advantage: the electronics industry in South Korea and Taiwan', *Cambridge Journal of Economics*, 14(3), September: 291–314.

Nelson, Richard R. and Sidney G. Winter (1982) *An Evolutionary Theory of Economic Change*, Cambridge, MA: Harvard University Press.

North, Douglass C. (1990) *Institutions, Institutional Change, and Economic Performance*, Cambridge: Cambridge University Press.

Olson, Mancur (1982) *The Rise and Decline of Nations: Economic Growth, Stagflation, and Social Rigidities*, New Haven, CT: Yale University Press.

Pack, Howard and Larry E. Westphal (1986) 'Industrial strategy and technological change: theory versus reality', *Journal of Development Economics* 22(1), June: 87–128.

Putnam, R.D. with R. Leonardi and R.Y. Nanetti (1993) *Making Democracy Work: Civic Traditions in Modern Italy*, Princeton, NJ: Princeton University Press.

Ranis, Gustav and Syed A. Mahmoud (1992) *The Political Economy of Development Policy Change*, Cambridge, MA and Oxford: Blackwell.

Rhee, Yung Whee and Theresa Belot (1990) 'Export catalysts in low-income countries', Discussion Paper no. 72, Washington, DC: World Bank.

Richter, Josef (1992) 'Economic aspects of aging: review of the literature', in George

J. Stolnitz (ed.) *Demographic Causes and Economic Consequences of Population Aging*, New York: United Nations (ref. GV.E.92.0.4).

Stewart, F. and J. James (eds) (1982) *The Economics of New Technology in Developing Countries*, London: Frances Pinter.

United Nations (1985) *World Economic Survey*, New York: United Nations.

World Bank (1988) *Adjustment Lending: An Evaluation of Ten Years of Experience*, Washington, DC: World Bank.

—— (1993) *The East Asian Miracle: Economic Growth and Public Policy*, New York: Oxford University Press.

NAME INDEX

SUBJECT INDEX